BRITISH ENLIGHTE]

C000261989

In this groundbreaking work, Bridget Orr shows that popular eighteenth-century theatre was about much more than fashion, manners and party politics. Using the theatre as a means of circulating and publicizing radical Enlightenment ideas, many plays made passionate arguments for religious and cultural toleration, and voiced protests against imperial invasion and forced conversion of indigenous peoples by colonial Europeans. Irish and labouring-class dramatists wrote plays, often set in the countryside, attacking social and political hierarchy in Britain itself. Another crucial but as yet unexplored aspect of early eighteenth-century theatre is its connection to freemasonry. Freemasons were pervasive as actors, managers, prompters, scene painters, dancers and musicians, with their own lodges, benefit performances and particular audiences. In addition to promoting the Enlightened agenda of toleration and cosmopolitanism, freemason dramatists invented the new genre of domestic tragedy, which criticized the effects of commercial and colonial capitalism.

BRIDGET ORR is an Associate Professor in the Department of English at Vanderbilt University. She is the author of *Empire on the English Stage, 1660–1714* (Cambridge University Press, 2001) and co-editor of *Voyages and Beaches: Cultural Contact in the Pacific, 1769–1840* (1999). She is editor of a special Pacific issue of *The Eighteenth Century: Theory and Interpretation* and has published many essays on Restoration and eighteenth-century drama and New Zealand, Maori and Pacific writing and film. Among other awards she has won Fellowships from the National Endowment for the Humanities and the American Council of Learned Societies.

BRITISH ENLIGHTENMENT THEATRE

Dramatizing Difference

BRIDGET ORR

Vanderbilt University, Tennessee

CAMBRIDGE
UNIVERSITY PRESS

University Printing House, Cambridge CB2 8BS, United Kingdom

One Liberty Plaza, 20th Floor, New York, NY 10006, USA

477 Williamstown Road, Port Melbourne, VIC 3207, Australia

314-321, 3rd Floor, Plot 3, Splendor Forum, Jasola District Centre, New Delhi - 110025, India

103 Penang Road, #05-06/07, Visioncrest Commercial, Singapore 238467

Cambridge University Press is part of the University of Cambridge.

It furthers the University's mission by disseminating knowledge in the pursuit of education, learning and research at the highest international levels of excellence.

www.cambridge.org
Information on this title: www.cambridge.org/9781108731188
DOI: 10.1017/9781108584494

© Bridget Orr 2020

First published 2020
First paperback edition 2021

A catalogue record for this publication is available from the British Library

Library of Congress Cataloging in Publication data
NAMES: Orr, Bridget, author.
TITLE: British Enlightenment theatre : dramatizing difference / Bridget Orr.
DESCRIPTION: Cambridge, United Kingdom ; New York, NY : Cambridge University Press, 2019. | Includes bibliographical references and index.
IDENTIFIERS: LCCN 2019019475 | ISBN 9781108499712 (hardback) | ISBN 9781108731188 (paperback)
SUBJECTS: LCSH: Theater–Great Britain–History–18th century. | English drama–18th century–History and criticism. | Enlightenment–Great Britain. | Great Britain–Intellectual life–18th century.
CLASSIFICATION: LCC PN2593 .O77 2019 | DDC 822/.509355–dc23
LC record available at https://lccn.loc.gov/2019019475

ISBN 978-1-108-49971-2 Hardback
ISBN 978-1-108-73118-8 Paperback

To Jonathan

Contents

Illustrations

Acknowledgements

This book would not have been written without the generous assistance of my home institution, Vanderbilt University, which has supported me with leave and with research funding from the Poindexter Fund. I am also grateful to Clare Hall, University of Cambridge, which has provided me with study space during my leaves and summers, giving me quiet space to work and invaluable proximity to the University Library. The American Council of Learned Societies really made the book happen by providing a yearlong fellowship for its final stage.

I owe debts to many colleagues, but first among them is to Felicity Nussbaum who has been for me, as for many others, a mentor, an inspiration and of immense practical and intellectual assistance. Like everyone else involved in research on Georgian freemasonry, I owe a large debt to Andrew Pink, and I would also like to thank Martin Cherry, of the Grand Lodge Library, who enabled me to discover George Lillo's lodge membership.

I have presented versions of parts of this book to many different groups, and I would like to thank those who organized such occasions. These include Larry Klein, whose Eighteenth-Century Seminar at Cambridge heard a very early version of the first chapter; Susan Bruce, who invited me to the English Department at Keele University to talk about Amerindian plays; Markman Ellis, who arranged for me to address the Eighteenth-century Seminar at Queen Mary College on spiritual dragooning; and Peter Lake and Samira Sheik, in whose Performance Seminar in the History Department at Vanderbilt I talked about freemasonry and Georgian theatre. I would like to underscore particular gratitude to that most energetic of Irish *dix-huitièmistes*, David O'Shaughnessy, who has included me in two conferences, both of which changed my thinking in significant ways.

The team at Cambridge University Press, Kate Brett especially, could not have been more helpful and efficient.

My greatest debts are to my whānau. Betty and Carl Pforzheimer have been my friends in America for many decades, and to Betty in particular I express my thanks and gratitude for fun, kindness, generosity and wisdom. Friends in Cambridge who have talked me through the project with just the right degree of encouragement include Ulinka Rublack and Chris Clark. For wonderful companionship, thanks to Pete and Christine, Simon and Anita, Chris and Trudi, Mary and Ed and Helen and Alan. Thanks to Paul and Andy, superb godfathers both.

Thanks to my dearest friends Jane Wild and Frances Walsh, to whom I owe more than I can say. Recent extensive support has come my way from the amazingly creative and energetic Dave Launder and Isobel Gabites, who have together made the beautiful space at Takahoa in which the last sections of this book were composed – thank you both.

My remarkable mother Elizabeth published a book in her eighty-ninth year (perhaps to remind me how it's done) and has been an enthusiastic supporter from the outset. My father Gordon's work for the Waitangi Tribunal was a continuing influence in thinking through the issues addressed in this project. My son Charlie has grown up in the years during which the book was written, providing me with parallel kinds of education, inspiration and pleasure.

My greatest debt is owed to my husband, Jonathan Lamb. There is a certain overlap in the key words for book, partner and relationship – sympathy, empathy, interlocution, dialogue, new world/old world, voyaging, rusticity – sentimental comedy.

Introduction: Dramatizing Enlightenment

In the first half of the eighteenth century, English theatres staged large numbers of plays that dramatized the most important issues of the early Enlightenment. These contentious topics included the advocacy of religious tolerance, indigenous critiques of colonialism and plebeian attacks on social hierarchy and political corruption. These arguments were frequently presented in new dramatic genres such as sentimental comedy and domestic tragedy, ballad and later comic opera, and they made novel appeals to audiences by establishing sympathetic identification with protagonists of relatively modest social standing. In the midst of a burgeoning commercial theatre, the masonic affiliations of a plurality of performers and many other theatre professionals ranging from prompters and theatre managers to dramatists ensured that the preoccupations of 'the shock troops of the Enlightenment', as Margaret Jacob has called them, shaped both the repertory and the dramaturgy of the Georgian playhouse – in England and in her colonies.[1]

While the subversive and oppositional dimensions of John Gay's and Henry Fielding's theatrical writing have long been recognized, much of the radicalism of England's late Stuart and early Georgian theatre has been occluded by the tendency to read the drama's politics in narrow partisan terms as well as the long-standing refusal to recognize that there was such a thing as an English Enlightenment. Postmodernist, postcolonial and *marxisant* suspicion of the Enlightenment has generated suspicion of any claims to a progressive politics in this era, certainly as far as the culture of sentiment is concerned. But the recent intensification of research into the performative history of the period, notably by Felicity Nussbaum and Joseph Roach, has led to a new understanding of the extraordinary power of Georgian theatrical celebrities and the importance of theatre in the

---

[1] Margaret C. Jacob, *Living the Enlightenment: Freemasonry and Politics in Eighteenth-Century Europe* (New York: Oxford University Press, 1991), 3.

culture at large.[2] Revived interest in performance has put pressure on the long-standing tendency to dismiss eighteenth-century dramaturgy as degraded, uninteresting and ineffective in comparison with new developments in acting, production and scenography. Lisa Freeman's *Character's Theater* (2002), a compelling account of the central cultural role of generic innovation in Georgian theatre, has been especially important in reframing our conceptions of eighteenth-century dramaturgy. Without denying the central role of celebrity performance in creating theatrical success, the revisionist focus on playwriting helps explain why innovative texts like Aaron Hill's *Zara* (1735), Sir Richard Steele's *The Conscious Lovers* (1721), George Lillo's *The London Merchant* (1731) and Robert Dodsley's *The King and the Miller of Mansfield* (1737) not only were star vehicles but stayed in the repertory for decades.

Clearly, not all early eighteenth-century theatre can be seen as 'enlightened', in intention or effect. The theatres were commercial institutions, vulnerable to financial imperatives as well as sites of continuing controversy over their moral and political consequences. Governmental control was asserted in the Licensing Act of 1737, creating an onerous censorship regime that took dexterity to circumvent and to which plays fell victim. Theatrical apologists and defenders were by no means radicals, arguing for a national stage that would unify and uplift the fractious and newly united kingdom, celebrating both British identity and her expanding empire. But the substantial, cross-party support for religious toleration, and public hostility to absolutism, created ideological space for plays in which distinctly subversive and utopian visions of interreligious and intercultural dialogue, and social and political justice, could and would be written and performed.

The Enlightenment Stage in a Universal Frame

In 1749 veteran Drury Lane prompter and probable freemason William Chetwood published *A General History of the Stage*. The book has long been recognized as an invaluable source of information about the early Georgian British and Irish stages, but Chetwood's text was original as well as informative. Like other defenders of the theatre, Chetwood made the Greek invention of and Roman support for the stage central to his

---

[2] Felicity Nussbaum, *Rival Queens: Actresses, Performance, and the Eighteenth-Century British Theater* (Philadelphia: University of Pennsylvania Press, 2010) and Joseph Roach, *Cities of the Dead: Circum-Atlantic Performance* (New York: Columbia University Press, 1996) and *It* (Ann Arbor: University of Michigan Press, 2007).

recuperation of the institution as a patriotic nursery of virtue, before citing the Elizabethan and early Stuart efflorescence of dramatic talent. But prior to proceeding to a history of the British stage that gives novel prominence to Irish theatres and performers, Chetwood supplements his argument from the ancients with a highly unusual invocation of Chinese theatre. Moving from contemporary European instances of theatrical grandeur, he cites East Asian practice:

> I saw, in my youth, a *Chinese* performance at *Canton*, where the *Scenes*, *Machines*, and *Habits*, were surprising and magnificent ... Tavernier in his Travels to the *East-Indies* informs us, that Theatres have been Many Ages the Diversion of the *Chinese*, and more magnificent than those of *Europe*. He relates a long description of them; and the more to illustrate the Account, gives you the *Plan* and *Picture* of one engrav'd, with the *Scenes* and *Machines*.[3]

Chetwood is less impressed with Chinese dramaturgy, suggesting that Du Halde's translations of 'Chinese Dramatic Authors ... seem plann'd mostly like – A Prince secreted in his youth by an Evil Minister and counterplotted by a Good one' (14). But his account stresses the antiquity, splendour and patriotic purposes of Chinese theatre, identifying the same functions that justified ancient and contemporary European drama in the culture of a great contemporary Asian state. Pursuing this comparativist argument from the old world to the new, Chetwood remarks that 'the People of *America* had their *Theatre*, according to *Acosta*' (15). In an extended footnote dedicated to that American theatre, he amplifies the report:

> *Acosta*, the *Spaniard*, that wrote the *History of the West Indies*, before *Cortez* had conquered it all, says, the *Amantas*, or *Indian Philosophers*, were also Poets, and invented *Comedies* and *Tragedies*, which were acted in their Festivals before the King, the Royal Family, and the Court; the Actors being the Noblemen and great officers of the Army. The Subject of their *Tragedies* were the Victories and great Actions of their Ancestors, which seemed to be the best means they had of preserving the Memory of what was past. In their Comedies, their Husbandry, their Household Affairs and Commerce were represented, and the most remarkable Follies in Life expos'd. The Poets taught them what they had to say, not by Writing, but by Memory; for Orthography was not known among the *Indians* until after the Conquest. (15)

And he goes on to explain that 'according to *Lopez de Vega*, the Christian Religion was propagated among the *Americans* by the Theatre' (15).

---

[3] William Rufus Chetwood, *A General History of the Stage from Its Origin in Greece Down to the Present Time* (London: W. Owen, 1749), 13–14.

As with the account of Chinese drama, Chetwood is at pains to suggest the high moral purpose, longevity and courtly associations of new world theatre, characterizing the stage as an institution in which the very genres of tragedy and comedy appear to be as universal as its noble avatars, allowing his complacent conclusion 'that polite Nations allow the *Theatre* a wise and instructive Amusement' (15).

Chetwood's claims for the usefulness of the stage are in no way unusual, but his use of Asian and American evidence to universalize his arguments is striking. Writing in the wake of the Anglophone publication of Jean-Frederic Bernard's and Bernard Picart's groundbreaking tolerationist analyses of global religions, and a year after the appearance of Montesquieu's initiation of comparative political anthropology in *L'esprit des lois* (1748), Chetwood's gestures towards non-European parallels for the theatre may seem banal.[4] But in the context of British stage history, in which writers from John Dryden through Thomas Rymer, Charles Gildon, John Dennis, Colley Cibber, Thomas Wilkes, Benjamin Victor, Francis Gentleman, William Guthrie and Samuel Foote are uniformly concerned to legitimate and celebrate English achievement within a competitively European framework of ancient and modern antecedents, Chetwood's invocation of Asian and American parallels stands out.[5] It suggests that the redefinition of the classical world proposed by Sir William Temple, in which knowledge of Near Eastern, Greek and Roman antiquity should be extended to include the histories of China, Peru, Scythia and Arabia, could become a presumption for theatre practitioners as well as cultural historians and critics. For Temple, the restriction of 'the stage' of heroic virtue to Assyria, Persia,

---

[4] Bernard Picart, *The Ceremonies and Religious Customs of the Various Nations of the Known World*, 7 vols. (London: William Jackson, 1733). For recent commentary on the cosmopolitanism and cultural relativism of 'the book that changed Europe', see Lynn Hunt, Margaret Jacob and Wijnand Mijnhardt (eds.), *Bernard Picart and the First Global Vision of Religion* (Los Angeles: Getty Institute, 2010). For feminist and postcolonial critiques of the way Montesquieu's innovative universalist history helped justify control over non-European peoples by claiming to emancipate them from oppressive governmental and gender regimes, see Felicity Nussbaum's *Torrid Zones: Maternity, Sexuality and Empire in Eighteenth-Century English Narratives* (Baltimore: Johns Hopkins University Press, 1995) and chap. 5 in Betty Joseph's *Reading the East India Company, 1720–1840: Colonial Currencies of Gender* (Chicago: University of Chicago Press, 2003).

[5] Dryden's patriotic championing of English drama against ancient and contemporary European rivals in his 'Essay of Dramatick Poesy' continued in eighteenth-century commentary. See John Dryden, *The Works of John Dryden*, ed. H. T. Swedenberg Jr. et al., 19 vols. (Berkeley: University of California Press, 1956), 17:63. See, for example, Samuel Foote, *The Roman and English Comedy Consider'd and Compar'd with Remarks upon the Suspicious Husband* (Dublin: A. Reilly, 1747) and William Guthrie, *An Essay upon English Tragedy* (London, 1757). There are various recurring tropes: in Charles Gildon's *A Comparison between the Two Stages* (London, 1702) English 'Life' and 'Spirit' are contrasted with the respectful decorum of French, Spanish and Italian drama and Shakespeare's violations of neoclassic rules became a topos for England's aesthetic and political liberty (122).

Greece and Rome provided 'but a limited compass of earth that leaves out many vast regions of the world, the which, though accounted barbarous and little taken notice of in story or by any celebrated authors, yet have a right to come in for their voice, in agreeing upon the laws of nature and nations (for aught I know) as well as the rest that have arrogated it wholly to themselves'.[6] Temple's enlightened curiosity about societies neglected by the ancients and moderns venerated in his own culture extended to an unusual respect for orature, doubt as to 'whether [books] are necessary for learning or no', given that 'in Mexico and Peru, before the least use or mention of letters, there was remaining among them the knowledge of what had passed in those mighty nations and governments for many ages' (433).

Contemptuous of the restricted knowledge gained of these great states by modern nations preoccupied by the pursuit of 'endless gains and wealth' (456) whose 'most penetrating Genii' have been 'overwhelmed in the abyss of disputes about matters of religion' (465–466), the deist Temple famously provided his own potted panegyrics to the neglected empires in his essay 'Of Heroic Virtue'. As Samuel Monk points out, his views are legible in a broad range of early eighteenth-century essays and criticism, notably those of Addison and Steele (xxxiii). But this new kind of 'universal classicism' is even more visible, indeed spectacularly so, in the expanded choice of settings for serious drama.[7] While dramatists continued to write plays set in the familiar terrain of the Ottoman Empire, Persia, Egypt, North Africa, Greece and Rome, successful playwrights including John Hughes, James Thomson, Aaron Hill, Henry Brooke and Arthur Murphy, among others, produced tragedies set in Syria, China, Arabia and the Inca Empire – 'from China to Peru', as Samuel Johnson put it in *The Vanity of Human Wishes*. In choosing these settings for tragic actions, dramatists implicitly granted these societies a kind of cultural equivalence to the noble, if archaic, Graeco-Roman past that the British claimed for themselves.[8] But the settings were also intended to inform spectators about cultures and histories about which they might be

---

[6] Sir William Temple, 'Of Heroic Virtue', in *Five Miscellaneous Essays by Sir William Temple*, ed. Samuel Holt Monk (Ann Arbor: University of Michigan Press, 1963), 105–106.

[7] For a lapidary treatment of 'the burgeoning interest in human universality amidst contact with other peoples' in the late seventeenth century, see Srinivas Aravamudan, *Enlightenment Orientalism: Resisting the Rise of the Novel* (Chicago: University of Chicago Press, 2012), 1–18.

[8] Early eighteenth-century British attitudes to the Romans in particular are contested: for an emphasis on negative perspectives, see Howard D. Weinbrot, *Britannia's Issue: The Rise of British Literature from Dryden to Ossian* (Cambridge: Cambridge University Press, 1993), with a contrasting view in Phillip Ayres, *Classical Culture and the Idea of Rome in Eighteenth-Century England* (Cambridge:

ignorant, for while most of the more educated members of the audiences would be recognize the passages of Ottoman or Roman history dramatized in David Mallet's *Mustapha* (1739) Samuel Johnson's *Irene* (1749) or Addison's *Cato* (1713), they would be far less familiar with the Incan, Chinese and Arabian histories invoked by Temple that now appeared on the London stage. Arguing for the utility of theatre a few years after Chetwood, Thomas Wilkes quotes Aaron Hill on the culturally enlightening effects of tragedy: "'We are humanized,' says Aaron Hill, "without suffering; we become acquainted with the manners of nations, acquire a fine polish without travelling; and without the trouble of studying, imbibe the most pleasing, the most useful lessons.'"[9] Although he had limited success in practice, Hill argued that stage scenery and costume should reinforce the ethnographic information conveyed by the dramatic action, imaginatively anticipating the creation of 'vicarious voyages' generally associated with de Loutherbourg's scenography in the last decades of the eighteenth century.[10] Like Voltaire, he wanted the customs and manners of the exotic locales he was dramatizing to be given sartorial and scenic specificity in performance: 'An old Roman could never with any propriety be made to look like a modern Frenchman; nor a Dutch burgomaster's wife like the Queen of Great Britain.'[11]

The extended eighteenth-century dramatization of East Asian, Arabian and new world empires was inflected by new economic and intellectual engagements, as trade expanded and challenges to Christian doxa (such as biblical chronology) emerged in the light of Egyptian and Chinese

---

Cambridge University Press, 1997). Unlike Persia, Syria and Latin America, China's role in the eighteenth-century English imaginary has recently attracted scholarly attention, in studies that include analysis of versions of Du Halde's 'Chinese tragedy, call'd Chau shi ku eul, or the little orphan of the family of Chau' published in Jean-Baptiste Du Halde, *A Description of the Empire of China and Chinese Tartary, Together with the Kingdoms of Korea, and Tibet*, 2 vols., trans. Emanuel Bowen (London, 1738, 1741), I, 248. For an early perspective, see Chen Shouyi, 'The Chinese Orphan: A Yuan Play: Its Influence on European Drama of the Eighteenth Century', in *The Vision of China in the English Literature of the Seventeenth and Eighteenth Centuries*, ed. Adrian Hsia (Hong Kong: Chinese University Press, 1998), 359–382; and for more recent accounts, see Ros Ballaster, *Fabulous Orients: Fictions of the East in England 1662–1785* (Oxford: Oxford University Press, 2005), 208–218, and Chi-Ming Yang, *Performing China: Virtue, Commerce and Orientalism in Eighteenth-Century England, 1660–1760* (Baltimore: Johns Hopkins University Press, 2011), 148–183.

9 Thomas Wilkes, *The History of the Theatres of London and Dublin*, 2 vols. (Dublin: G. Faulkner and J. Exshaw, 1761), 4.

10 For a recent survey of this issue, see Kathryn R. Barush, 'Painting the Scene', in *The Oxford Handbook of the Georgian Theatre, 1737–1832*, ed. Julia Swindells and David Francis Taylor (Oxford: Oxford University Press, 2014), 265–285.

11 Aaron Hill, *The Prompter (1734–1736)*, ed. William W. Appleton and Kalmain A. Burmin (New York: Bejamin Bloom, 1966), 22, 26.

antiquity. Oriental dramas of state, as Ros Ballaster calls them, retained their ancient capacity to allegorize contemporary politics and to present fascinating forms of alterity, constructing versions of Confucian or Islamic states that were both recognizable and exotic, if not referentially plausible.[12] The natural religion of the Incas, the enthusiastic monotheism of early Islam and the sophisticated Confucianism of the Chinese could all be dramatically rendered in terms that exploit fascinating difference but ultimately reveal similitudes. Still awaiting analysis, however, are those dramatic texts that use the novel settings and actions they present to make challenging arguments for religious and cultural toleration, while attacking imperial aggression. Such texts and productions stand as evidence that the late Stuart and early Georgian theatre was not just the scene of narrowly partisan political debate and thrusting commercial novelties but also an institution in which radical as well as moderate Enlightenment ideas were presented, debated and circulated.

English Enlightenment

Folding theatrical development into the universalist accounts of 'the science of man' is rare, but it has long been understood that the theatre was a privileged site for Enlightenment debate in France and Germany, if only because of the massive presences of Voltaire and Lessing.[13] Christopher Balme has recently made a claim for theatre to be seen as an important aspect of the public sphere, and Gillian Russell has contested Habermas's diminution of its role in social, political and cultural debate in the later Georgian era.[14] Generally, however, histories of English Enlightenment (itself a term until recently considered almost oxymoronic) have almost never included the theatre. The ideological contours of English Enlightenment are contested: influentially, J. G. A. Pocock has described a conservative, Anglican Enlightenment, one developed through connections to continental Protestants and conducted by academics, clerics and

---

[12] See Ballaster, *Fabulous Orients*, 208–217.
[13] For the authoritative overview of Voltaire's relation to Enlightenment theatre, see Marvin Carlson, *Voltaire and the Theater of the Eighteenth-Century* (Westport, CT: Greenwood, 1998); for a recent argument for Lessing's continuing contribution to interfaith toleration, see Eva Urban, 'Lessing's Nathan the Wise: From the Enlightenment to the Berliner Ensemble', *New Theatre Quarterly* 30.2 (May 2014): 183–196.
[14] Christopher Balme, *The Theatrical Public Sphere* (Cambridge: Cambridge University Press, 2014) and Gillian Russell, *Women, Sociability and Theatre in Georgian London* (Cambridge: Cambridge University Press, 2007).

intellectual politicians.[15] By contrast, John Robertson argues for a more unified account of the Enlightenment, despite richly particular manifestations in places as distinct as Naples and Scotland, in an overview in which England fares rather poorly.[16] Roy Porter's *Enlightenment: Britain and the Creation of the Modern World* (2000) argues for a nativist version, rooted in late seventeenth-century scientific and political revolutions, while B. W. Young focuses on the liberal, scientifically informed late Latitudinarians who promoted freedom of conscience and reason over dogma and church authority.[17] In assessing these characterizations, Karen O'Brien suggests that the English Enlightenment encompassed 'a fruitful, if sometimes unstable, mixture of Anglicanism and Dissent, Whiggism and radicalism'.[18]

Other accounts of English Enlightenment that have stressed the radical dimensions of the phenomenon include John Marshall's demonstration of the emergence of toleration as a central value in the late seventeenth-century 'Republic of Letters' in France, Piedmont, England, Ireland and the Netherlands.[19] In these contexts, he argues, religious toleration intersected with arguments for and against political tyranny (1–3). Exploring specifically English radicalism, Justine Chapman has demonstrated the extent of freethinker John Toland's influence in the years leading up to the South Sea Bubble, in order to argue against the notion of English Enlightenment as underpowered and conservative.[20] Although her work includes England in a broadly comparativist perspective, Margaret Jacob provides more evidence of Britain's radical Enlightenment in her account of freemasonry understood as a constitutionalist, democratic, ecumenical and ethnically inclusive institution, modelling a modern, broadly egalitarian and tolerant society.[21] Jonathan Israel's *Radical Enlightenment* (2001)

[15] J. G. A. Pocock, 'Clergy and Commerce: The Conservative Enlightenment in England', in *L'età dei lumi: Studi storici sul Settecento europeo in onore di Franco Venturi*, 2 vols., ed. Rafaelle Ajello et al. (Naples, 1985).

[16] John Robertson, *The Case for the Enlightenment: Scotland and Naples, 1680–1760* (Cambridge: Cambridge University Press, 2005).

[17] Roy Porter, *Enlightenment: Britain and the Creation of the Modern World* (London, 2000) and Brian Young, *Religion and Enlightenment in Eighteenth-Century England: Theological Debate from Locke to Burke* (Oxford: Oxford University Press, 1998).

[18] Karen O'Brien, *Women and Enlightenment in Eighteenth-Century Britain* (Cambridge: Cambridge University Press, 2009), 5.

[19] John Marshall, *John Locke, Toleration and Early English Enlightenment Culture* (Cambridge: Cambridge University Press, 2006), 1.

[20] Justin Champion, *Republican Learning: John Toland and the Crisis of Christian Culture, 1696–1722* (Manchester: Manchester University Press, 2003), 1–6.

[21] Among other publications, see Jacob, *Living the Enlightenment*.

seeks to revise what he sees as an excessive stress on the role of Locke and Newton in the formation of the early Enlightenment thought, redirecting attention to the pervasiveness of Spinoza's European influence in Europe generally and in the work of English deists Blount, Temple, Toland, Collins and Tindal in particular.[22]

Although the word scarcely appears in his book, Steven Pincus's *1688: The First Modern Revolution* (2009) reminds us why late seventeenth-century and early eighteenth-century Europeans – including, most famously, Voltaire – thought Britain was in fact the model for the contemporary Enlightened state. Pincus argues that the Glorious Revolution was neither an oligarchical conspiracy nor an invasion but a broad-based event generated by those who believed that England's future lay in encouraging political participation rather than absolutism, religious toleration rather than Catholicism and manufacturing rather than landed empire.[23] For Pincus, much of the groundwork of the Revolution can be found in the sophisticated communications networks and media formations that informed and extended the political nation and those out of doors, as people in far-flung provinces consumed up-to-date and opinionated print reports of current events at home and abroad and discussed them in coffeehouses (78–81).

Pincus's stress on the importance of England's unique newspaper and coffeehouse culture (whose origins he locates in the late seventeenth century, rather earlier than Habermas) takes us to another critical aspect of Enlightenment culture, that of print.[24] For many recent scholars, the expansion of print in new forms such as the periodical essay and the novel is as central to Enlightenment culture as conjectural history and the science of man.[25] Though dispersed temporally and spatially, the 'postal principle' allowed disparate readers of fiction, newspapers and philosophical critique to experience new forms of subjectivity, interiority and community.[26]

---

[22] Jonathan Israel, *Radical Enlightenment: Philosophy and the Making of Modernity 1650–1750* (Oxford: Oxford University Press, 2001), esp. 515–527 and 599–623.

[23] Steven Pincus, *1688: The First Modern Revolution* (New Haven, CT: Yale University Press, 2009), 3–10.

[24] In many ways Habermas's depiction of the Enlightenment as a model for disinterested political debate by citizens in his *The Structural Transformation of the Public Sphere: An Inquiry into a Category of Bourgeois Society*, trans. Thomas Burger with Fredrick Lawrence (1962; repr., Boston: MIT Press, 1991) galvanized Anglophone scholarly interest in the phenomenon. See John Bender, *Ends of Enlightenment* (Stanford, CA: Stanford University Press, 2012), 3–11.

[25] Israel, *Radical Enlightenment*, places particular stress on the importance of learned journals: see 142–156.

[26] See John Guillory, 'Enlightening Mediation', in *This Is Enlightenment*, ed. Clifford Siskin and William Warner (Chicago: University of Chicago Press, 2010), 37–63.

For Benedict Anderson, these forms of dispersed 'imagined community' would be the necessary precondition for establishing the modern nation.[27] Print's role in creating modern national communities sits uneasily aside the Enlightenment's famously cosmopolitan 'Republic of Letters.' Until recently Enlightenment learning, although universalist in scope, has been understood as peculiarly and specifically European, indeed sinisterly so in the critique proposed by Adorno and Horkheimer. In *The Dialectic of Enlightenment* (1944), the former argue that the categorizing, universalizing principles and techniques at work in Enlightenment discourse manifest a dominating relation to the world and its peoples that resulted, notoriously, in the catastrophes of the Holocaust.[28] This account of the Enlightenment is vigorously contested, notably by Jürgen Habermas, who famously identified the growth of coffeehouses, print culture and salons in early eighteenth-century England as scenes of the first public sphere, in which citizens could participate in principled discussion of political, cultural and social issues in open and egalitarian contexts.[29] Other scholars who openly identify with the liberal inheritance of the Enlightenment include Anthony Pagden, whose broad-ranging survey stresses the extent to which the values of humanity, universal rights, democracy, religious tolerance and critique are Enlightenment inheritances.[30] Dennis C. Rasmussen offers a more focused analysis of what he calls the 'pragmatic Enlightenment' thought of Hume, Smith, Montesquieu and Voltaire, and which he characterizes as nonfoundational and comparativist, committed to limited government, religious tolerance, commerce and humane criminal laws.[31]

Recent historians of early eighteenth-century English culture tend now to be thoroughly sceptical of a public sphere constituted by rational and disinterested actors capable of transcending partial interests for the greater good; as Lisa Freeman comments, 'The discursive culture of the day was one in which even rhetorical claims to civility and politeness could be read

[27] Benedict Anderson, *Imagined Communities: Reflections on the Origin and Spread of Nationalism*, rev. ed. (New York: Verso, 1998).

[28] Theodor Adorno and Max Horkheimer, *The Dialectic of Enlightenment* (1944; repr., London: Continuum, 1994).

[29] Habermas, *Structural Transformation of the Public Sphere*.

[30] Anthony Pagden, *The Enlightenment and Why It Still Matters* (New York: Random House, 2013), preface, ix–xviii.

[31] Dennis C. Rasmussen, *The Pragmatic Enlightenment: Recovering the Liberalism of Hume, Smith, Montesquieu and Voltaire* (Cambridge: Cambridge University Press, 2013).

rancorously as strategic power plays.'[32] In another recent revision of the way we understand debate over political, religious and cultural issues in this period, William Bulman argues that both the most fierce radicals of the English Enlightenment and their clerical opponents were actually united in their mutual fear that the bloody sectarian conflicts of the seventeenth century might recur and that their disagreements arose from different prescriptions about the best way to avoid a repetition of those struggles. In making arguments about the most effective route to follow, he suggests that proponents of very different policies (such as Matthew Tindal and Lancelot Addison) were all grappling with ideas about history, nature, civilization and humanity that had been reshaped by civil war and imperial expansion. They were united, Bulman argues, by a shared recognition that new prescriptions for national and global redemption had to be acceptable to very different audiences with very different forms and degrees of belief and scepticism.[33]

Complicating these new characterizations of the public sphere as divided, various and contested are those scholarly accounts that have revisited the question of Enlightenment cosmopolitanism to explore European intellectual exchanges and appropriations of non-European culture and learning. While on the one hand, as Bulman demonstrates, imperial adventurism ensured that even the most traditionalist supporters of the established Church were increasingly privy to non-Christian and non-European beliefs and cultures, and incorporated such knowledge in their theodicy, the colonial expansion with which Enlightenment was continuous has been seen also as the material manifestation of the phenomenon, codified in such state-sanctioned scientific and exploratory expeditions as Cook's Pacific voyages.[34] At the same time that invasive voyaging was hymned as an enlargement of knowledge, the emissary of Christianity and the extension of commerce and sovereignty, however, Enlightenment thinkers were frequently critical of European expansion and the slavery, genocide, theft and oppression that characterized colonialism.[35] Debate continues over the efficacy of such critique: while Sankar Muhtu argues

---

[32] See Gary De Krey, *A Fractured Society: The Politics of London in the First Age of Party* (Oxford: Clarendon, 1985), 218 and Lisa Freeman, *Antitheatricality and the Body Public* (Philadelphia: University of Pennsylvania Press, 2017), 102–103.

[33] William J. Bulman, *Anglican Enlightenment: Orientalism, Religion and Politics in England and Its Empire, 1648–1715* (Cambridge: Cambridge University Press, 2015), 11–13.

[34] See, for example, Peter Hanns Reill and David Phillip Miller (eds.), *Visions of Empire: Voyages, Botany and Representations of Nature* (Cambridge: Cambridge University Press, 1996).

[35] See Simon Davies, 'Reflections on Voltaire and His Idea of Colonies', in *Studies on Voltaire and the Eighteenth Century* 332 (1995): 61–69; Gregory Jusdanis, 'Enlightenment Postcolonialism',

that in the late Enlightenment Diderot, Kant and Herder mounted powerful (if underappreciated) critiques of empire, the scholars collected in Daniel Carey's and Lynn Festa's *Post-colonialism and Enlightenment* (2013) come to a shared conclusion that Enlightenment critique tended to confirm notions of European superiority.[36] Hume's notorious racist footnote has subsumed critiques of racial oppression elsewhere in his writing, and Christopher Miller has explored the limitations of Voltaire's critique of slavery.[37] In addition to the fact that Voltaire held shares in a slaving company, Miller points out that wealthy slave traders included the author's works in their libraries and that one slave master even performed his *Alzire* on the deck of a slave ship, suggesting the writer's work had very little real critical effect on economic and political practices.[38]

Complicating the question of enlightened critique of empire, scholars have recently become attentive to European dependence on the societies they encountered and the ways in which English 'modernity' was constructed through (often) unacknowledged appropriation from non-Western cultures. These appropriations range from the technological, such as the East India Company's use of superior mortar techniques in Madras documented by Rajani Sudan, to Ros Ballaster's extensive account of anglophone reiterations of oriental narratives and Srinivas Aravamudan's argument for the realist novel's secondariness to the forms of fictionality textualized in the *Thousand and One Nights*.[39] This new attention to the non-European sources of Enlightenment includes drama, with the repeated adaptations of *The Orphan of China* incisively analysed by Chi-Ming Yang in *Performing China* (2011), an account that focuses on the more general proclivity in eighteenth-century England to spectacularize 'imports' of Chinese culture in order to negotiate tensions over consumption, class and national identity.[40] Wendy Belcher characterizes English

Research in African Literatures 36.3 (Fall 2005): 137–150; and Sankar Muthu (ed.), *Empire and Modern Political Thought* (Cambridge: Cambridge University Press, 2012).

[36] Sankar Muthu, *Enlightenment against Empire* (Princeton, NJ: Princeton University Press, 2003), esp. 259–283. See also Daniel Carey and Lynn Festa (eds.), *Post-colonialism and Enlightenment: Eighteenth-Century Colonialism and Postcolonial Theory* (New York: Oxford University Press, 2013).

[37] For discussions of Hume's attitudes to race, see Richard H. Popkin, 'Hume's Racism Reconsidered', in *The Third Force in Seventeenth-Century Thought* (Leiden: Brill, 1992), 71–72, 75; and Aama Garnett, 'Hume's 'Original Difference': Race, National Characteristics and the Human Sciences', *Eighteenth-Century Thought* 2 (2004): 127–152.

[38] Christopher L. Miller, *The French Atlantic Triangle: Literature and Culture of the Slave Trade* (Durham, NC: Duke University Press, 2008).

[39] See Rajani Sudan, *The Alchemy of Empire: Abject Materials and the Technologies of Colonialism* (New York: Fordham University Press, 2016) and Aravamudan, *Enlightenment Orientalism*, 1–30.

[40] Yang, *Performing China*, 1–31.

dependence differently, by arguing that Samuel Johnson was spiritually possessed by Abyssinian Habesha discourse and that his writing can be understood as energumen, 'texts animated by the other's discourse'.[41] Thus not just his translation of Pere Lobo's *Voyage to Abyssinia* (1735) and *Rasselas* (1759) but Johnson's oriental tragedy, *Irene*, can be read as instances of Habesha discourse, recirculating texts that generate more spiritual possession and produce other energumens. In a further important contribution to the reassessment of the sources of radical religious thought in the period, Humberto Garcia argues that Islam offered English thinkers a model of monotheism whose egalitarianism and tolerance formed an attractive alternative to Christianity and contributed to reformulations of Whig thought.[42] The peculiar advantages Islam offered to women, he argues, are depicted spectacularly in Delarivier Manley's play *Almyna* (1707).

Thus, while past scholarship generally treated the non-European origins of Enlightenment writing and performances as passive 'sources' reshaped by the creative activity of Western authors, we can see current scholars rethinking the relationship between Amerindian or Asian or African and European texts to explore the agency of cultural materials occluded by colonialist presumptions. While the relationship between certain texts and their European reiterations may indeed be best understood as an exploitation of an indigenous or exotic (re)source, other Occidental versions of non-European texts may be mixed or hybrid or even determined by the originary performance, text or speaker. In considering this issue, it is important to consider that the primary concerns of early Enlightenment thinkers, religious tolerance and the critique of authoritarian, hierarchical political structures, were frequently, if not always, voiced by cultural outsiders, such as Montesquieu's Persian traveller or Lahontan's Adario. The alterior position of these critics was not simply a useful fiction implying an impersonal and objective spectator without a stake in the culture observed – these figures do in fact often articulate non-European perspectives. The critiques of religious and political oppression that such outsiders voiced were surprisingly assimilable in Britain because (limited) toleration and constitutionalism were central planks of the Whig project. While anti-clericalism and the critique of absolutism had their own particular significance in Gallican France, in post-Revolutionary Britain

---

[41] Wendy Belcher, *Abyssinia's Samuel Johnson: Ethiopian Thought in the Making of an English Author* (Oxford: Oxford University Press, 2012), 17.
[42] Humberto Garcia, *Islam in the English Enlightenment, 1670–1840* (Baltimore: Johns Hopkins University Press, 2011).

these views were broadly shared in a nation that not only served as an implicit political model for writers like Voltaire but had individuals and communities who sympathized with the more radical views of the *Lumières*.[43]

England's Enlightened Theatre

While the revolutionary effects of print culture are undeniable, the burgeoning studies of the history of the book have been a mixed blessing for theatre studies, tending to reinforce the traditional belief in the 'rise of the novel' as the most salient aspect of literary culture in the Enlightenment. Recent scholarship has modified this assessment radically, showing how developments in theatre including dramaturgy, scenography, new modes such as pantomime and spectacle and the cults of celebrity performers and their commodification all reveal the continuing cultural salience of the stage in eighteenth-century culture, rather than its decline and eclipse by fiction. Not only was there considerable overlap between writers of plays and fiction, the emergent novel drew on a wide variety of dramatic techniques, ranging from character types to dialogue, gesture and scene to structure and embody narrative.[44]

It is well understood by drama historians that English theatre was one of the most important venues in which political disputes over the Revolution and the late Stuart and Hanoverian regimes were played out for the public. A scholarly legacy in which John Loftis's foundational work has been extended by Jean Marsden, Richard Braverman, Elaine McGirr, Brett Wilson and others has made it clear how debates over legitimate sovereignty, foreign and colonial policy, threats of counterrevolution, the nature of patriotism and the proper role of religion in the state were repeatedly depicted on stage.[45] But just as the Whig values of tolerance and hostility to despotism, classically articulated by Addison and Steele in their

---

[43] There is continuing dispute over the nature and extent of English influence in the early Enlightenment: for a recent overview and revisionist view, see Israel, *Radical Enlightenment*, 515–527 on 'Anglomania'.

[44] Among a number of recent studies on the interconnection of stage and page, see Anne F. Widmayer, *Theatre and the Novel from Behn to Fielding*, Oxford Studies in the Enlightenment (Oxford: Voltaire Foundation, 2015).

[45] John Loftis, *The Politics of Drama in Augustan England* (Oxford: Clarendon, 1963), established terms for reading the drama that remain influential. See also Richard Braverman, *Plots and Counterplots: Sexual Politics and the Body Politic in English Literature, 1660–1730* (Cambridge: Cambridge University Press, 1993); and Elaine McGirr's astute *Heroic Mode and Political Crisis, 1660–1745* (Newark: University of Delaware Press, 2009).

periodical papers, are seldom identified as 'enlightened', so too the extensive early eighteenth-century theatricalization of arguments for cultural
and religious diversity and the critique of oppressive European invasions
and colonial regimes by 'noble savages' has passed largely unobserved.
While drama historians focused on late Georgian and Regency theatre
have been alert to the subversive dimensions of plays written and produced
(and censored) in the context of repeated revolution, abolitionism and
reaction, there has been less attention to the radical dimensions of late
Stuart or early Georgian texts, with the important exception of gender.[46]
This study redirects attention to the extensive body of early and mid-
eighteenth-century dramatic texts and performances in which questions of
religious difference, cultural diversity, indigenous protest and class hierarchy are at issue.

My argument begins with the claim that Whig dramaturgy, as exemplified by Sir Richard Steele, Joseph Addison, John Dennis, John Hughes
and James Thomson, among others, was concerned with creating a community of spectators joined by national feeling – that the theatre was the
site in which English (and British) audiences learned to feel together as
Britons but also to feel for various people outside their own community.
My account builds both on Freeman's account of generic development and
national character and on Brett Wilson's demonstration of the ways in
which Shaftesbury's ideas of the *sensus communis* were mobilized by
dramatists seeking to unify their audiences in public feeling, both nationally and across cultural divides.[47] Wilson's explanation of Shaftesbury's
role in this process emphasizes the latter's centrality to Whig thought but
as Anthony Pagden points out, Shaftesbury's drive to create a theory of
human mind shaped by more than self-interest was a European-wide
project.[48] Pufendorf was one of the first who sought to replace Hobbes's
and Grotius's unconsoling accounts of the origins of sociability with a new
focus on 'feelings' and 'sentiments'.[49] This central and long-familiar aspect
of Enlightenment thought shaped novels as much as drama, but it is

---

[46] See, among others, Betsy Bolton, *Women, Nationalism, and the Romantic Stage: Theatre and Politics in Britain, 1780–1800* (Cambridge: Cambridge University Press, 2001); David Worrall, *Harlequin Empire: Ethnicity and the Drama of the Popular Enlightenment* (London: Pickering and Chatto, 2007); and Daniel O'Quinn, *Staging Governance: Theatrical Imperialism in London, 1770–1800* (Baltimore: Johns Hopkins University Press, 2005).

[47] Brett Wilson's important study, *A Race of Female Patriots: Women and Public Spirit on the English Stage, 1688–1745* (Lewisburg, PA: Bucknell University Press, 2012) is a groundbreaking analysis of Whig dramaturgy in terms of its attempts at evoking public feeling.

[48] See Pagden, 'Bringing Pity Back In', in *The Enlightenment and Why It Still Matters*, 65–95.

[49] Pagden, 'Bringing Pity Back In', 81.

important to note that literary sentiment (as Ernest Bernbaum pointed out long ago) appears in English theatre as early as, if not prior to, fiction.[50]

Within a context in which Shaftesbury is generating ideas of our innate or instinctual capacity for 'pity' (as Smith and Rousseau would call it) or Diderot's 'natural commiseration', Sir Richard Steele was theorizing and creating the novel genre of sentimental comedy and supporting serious drama that promulgated tolerance through sympathy.[51] Mathew Kinservik has argued that Steele served as an informal censor during the first three decades of the eighteenth century, presiding over a gradual shift from the biting satire of the Restoration to a more sympathetic mode that remained preeminent through much of the century.[52] Kinservik points to Steele's early consistent self-fashioning as a moral reformer, a crucial aspect of his public identity. Equally important however, and generally ignored in assessments of his cultural importance, was his position as an Anglo-Irishman, a problematic status that gave him a peculiarly intense investment in a unified but heterogeneous British identity.[53] As John Marshall trenchantly puts it, toleration is the political solution to the problem of 'the other': sympathy is the social answer. For all his closeness to the Whig establishment, Steele always was, to a degree, that 'other', vulnerable to attack on the grounds of his nationality. For him the theatre provided a crucial space in which Britons divided by political, religious and national affiliations could become one in their responses to affecting drama.

As Wolfram Schmidgen argues in his recent account of the cultural value of 'mixture' in early eighteenth-century Britain, however, Steele was not alone in insisting on the value of the heterogenous elements that constituted the United Kingdom.[54] The effectiveness of Steele's new model comedy as a vehicle for harmonizing sectarian and national differences can be seen in later sentimental texts, such as Colman's recuperation of Jacobites in *The English Merchant* (1767) and Cumberland's rehabilitation of creoles in *The West Indian* (1771). These texts are conservative in

---

[50] Ernest Bernbaum, *The Drama of Sensibility: A Sketch of the History of English Sentimental Comedy and Domestic Tragedy, 1696–1780* (Gloucester, MA: Peter Smith, 1958).

[51] Pagden, 'Bringing Pity Back In', 88.

[52] See Mathew Kinservik, *Disciplining Satire: The Censorship of Satiric Comedy on the Eighteenth-Century London Stage* (Lewisburg, PA: Bucknell University Press, 2002), 19–54.

[53] An important exception is Charles Knight's recent study, *A Political Biography of Richard Steele* (London: Pickering and Chatto, 2009). Knight sees what he describes as Steele's 'politics of sympathy' arising from his outsider status.

[54] Wolfram Schmidgen, *Exquisite Mixture: The Virtues of Impurity in Early Modern England* (Philadelphia: University of Pennsylvania Press, 2012).

tenor, modelling processes by which unruly or indeed subversive but valued members of Britain's varied imperial community can be incorporated into the body politic. As Michael Ragussis has shown recently in detail, comedy provided a broad-ranging means of negotiating the presence of heterodox communities, both policing entryism by Jews, Irishmen and other 'outlandish Englishmen' and 'writing back' from a minority perspective against theatrical racism.[55] But in the theatrical campaign for abolition, it is unsurprising that sentimental comedy in the form of *Inkle and Yarico* (1787) served as the primary vehicle for generating hostility to the trade, as Colman the Younger revisited Steele's fiction to create a text that again depicted the British Empire as benevolently inclusive.

There has been a degree of consensus over the last twenty years that late sentimental plays that seek to recuperate their exotic subjects (Arabs, Jews, enslaved Africans) frequently if not uniformly depict them as pathetic victims, reiterating their inferior status despite the apparent establishment of bonds of human feeling, fraternity and equality.[56] In their own context, however, texts such as Richard Cumberland's *The Jew* (1794) and George Colman's *Inkle and Yarico* not to mention Elizabeth Inchbald's *Such Things Are* (1780) were reformist. Arguing for the counterhegemonic potential of sympathy, Ramesh Mallipeddi has recently argued that sentimentalism, rather than serving solely as a means of assuaging imperial guilt through degrading patronage, should in fact be seen as providing a mode of protest against the dehumanizing effects of commercial capitalism whose most horrific innovation was chattel slavery. Suggestively, Mallipeddi's study turns from delineating the early articulation of metropolitan sympathy in Aphra Behn's *Oroonoko* to analyse the uses of 'melancholic memory' by those who were themselves enslaved, demonstrating the utility of sentimental discourse for the victims and resisters of slavery.[57]

While abolitionist argument became a theatrical preoccupation in British drama from the 1760s forward, however, prior to this decade, and before 1737 especially, radical critique focused much more on religious

---

[55] Michael Ragussis, *Theatrical Nation: Jews and other Outlandish Englishmen in Georgian Britain* (Philadelphia: University of Pennsylvania Press, 2010).

[56] For a powerful critique of sentimentalism's facilitation of empire, see Lynn Festa, *Sentimental Figures of Empire in Eighteenth-Century Britain and France* (Baltimore: Johns Hopkins University Press, 2006), 14–66; and George Boulukos, *The Grateful Slave: The Emergence of Racism in Eighteenth-Century British and American Culture* (Cambridge: Cambridge University Press, 2008).

[57] Ramesh Mallipeddi, *Spectacular Suffering: Witnessing Slavery in the Eighteenth-Century British Atlantic* (Charlottesville: University of Virginia Press, 2016), 1–24.

persecution, social hierarchy and imperial conquest.[58] As we have noted above, religious toleration was not only a central plank of Whig orthodoxy but also, John Marshall argues, *the* central issue of early Enlightenment dispute. Despite his authorship of the highly orthodox *The Christian Hero* (1701), Steele like Addison was a staunch advocate of toleration, with the latter castigating religious persecution in *Tatler* 161. Less familiar, however, is Steele's patronage of John Hughes and the latter's *The Siege of Damascus* (1717–1718), a play depicting the Arab capture of the city from Christians and the subsequent religious testing of its hero. The production of Hughes's text (which remained an important part of the repertory throughout the century), one among a number of serious plays representing the evils of 'spiritual dragooning' in the first half of the century, provides an object lesson in the process by which a Whig place-man with radical views used the theatre to put a respectful and learned account of Arab history into wide circulation. Hughes used the work of pioneering Arabist Simon Ockley as the basis for his tragedy and in so doing introduced Ockley's admiring and revisionist perspective on Arab history to a broad public. Other plays that also used episodes from Near Eastern history with a similarly tolerationist agenda include Aaron Hill's adaptation of Voltaire's *Zaire* (1732) and Thomson's *Edward and Eleonora* (1739).

Plays critical of 'spiritual dragooning' theatricalize one core argument of the early Enlightenment, while dramas that represent European oppression in the new world depict another. From John Dennis's *Liberty Asserted* (1704) through Hill's *Alzira* (1736) to Arthur Murphy's *Alzuma* (1767), playwrights present actions highly critical of European colonialism. More than reiterations of the black legend of Spanish Conquest codified in Dryden's *Indian Emperor* (1665), these plays served like Hughes's text to put into circulation indigenous perspectives on European invasion. Without claiming that *Liberty Asserted* and *Alzira* are the products of spiritual possession, it is plausible to see these texts and their performances as instances of energumen, or rearticulated discourse of the other, especially when authored by Irishmen such as Henry Brooke and Arthur Murphy, who had their own critical take on British colonialism. As Dennis makes clear, *Liberty Asserted* was inspired by and incorporated considerable material from Lahontan's celebrated *Dialogue* with Adario, the canonical

---

[58] For an unusually strenuous argument that theatre in London under Walpole was indeed politically threatening, see Julia Swindells, 'The Political Context of the 1737 Licensing Act', in Swindells and Taylor, *Oxford Handbook of the Georgian Theatre*, 107–122.

Enlightenment 'noble savage', while Hill's Englishing of Voltaire's *Alzire* likewise depends on *The Royal Commentaries of Peru* (1609–1617) written by the half-Incan Garcilaso de la Vega.[59] Reluctant to acknowledge that noble savage discourse is anything other than Western ventriloquism, scholars have concurred in characterizing such writing as pure projection. Robert Stam and Ella Shohat have challenged this position, however, by arguing that we should take seriously the claims made by such writers as Montaigne and Lahontan that their discourse was the result of real dialogue and interlocution.[60] Certainly the historical record suggests that Lahontan's articulation of 'Adario's' arguments was based on extended, serious and well-recorded engagement.[61]

Analysing the shaping role of indigenous discourse in dramatic performances of 'noble savagery' underscores the radical potential of plays that tried to establish the universality of Whig values of religious and political liberty by 'speaking the other'. In serious plays, such attempts were caulked on authoritative texts that reported or were authored by indigenes, while comedies such as James Miller's *Art and Nature* (1735) used Amerindian visits, with all their attendant publicity, to voice more generalized versions of 'savage' critique. Following the collapse of the South Sea Bubble, however, a new dramatic genre that depicts the dangers of an expansionist commercial empire from within was invented by a series of London playwrights who were also freemasons. Freemasonry emerged in London in the late 1710s as a form of sociability with a commitment to tolerant, cosmopolitan constitutionalism of a characteristically Enlightenment cast.[62] Quickly proscribed by the French as anti-clerical and anti-absolutist, Hanoverian freemasonry was intimately connected with the stage.[63] Famous actors such as James Quin were masons; stage managers such as Steele were members of the lodge, and so too were dramatists, notably George Lillo. In practical terms, freemasonry offered a kind of social and economic insurance against the rigours of a brutal market

---

[59] Dennis's play appeared a year after the publication of *New Voyages to North America* by Louis-Armand de Lom d'Arce, Baron de Lahontan (London: printed for T. Goodwin, M. Wotton, B. Tooke, 1703).

[60] Robert Stam and Ella Shohat, 'Where and Whither Postcolonial Theory', *New Literary History* 43 (2012): 376.

[61] See Gordon Sayre, *The Indian Chief as Tragic Hero: Native Resistance and the Literature of the Americas from Moctezuma to Tecumseh* (Chapel Hill: University of North Carolina Press, 2005).

[62] See Jacob, *Living the Enlightenment*, esp. introduction.

[63] For the best account of theatre and freemasonry in this period, see Andrew Pink's splendid dissertation, 'The Musical Culture of Free-Masonry in Early Eighteenth-Century London' (PhD diss., Goldsmiths College, University of London).

economy: more idealistically, it promoted religious and cultural toleration and fraternity, with the promise of a degree of equality rare in a thoroughly hierarchical society. Not only did freemasonry model Hanoverian constitutionalism but its cultural expressions in songs and in drama articulated the same values of communal sympathy and benevolence that were so central to Whig dramaturgy generally. In the critique of commercial society and colonial trade legible in domestic tragedies by David Mitchell, Aaron Hill, George Lillo and George Moore, author of the later, highly successful *The Gamester* (1753), families founder financially and friends provide succour; the tragic action explains the need for freemasonry and the supportive helpers mirror the fraternal support offered by the lodge. It is suggestive that George Lillo wrote *The London Merchant* (1731) in the same year he attended his first lodge meeting.

Religiously, ethnically and socially inclusive and constitutionally governed but with upper ranks dominated by royalty, aristocrats and wealthy merchants, freemasonry expresses the tensions of English Enlightenment. The lodges modelled the Whig agenda, helping create new social and economic relationships between men of different religious convictions, ethnicities and ranks, but they did not have any interest in destroying social or political hierarchy. The domestic tragedies produced by the masonic playwrights provide a searching critique of new forms of property relations, capital accumulation and enterprise, but their implied solutions are not revolutionary. In some ways, the most radical internal critique of Georgian England seen on stage came from writers whose origins would have generally precluded their being considered capable of Enlightenment. Noble savages were mostly figures of chiefly, aristocratic or royal status, but Enlightenment thinkers were also fascinated by 'wild men within'. Such figures included wild children raised outside civil society, those excluded from civility for extended periods by shipwreck, figures from the borders of the metropolitan state such as the Irish and of course rustics. Among the latter group (perhaps the most despised of all), enterprising intellectuals sought out signs of 'natural genius', men (and even less usually, women) of striking cognitive or creative capacities, several of whom went on to have notable literary careers.

What we might call 'internal savages' of many kinds appear in considerable numbers on the eighteenth-century stage, particularly visible in the vastly increased number of plays and comic opera that depict rural life. While establishment Whig dramatists such as Addison contributed to this oeuvre, doing dramatic battle in plays such as *The Drummer* (1714) for territory regarded as quintessentially Tory, many more country plays were written by playwrights of plebeian, middling or Irish origins. It is no accident that Richardson's depiction of cross-class romance in *Pamela* (1740) is set on a country estate – despite its image as Sir Roger de Coverley land, the English shires provided dramatic locations in which relations between the labouring classes and their landed betters were most vividly explored and criticized. Plays such as Charles Johnson's perennially popular *The Country Lasses* (1715) revised the general late seventeenth-century contempt for the countryside, both by deploying rural mockery of urban artifice and by demonstrating the continuing vitality of the civilized 'country house ethos'. But rural plays were often quite radical: George Farquhar's *The Recruiting Officer* (1706) was attacked as a seditious under-mining of enlistment, as was Sir John Burgoyne's reworking of the recruitment topos in *The Lord of the Manor* (1780). Rural plays and comic operas such as Lillo's *Sylvia; or, The Country Burial* (1730) denounced the stultifying drudgery of labouring-class country life, especially for women, and implicitly defended plebeian women's decisions to market their sexu-ality as profitably as possible. Perhaps the most swinging critique is articulated in Dodsley's *The King and the Miller of Mansfield* (1737), a play written by a former footman: while its anti-Walpolean dimensions are clear, the text moves beyond factional politics to attack social hierarchy in general terms, not least by rendering its rustic characters as intelligent, sympathetic agents.

It is hardly surprising that the countryside should provide such a compelling scene for Enlightenment dramaturgy – as Jonathan Israel points out, the preoccupation with 'natural man' and the associated ideas of equality, democracy and liberty all depended on the presumption of an original collective ownership of land.[64] Israel argues that the most influen-tial articulation of this nexus was Baron de Lahontan's *Nouveaux Voyages* (1703) (which he characterizes as Spinozan) dramatized in Dennis's *Liberty Asserted*. At midcentury, Jean-Jacques Rousseau's extension of this critique, deploying rural simplicity against the corruptions of commercial society was well-known in Britain, but it is telling that the pastoral opera he authored on the theme – *Le Devin du Village* (1752) – and which David Garrick believed might counter the enormous success of Isaac Bickerstaff's *Love in a Village* (1762), was a flop in London. Reading Charles Burney's adaptation, *The Cunning Man* (1766), one is hardly surprised. Anodyne as

---

[64] Israel, *Radical Enlightenment*, 272.

it might appear today, Bickerstaff's musical was accused of Wilkite tendencies and its dramatization of cross-class infatuation echoes the way its dramatic predecessors explore status and property tensions in a rural setting. By contrast, Rousseau's text shows no interclass interaction and simply asserts the superiority of a pastoral existence: ironically, any political resonance seems completely subordinate to anodyne pastoralism. As we see in the huge success of Oliver Goldsmith's *She Stoops to Conquer* (1773), British audiences had come to expect and responded enthusiastically to depictions of rural life that were animated by 'local savages' such as Tony Lumpkin. Not infrequently identified with Caliban, the archetypal ignoble indigene, Tony's dominion over both dramatic action and spectators suggests the continuing fascination with active resistance to urbanity, politeness, fashionable consumption, social hierarchy and normative sexuality.

As the recent efflorescence in theatre studies has shown, the late Stuart and Georgian stage served multiple cultural, economic, social and political functions. The managers who ran the theatres were motivated by profit, and their choice of repertory and performers was always governed by that imperative. Much recent scholarship has been devoted also to demonstrating the increasingly important role of actors and actresses, the first modern celebrities whose characteristics in performance helped shaped dramaturgy and repertoire.[65] The later proliferation of 'illegitimate' genres (and theatres) has been revisited, so that we understand pantomime, harlequinades, burlettas and comic operas not just in the jaundiced terms of hostile contemporary critics as symptoms of theatrical decline but as creative responses to an onerous censorship regime as well as entrepreneurial opportunism.[66]

The recent scholarly stress laid on the commercial imperatives driving theatrical developments in the late Stuart and early Georgian theatre might seem at odds with the high-minded aims of tragedians pursuing an explicitly 'enlightened' agenda. In fact, however, as Al Coppola has recently shown, even such an emblem of theatrical decadence as John Rich's hugely successful *The Necromancer* (1723) depended for its compulsive appeal on the public fascination with the cynosure of British Enlightenment,

---

[65] See esp. Nussbaum, *Rival Queens* and Russell, *Women, Sociability and Theatre.*
[66] See John O'Quinn, *Harlequin Britain: Pantomime and Entertainment, 1690–1760* (Baltimore: Johns Hopkins University Press, 2004); and for the later Georgian period, see Jane Moody, *Illegitimate Theatre in London, 1770–1840* (Cambridge: Cambridge University Press, 2000).

Newtonian natural philosophy. Coppola convincingly demonstrates that *The Necromancer* was so compelling to audiences because Harlequin Faustus served as an ironic double for the radical new command over the physical world displayed by Newtonian practitioners of public science, such as Frances Hauksbee, William Whiston and John Theophilis Desauguliers. These popularizers of Newtonianism were themselves showmen, generating income at lectures by producing spectacular performances of natural wonders that caused hostile commentators like Defoe to compare them to conjurors. The notorious deism of the heterodox Whiston, ejected from his Lucasian Chair at Cambridge for denying the Trinity, reinforced the suspicions of those like Defoe, who saw the advocates of the new natural philosophy not as supporters of established power but as destructive infidels. Like both Defoe's *A System of Magic* (1731) and Desauguliers's pamphlet arguing the case for a steam engine on the Thames to pump water for new housing in Westminster, *The York-Buildings Dragons* (1725–1726), Rich's own spectacular demonstration of human command over the laws of attraction in *The Necromancer* is linked to public science.[67]

A further dimension of this complex of associations unmentioned by Coppola is the fact that John Rich, unlike the managers at Drury Lane, was not a freemason. The masons had a demonstrable loyalty to Drury Lane, so it is not surprising that a pantomime that deploys the new science for satiric as well as spectacular purposes, with Desauguliers a main target, premiered at Covent Garden. Most of London's leading actors and the theatre managers at Drury Lane were freemasons, and Desauguliers was himself the first Grand Master of the newly constituted Grand Lodge. The occult reputation that rapidly attached itself to freemasonry (whose association with Newtonian cosmology was strong) provides another suggestive link between the public spectacle of science and its demonic pantomimic repetition.

Focused on broadly Whig, sometimes radical dramaturgy, this book suggests that eighteenth-century English theatre, from pantomime to tragedy, should be seen as an important site of the critical questioning of received wisdom about church, state, society, empire and human nature associated with the Enlightenment. Given the close control exerted over the theatres after 1737 in particular, this might seem an implausible claim,

---

[67] Al Coppola, 'Harlequin Newton: John Rich's *Necromancer* and the Public Science of the 1720s', in *'The Stage's Glory': John Rich, 1692–1761*, ed. Berta Joncus and Jeremy Barlow (Newark: University of Delaware Press, 2011), 238–252.

for even prior to the passing of the Licensing Act the management of the dominant theatres was politically sensitive. In the first decades of the century, however, there was a degree of coincidence between fundamental tenets of Enlightenment belief – the importance of religious tolerance and an associated hostility to absolutist forms of government – with central planks of Whig ideology. In this context, deist and cosmopolitan critiques of fanaticism and persecution and indigenous protests against unlawful invasion, oppression and slavery could sometimes be articulated – indeed, such statements could be seen as the guarantors of Britain's much-lauded liberty. The periodical papers in which such arguments were circulated provided a model for tolerant and inclusive communal discussion that self-consciously opposed the 'reasoning by violence' of absolutist regimes, a model of sympathetic persuasion that Whig dramatists sought to re-create on the stage. Rather than dismiss such periodical and dramatic protest as hypocritical, constructed to claim a liberal virtue that actually facilitated an expansionist empire, theatrical critique written and performed during the English Enlightenment remains important as an archive of interlocution between Europeans and indigenous Americans, Christians and Muslims. Further, by recognizing the links between freemasonry and domestic tragedy, we see the Enlightenment utopianism of the Craft shaping the internal critique of a commercial, colonial society encoded in this new form. One of the other great innovations of eighteenth-century drama, the rural play and comic opera, provides a final example of socially and ethnically marginal authors voicing local 'savages' to protest hierarchy and convention in the name of other less constrained life ways and values.

It scarcely needs saying that this progressive programme was partial and from a contemporary perspective, the marginality of critiques of slavery is particularly glaring. The two perennially popular dramatic depictions of enslavement from the Restoration and early eighteenth century, South-erne's *Oroonoko* (1696) and Young's *The Revenge* (1721), are ambivalent in their characterizations of royal slaves and the degree of their hostility to slavery as an institution has proved hard to parse. Steven Pincus has revealed that politically active Whigs before 1714 and Patriots afterwards did believe the acquisition of slave colonies was ethically and economically problematic, but such views were not vented in the playhouse as frequently as attacks on religious intolerance or imperial oppression.[68]

---

[68] Steven Pincus, 'Addison's Empire: Whig Conceptions of Empire in the Early Eighteenth Century', *Parliamentary History* 31.1 (February 2012): 99–117.

While Enlightened concern over slavery does appear in such early eighteenth-century sentimental classics as Steele's *Inkle and Yarico,* widespread theatricalization of abolitionism would not appear until much later in the century, whereupon – as Jenna Gibbs's *Performing the Temple of Liberty* (2014) has shown us – the campaign to end the slave trade finally does become a central theatrical preoccupation.[69]

---

[69] Jenna M. Gibbs, *Performing the Temple of Liberty: Slavery, Theater and Popular Culture in London and Philadelphia, 1760–1850* (Baltimore: Johns Hopkins University Press, 2014).

CHAPTER I

Addison, Steele and Enlightened Sentiment

According to the twelfth anecdote recorded in *Addisoniana* (1803), 'The Inquisition was pleased in their great wisdom to burn the predictions of Isaac Bickerstaffe, Esq., for the year 1708, and to condemn the authors and readers of them.'[1] Such absolutist and Roman Catholic hostility might seem surprising to contemporary scholars, who tend to characterize *The Tatler* and *The Spectator* as emollient celebrations of politeness and commerce. But as the Inquisitors apparently concluded, no purveyors of Enlightened culture in late Stuart England were more important than Joseph Addison and Sir Richard Steele. Recognized as central to the development of print culture and the public sphere in the first decades of the eighteenth century, their complex commentary on commercial society, manners, fashion and gender, particularly through their critical avatar Mr Spectator, has been very fully explored in recent years.[2] But other aspects of their essays that derive from and promulgate an Enlightenment agenda have been relatively neglected. *The Tatler* and *The Spectator* include numerous essays that attack religious intolerance, extractive colonies, oppressive superstition and prejudice and that celebrate advances in natural history and support the extension of education, on the presumption that human intelligence is a universal characteristic of the species. Exploring these aspects of their periodical production reveals how such issues were not simply the concern of radical continentals and subversive Dissenters but figured in the nation's most polite and improving literature.

[1] Joseph Addison, *Addisoniana* (London: R. Phillips, 1803), 10.
[2] The classic Whiggish account is Edward Bloom and Lillian Bloom, *Joseph Addison's Sociable Animal* (Providence: Brown University Press, 1971). See also Terry Eagleton, *The Function of Criticism from the Spectator to Post-structuralism* (London: Verso, 1984); Scott Paul Gordon, 'Voyeuristic Dreams: Mr Spectator and the Power of Spectacle', *Eighteenth Century: Theory and Interpretation* 36 (1995): 3–23; Shawn Lisa Maurer, *Proposing Men: The Dialectics of Gender and Class in the Eighteenth-Century English Periodical* (Stanford, CA: Stanford University Press, 1998); and Erin Mackie, *Market a la Mode: Community and Gender in* The Tatler *and* The Spectator (Baltimore: Johns Hopkins University Press, 1997).

Further, while their periodicals were of central importance culturally, it is crucial to recall that (like Voltaire) to their contemporaries Addison and Steele were known equally as playwrights. As Julie Ellison has argued, Addison's *Cato* (1712–1713) created a discourse of softened Stoicism that has informed Anglo-American political rhetoric to this day, while Steele functioned as an informal dramatic censor.[3] Steele was further celebrated as the architect and popularizer of sentimental comedy, a form that worked deliberately to unify the fractious members of audiences who reflected a society and a state divided by nation, ethnicity, religion, class and gender.[4] Implicitly appealing to a theatrical spectator as polite and sympathetic as his periodical reader, Steele developed a dramatic genre that sought to unify audiences through pathos and extended the community of benevolent feeling to ethnic, religious, class and racial others. In a recent rearticulation of a long tradition of scepticism regarding the mode, sentiment has been recently characterized as a specifically imperial form of 'emotional piracy', as patronizingly ineffectual as Mr Spectator's tears of sympathy for Yarico, complicit with colonial exploitation.[5] But plays depicting and establishing empathetic relations between Christians and Muslims and Europeans and Amerindians in the first decades of the eighteenth century also revised and criticized earlier negative representations of cross-cultural encounters and opened up new possibilities of respectful relationship.

London *Lumières*

Until recently, Addison and Steele were not regarded as participants in Enlightenment. That perception of their role flows in large part from Habermas's characterization of the formation of the public sphere in early eighteenth-century Britain, which became available to Anglophone readers only in the 1980s, prompting a reconsideration of *The Spectator* and *The*

---

[3] See Julie Ellison, *Cato's Tears and the Making of Anglo-American Emotion* (Chicago: University of Chicago Press, 1999), 1–74; and Kinservik, *Disciplining Satire.*

[4] For an earlier version of this argument, see Bridget Orr, 'Empire, Sentiment and Theatre', in Swindells and Taylor, *Oxford Handbook of the Georgian Theatre*, 621–637.

[5] Festa, *Sentimental Figures of Empire*, 5. Festa's is the most recent and incisive account of sentiment's imbrication in oppressive institutions it overtly decries, although suspicion of the phenomenon emerges at its origins. For an older account of contemporary criticism of sentiment, see R. F. Brissenden's *Virtue in Distress: Studies in the Novel of Sentiment from Richardson to Sade* (London: McMillan, 1974), and for the first recent critique of Steele's Inkle and Yarico, see Martin Wechselblatt, 'Gender and Race in Yarico's Epistles to Inkle: Voicing the Feminine/Slave', *Studies in Eighteenth-Century Culture* 19 (1989): 197–223.

Tatler as more than genial purveyors of Whig axioms.[6] Attention to the early periodicals is also central in the early eighteenth-century efforts to create a culture of 'politeness' documented by scholars including J. G. A. Pocock, John Brewer, Peter Clark and Lawrence Klein, who have tracked competing discourses of political virtue and commerce through philosophy, cultural networks and new forms of sociability.[7] Historical research has been matched by literary scholarship that has begun to recover writing long occluded by an uncritical acceptance of Scribblerian disdain for their political opponents, as Christine Gerrard's study of the literary dimensions of the Patriot Opposition to Walpole, Abigail Williams's account of Whig poetry and Brett Wilson's analysis of Whig dramaturgy have extended our understanding of 'Augustan' culture, although only Karen O'Brien's survey of women and progressive thought actually characterizes eighteenth-century British society as 'Enlightened'.[8]

Within this new context there is continuing debate over the way *The Tatler* and *The Spectator* contributed to early Enlightenment English culture. Erin Mackie influentially argued that the periodicals depend on and reiterate the corrupt forces of commerce they attempt to reform, while more recently Anthony Pollock has claimed that *The Spectator* creates an image of the public sphere as unmanageable, with spectators necessarily confined to a position of impotent if sympathetic neutrality.[9] Recent critics thus tend to be not only sceptical that Addison's and Steele's publications contributed to an early version of a potentially open and democratic political process but doubtful that periodicals intended to reform and control their readers were successful in their overt aims of moral and social improvement. Informed by the current scepticism about

---

[6] See Bender, *Ends of Enlightenment*, 1–12.

[7] See Lawrence E. Klein, *Shaftesbury and the Culture of Politeness: Moral Discourse and Cultural Politics in Early Eighteenth-Century England* (Cambridge: Cambridge University Press, 2004); J. C. D. Pocock, *Virtue, Commerce and History: Essays on Political Thought and History, Chiefly in the Eighteenth Century* (Cambridge: Cambridge University Press, 1985); Peter Clark, *British Clubs and Societies, 1580–1800* (Oxford: Oxford University Press, 2000); and John Brewer, *The Pleasures of the Imagination: English Culture in the Eighteenth Century* (New York: Farrar, Straus & Giroux, 1997).

[8] See Christine Gerrard, *The Patriot Opposition to Walpole: Politics, Poetry, and National Myth, 1725–1742* (Oxford: Clarendon, 1994); Abigail Williams, *Poetry and the Creation of a Whig Literary Culture, 1681–1714* (Oxford: Oxford University Press, 2005); Wilson, *Race of Female Patriots*; and O'Brien, *Women and Enlightenment*.

[9] See Mackie, *Market a la Mode* and Anthony Pollock, 'Neutering Addison and Steele: Aesthetic Failure and the Spectatorial Public Sphere', *English Literary History* 74.3 (Fall 2007): 707–734. Other important accounts include Kathryn Shevelow's *Women and Print Culture: The Construction of Femininity in the Early Periodicals* (London: Routledge, 1989); and Lawrence Klein, 'Enlightenment as Conversation', in *What's Left of Enlightenment: A Postmodern Question*, ed. Keith Michael Baker and Peter Hanns Reiss (Stanford, CA: Stanford University Press, 2001).

the eirenic capacities of periodical literature however, Scott Black avoids characterizing Addison as an 'ideologue of the bourgeoisie', whose essays modelled identities structured by republicanism, capitalism or the Protestant ethic, instead arguing that *The Spectator* was humanist, commercial and modern, providing the formal conditions by which the metropolitan world became self-reflective.[10] Black's sense of the open and self-reflexive nature of essayistic practice in *The Spectator* is demonstrated by Tony Brown's analysis of the role played by China, more specifically Temple's accounts of Chinese gardens, in Addison's aesthetics. Significantly, Brown is concerned not with *The Spectator* as instrument of domestic discipline but with Addison's use of China to think through aesthetic questions. Brown explores the consequent revelation of the (English) self's incompletion, thus recasting the standard approach to eighteenth-century aesthetics as an internal European development.[11] While Brown's essay participates in the ongoing rethinking of Enlightenment cosmopolitanism as a process of intercultural interlocution, however, Richard Braverman's essay on a *Spectator* paper's depiction of the Jews suggests a less open engagement with non-Christian peoples in Addison's writing. Discussing the turns of *Spectator* essay 495, Braverman observes that in the course of the essay Addison departs from a relatively tolerant characterization of Jews, a discourse that stresses their vital role in the maintenance of commerce and hence civility, to a much more negative assessment shaped by anti-Semitic Christian apologetics.[12]

Although these issues have attracted relatively little scholarly attention, there is nothing occasional about *The Spectator*'s engagement with Chinese culture and Jewish religion. The recent emphasis on the periodical's negotiation of conflict between monied and landed interests, its promulgation of values suited to a commercial and colonizing society and its particular focus on regulating female conduct have to a large extent occluded Addison's and Steele's preoccupation with questions of natural religion, natural philosophy, natural genius and religious difference, all issues central to enlightened discourse. Although *The Spectator* is now seen largely through a prism of national social reformation and the recuperation of commerce, early commentators recognized that it had an intimate relation to continental enlightened culture, at one level functioning as a

---

[10] Scott Black, *Of Essays and Reading in Early Modern Britain* (London: Palgrave Macmillan, 2006), 86–106.
[11] Tony C. Brown, *English Literary History* 47.1 (Spring 2007): 171–176.
[12] Richard Braverman, 'Spectator 495: Addison and the "Race of People called the Jews"', *Studies in English Literature, 1500–1900* 34.3 (Summer 1994): 537.

popularization of Pierre Bayle's famously subversive *Dictionnaire historique et critique* (1697), the scourge of intolerance and absolutism. The *Addisoniana* records that 'old Jacob Tonson used to tell, that he seldom called on Addison when he did not see Bayle's Dictionary lying upon his table',[13] while De Quincey accused Addison of actually plagiarizing from the *Dictionnaire.*[14] Donald Bond observes that many of the historical anecdotes in the papers can be traced to Bayle, and Addison himself repeatedly refers to the *Dictionnaire* both playfully and with respect. In *Spectator 92*, June 15, 1711, responding jokingly to a letter requesting help in assembling a lady's library, Addison suggests that along with such clearly inappropriate tomes as *Dalton's Country Judge*, *The Compleat Jockey* and *Mr Mede Upon Revelations*, 'Mr Jacob Tonson Junr. Is of Opinion, that *Bayle's Dictionnary* might be of very good Use to the Ladies, in order to make them good Scholars' (1:390). In an entirely different tone, however, in *Spectator 121*, July 19, 1711, he quotes the *Dictionnaire* to bolster an argument about the divinely inspired nature of animal instinct:

> To me, as I hinted in my last paper, [Instinct] seems the immediate Direction of Providence, and such an Operation of the Supreme Being as that which determines all the Portions of Matter to their Proper Centers. A modern Philosopher, quoted by Monsieur *Bayle*, in his Learned Dissertation on the Souls of Brutes, delivered the same Opinion, though in a bolder form of Words, when he says *Deus est Anima Brutus,* God himself is the Soul of Brutes. (1:493)

The Tatler and *The Spectator* did more than draw from Bayle's survey of the evils of persecution and intolerance. In accordance with the enlightened English fascination with the new science, *Spectator 121* is one of a number of papers in which Addison channels texts such as Locke's *Essay on Human Understanding* (1690) and Newton's *Opticks* (1704) to promulgate the most recent developments in natural philosophy. He always does so in accordance with Newton's own adherence to Anglican belief – stressing here for example that instinct should be understood as 'an immediate Impression from the first Mover, and the Divine Energy acting in the Creation' (1:493). As the success of John Rich's *The Necromancer* made clear, however, while practitioners might have characterized the new science as evidence of Providential Design, there were plenty among the devout and the credulous (including Defoe) for whom the heady

---

[13] Addison, *Addisoniana*, 1:207.
[14] See Donald Bond (ed.), *The Spectator*, 5 vols. (Oxford: Clarendon, 1965), 1:xcix. All quotations are from this edition and are cited in the text by volume and page number.

discoveries and speculations generated suspicion and fear. That Addison was aware of such responses seems borne out by his essays on the supernatural, for while he describes himself as 'neutral' in regard to ghosts, his discussion of witches is an unambiguous attack on the superstition that results in aged, infirm and mentally fragile women being persecuted when they are in most need of charity (*Spectator* 117, July 14, 1711: 1:482).

In representing new epistemological or ontological arguments, Addison has recourse to a heterodox series of authorities, complicating his invocation of orthodox Providentialism by routing it through radical discourse like Bayle's or, in another instance, the Koran. In explaining Locke's ideas on the variability of our perception of duration, in Paper 94, June 18, 1711, he invokes a 'very pretty Story in the *Turkish Tales* which relates to that Passage of that famous Imposter, and bears some affinity to the Subject' (1:401). Addison's citation from *The Turkish Tales* (not coincidentally brought out a couple of years earlier by Kit-Kat Club stalwart and Bayle printer Jacob Tonson) tells the story of a sultan who falls asleep and dreams he lives for many years in a distant land in pinched circumstances. When he awakes he is furious with his doctor, whom he thinks has enchanted him but is mollified by realizing he has simply been asleep. The story ends with the following homily:

> The *Mahometan* Doctor took this Occasion of instructing the Sultan, that nothing was impossible with God; and that *He*, with whom a Thousand Years are but one Day, can if he pleases make a single Day, nay a single Moment, appear to any of his Creatures as a Thousand Years. I shall leave my Reader to compare these Eastern Fables with the Notions of those great Philosophers [Mallebranche and Locke] whom I have quoted in my Papers. (1:401)

The implication here is that the oriental tales, caulked on the *Alcoran*, articulating the dogma of the 'Great Imposter' nevertheless provide the same insight as 'the great Philosophers'.

In another paper that begins by Mr Spectator claiming affinity with 'Mahometans', Addison explains that 'I have so much of the *Musselman* in me that I cannot forebear looking into any Printed Paper which comes in my way' (Number 85, June 7, 1711: 1:361). The complex trajectory of this essay involves an implicit equation between the potentially undignified fate of both the Koran and Christian theological writings, as Mr Spectator explains that 'I have lighted my Pipe more than once with the Writings of a Prelate' and that 'I once met with a Page of *Baxter* in a *Christmas* Pye' before proceeding to celebrate the value of old English ballads, often found serving the same ignominious purposes as redundant homiletics as linings for hatboxes, wall-paper and so forth (1:361). Addison's vindication of ballads, celebrated as providing a true 'copy of nature', is being deployed here against Tory polemicist William Wagstaffe's attack on texts that the latter despised for their 'unpolished homeliness of dress' (1:391) but which *The Spectator* consistently celebrates for their rough but vigorous indigeneity. The essay proceeds therefore by subjecting the common reverence shared by different 'people of the Book' for religious writing to a materialist critique that suggests that indigenous and demotic forms of orature have a vitality – perhaps even a truth to nature – that theological writings, whether Islamic or Christian, may lack.

Addison's *Spectators* suggest a consistent attempt to invoke Islamic parallels, both to illustrate apparent universals and at other moments, much more subversively, to question the possibility of accessing any such possible truths. The power of oriental materials in negotiating this ambivalently relativist programme is signalled most spectacularly by the success of 'The Vision of Mirza', one of the most frequently cited and translated papers, contained in *Spectator* 159, September 1, 1711. The 'Vision' is a manuscript supposedly picked up by the writer 'at the *Grand Cairo*', in which the visionary is led to a high hill above 'Bagdat' where he sees a panoramic view of human existence. Life is shown as a progress over a rickety bridge in a dark tide of waters, ending in an inevitable fall into seas that sweep the fallen towards either a paradise of edenic islands or to a cloud-shrouded bank where their fate is obscured. The sublime evocation of life as a 'vale of Misery', a brief sojourn in watery turbulence, hopefully rewarded by eternal life on happy isles, clearly appealed to the British, for whom both the oceanic and the insular were master tropes of national identity. The paper was republished in collections and in Steele's *The Conscious Lovers*, the hero Bevil Jr. introduces himself to the audience by apostrophizing 'this charming Vision of Mirza', going on to remark that 'such an author consulted in a morning sets the spirit for the vicissitudes of the day better than the glass does a man's person' (Act 1, Scene 11). The friendly compliment to his former collaborator aside, Steele's invocation of the Vision not only underscores Bevil Jr.'s polite virtue but invokes the tumultuous, obscure and maritime circumstances in which the heroine Indiana Sealand and her family have been enveloped and from which she must emerge onto safe (English) ground.

The 'Vision of Mirza' is carefully characterized as a found object, for which no truth claims are advanced – as is the case with the degraded texts in Paper 85, the reader must decide herself what status it occupies. Policing the cultural/religious boundary, deciding how to respond to this Islamicist reverie thus becomes the responsibility of each particular reader. In a fashion demonstrated repeatedly in Ballaster's *Fabulous Orients,* far from modelling an uncritical collapse into emotionally ineffective passivity, *Spectators* 85 and 159 invite their readers to enter into another imaginary, one both alike and yet still markedly different to their own, thereby creating the possibility of self-reflective critique. This education in empathy is matched by Addison's emphatic hostility to zeal, which is carefully characterized as the accompaniment of all religion, not simply Catholicism, Islam or Judaism:

> It is certain where [zeal] is at once Laudable and Prudential it is an hundred times Criminal and Erroneous, nor can it be otherwise if we consider that it operates with equal Violence in all Religions, however Opposite they may be to one another, and in all the subdivisions of each Religion in particular. (Number 185, October 2, 1711: 2:227)

Addison goes on to quote Bayle to the effect that 'some of the *Jewish Rabbins*' say that 'the first Murder was occasioned by a Religious Controversy', casting doubt about the justification of religious belief tout court: for 'if we had the whole History of Zeal from the Days of *Cain* to our Times, we should see it filled with so many Scenes of Slaughter and Bloodshed, as would make a wise Man very careful how he suffers himself to be actuated by such a Principle, when it only regards matters of Opinion and Speculation' (2:228).

Addison's revulsion from zeal is the flipside to his attraction to genial persuasion and the establishment of empathy. In *Spectator* 239, December 4, 1711, he again alludes to Bayle while writing passionately, one might almost say violently, against 'what we may call *Arguing by Terror*' (2:430). The immediate context is the controversy over the presence of refugees from the Palatine (and the long-standing presence of Huguenots displaced by Louis XIV), but for Addison, as for other Whigs, violent persecution and attempts at the forced conversion of religious dissenters was a fundamental evil, against which Toleration stood as a bastion of humane reason.

> Arguing by Terror ... is a Method of Reasoning which has been made use of by the poor Refugees and which was so fashionable in our Country during the Reign of Queen *Mary,* that in a Passage of an Author quoted by Monsieur *Bayle,* it is said, the Price of Wood was raised in England, by reason of the Executions made in Smithfield. These Disputants convince their Adversaries with a Sorites commonly called a Pile of Faggots. The Rack is also a kind of Syllogism which has been used to good effect, and has made multitude of Converts. Men were formerly disputed out of their

Doubts, reconciled to Truth by form of Reason, and won over to Opinions by the Candour, Sense and Ingenuity of those who had Right on their Side; but this method of Conviction operated too slowly. Pain was found to be more Enlightening than Reason. (2:430–431)

The Spectator is obviously intended to model a truly 'Enlightening' form of suasion, directly opposed to such persecution. Louis XIV, who, Addison points out, 'writ upon his great Guns – *Ratio ultima Regnum* – The Logick of Kings' (2:431), was the primary contemporary instance of such intellectual and material violence. As so often, Addison's source here is the *Dictionnaire*, in which Bayle wrote in his note B on the Anabaptists 'What is said of Artillery, that it is the last Reason of Kings, *Ratio ultima Regnum*, may be applied to the Penal Laws; they are the last Reason of Divines, their most powerful Argument, their *Achilles*, etc.' (quoted by Bond, 2:431). Limited as Toleration may have been in post-Revolution Britain, from an enlightened Whig perspective it was clearly preferable to the spiritual dragooning of an absolutist Catholic.

By contrast with Romish violence, the authors of *The Spectator* saw their own project of 'Enlightening' as one that proceeded through 'Candour, Sense and Ingenuity.' Privileging the imaginative inhabitation of a cultural other's perspective as a rhetorical strategy that rendered alterity intimate while defamiliarizing the domestic was a favoured device not just in respect of the Orient but in the equally famous papers on the Four Indian Kings. *The Spectator* that ventriloquizes the Iroquois sachems who visited London in 1711 has long served as a brief resume of an emergent cultural relativism, in which noble savages function to remind Europeans of the specificity of their own customs and manners. The dismissiveness of this response should be modified however by Kate Fullagar's recent account, *The Savage Visit* (2012), which makes clear the breadth and intensity of interest in the sachems and the political implications of their presence in London.[15] Political partners in the Canadian arm of the war against the French, the Iroquois served as the fulcrum for debate over the virtues of landed or commercial society. Such differences had significant political implications. Steven Pincus has recently demonstrated that far from sharing mercantilist presumptions about the landed basis of national wealth that shaped a common approach to empire, Whig and Tory colonial policy developed along very different lines after 1688. For Whigs human labour and ingenuity, industry and trade generated wealth, and

---

[15] Kate Fullagar, *The Savage Visit: New World People and Popular Imperial Culture in Britain, 1710–1795* (Berkeley: University of California Press, 2012), 37–64.

colonies and other nations were best seen as trading partners in a virtuous circle of ever-growing commerce. For Tories, however, guided by strict mercantilists such as Charles Davenant, there was only a limited amount of global wealth and the best way to secure Britain's position was by plunder.[16]

If, as Pincus demonstrates, Addison is the voice of a Whig colonial policy actively hostile to conquest, resource extraction and slavery, his periodical representation of indigenous Americans in 'The Vision of Marraton', *Spectator* 56, May 4, 1711, has highly topical implications. 'The Vision of Marraton' recounts the dream of the paradisal afterlife imagined by an Indian sachem, replete with happy hunting grounds and arcadian uplands. The sole negative feature is a lake of molten gold in which the Indians recognize avaricious Europeans dying a horrible death of the element that they have fetishized. The obvious axis of the story is a division between the pastoral existence of the Indians, natural man in an environment uncorrupted by the evils of civil society and the contrasting representation of modern Europeans as (*pace* Temple) focused exclusively and destructively on the pursuit of wealth. But 'Marraton' had a more specific moral for his readers. In 1711 Whigs were infuriated by the Tory obsession in negotiations to end the War of Spanish Succession with demanding more territory from France – and in particular with gaining access to Latin American mines – rather than ensuring guarantees of trading rights. From the Whig point of view, access to extraction and extended territory colonial was worth little in comparison with an amplified ability to trade, and further, the emulation of Spanish colonial policies, notoriously based on policies of conquest, forced conversion and enslaved labour, was regarded as morally deplorable.[17] As 'Marraton', Addison spoke in a voice that combined Whig disgust for an ethically degraded and economically distorted colonial policy with the horror of an indigene whose way of life was immediately threatened if not already extirpated by such action.

'The Vision of Marraton' is then one of many *Spectator* essays whose invocation of such tropes as the rational Muslim, the noble savage or the persecuted woman is intended to model critique and to affect opinion and policy. One of the most important questions raised by *The Tatler* and *The Spectator* is the extent to which their sophisticated evocation of pity (for betrayed women, for exploited indigenes) can be seen as creating the

---

[16] Pincus, 'Addison's Empire'.   [17] Pincus, 'Addison's Empire', 100–105.

means of critique of or (by contrast) facilitating commercial and colonial empire.

As we have seen, Anthony Pollock has recently argued persuasively that the creation of the reader's avatar in the neutral and neutered form of Mr Spectator produced a model of citizenship capable of passive sympathetic witness that also precluded active intervention to rectify injustice. It is hardly surprising that Pollock, one of a long line of critics who have used the story of Inkle and Yarico as a testing ground for such speculations, agrees with the generally sceptical view of sentiment's capacities for effecting reform. The connection between abolitionism and sentiment in particular has long been familiar, canvassed many years ago by Wylie Sypher as well as by Markman Ellis, Deirdre Coleman, George Boulukos and others.[18] In *Sentimental Figures of Empire*, Lynn Festa argues that sentimentality replaced epic in the eighteenth century as the dominant literary mode of empire by magnifying and mystifying colonial relations and by generating the tropes that render relations with distant others thinkable.[19] For Festa, sentimentality structured flows of affect between metropolitan subjects and colonial objects, not only by refashioning scenes of violence for facile consumption but by facilitating the constitution of the modern (metropolitan) self through repeated acts of emotional violence.

By contrast, I contest the view that the *Spectator* papers functioned only to establish 'solidarity-in-guilt', modelling their readers as witnesses to scenes of social violence to which no response except passive sentiment was required. Addison and Steele constructed their essays in a context in which reasoned forms of argument and sympathetic identification with various social, political, religious and ethnic others were deliberate strategies deployed to support an enlightened vision of society that – highly unusually, in an early modern European context – privileged tolerance. Although *Spectator* 262 (December 31, 1711) disingenuously claims that the paper 'has not in it a Single Word of News, a Reflection in Politicks,

---

[18] Wylie Sypher's *Guinea's Captive Kings: British Anti-slavery Literature of the XVIIIth Century* (New York: Octagon Books, 1969) is still an important survey of the relevant literature. See also the more recent studies by Markman Ellis, *The Politics of Sensibility: Race, Gender and Sensibility in the Sentimental Novel* (Cambridge: Cambridge University Press, 1996); Deirdre Coleman, *Romantic Colonization and British Anti-slavery* (Cambridge: Cambridge University Press, 2005); and Brycchan Carey, *British Abolitionism and the Rhetoric of Sensibility: Writing, Sentiment and Slavery, 1760–1807* (New York: Palgrave Macmillan, 2005). For a recent discussion of the role of abolitionism in relation to national character, see Srividhya Swaminathan, *Debating the Slave Trade: Rhetoric of British National Identity, 1759–1815* (Farnham: Ashgate, 2009).

[19] Festa, *Sentimental Figures of Empire*, 2–8.

nor a Stroke of Party', and that there are 'no fashionable Touches of Infidelity' (2:517), the papers do in fact address pressing issues such as opposing territorial expansion, continuing the admission of religious refugees, maintaining toleration, questioning religious authority and increasing education and social opportunity. Yet another aspect of the neglected critical programme of *The Spectator* is in fact its extended argument for a meritocratic society in which all (men) receive an education appropriate to their talents, regardless of rank or race.[20] This position was most frequently articulated by Steele but occasionally voiced also by Addison. In Number 214, for instance, Steele attacks clientage relationships and the unthinking presumption of superiority that accompanies preferment, remarking approvingly that 'I know a Man of good Sense who put his Son to a Blacksmith, tho' an Offer was made him of his being received as a Page to a Man of Quality' (November 5, 1711: 2:333), and Budgell continues the argument in Number 307 (February 21, 1712), lamenting the waste of talent through educational misapplication, claiming, 'I have known a corn-cutter, who with a right Education would have been an excellent Physician' and going on to say, 'In like manner, many a Lawyer, who makes but an indifferent Figure at the Bar, might have made a very elegant Waterman, and have shined at the *Temple* Stairs, tho' he get no Business in the House' (3:109).

One of the most extended treatments of the topic is Addison's Paper 215, November 6, 1711, in which he recounts a 'kind of wild tragedy' concerning three Africans enslaved on a plantation in the Leeward Islands. The two men are in both in love with the same woman and as they are unable to decide which should marry her, they kill her together and then themselves. Addison's motto is from Ovid, to the effect that 'Liberal arts, where studied faithfully, soften the manners and prevent cruelty.' He frames the story by comparing human nature generally to marble, suggesting that only education is capable of drawing out 'every latent Vertue and Perfection' (2:338) and draws a comparison between those at the bottom of European societies and the uncivil:

> The Philosopher, the Saint, or the Hero, the Wise, the Good, or the Great Man, very often lie hid and concealed in a Plebean, which a proper

---

[20] One recent commentator who does stress the egalitarian and individualistic aspect of Addison's and Steele's periodical writing is Brian McCrea in *Addison and Steele Are Dead: The English Department, the Canon, and the Professionalization of Literature* (Newark: University of Delaware Press, 1990), 23 and 29.

Education might have disinterred, and brought to Light. I am therefore much delighted with reading the Accounts of Savage Nations, and with contemplating those Vertues which are wild and uncultivated; to see Courage exerting itself in Fierceness, Resolution in Obstinacy, Wisdom in Cunning, and Patience in Sullenness and Despair. (2:338–339)

While Addison's conviction of his own cultural superiority shapes his belief that 'savage nations' are less capable of producing men of great learning, devotion or heroism, he is emphatic that human beings of all races are endowed with identical capacities, identifying a 'Savage Greatness of Soul' in slaves who reportedly suicide after their master's death and lamenting that their virtues are not 'rightly cultivated'. He goes on to attack 'the Contempt with which we treat this Part of our Species' and question 'that we should not put them upon the Common foot of Humanity, that we should only set an insignificant Fine upon the Man who murders them; nay, that we should, as much as in us lies, cut them off from the Prospects of Happiness in another World as well as in this?' (2:339).

Addison is certainly adamant that it is 'an unspeakable Blessing to be born in those Parts of the World where Wisdom and Knowledge flourish' (2:340), but he is equally frank about the inequity of education's distribution in both the metropolis and Britain's colonies. However, we should note that far from encouraging a passive acceptance of this unjust status quo, he wrote the essay in the months following the signing of the Treaty of Utrecht, which we have seen was deplored by Whigs for its mistaken (and immoral) preoccupation with gaining slave trading rights and colonies and access to centres of extraction in Latin America. Further, the essay was published on the day after Bonfire Night, (November 5), still celebrated for the failure of Guy Fawkes and his fellow Catholic aristocrats to blow up the Houses of Parliament. Identifying ignorance with perverted 'greatness of soul', Addison is surely denouncing the zeal or violent extremism inculcated in Roman Catholics of whatever rank by what he saw as a misguided education.[21]

---

[21] Further evidence of Addison's hostility to social hierarchy and its concomitant psychic injuries can be found in the anecdote about James Craggs (1686–1721), to whom Addison dedicated his works a few days before his death. Craggs, whose father had risen to be postmaster general and home agent of the Duke of Marlborough and was himself a leading member of the Stanhope-Sunderland ministry in the Commons after a distinguished diplomatic career, was nevertheless tormented by the remembrance that his grandfather was a barber. Addison styled this misery 'a vicious modesty'. Addison, *Addisoniana*, 1:166.

The Spectator's own didacticism was aimed at establishing sympathy as a counter to zeal, modelling the imagining of fellow feeling rather than entrenching differences likely to encourage violence, while underlining the ethical claims of Whig policies and circulating contemporary advances in philosophy and science. Given that the model offered in *The Spectator* is that of the viewer, and that 'Mr Spectator' identifies the theatre as his one sphere of influence, it's unsurprising that Addison and Steele regarded the stage as the other great scene of action for sympathy. It's important to note that their condescension to 'plebean' intelligence does not extend to dramatic spectatorship: in stressing the universality of literary appeal, Steele famously cites the anecdote recording Moliere's dependence on his housekeeper's judgement of his comedies while in *Spectator* 235, November 29, 1711, Addison celebrates the taste-making capacity of the Trunk-maker in the Upper-Gallery, 'a large black man, whom no-body knows' (2:414). 'Black' here might signal the man's hair colour, low rank, swarthiness or Irish ethnicity but is unlikely to suggest a non-European identity. This paper suggests, in fact, a rather remarkable coincidence between the role of the Spectator, for whom nothing lies more within his Province than 'Publick Shows and Diversions', and the plebeian censor of the upper gallery, who has 'saved many a good Play, and brought many a grateful Actor into Reputation', by ruling the audience like the 'Director of a Consort', or 'Virgil's Ruler of the Winds' from his perch high up in the cheap seats (2:416). Mr Spectator explains in Number 370, May 15, 1712, that 'It is, with me, a Matter of the highest consideration what Parts are well or ill-performed, what Passions or Sentiments are indulged or cultivated, and consequently, what Manners and Customs are transferred from the Stage to the World, which reciprocally imitate each other' (3:242). In assuming just such a censorial role and successfully imposing his judgments on players and audience alike by means of his patriotically oaken staff, the Trunk-maker's exhibition of faultless if untutored taste foreshadows the opening of the Enlightenment stage to natural genius.

Sentiment and the Stage

Rather than presuming that sentiment originates in fiction, and that its earliest texts then 'migrated' to the playhouse, we might explore an alternative story of sentiment, empire and Enlightenment. To do so requires returning to an older scholarship, in which the origins of sentimental discourse are shown to lie in the theatre as well as the formulations of the Cambridge Platonists or Shaftesbury.[22] Arguing that Steele served as unofficial censor for many of the first three decades of the century, Kinservik has shown that Restoration satire morphed into politer forms in which reform was to be effected by sympathetic identification with transgressors, rather than contemptuous disavowal. Tracking the overlap of Shaftesbury's claims for the *sensis communis* in the early Whig drama of patriotic public feeling, Brett Wilson makes a parallel case for the power of sympathy in serious plays of the period.

While Addison had a particularly prominent part in articulating the tolerationist and rationalist agenda of *The Spectator*, in which the reader was interpellated as a feeling viewer encouraged to adopt politically and culturally charged opinions, Steele had the more prominent role in the construction of dramatic sympathy. Self-described as an 'Englishman born in Dublin', Steele was personally invested in creating dramatic vehicles intended to meld together the heterogenous audiences who literally embodied the recently united kingdom. As Joseph Roach has suggested in *Cities of the Dead*, the late Stuart theatre was an early scene of imagined community, one in which one's fellow subjects are physically proximate rather than virtually united by the simultaneous but spatially distinct consumption of print.[23] The early eighteenth-century stage was understood by contemporaries to model the kingdom as a whole, its fractious heterogeneity as much as its aesthetic peculiarities an index of the nation's historical vicissitudes but also its great particularities – the Enlightened English shibboleths of political liberty and religious toleration. For Colley Cibber, Steele's ally in the promulgation of Whig dramaturgy, theatre's unique capacity to raise strong common feeling among divided spectators was the key to its national importance, as we see in his remarks on Addison's *Cato* (1713):

> When the Tragedy of *Cato* was first acted, let us call to mind the noble Spirit of Patriotism, which that Play then infus'd into the Breasts of a free People, that crowded to it; with what affecting Force, was that most elevated of Human Virtues recommended? Even the false Pretenders to it felt an unwilling Conviction, and made it a Point of Honour to be foremost, in their Approbation; and this too, at a time when the fermented Nation had their different Views of Government. Yet the sublime

---

[22] See Bernbaum, *Drama of Sensibility*. Important advances to this discussion have been made by Lisa Freeman in *Character's Theater: Genre and Identity on the Eighteenth-Century English Stage* (Philadelphia: University of Pennsylvania Press, 2002) and Brett Wilson, whose 'Race of Female Patriots' also identifies early Whig dramaturgy with ideals of sentimental union.

[23] Roach, *Cities of the Dead*.

Sentiments of Liberty, in that venerable Character, rais'd, in every sensible Hearer such conscious Admiration, such compell'd Assent to the Conduct of a suffering Virtue, as even *demanded* two almost irreconcilable Parties to embrace, and join in their Applause of it. Now, not to take from the Merit of the Writer, had that Play never come to the Stage, how much of this valuable effect of it must have been lost?[24]

David Marshall has stressed the importance of theatrical modelling in Adam Smith's account of sentiment, a theoretical framework for social bonding that cultural historians now argue constitutes a characteristically British way of understanding national identity.[25] It was by watching theatrical performances of the emergent modes of pathetic and sentimental drama that audiences learned to become unified by a common, national feeling.

As he pursued a career as a cultural impresario in late Stuart/early Hanoverian Britain, Steele's Irish origins shaped his embrace of reforming Whiggery's projects of politeness and piety, a cultural and political pro-gramme that could include and manage the relations of individuals and groups divided by ethnicity, rank, religious belief and political loyalties. In working to invent a sympathy machine that would reduce all his audience, generals included, to tears, Steele was not simply aiming at a reconciliation of trade and land, or the promulgation of middle-class morality. The union he sought to create was one that might sink ethnic, religious or national differences in proper feeling, ideally what Cibber called 'the noble Spirit of Patriotism'. To succeed in this venture he turned to old plays and in particular, the she-tragedies of Banks. In *The Conscious Lovers* (1721) he created a template that would be used repeatedly by dramatists seeking to recuperate all those heterogenous groups who were part of but marginal to the United Kingdom and empire – Jacobites, Jews, the Irish, Scots, nabobs, creoles and African slaves. As we have noted above, the extent to which dramatic sentiment actually succeeded in that later, more extensive project of 'humanization' is as much contested now as it was in the eighteenth century: George Boulukos argues that sentimental depictions

---

[24] Colley Cibber, *An Apology for the Life of Colley Cibber with an Historical View of the Stage during His Own Time Written by Himself* (1740), ed. B. R. S. Fone (Ann Arbor: University of Michigan Press, 1968), 196. Characteristically, Cibber stresses the moving effect of the play in performance.

[25] See David Marshall, *The Figure of Theatre: Shaftesbury, Defoe, Adam Smith, and George Eliot* (New York: Columbia University Press, 1986). Recent work on the way in which Scottish Enlightenment theories of sympathy created 'national feeling' in the later eighteenth century include Evan Gottlieb, *Feeling British: Sympathy and National Identity in Scottish and English Writing, 1707–1832* (Lewisburg, PA: Bucknell University Press, 2007); and Juliet Shields, *Sentimental Literature and Anglo-Scottish Identity, 1745–1820* (Cambridge: Cambridge University Press, 2010).

of 'the grateful slave' actually made racist discourse conventional, while David Worrall argues that anti-slavery plays popularized the abolitionist juggernaut.[26] What is certain however is that eighteenth-century British dramatists repeatedly turned to pathos and sentiment in attempting to generate religious toleration, cultural rapprochement and national reconciliation.

Anglo-Hibernus

Steele's investment in an expansive and inclusive United Kingdom was shaped by his own colonial background. His grandfather's career as a dashing East India Company merchant commissioned to open up the Persia trade, and celebrated as a friend of the Great Mughal, was memorialized by Coryat. Steele's grandmother and her children (one of whom was born in India) were settled by the family patriarch in a plantation near Ballyinaskill and experienced a terrible siege in the castle there during the Irish Confederation uprising of 1641. Orphaned at ten, Steele was removed to school in England but never hid his antecedents, functioning as a Steward for example during the memorial processions for the 1641 rebellion.[27] His always shaky finances received a very substantial boost when he inherited a Barbadian plantation from his first wife – who had herself inherited when her brother was captured by French privateers. The estate, worth at least £850 a year, was worked by two hundred slaves and Steele sold it after his first wife's death to facilitate his second marriage.[28] He was friendly with several West Indians and was the first subscriber to offer books to the library at the newly established Yale College in Connecticut.

Steele was thus connected to at least three main arenas of colonial activity but by no means consistently in positions of profit, mastery or virtue. His Irish origins were an obvious source of vulnerability when he sought to establish himself as a figure of political as well as cultural authority. Unlike Addison however, who achieved high office through

---

[26] See Boulukos, *Grateful Slave*. Boulukos argues that while the (trope of) the slave's gratitude humanized him or her, it suggested a willingness to accept subservience, which implied inferiority, enabling ameliorationist arguments to become dominant at the expense of abolition. The argument is compelling but fails to take account of the effect of reaction to the French Revolution. In *Harlequin Empire*, David Worrall demonstrates the huge reach of abolitionist drama and the greater acceptance of black actors on British stages in the late Georgian period.

[27] See Knight, *Political Biography of Richard Steele*, 10.

[28] Details of the West Indies estate are in George A. Aitken, *The Life of Richard Steele*, 2 vols. (London: Wm. Isbister, 1889), 1:132–133.

patronage, Steele sought to become an increasingly visible political player. As part of this process, he gradually abandoned the increasingly transparent personae of Isaac Bickerstaffe, Tatler and Censor, Mr Spectator and Nestor Ironside to appear in his later periodicals without disguise, under his own name as 'an Englishman born in Dublin'. Regarded no longer as an impartial observer above the fray but as an engaged participant in political and cultural conflict, Steele became the subject of evermore vituperative attack, with the publication of *The Importance of Dunkirk Consider'd* (1713) in particular producing highly personal responses. Steele's financial problems, his drunkenness, his supposed ingratitude to patrons and his alchemical projects were all canvassed by opponents, but as Charles Knight and Rae Blanchard have noted, the primary focus of these negative characterizations is his nationality.[29]

In several of the hostile accounts of Steele, the dramatist figures as a fortune-hunting stage Irishman, an Irishman moreover whose profitable marriage to a Barbadian heiress taints him with a certain creole arrogance – Defoe accused him of addressing the Queen 'just as an imperious Planter at Barbadoes speaks to a Negro Slave'.[30] John Lacy attacks him in similar terms in *The Ecclesiastical and Political History of Whigland* (1714):

> Many Years ago, *Don Ricardo* had Ingenuity enough to make his own Fortune, by that Qualification, which seems to be more particularly innate to him, than any of his Countrymen, who are famous for a constant and diligent Impudence, the Practice of which, in the most flagrant Degree, gives them a Dominion over the weak Sex; who are unable, tho' they even hate, to resist such violent and unnatural attacks as they usually make upon 'em, till they are forced to be their Wives, as the only Way to get Rid of 'em. A West-Indian Beauty, attacked in this Manner, gave herself and with her Person, more Mines of Gold, than would have made a plentiful Fortune for a worthier Mortal than *Don Ricardo*.[31]

Lacy goes on to claim that Steele's infidelity caused his wife's death, an accusation already canvassed by Delarivier Manley in her *New Atalantis*, describing him as 'thick set, his Eyes lost in his head, hanging Eye-Brows,

---

[29] The most recent survey of this aspect of Steele's career is found in Knight's excellent *Political Biography of Richard Steele*, which has guided my account. For Blanchard's commentary, see Richard Steele, *Tracts and Pamphlets* (1714), ed. Rae Blanchard (Baltimore: Johns Hopkins University Press, 1944).

[30] Daniel Defoe, *The Honour and Perogative of the Queen's Majesty Vindicated and Defended against the Unexampled Insolence of the Author of the Guardian: In a Letter from a Country Whig to Mr Steele* (London: J. Morphew, 1713), 8.

[31] John Lacy, *The Ecclesiastical and Political History of Whig Land, of Late Years* (London: John Morphew, 1714), 12.

broad Face and tallow Complexion ... has an inexhaustible fund of Dissimulation, and does not bely the Country he was born in, which is fam'd for falsehood and Insincerity.'[32] In a dialogue with a Mrs Tofts later in the *Memoirs*, the lady remarks to Don Phoebo (Steele) of his dead wife that 'Your Fame is not quite so clear in Reference to that ugly and odd Misfortune, that was so fatal to her, occasion'd by your Sister.'[33] When focusing on Steele's activities as a political author, the pretentions of an Irishman to English identity and authority are a recurring trope – as William Wagstaffe writes in *A Letter from the facetious Doctor Andrew Tripe at Bath*: 'Sir, I more particularly remember they said of you ... that you attempted to make an Englishman of Teague.'[34] Swift's is perhaps the most extreme instance of such exclusionary language, when at the end of *The Publick Spirit of the Whigs* he suggests that 'I agree with this Writer, that it is an idle thing in his Antagonists to trouble themselves upon the Articles of his Birth, Education or Fortune; for Whoever writes to his Sovereign, to whom he owes so many personal Obligations, I shall never enquire whether he be a GENTLEMAN BORN, but whether he be HUMAN CREATURE.'[35]

Occasionally Steele fought back in kind. In his 'Apology for Himself and His Writings' (1714), in which he defended himself from the charges of seditious libel that had led to his expulsion from the House of Commons early in 1714, he described Thomas Foley, an in-law of Harley's, who led the attack against him as follows:

> The Man I mean was of an Enormous Stature and Bulk, and had the Appearance, if I may speak so, of a Dwarf-Giant. His Complection Tawny, his Mein disturb'd, and the whole Man something particularly unfamiliar, disingenuous, and shocking to an English Constitution. I fancied, by his exotick Make and Colour, he might be descended from a Moor, and was some Purchase of our African, or other trading Company, which was manumised. This Man, thought I, was certainly bred in Servitude, and being now out of it, exerts all that he knows of Greatness in Insolence and Haughtiness.[36]

---

[32] Delarivier Manley, *Secret Memoirs and Manners of Several Persons of Quality of Both Sexes. From the New Atalantis, an Island in the Mediterranean*, 6th ed. (London: John Morphew, 1720), 4:e302.

[33] Manley, *Secret Memoirs and Manners*, 4:307.

[34] William Wagstaffe, *A Letter from the Facetious Doctor Andrew Tripe at Bath to the Venerable Nestor Ironside* (London: B. Waters, 1714), 28.

[35] Jonathan Swift, *The Publick Spirit of the Whigs* (London: T. Cole, 1714), 39.

[36] Richard Steele, 'An Apology for Himself and His Writings', in Blanchard, *Tracts and Pamphlets*, 295.

This invention of a fantastic history for Foley involving North African ancestry, enslavement, manumission and illegitimate entry into Parliament reworks many of the tropes employed in the attacks on Steele himself: blackness, creole arrogance, profoundly un-English origins and a passage from colonial obscurity to the nation's seat of power. The biography that Steele creates for his accuser mirrors the delegitimating narrative projected onto him by the pamphleteers. But while its primary target is personal, the passage also implies that the slave trade has the capacity to fundamentally disfigure and denature the English constitution, evoked here in both its bodily and political dimensions. Unlike the mutually enriching operations of *doux commerce*, maritime trade has here injected an alien body into the nation's political heart – a heart unnaturally hardened, Steele goes on to suggest, by his accuser's unjust cruelty. As the tide seemed to be turning in Steele's favour, 'The untam'd Creature stood up to turn off the merciful Inclination which he saw grow towards the Member accus'd', suppressing their natural inclination to tenderness.[37] In the miniature sentimental narrative Steele has constructed for his readers, the manumitted slave's mimicry of his former masters' tyranny triumphs over the natural benevolence of the nation's representatives. In his hostility to slavery understood not as Aristotelian metaphor but as a trade, we see the same emergent Whig hostility to the institution notable in Addison's views of colonial policy.

Steele continued his campaign against the Harleys in *The Lover*, in terms that seem to underscore his sensitivity to the specifically ethnic nature of the attacks in *The Examiner* and elsewhere. At the close of *Lover* 14, March 27, 1714, for example, 'Ephraim Cattlesoap' concludes his account of 'the Exotick and Comick Designs of this unaccountable Race' the Crabtrees (Oxford, his brother Edward, and Foley) who are, he writes, '(according to their own different Accounts of their Parts and Births) occasionally Syrians, Egyptians, Saxons, Arabians, and every thing but Welch, British, Scotch, or anything that is for the Interest of these Dominions'.[38] The obscurely and exotically ancestored Harleys are contrasted to those whose positively valenced British identities actually exclude the English. The valorization and claim to a Cambro-British heritage starts to replace Steele's self-described English identity. In 1720, for example, he claims, 'I was begot in Dublin by a Welsh gentleman upon a Scots Lady of

[37] Steele, 'Apology for Himself', 295.
[38] Rae Blanchard (ed.), *Richard Steele's Periodical Journalism 1714–16* (Oxford: Clarendon, 1959).

Quality', reinscribing his suspiciously hybrid Anglo-Irishness as a rich compendium of the United Kingdom's ancient nations.[39]

Although biographers other than Charles Knight have passed over the attacks and critics by and large disregard the topic, it would have been near impossible for Steele's ethnicity to have been ignored in the pamphlet wars of the 1710s. A brief inspection of the recent historiography of British national identity in the eighteenth-century makes it clear why Steele's position was so confused and vulnerable. In *Britons* (1992), Linda Colley argues that the eighteenth-century British were united by their Protestantism, their hostility to Catholic enemies, their commitment to trade and their common interest in imperial expansion.[40] But she pays rather less attention to the religious and national or ethnic differences that continued to divide the Scots, Irish, Welsh and English under the later Stuarts and Hanoverians.[41] While nativist traditions drawing on Celtic pasts were variously deployed from the seventeenth century on to stress cultural distinctiveness, Colin Kidd has shown the extent to which various theological and antiquarian arguments about pan-European Gothicism provided rhetorical resources for those who sought to underline the essential historical unity of the British as well as their ancestral links to other modern Europeans.[42] As Gothicism was incorporated into popular Whig apologetics in the post-Revolutionary period, it provided a specifically historical justification for understanding the component kingdoms of the British Isles as the common inheritors of the Teutonic legacy of liberty. Steele himself provides a classic articulation of this *idée reçu* in *The Englishman* 28, from December 8, 1713:

> If LIBERTY be then so valuable, those Nations whose Government has appear'd to be founded on its Maxims the most conducive to its Preservation, though not conversant in the politer parts of Learning, are so far from being deserving to be stiled *Barbarous*, that they justly merit as glorious Panegyricks as ever came from the Mouth of *Tully* or *Demosthenes*.
>
> AMONGST those may be reckoned the ancient Inhabitants of the Northern Parts of *Europe*, out of which in different Ages have gushed those mighty swarms of *Goths, Vandals, Saxons, Angles, Franks, Huns, Danes* and *Normans*, which subdu'd all the Western Parts of *Europe*.

[39] Steele apparently made the claim in a debate on classifying Irish cloth as a foreign manufacture. See British Museum, Addison Manuscripts, 47, 029, 23–24.
[40] Linda Colley, *Britons: Forging the Nation* (New Haven, CT: Yale University Press, 1992).
[41] For a more comprehensive account, see James Smyth, *The Making of the United Kingdom: State, Religion and Identity in Britain and Ireland* (London: Longmans, 2001).
[42] Colin Kidd, *British Identities before Nationalism: Ethnicity and Nationhood in the Atlantic World 1600–1800* (Cambridge: Cambridge University Press, 1999).

THE grand Northern HIVE from whence they came, has by some Authors been stiled *Officina Gentium*, the Shop of Nations; and might with as much Justice have been called *Officina Libertatis*, the Shop of Liberty.

In the case of those we now call the Anglo-Irish, including Steele and Swift, the sense of an English identity that survived transplantation to Ireland was even more distinct, as new settlers distinguished themselves from the 'mere Irish' – the dispossessed Catholics – despite the fact that the metropolitan English refused to recognize such differences.[43] The irony for the Anglo-Irish – like other settlers – was that in colonizing, the 'West British' became colonials.

Steele's investment in the Whig project thus has a cultural and political specificity conditioned by his Irish antecedents. His admiration for William III was arguably informed by a positive attachment to the idea that what mattered in a 'Christian hero' was that he was a hero of the Protestant interest and that his non-English origins were decidedly irrelevant to his role as national saviour. Writing in *The Englishman* 3, October 10, 1713, Steele explains,

> When I say an *Englishman*, I mean every true Subject of her Majesty's Realms, the *Briton* of the North as well as he of the South; and know no Reason for saying *Englishman* instead of *Scotsman*, but that latter Appellation is drawn into the former from the Residence of the Queen in the Southern Part of *Great Britain*. I abhor the Distinction, and think it absolutely necessary for our mutual Honour and Safety, as far as it is possible, to abolish it. It is below the Sincerity of Heart and innate Honesty of a true *Englishman* to enter into a partial Friendship; and it is a Matter of Lamentation, to observe the cool Distance, that is maintained towards Men who have resigned great Immunities, and placed themselves irrevocably under the same Soveraignty with us, in order to our mutual Wealth, Glory and Happiness.[44]

But as we have seen, the 'mere English' did not necessarily share Steele's views, not in politics, nor in the playhouse. John Dennis believed the stage's contemporary decline was caused by venal and low-bred actor-managers supplanting theatrical management by nobles but he also cited demographic shifts in the audience consequent on the more general political and social changes that followed the golden age of the Restoration:

---

[43] See Kidd, *British Identities before Nationalism*, chaps. 7–10.
[44] Rae Blanchard (ed.), *The Englishman: A Political Journal by Richard Steele* (Oxford: Clarendon, 1955), 14.

> The Audiences were *English* all or most of them, audiences that understood what they saw and heard; and we had the none of those shoals of exoticks, that came in by the Revolution, the union, and the *Hanover* Succession, which tho They were events that were necessary all, and without which we had been undone; yet they have hitherto had but an evil Influence upon the genuine Entertainments of the stage, and the studies and arts of Humanity.[45]

For in addition to the 'shoals of exoticks' who require a dumbed-down theatre, Dennis is incensed by the undiscriminating ignorance of successful military men and stock-jobbers: 'a new and numerous Gentry has risen among us by the Return of our fleets from sea, of our Armies from the Continent, and from the wreck of the South Sea. All these will have their Diversions and their easie Partiality leads them against their own palpable interest to the Hundreds of Drury'.[46] For Dennis a vicious cycle had emerged, whereby a newly heterogenous and uneducated spectatorship was pandered to by equally low, ill-informed and in Steele's case un-English theatrical managers. In his 'Picture of Sir John Edgar', he describes Steele as follows:

> He was a Gentleman born, Witness himself; of a very Honorable Family, certainly of a very Ancient one. For his Ancestors flourish'd in *Tipperary* long before the *English* ever set foot in *Ireland*. He has Testimony of this more Authentick than the *Herald's* office or than mere Human Testimony; for God has mark'd him more abundantly than *Cain*, and stamp'd his Native Country upon his Face, his Understanding, his Writings, his Actions, his Passions, and above all, his Vanity. The *Hibernian* Brogue is still upon all these, tho long Habitude and Length of Days has worn it from off his Tongue.[47]

It is these Tipperary origins that Dennis cites obsessively as the source of Steele's imputed shameless avarice, his philandering, his nonsensical projects and his plagiary.

We have seen that Steele responded to the directly political attacks upon his nationality by constructing and circulating discursive accounts of himself as a sympathetic subject and by reconstructing his enemies as

---

[45] John Dennis, 'The Causes of the Decay and Defects of Dramatick Poetry, and of the Degeneracy of the Publick Taste' (1725), in *The Critical Works of John Dennis*, 2 vols., ed. Edward Niles Hooker (Baltimore: Johns Hopkins University Press, 1943), 2:276.
[46] Dennis, 'Causes of the Decay', 278.
[47] Dennis, 'The Character and Conduct of Sir John Edgar, call'd by Himself Sole Monarch of the Stage in Drury-Lane; and His Three Doughty Governors' (1720), in Hooker, *Critical Works*, 2:181.

objects of ethnic and religious antipathy. Charles Knight has argued that what he calls Steele's 'double vision' (Irish and English) shaped his 'politics of sympathy'.[48] Certainly, in episodes such as the debates over whether to execute or pardon peers who joined the Jacobite Rebellion in 1715, Steele was emphatically on the side of mercy. In 'A Letter to a Member, etc. Concerning the Condemn'd Lords' (1716), he wrote, 'I never talked of Mercy and Clemency, but for the Sake of my King and Country, in whose Behalf I dare to say, That to be afraid to forgive, is as low as to be afraid to punish; and that all noble Geniuses in the Art of Government have less owed their Safety to Punishment and Terror, than Grace and Magnanimity'.[49] It seems likely that the sympathy he extended to the Scots Lords in that episode was a factor in his appointment to the Committee for Sequestrations in the aftermath of the rebellion, as his reputation for clemency would have made him more acceptable in the north. But the stress here on pity as a characteristic of political genius had an ideological as much as a tactical import. In *The Englishman* 32, Steele uses the familiar analogy of the kingdom as 'a great Family' to stress that a ruler needs to treat his subjects with 'Love, Tenderness, and Compassion', without which his authority will soon decay.[50] In a slightly later issue, he returns to the familial analogy to amplify his critique of absolutist monarchy:

> To say, therefore, that the Nature of Government requires an absolute Submission in the whole governed Society, even to a Degree of total Ruin, when that shall seem fit to the governing Part, is just as if it should, with great Gravity be affirmed, That the Nature of Government requires, that the very End for which only it was instituted, should be frustrated, and wholly destroyed . . .
>
> It is as if it should be said, That the Nature of a Guardianship requires, that the Children, for whose Good it was settled, must, without Limitation, submit, should a Guardian sell them to the Slavery of the Galleys . . .[51]

Steele's example of illegitimate, despotic governance uses the same figure of literal enslavement that he invoked in his defence of his conduct in the 'Apology', in which, as we saw, he characterized his parliamentary tormentor as a brutalized former slave. Literal enslavement often appears in Steele's polemical writing as the horrific *telos* of the political domination he

---

[48] Knight, *Politics of Sympathy*, 12.

[49] 'A Letter to a Member, etc. Concerning the Condemn'd Lords, in Vindication of Gentlemen Calumniated in the St. James's Post of Friday March the 2nd', in Steele, *Tracts and Pamphlets*, 415.

[50] *The Englishman*, 32, December 17, 1713, in Blanchard, *The Englishman*, 129.

[51] *The Englishman*, 22, September 23, 1715, in Blanchard, *The Englishman*, 337.

associates with absolutism, while an inclusive compassion is good government's virtuous antithesis. But in his 'Apology', as clearly as in the
celebrated fable of Inkle and Yarico, the invocation of slavery actually
collapses that crucial opposition between the free trading nation and its
tyrannic rivals. Feeling himself not only humiliated but literally cast out of
the political nation by his expulsion from the House, Steele's rhetorical
misrecognition of his accuser as a depraved denizen of the slave trade recurs
to a fundamental contradiction in his beloved 'English constitution',
identifying slavery as a delegitimating canker on the British body politic.
The dark body and 'exotick' origins that he shares with his Accuser,
rhetorically at least, continually threaten entry to or expulsion from the
idealized, free Protestant nation into a condition of slavery, whether
material or political.

Play Making

It's unsurprising that Steele, forced to reflect repeatedly upon his own and
others' nationalities, seems peculiarly sensitive to the shifting, contingent
and hierarchical nature of ethnic and national identities and affects. With
multiple national affiliations and residencies, he was in pole position to
originate literary techniques that manage difference and distance. While
the flow of sympathy in sentimental drama (or novels) may help constitute
and consolidate identities, it also blurs boundaries, whether one figures the
sympathetic self as subjugated by feeling or aggressively appropriative of
another's most intimate experience via identification. Given Steele's own
always uncertain hold upon an 'English Constitution', it makes sense he
should find the 'universal' appeal of virtuous sympathy – in which
national, party and even gender differences are putatively sunk – so
compelling.

Steele was not of course alone in his attempts at constructing sentimental union. Following Shaftesbury's early articulation of a common 'moral
sense', Scottish historians and philosophers Francis Hutcheson, David
Hume and eventually Adam Smith began theorizing the sympathetic
exchanges that they believed bound together families, communities and
nations.[52] In developing the notion of an innate capacity of feeling for

---

[52] For an excellent discussion of public feeling in Shaftesbury, see Wilson, *Race of Female Patriots*,
15–19. For two accounts of sentimental fiction and the formation of British identity, see Gottlieb,
Feeling British, and Shields, *Sentimental Literature*. For a stimulating account of what he calls the
'multi-ethnic spectacle' on British stages in this period, see Ragussis, *Theatrical Nation*.

others, the Scots all include what seemed to them our natural feeling for our fellow citizens as aspects of our intrinsic benevolence. Francis Hutcheson claimed that among our strongest motivations 'we shall find strong natural affections, friendships, national love, gratitude'.[53] Bracketing the more usual explanations for national characteristics based on geography and climate, Hume suggested that to sympathy 'we might ascribe the great uniformity in the humours and turn of thinking of those of the same nation'.[54] Although he never offers a hard and fast definition of sympathy, Hume's accounts of its workings suggest an almost physical transmission of feeling from one individual to another: 'As in strings equally wound up, the motion of one communicates itself to the rest; so the affections readily pass from one person to another, and beget corresponding movements in every human creature' (576). Adam Smith would argue that sympathy works in a more mediated fashion, through the visual impressions of another's experience, a copy of which will convey only a partial version of the original experience and whose intensity depends to quite some degree on the willingness of the spectator to extend sympathy. This model of sympathy corresponds particularly well to theatrical experience – a favourite analogy in his analysis of sympathy's workings – not least because the theatrical contract implies a heightened willingness to be moved by exhibitions of suffering.

Only Shaftesbury's meditations on sympathy were available to Steele, although prior to his finally producing *The Conscious Lovers*, generally accepted as the fullest exemplum of the sentimental comedy, he had been theorizing the genre for years. In *Tatler* 172 he argues against the recourse to the 'History of Princes and Persons who act in high Spheres', believing in 'the great Use (if any Body could hit it) to lay before the World such Adventures as befall Persons not exalted above the common Level'.[55] He rejected 'poetical justice' and preferred plays 'in which the persons are all of them laudable, [in which] their misfortunes arise from unguarded virtue than propensity to vice' (*Tatler* 98). The aim of the dramatist was to unite the audience in a sympathetic response to suffering virtue, the sign of such pity being tears.

[53] Francis Hutcheson, 'Reflections on Our Common Systems of Morality', in *On Human Nature*, ed. Thomas Moutner (Cambridge: Cambridge University Press, 1993), 100.
[54] David Hume, *A Treatise of Human Nature*, 2nd ed., ed. L. A. Shelby-Bigge and P. H. Nidditch (Oxford: Oxford University Press, 1978), 316.
[55] Richard Steele, *The Tatler: The Lucubrations of Isaac Bickerstakke, Esq.*, 4 vols. (London: H. Lintott et al., 1754), 3:246.

Where was the model for such a dramaturgy? Steele identifies it in the practice of John Banks, author of oriental heroic plays before he started composing a run of she-tragedies with subjects drawn exclusively from British history in the 1680s. For Steele, the great virtue of Banks's plays that they were tear pumps, as he remarks (not altogether admiringly) in *Tatler* 14:

> Yesterday we were entertain'd with the Tragedy of the *Earl of Essex*, in which there is not one good line, and yet a Play which was never seen without drawing Tears from some part of the Audience; a remarkable instance, that the Soul is not to be mov'd by Words, but Things; for the Incidents in this Drama are laid together so happily, that the Spectator makes the Play by Himself, by the Force which Circumstance has upon his Imagination.[56]

Colley Cibber, also a contender for the title of first sentimental dramatist, makes precisely the same point about Banks. Exhorting would be playwrights to remember the primacy of plot, Cibber invokes Banks's example:

> There are three Plays of his, The Earl of Essex, Anna Bullen, and Mary Queen of Scots, which tho' they are all written in the most barren, barbarous Stile, that was ever able to keep the Stage, have all interested the Hearts of his Auditors. To what then could this Success be owing, but to the Intrinsik, and naked Value of the Tales he has simply told us? There is Something so happy in the Disposition of all his Fables; all his chief Characters are thrown into such natural Circumstances of Distress, that their Misery or Affliction, wants very little Assistance from the Ornaments of Stile, or Words to speak them ... At such a Time, the attentive Audience supplies from his own Heart, whatever the Poet's Language may fall short of, in Expression, and melts himself into every pang of Humanity, which the like Misfortunes in real life could have inspired.[57]

Banks's she-tragedies, several of which were suppressed in the 1680s, all held the stage through the eighteenth century.[58] Although recent commentators, such as Louise Marshall and Christine Gerrard, stress Elizabeth's

---

[56] Steele, *The Tatler*, 1:85.   [57] Cibber, *An Apology*, 190.

[58] In his *Memoirs of the Life of David Garrick, Esq.* (London: Printed for the Author, 1780), Thomas Davies echoes Steele's and Cibber's praise of Banks: 'The Tragedy of the Earl of Essex, by Banks, had lain long neglected, though no play had ever produced a stronger effect upon an audience: for though the language is a wretched compound of low phrase and bombast expression, and is indeed much below criticism; yet in the art of moving the passions Banks has no superior' (294).

continuing value as an emblem of proper Protestant rule in the plays produced under the Hanoverians, John Watkins argues that the Elizabeth depicted in Banks's drama is a repudiation of her status as a great sovereign as she is refigured as a suffering tragic heroine whose miseries are essentially private.[59] In an account consonant with other recent readings of pathetic tragedy, Watkins argues that Elizabeth's tragic suffering models the conflicted interiority of the emergent bourgeois subject.[60] Without contesting the centrality of class mediation in these texts, I want to suggest that Banks's tragedies were also successful over a period of decades in moving significant portions of audiences because his heroines were domestic in both senses – primarily concerned with private passions but equally important, characters in the national narrative. Although his female protagonists were royal, they were figures from a shared and not too distant British past, thus diminishing the distance from the audience who were simultaneously united in watching a common history unfold.[61] Banks was himself very emphatic about the importance his choice of domestic subjects, writing in the 'Preface to Anna Bullen' (1682) that unlike those of his fellow dramatists, 'His *Heroes* all to *England* are confin'd', suggesting further that this should ensure the spectators' approbation: 'To your own *Fathers* sure you will be kind.'[62]

Although *The Unhappy Favorite* and *The Island Queens* were both suppressed by the Lord Chancellor in the 1680s, Banks insisted that his plays were innocent of parallels. While it is hard to see dramas in which a Protestant ruler executes a Catholic Stuart heir as entirely free of contemporary reference, the subsequent reception history of these texts suggests that they were valued for their ability to unify audiences by means of specifically British subjects and affects.

---

[59] Gerrard, *Patriot Opposition to Walpole*; Louise H. Marshall, *National Myth, Imperial Fantasy: Representations of British Identity in the Early Eighteenth Century* (London: Palgrave, 2008); and John Watkins, *Representing Elizabeth in Stuart England* (Cambridge: Cambridge University Press, 2002), 185–186.

[60] See Laura Brown, 'The Defenceless Woman and the Development of English Drama', *Studies in English Literature, 1500–1900* 22.3 (Summer 1982): 429–443.

[61] Mark Sabor Phillips has tracked this process in historiography from the midcentury. See his *Society and Sentiment: Genres of Historical Writing in Britain, 1740–1820* (Princeton, NJ: Princeton University Press, 2000). For a wide-ranging discussion of the pleasures recollections of Mary Queen of Scots provided through the eighteenth century, see Jayne Lewis, '"The Sorrow of Seeing the Queen": Mary Queen of Scots and the British History of Sensibility, 1707–1789', in *Passionate Encounters in a Time of Sensibility*, ed. Maximillian E. Novak and Anne Mellor (London: Associated University Presses, 2000).

[62] John Banks, *Preface to a New Play called Anna Bullen* (London: Allan Banks, 1682).

Sentimental Comedy

Steele's choice of Terence's *Andria* as a model for his new kind of comedy has been acutely explained as a useful classical analogue that authorized the creation of what was seen as an un-English kind of text.[63] This seems highly plausible and not least because one is tempted to consider that Steele may have identified with Terence. A manumitted slave from Carthage, darkly complexioned, educated in the metropolis through the benevolence of his master and subject to suggestions that he plagiarized the nobles with whom he was intimate, Terence may have seemed to model a difficult outsider career as well as a play. The humane feeling with which Terence's plays were associated, possibly a function of his experiences of loss, dislocation and compassion, provides another point of concurrence.

When Steele came to write *The Conscious Lovers* (possibly as early as 1713), although the play appeared only in 1721, he created a comic form that skirts tragedy. This allowed him to use figures 'not above the common level', closer to the audience than Banks's British queens but capable of generating a similar pathos. In the rough notes that Steele drew on for his Preface, he writes that 'Addison told me I had a faculty of drawing Tears- and bid me compare the Places in Virgil wherein the most judicious Poet made his Hero weep', and while he himself thought Bevil's refusal to fight in the fourth act the play's most important scene, audiences and critics were agreed that the recognition scene in which Indiana is reunited with her father was the affective climax of the drama.[64]

The action of the play is focused on Indiana, long-lost daughter of the East Indies merchant Sealand. Rescued from a lecherous French captor, Indiana has come penniless to London where she is under the protection of the virtuous hero, Bevil Jr.. Bevil's father wishes his son to marry the wealthy Lucinda, beloved by Bevil's friend Myrtle. The forced marriage is averted by Sealand's recognition of Indiana, thus paving the way for her match with Bevil Jr.. Recent critics of *The Conscious Lovers* have focused on the interrelated issues of the play's thematic reconciliation of monied and landed interests and the question of aesthetic legitimacy raised by the novel sentimental form in which the action is cast. Lisa Freeman has argued that Steele's project of inculcating 'good breeding' by means of an exemplary

---

[63] See Malcolm Kelsall, 'Terence and Steele', in *Essays on the Eighteenth-Century English Stage*, ed. Kenneth Richards and Peter Thomson (London: Methuen, 1972), 11–27.

[64] Quoted in Aitken's *Life of Richard Steele*, 1:277.

comedy was challenged by accusations that his new genre was an illegitimate hybrid whose curbing of humour embodied a threat to liberty.[65] Nicole
Horejsi reverses Freeman's account of the play's positive vision of overseas
trade by stressing Indiana's vulnerability to accidents contingent on East
Indian trafficking.[66] Peter Hynes revisits the question of legitimacy by
analysing how Terence's cultural authority as a classical progenitor of
tender comedies was invoked to defend Steele's text and larger project of
dramatic reform.[67]

These readings suggest that Steele's cultural authority was fractured by
his own hybrid national status, particularly after 1714. The fusillade of
attacks on the play by Dennis follow the practice of earlier pamphleteers in
focusing on Steele's Irishness. In 'A Defence of Sir Fopling Flutter, a
Comedy by Sir George Etheridge' (1722), Dennis's argument about
literary authority turns on nativism as much as genteel status: 'I shall only
add, that I would advise for the future, all the fine Gentlemen, who travel
to *London* from *Tipperary*, to allow us *Englishmen*, to know what we mean,
when we speak our own Language.'[68] As Freeman notes, Dennis is
particularly incensed by what he sees as Steele's violation of Thalia because
of his conviction that comic excellence is a peculiarly national trait: 'the
very Boast and Glory of the *British* Stage is Comedy, in which *Great
Britain* excels any other Country: Nay, we can show more good and
entertaining Comedies than all the rest of *Europe*.'[69] In attacking *The
Conscious Lovers*, Dennis invokes two kinds of authority: classical poetics
and insider knowledge of overseas trade. The first, extended critique of the
play uses an Aristotelian standard of verisimilitude to indict the text for
repeated failures in the probability necessary to create plausible social
representation:

> But now this whole Dramatick Performance seems to me to be built upon
> several things which have no Foundation, either in Probability, or in
> Reason, or in Nature. The Father of *Indiana*, whose Name is *Danvers*,
> and who was formerly an eminent Merchant at *Bristol*, upon his Arrival

[65] Freeman, *Character's Theater*, 193–234.
[66] Nicole Horejsi, '(Re)valuing the 'Foreign-Trinket': Sentimentalizing the Language of Economics in Steele's Conscious Lovers', *Restoration and Eighteenth-Century Theater Research* 18.2 (Winter 2003): 11–36.
[67] Peter Hynes, 'Richard Steele and the Genealogy of Sentimental Drama: A Reading of *The Conscious Lovers*', *Restoration and Eighteenth-Century Theater Research* 40.2 (Spring 2004): 142–166.
[68] John Dennis, 'A Defence of Sir Fopling Flutter, a Comedy by Sir George Etheridge', in Hooker, *Critical Works*, 245.
[69] John Dennis, 'Remarks on a Play, Call'd The Conscious Lovers, a Comedy' (1723) in Hooker, *Critical Works*, 252.

from the *Indies*, from whence he returns with a great Estate, carries on a
very great Trade at *London*, unbeknownst to his Friends and Relations at
Bristol, under the Name of *Sealand*. Now this Fiction, without which there
would be no Comedy, nor anything call'd a Comedy, is not supported by
Probability, Reason or Nature.[70]

Dennis queries the strategy of concealment, the implausibility of Sealand's
never sending for news of his missing wife, sister and child from Bristol
and in particular, the unlikelihood of a merchant returning 'from the
Indies with a vast Estate, and the World should not know either what he
is, or what he was when he went thither, especially when he traded to every
Part of the Globe. Or was there ever any great Merchant of *London* whose
Family and Original was not known to the Merchants of *Bristol?*[71] For
Dennis, the trading world is too transparent, secure and well-networked to
allow women to be taken prisoner and 'disappeared'. He calls Indiana's
capture 'Pregnant with Absurdity' (268) because "Tis highly improbable,
that an *East-Indies* Vessel, which had Force enough to venture without a
Convoy, should be taken by a Privateer' (268). He finds it ridiculous that
Indiana's aunt could send no letters from France asking for help and insists
that even were she unable to write, not only 'the whole *East*-India
Company but all *London* would have known what was become of the
Ship, at a time when so many News-Writers contended which could
furnish the Town with the freshest News' (268).

Dennis has other complaints, about Indiana's dubious claims to modesty and Bevil's unbelievable filial piety, although his emphasis falls heavily
on what he regards as a travesty of overseas trade. But the incidents from
which Steele has constructed his action are not simply romance tropes
recycled from Terence's *Andria* – they are reminiscent of events in his own
family history. One of his aunts was born in South Asia and named
Indiana; his first wife's brother was captured by French privateers while
sailing from the West Indies and was killed. Steele's dead brother-in-law
left a 'Negro woman' and numerous children, all of whom were manumitted on his death but received no inheritance, being reduced to indigence.
Steele was able to bring his own marriage plot to a happy conclusion when
the West Indian inheritance of a plantation and slaves he gained from his
first wife facilitated his marriage to a woman who brought him a small
landed estate in Wales.

Anglo-Irish adventurism was not, it seems, hard to cloak in the tropes of
romance or Terentian antecedent. The point was to bring the audience

---

[70] Dennis, 'Remarks on a Play', 263.   [71] Dennis, 'Remarks on a Play', 263.

into collusion with this particular version of the trials and triumphs of 'the new and numerous Gentry' deplored by Dennis as he warned of Irish cultural corruption: 'The Sentiments in *The Conscious Lovers* are often frivolous, false, and absurd; the Dialogue is awkward, clumsy, and spiritless; the Diction affected, impure, and barbarous, and too often *Hibernian*. Who, that is concern'd for the Honour of his Country, can see without Indignation whole Crowds of his Countrymen assembled to hear a Parcel of *Teagues* talking *Tipperary* together, and applauding what they say?' (274).

Steele is able to effect the triumph of what Danvers/Sealand also identifies in a famous speech as a new 'species of gentry, that have grown into the world this last century' (4.2.52) by yoking affiliation to sentiment. Cibber's commentary on the reception of *Cato* makes it clear that the expression and avowal of a feeling response to Addison's play in performance was mandated – to remain unmoved would be to mark oneself not just undiscriminating but profoundly unpatriotic. Ten years later, *The Conscious Lovers* sought to exercise a similar power; the play's ostensible programme of elite reconciliation, extreme filial piety, rakish reform and exemplary benevolence was to be enforced by the spontaneous, communal response to Indiana's reunion with her father. Commentators through the eighteenth century bear out the claim that the play moved audiences: an early sonnet 'To Sir Richard Steele' (1726) remarks, 'At Sealand's Feet to see his Daughter lie / Each tender Heart o'erflows with Tears of Joy'.[72] Another commentator, writing several decades, recalls a famous anecdote:

> We have already observed, that it is impossible to witness the tender scenes of this comedy without emotion; that is, no man who has experienced the delicate solicitudes of love and affection, can do it. Sir Richard has told us, that when one of the players told Mr Wilks, that there was a general weeping for Indiana, he politely observed 'that he would not fight the worse for it.'[73]

The early panegyrics to Steele that celebrated the play were equally emphatic about the play's patriotic effect: 'The *British* Fair, thy finish'd Model shown, / By *Indiana's* Conduct set their own' declaims one celebrant, 'What *Briton* now, will reckon Vertue dull?' asks another.[74] By

[72] James Heywood, 'To Sir Richard Steele, on His Comedy, call'd *The Conscious Lovers*', in *Letters and Poems on Several Subjects* (London: W. Meadowes, T. Worral, J. Ashford, 1726), 207.

[73] *The Theatre: or, Select Works of the British Dramatick Poets*, 12 vols. (Edinburgh: Martin and Wotherspoon, 1768), 6:xiv.

[74] Anonymous, 'To Sir Richard Steele, on His Comedy, The Conscious Lovers', in *Miscellaneous Poems by Several Hands* (London: D. Lewis, 1722), 68; and Joseph Mitchell, 'To Richard Steele on

weeping, the audience demonstrated their incorporation of and assent to the sentimental norms modelled on stage. No response could distinguish one weeping spectator from another except an indifference that would mark the viewer as uncivil – self-condemned to unfeeling isolation. Almost maddened by his sense of alienation from this community of taste and feeling, Dennis proclaimed wildly in his 'Remarks on a Play call'd The Conscious Lovers' that 'I am as to this Matter, in a State of Nature with these Persons.'[75] In a deliberate, direct riposte to the ethnic aspersions that follow, Benjamin Victor praised Steele's multiple hybridity: 'the greatest Panegyrick upon you, is the unprejudic'd and bare Truth of your Character, the Fire of Youth, with the Sedateness of a Senator, and the modern Gayety of an *English* Gentleman, with the Noble Solidity of an Ancient *Briton*'.[76] Refusing the ethnocentric singularity of Dennis's definitions of comedy and national identity, Victor celebrates Steele's personal combining of opposites as a model of contemporary British manhood. The value of the sentimental drama was equivalent, as its novel union of dramatic elements succeeded in erasing ethnic as well as sectarian, status or party differences in a temporary community of proper feeling.

Both before and after the decades following the great success of *The Conscious Lovers*, other writers adopted pathetic and sentimental scenarios in pursuit of agendas that reiterated but also stretched beyond Steele's conventional unionist, latitudinarian Anglican and Whig apologetics. Deist sympathizers such as John Hughes, Aaron Hill and James Thomson wrote highly pathetic philo-Islamic plays that implicitly supported universal toleration: George Coleman the Elder adapted Voltaire's sentimental *L'Ecossaise* to rebuke contemporary Scotophobia and encourage interunion harmony. Plays about cruelly treated Indians reiterated the black legend of Spanish Conquest in America and set up an implicit contrast with British colonial policy. As abolition became a heated topic of cultural and political debate from the 1760s on, Southerne's *Oroonoko; or, The Royal Slave* was repeatedly revised to excise its comedy, heighten its pathos and drive home an abolitionist message. Just how successful anti-slavery drama was in confirming rather than undermining African humanity is an open question, but there is no doubt that contemporary commentators themselves believed it to be an effective weapon, remarking of Coleman's

the Successful Representation of His Excellent Comedy call'd, *The Conscious Lovers*', in *Poems on Several Occasions,* 2 vols. (London: L. Gilliver, 1729), 2:257.

[75] Dennis, 'Remarks on a Play', 257.

[76] Benjamin Victor, *An Epistle to Richard Steele, on His Play call'd* The Conscious Lovers, 2nd ed. (London: W. Chetwood, S. Chapman, J. Stagg, J. Brotherton, Th. Edlin, 1722), 29.

sentimental *Inkle and Yarico* that it was 'as capable of *writing* a petition for the abolition of the slave-trade as any of those associated bodies who have taken so much pains for that laudable purpose'.[77] It is equally clear that pathetic and sentimental drama worked persistently to confirm spectators in their own sense of national superiority, not least their possession of that most vital of Enlightenment virtues, humane feeling.[78] What seems more surprising is that they convinced others of it too: in a letter about *Oroonoko* sent by a French traveller to a friend back home, Jean Bernard Le Blanc commented, 'The author has painted the strongest of all virtues in it, with the strongest and most moving strokes; and let us say to the honour of the English, that which is the peculiar characteristic of their nation, humanity'.[79] If sentimental drama did not succeed in abolishing the slave trade, it certainly assisted in the construction of a national imaginary in which humane feeling assumed a central role.

---

[77] *The Theatrical Register* (York, 1788), 12–13, quoted by Worrall in *Harlequin Empire*, 1.

[78] For a recent discussion of the importance of humanity to British identity in the later eighteenth century, see Swaminathan, *Debating the Slave Trade*.

[79] Jean Bernard Le Blanc, *Letters on the English and French Nations*, 2 vols. (London: J. Brindley, R. Francklin, C. Davis, J. Hodges, 1747), Letter LVI, vol. 2, 58.

CHAPTER 2

Fair Captives and Spiritual Dragooning
Islam and Toleration on Stage

In *Tatler* 41 (July 26, 1709), Richard Steele depicts a city merchant he calls Aurengzebe, Mughal of India and hero of Dryden's eponymous play, relaxing daily in an elaborate oriental performance staged in a Drury Lane brothel. 'Here it is, that when *Aurengzebe* thinks to give a Loose to Dalliance, the Purveyors prepare the Entertainment; and what makes it more august is, that every Person concerned in the Interlude has his set Part, and the Prince sends before-hand Word what he deigns to say, and directs also the very Answer which shall be made to him.'[1] 'Aurengzebe' is decorated by a huge diamond, 'the largest Stone [India's] rich Earth produced' (1:329) and after entering the 'seraglio', is presented to the brothel-keeper and her two assistants. They are followed by 'an unhappy Nymph, who is to be supposed just escaped from the Hands of a Ravisher, with her Tresses dishevel'd, runs into the Room with a dagger in her Hand, and falls before the Emperor' (1:330). This woman (who feigns suicide after lamenting her supposed ravishment) is followed by 'others of different Characters' to all of whom the client is finally 'revealed' as 'the Great Mogul' (1:330).

While the primary object of Steele's satire here is Thomas Coulson, a merchant whose aged and impotent depravity is enabled by the wealth he has accumulated in the East India trade, signalized by his enormous diamond, the sketch is equally concerned with criticizing the bordello's provision of erotic theatricality. Many of Steele's readers would have had no difficulty in recognizing the original of the ravished nymph at 'Aurengzebe's' feet as Morena, the Turkish virgin whose rape by Ibrahim the Thirteenth in Mary Pix's eponymous tragedy was orchestrated by the head

---

[1] *The Tatler*, 3 vols., ed. Donald F. Bond (Oxford: Clarendon, 1987). All other quotations are from this edition and are cited in the text by volume and page number.

of his harem, a woman called Sheker Para.[2] Located as it was in Drury Lane, the brothel's reenactment of a climactic scene from Pix's play suggests a morally dubious traffic in representations of exotic sexuality between the theatre and the licentious places of entertainment in its immediate vicinity, as theatre audiences domesticate and re-consume the luscious spectacles on offer in the playhouse. Steele makes his hostility to such enflaming dramatic scenes clear in *Spectator* 51 (April 28, 1711), arguing that 'no one ever writ Bawdy for any other Reason but the Dearth of Invention' (3:121) and suggesting that women dramatists were particularly notable for such erotic padding. Significantly, he again invokes Mary Pix's Turkish tragedy as an example of licentious female stagecraft: 'It is remarkable, that the Writers of least Learning are best skilled in the luscious way. The Poetesses of this Age have done Wonders in this kind; and we are obliged to the Lady who writ *Ibrahim*, for introducing a preparatory Scene to the very Action, when the Emperor throws down his Handkerchief as a Signal for his Mistress to follow him to the most retired part of the Seraglio' (3:218).

Steele's hostility to the contaminating salaciousness of harem drama points to a crucial element in the continuing appeal of plays set in the Ottoman or North African states.[3] The seraglio was a focus for European sexual fantasy before, throughout and after the eighteenth century, and plays that focused on sexually vulnerable Christian women immured in the harem appeared regularly on English stages.[4] At the same time, however, rather more sober dramas of state, such as David Mallet's *Mustapha* (1736), also retained a place in the repertory. *Mustapha* resembled the heroic plays of the Restoration, allegorizing domestic political tensions in an oriental vehicle that also registered the greatness of historical figures such as Solymon the Magnificent.[5] From the 1710s on however, oriental

---

[2] *Ibrahim* was first produced in 1695–1696 and was sufficiently successful to be revived three times, in 1702, 1704, and finally 1715. For a recent summary of the now fairly extensive criticism of the play, see Bernadette Andrea (ed.), *Delarivier Manley and Mary Pix: English Women Staging Islam* (Toronto: ITER, 2012), 261–264.

[3] Jean Marsden's account of the anti-theatricality attacks associated with Collier suggests that Steele's attack on salaciousness in serious plays was unusual, as she argues that it was largely comedy rather than she-tragedies that attracted opprobrium. See *Fatal Desire: Women, Sexuality, and the English Stage 1660–1720* (Ithaca, NY: Cornell University Press, 2006), 62–63.

[4] For a more general discussion of the harem's fascination for Westerners, see Alain Grosrichard, *The Sultan's Court: European Fantasies of the East*, trans. Liz Heron (London: Verso, 1998); and Ruth Yeazell, *Harems of the Mind: Passages of Western Art and Literature* (New Haven, CT: Yale University Press, 2000).

[5] For recent commentary, see Mita Choudhury, *Interculturalism and Resistance in the London Theater, 1660–1800: Identity, Performance, Empire* (Lewisburg, PA: Bucknell University Press, 2000), 61–86; and Ballaster, *Fabulous Orients*.

tragedies with a somewhat different focus began to emerge, as serious plays engaged with the questions of religious tolerance and governance that fomented deistic controversy, informed party rage and justified continuing hostility to Catholic powers. From John Hughes's *The Siege of Damascus* (1719–1720) to James Thomson's *Edward and Eleonora* (1737), playwrights used episodes from the expansive history of Islamic interaction with Christians to explore and often to criticize the demands of religious orthodoxy. These texts do more than reiterate a conventional Whig condemnation of fanatic cruelty; their characterization of Islamic-Christian interaction carries the radical implication that universal toleration is both desirable and possible. They thus exemplify Wayne Hudson's suggestion that there was much more overlap between the varied positions of reformist deists and Protestant Whiggery than has been recognized.[6] Hudson suggests that for the majority of English deists, who remained socially conformist to Protestantism and Whiggism, reform involved reshaping 'the schemes human beings used to navigate their path through history' and trying 'to eliminate tyranny, priestcraft and superstition'.[7] The authors of the philo-Islamic tolerationist plays such as John Hughes, Aaron Hill and James Thomson shared a sympathetic interest in deism while remaining well-connected members of established literary and social communities. Further, it is telling that while most of these plays remained in the repertory, the last of them, James Miller's and James Hoadley's version of Voltaire's *Mahomet*, was written and performed in 1744. The 1740s is generally reckoned to be the last decade in which deism was a prominent and innovative discourse in British culture, so it seems unsurprising that new texts with the characteristically deistic critique of bigoted belief and priestcraft should largely cease to be written after these years.[8]

   Whig support for toleration or a more radical hostility to priestcraft associated with freethinking aside, a variety of cultural and political factors produced a context in which Islamicist plays with a tolerationist ethos could be written, be produced and become popular. After the Battle of Karlowitz in 1699, European fear of an endless *jihad* diminished. The Ottomans were still a force to reckoned with, fighting victoriously against the Russians in 1710–1711, less successfully against the Austrians in 1716–1718 but taking territory from the Austrians in the Russo-Austrian-Turkish War of 1735–1739. These conflicts necessarily influenced

---

[6] Wayne Hudson, *Enlightenment and Modernity: The English Deists and Reform* (London: Pickering and Chatto, 2009), 1–29.
[7] Hudson, *Enlightenment and Modernity*, 20.   [8] Hudson, *Enlightenment and Modernity*, 141.

British strategic thinking, but there was distinctly less anxiety and awe directed at the supreme Porte than in the latter part of the seventeenth century, not least during the Tulip Period in which the Ottomans were relatively open to European influences. In addition, the British continued to trade with and make alliances with the Barbary States because their interests in the Mediterranean made them dependent on supplies from the Maghreb, to keep Gibraltar and Minorca garrisoned and fleets provisioned.[9] The cooperation this engendered in commercial and naval agents existed alongside a deep-seated popular fear of the Barbary corsairs, who continued their predation through the Mediterranean and beyond. As Linda Colley and others have pointed out, the very real terror and possibility of captivity and slavery haunted both Christian voyagers and coastal communities to whom North African pirates were a real and continuing threat.[10]

Hanoverian stages were favoured sites for enacting the seductions and terrors of the seraglio, but they also used Islamic locales to rehearse some of the most critical political-theological debates of the early Enlightenment. At the same time Britain was jockeying to secure its advantages in overseas trade, her intellectual classes were engaged in absorbing – or rejecting – the religious and political theses of Shaftesbury, Locke and Bayle.[11] Recent commentators have shown that Islam, as a politico-theological rival to Judaism and Christianity, was central to such debates. For Protestants, deists or freethinkers, the persecution of the Huguenots following the revocation of the Edict of Nantes in 1685 was simply the latest of a long series of acts of violence that demonstrated the Roman Catholic willing-ness to use the most immoral measures to ensure religious conformity. During this period, John Marshall suggests, the international 'Republic of Letters' served as a positive model of tolerant and humane communal interaction whose institutional antithesis was the Catholic Inquisition.[12]

Religious tolerance was the central issue in early Enlightenment think-ing, not least because it intersected with questions of governance, in societies that almost all enforced religious uniformity of one kind or another.

---

[9] See David Abulafia (ed.), *The Mediterranean in History* (London: Thames & Hudson, 2003); Virginia Aksan, *Ottoman Wars, 1700–1870: An Empire Besieged* (Harlow: Pearson Longman, 2007); and James D. Tracy, *The Rise of Merchant Empires: Long-Distance Trade in the Early Modern World* (Cambridge: Cambridge University Press, 1990).

[10] Linda Colley, *Captives: Britain, Empire and the World* (London: Pimlico, 2003).

[11] For a discussion of the role of Islam in the reception of such argument, see Garcia, *Islam in the English Enlightenment*.

[12] Marshall, *John Locke*, 1–12.

Arguments for greater tolerance had several origins, including the patristic and late medieval view that tolerance should be extended to Jews, Muslims and pagans who had not known God along with statist arguments, recognizing the vital role of Jewish finance in governance.[13] Philo-Islamic arguments had to contend with widespread popular disapprobation but focused on the similarities between anti-Trinitarianism and Islam. Among English thinkers, Edward Pococke and Isaac Barrow stressed the commonalities of Unitarian Christian and Islamic belief – providing common ground against atheists – while Stephen Nye and William Freke suggested Islam's rapid spread was due to its rejection of the Trinity. Although not everyone involved in the tolerationist debate agreed, as both Isaac Barrow and John Tillotson believed Islam was spread by force, many others thought that Turkey, peaceful, prosperous and tolerant, provided a positive model for humane, religiously various states.[14] Rycaut's positive account of Turkish toleration influenced both Pierre Bayle's description of Islam in the *Historical and Critical Dictionary* and Locke's argument for extending toleration to Jews and Muslims in the *Third Letter*. Bayle believed that Islam theoretically proposed conversion by force but had eschewed such policies in practice.[15]

The extent to which such heterodox views were adopted by the British political nation is uncertain.[16] Justin Champion has argued recently that John Toland, one of the five leading deists of the first half century, was in fact much closer to powerful individuals and networks than previously recognized, contributing significantly to the maintenance of the radical republican tradition in the 1710s and 1720s.[17] It is certainly the case that (degrees of) toleration remained an absolutely central plank of Whig ideology, and as is so often the case, no one makes the point more vividly than Addison. In *Tatler* 161 (April 20, 1710), Addison describes the cultural geography of toleration and tyranny. He records a dream of a fertile plain high in the alps, presided over by a Goddess who is not identified but seems celestial: she is flanked on one side by the Liberty-capped Genius of a Commonwealth, somewhat bold and cruel and on the other by the Genius of Monarchy, very beautiful and holding a British sceptre in her hand, with British lions at her feet. The Arts and Sciences are in Liberty's train and two other monarchs were visible, namely Plenty,

---

[13] Marshall, *John Locke*, 388–395.   [14] Marshall, *John Locke*, 470.
[15] Marshall, *John Locke*, 613.
[16] A powerful case for a broad-bottomed deistic influence can be found in Margaret Jacob, *The Radical Enlightenment: Pantheists, Freemasons and Republicans* (London: Allen and Unwin, 1981).
[17] Champion, *Republican Learning*.

seated on a verdant Hill, and Commerce, located on 'a little Island that was covered with Groves of Spices, Olives, and Orange Trees; and in a Word, the Products of every Foreign Clime' (2:201). Exploring the boundaries of the valley, the dreamer comes across two great armies trying to invade the paradisal upland.

> TYRANNY was at the Head of one of these Armies, dressed in an Eastern Habit, and grasping in her Hand an Iron Sceptre. Behind her was *Barbarity* with the Garb and Complexion of an *Ethiopian*; *Ignorance,* with a Turbant upon her Head; and *Persecution,* holding up a bloody Flag, embroidered in Flower de Luces. These were followed by *Oppression, Poverty, Famine, Torture,* and a dreadful Train of Appearances, that made me tremble to behold them. Among the Baggage of this Army, I could discover Rocks, Wheels, Chains and Gibbets, with all the Instruments Art could invent to make human Nature miserable. (2:203)

While Tyranny is readily legible as an Ottoman, followed by Asian and North African barbarians, Persecution is French, and attended by all the social, economic and institutional evils believed to follow from national policies of intolerance. In Addison's vision, the Turk and the French are politically equivalent in their brutal severity but Persecution figures a specifically elaborate and Catholic form of oppression. In his horror of the instruments of torture used to punish apostates and heretics, Addison echoes the condemnation voiced by Philipp van Limborch's (1633–1712) celebrated *History of the Inquisition* (1692) a work instigated by Locke.

The politico-theological critiques of the philosophes were matched by a revisionist historiography. The doyenne of Whig history was the Huguenot Rapin de Thoyras, whose *History of England* was translated by deist Nicholas Tindall in the 1720s.[18] Rapin was a French refugee who fought for William III, but his account provided the model and standard for most of his peers, whatever their ideological stripe, until Hume's work displaced all rivals. Crucial to Rapin's *History* was a contempt for barbarism and religion, the era of monkish superstition and untrammelled priestly power. Significantly for playwrights interested in revisiting the contest of Crescent and Cross, this implied considerable hostility to the whole project of the Crusades. In this respect his work precedes and informs the views of later 'anti-orientalist' Enlightenment historians including Hume, William

---

[18] For an account of Rapin within the ideological debates of early eighteenth-century historiography, see Laird Okie, *Augustan History Writing: Histories of England in the Early English Enlightenment* (Lanham, MD: University Press of America, 1991).

Robertson and Gibbon.[19] This revisionist Whig historiography of England was accompanied by historical and theological writing about the Islam and the Saracens, which would be particularly important for dramatist John Hughes.

Regency Issues

The originality of Hughes's *The Siege of Damascus* is particularly apparent when comparing it to Charles Johnson's *The Sultaness* (1717), which appeared just before the former's tragedy. Johnson's play was a fairly straightforward translation of Racine's *Bajazet* and is a striking example of the continuing attractions of the heroic palace intrigue, somewhat modified by the pathetic agonies of the female protagonist. The play focuses on the love triangle of Roxana, Sultan Amurat's Queen and Atalida, her attendant, who has acted as intermediary for Roxana in seducing Bajazet, the Sultan's attractive younger brother. In the process of the proxy wooing, Atalida and Bajazet have fallen in love. The Vizier Acomat has encouraged love between Bajazet and Roxana in hopes that the brutal Amurat will be supplanted by the nobler sibling. Although tortured by suspicion that Bajazet loves Atalida rather than herself, Roxana repeatedly ignores the absent Amurat's instructions to execute his brother. The action ends with all three dying; Bajazet finally falls victim to Roxana's mutes, Roxana is killed by janissaries angered by Bajazet's death and Atalida commits suicide.

Faithful as it is to Racine, the play's stress on the emotional anguish of the female characters is symptomatic of the early eighteenth-century predominance of she-tragedy, delineated by Jean Marsden.[20] But the tragedy's exploration of doomed passion and frustrated palace intrigue is more than pathos exoticized. Acomat's plotting is generated by the Sultan's brutality and absence, creating a political vacuum insecurely and erratically filled by Roxana, a woman whose emotions prove fatally easy to manipulate. Like many earlier Turkish plays, *The Sultaness* suggests parallels to current British politics; the division between jealous, unpopular, absent

---

[19] In an admiring account of Hume, Robertson and Gibbons, John Docker seems unaware of Rapin's earlier articulation of a similar critique. See 'Sheer Folly and Derangement: How the Crusades Disoriented Enlightenment Historiography', in *Representing Humanity in the Age of Enlightenment*, ed. Alexander Cook, Ned Curthoys and Shino Konishi (London: Pickering and Chatto, 2013), 41–52.

[20] Marsden, *Fatal Desire*.

Amurat and his compelling younger brother could be read as a version of the relationship between George I and the Prince of Wales, not least because their mutual hostility complicated Regency governance during the king's frequent, much-loathed absences in Hanover.[21] The play is equally concerned, however, with contemplating the vicissitudes of the resurgent Ottoman state, at that moment still engaged in a war with Austria. Addressing the female spectators as is customary after such plays, to stress the putative superiority of their own gender order, Mrs Santlow proclaimed,

> There where the Sultan, their half-vanquish'd Lord,
> Flies for Protection from *Eugenio's* Sword,
> To distant *Britain's* Prince, who wise and great,
> In equal Balance, holds *Europa's* Fate:[22]

Santlow is referring here to Prince Eugene of Savoy, who had just defeated the Ottomans at the Battle of Petrovaradin in 1716. Eugene had a European-wide reputation from fighting successfully against the Turks, but the British held him in especially high regard for having fought alongside Marlborough against the French at Blenheim, Oudenarde and Malplaquet.[23] Eugene would gain another victory against the Turks in 1718, paving the way for the British to join the French and the Austrians in the War of the Quadruple Alliance against the French. In reworking *Bajazet,* therefore, Johnson chose a text for the times that shows the Ottomans resurgent militarily but internally weak, riven by domestic and internecine conflict. By characterizing the Ottoman state in such divided, passional and feminocentric terms, the play hopefully implies that a full victory over 'half-vanquish'd' Vizier Damat Ali is assured – although Amurat's control of the action from offstage might be said to leave the issue open.

Clashing Superstitions

Glancing critically at both Britain's internal affairs and the embattled Ottomans, via a feminocentric vehicle that stressed the putative cultural

---

[21] For an account of these problems, see Brendan Simms, *Three Victories and a Defeat: The Rise and Fall of the First British Empire, 1714–1783* (London: Penguin, 2008), 127.

[22] Charles Johnson, *The Sultaness: A Tragedy* (London: W. Wilkins et al., 1717), n.p. All quotations are from this edition and are cited in the text by act, scene and page numbers.

[23] There were many contemporary lives of Eugene: see John Banks, *History of Francis-Eugene, Prince of Savoy ... Containing ... Military Transactions ...* (London: John Banks, 1741). For a more recent account of his career, see Nicholas Henderson, *Prince Eugen of Savoy* (London: Phoenix, 2002).

and political weakness of Turkish institutions, *The Sultaness* was consonant with many of its predecessors. By contrast, John Hughes's *The Siege of Damascus*, the next new oriental drama to be staged, was markedly original. Hughes chose an entirely novel subject, drawn from Simon Ockley's recently published and hitherto unexploited *Conquest of Syria* (1708), and focused his play on the dangers of religious and cultural fanaticism.[24] The production was great success in early 1720 and continued to be popular right through to 1785, with at least 117 performances in London and multiple editions of the text being printed.[25]

Hughes was from a dissenting family and may have pursued a career in letters because he couldn't take orders. Two of his poems, 'An Ode to the Creator of the World' (1712) and 'The Ecstacy' (1720), suggest deist sympathies, and he translated Fontenelle's *New Dialogues of the Dead* in 1708. He was not so wildly heterodox however that he couldn't write for *The Tatler*, *The Spectator*, and *The Guardian*, becoming friendly with Addison and Steele and other denizens of the Kit-Kat Club. Following the model identified by Abigail Williams, his efforts in Whig panegyric were rewarded with a 'place'; specifically, sometime after 1714 he became secretary to the Commission for Strengthening Fortifications of Royal Harbours.[26] In 1717, his main patron and Lord Chancellor Earl Cowper, appointed him secretary to the Commissions of the Peace in the Court of Chancery.

Hughes was thus comfortably situated and close to policy makers when he wrote *The Siege of Damascus*. The Prologue claims (rightly) that its subject is novel: 'the Story new. / Our opening Scenes shall to your sight disclose / How spiritual Dragooning first arose.'[27] The episode chosen was the conquest of Damascus by Khalid ibn al-Walid in August and September 635 CE, during the Rashidun Caliphate. Most of Syria had been taken by this date, but Emperor Heraclius sent an army to relieve the Damascenes. The Muslims withdrew but went on to defeat the Byzantines in a

---

[24] For a brief account of Ockley's career, see Ockley, 'The Pioneer', in *Oriental Essays: Portraits of Seven Scholars* (London: Allen & Unwin, 1960), and for a more recent overview, see G. J. Toomer, *Eastern Wisdom and Learning: The Study of Arabic in Seventeenth-Century England* (Oxford: Clarendon, 1996).

[25] Ben Ross Schneider Jr. (ed.), *The London Stage 1660–1800* (Carbondale: Southern Illinois University Press, 1979), 435.

[26] For an overview of Hughes's career, see Thomas N. McGeavy, 'John Hughes, 1668–1720', in *Oxford Dictionary of National Biography*, www.oxforddnb.com. For the entwined careers of literary and political 'placemen', see Williams, *Poetry and the Creation of a Whig Literary Culture*, 217.

[27] John Hughes, *The Siege of Damascus* (London, 1720), n.p. All other quotations are from this edition and are cited in the text.

battle at the nearby Yarmouk River. Most of the Damascenes apparently remained Christian after their incorporation into the Caliphate.[28]

In choosing to dramatize an episode from the first volume of Ockley's *The History of the Conquest of Syria, Persia and Aegypt by the Saracens*, Hughes was assisting the orientalist in his desire to inform the British about Arab culture and religion. Ockley was committed to educating his countrymen about the Saracens, for, he tells his reader, they were not 'sufficiently acquainted with that Nation, have entertain'd too mean an opinion of them, looking upon them as meer Barbarians, which mistaken Notion of theirs, has hinder'd all further Enquiry concerning them'.[29] As we have seen, philo-Islamic scholarship was often associated with hetero-doxy, but although he was associated briefly with William Whiston, who was banished from Oxford for his unorthodox views of the primitive church, Ockley seems to have made repeated efforts to distance himself from any freethinking. He was regarded by Harley as sufficiently respon-sible to translate letters from the Moroccan ruler Mawley Isma'il in 1714 but his government patronage ceased after Harley's fall. Unsuccessful as he was in worldly matters, the process by which Ockley's Saracen history was recirculated via the stage (and in a potted epitome when the play became successful) suggests a widespread public appetite for his theologic-ally charged subject matter.[30] The 'explaination' that was published to capitalize on the play's success suggests that its exoticism was also a draw: making a particular appeal to the female spectator, the pamphlet not only summarizes Ockley's historical narrative but explains terms like 'sopha'. A comparison much later in the century between a new oriental tragedy, William Hodson's *Zoraida* (1780), and Hughes's play suggests the con-tinuing power of the latter's Arabian enchantments:

> This management of local proprieties requires a taste and address not so happily displayed in the tragedy of *Zoraida*, just as in some other plays founded on Eastern stories. Part of the Turkish mythology is popular, and generally known. Such allusions are preferable to a parade of Oriental pedantry; as a proof of which, let the reader of *Zoraida* compare

[28] See Ross Burns, *Damascus: A History* (London: Routledge, 2005), chaps. 7 and 8.

[29] Simon Ockley, *The Conquest of Syria, Persia and Aegypt by the Saracens* (London, 1708), xi.

[30] Ockley's formal histories aside, in 1713 he also published *An Account of South-West Barbary*, a slave narrative intended to make money. The explanatory pamphlet is titled *An Explaination [sic] of the Several Arabick Terms us'd in The Siege of Damascus Written by Mr Hughes. With a Short Account of the Historical Seige, and the Life of Muhamet, as Far as It Is Necessary to Understanding the Story* (London: J. Brotherton et al., 1720).

Almaimon's description of the Mahometan paradise (p.28) to Caled's beautiful verses on the same subject in Hughes's *Siege of Damascus*.[31]

Hughes's play made one crucial change to the source. While most of the historical personages and the action follow Ockley's account, Phocyas himself is reconstructed. In *The Conquest*, Damascus is vigorously defended by one Thomas, a son of the Emperor, and betrayed for venal reasons by a corrupt priest called Josias. Phocyas is a minor figure. Hughes compounds Thomas and Josias in the figure of the virtuous Phocyas, creating a character who is racked by the competing claims of love and loyalty. In Hughes's play, Phocyas loves Eudocia, daughter of the governor, Eumenes; they plight their troth, Phocyas defeats the invaders and asks for Eudocia's hand. Eumenes refuses angrily and an agonized Phocyas and Eudocia decide to run away to Antioch, where Phocyas has an uncle. Unfortunately, Phocyas gets caught by the Saracens as he's leaving the city, although Eudocia gets back safely. Led by the brutal and threatening Caled, the Muslims try to convert Phocyas. On his refusal, his death is prevented by the humane Abudah, Caled's deputy. Abudah persuades Caled to accept Phocyas's offer to reveal a secret entry to the city in return for a promise of mercy to the citizens. The plan succeeds but Eudocia rejects Phocyas when he reveals his betrayal. As the Damascenes leave, Caled is enraged by the wealth they're removing; his slaughter of the refugees is halted by the humane Abudah and Phocyas kills Caled. Phocyas is reunited as he dies with Eudocia and Eumenes rues the discord, which has brought the Christians to this plight.

The Prologue is emphatic about the play's 'Moral': it begins by explaining it will show 'How Spiritual Dragooning first arose; / Claims drawn from Heav'n by a *Barbarian* Lord, / And Faith first propagated by the Sword.' The 'Faith' spreads because Araby's neighbours were 'By Faction weaken'd, and Disunion broke' – a fate that the British face if they 'grow supine with Liberty and Ease', but more importantly, if they give way to intolerance both internally and externally – 'forgo intestine Jars, / Then scorn the Rumours of Religious Wars.' The British need to keep their minds on maritime strength: 'speak loud in Thunder from your guarded Shores, / And tell the Continent, the Sea is Yours. / Speak on, ——— and say, by War, you'll Peace maintain.'

This set of injunctions is not hard to parse in the moment of the play's production. Hughes's position as Secretary for the Commission charged

---

with strengthening the royal harbours meant he had a professional appreciation of the importance of naval defence. Maritime power was critical as in the years of the play's production as Britain was embroiled in the War of the Quadruple Alliance, in which they were allied with the Dutch, the Austrians and the French against Spain. Extremely concerned about Spanish aggression in the Mediterranean and North America, the government also had to parry the Duke of Ormonde's Spanish-financed Jacobite invasion attempt in June 1719. However it might stick in the craw, the multiple threats provided by the Spanish required cooperating with other Catholic powers, even the French.[32]

How do such national security and imperial imperatives inform a play about the origins of 'spiritual dragooning' of an Islamic stripe? The play suggests that any form of fanaticism, irrationality and inhumanity is not only destructive but ineffective. The Muslim leader Caled – whose historic model was known as the 'Sword of God' for his militance – is motivated by violent fury, saying to his off-sider Daran 'I hate these Christian Dogs; and 'tis our Task, / As thou observ'd, to fight; our Law enjoins it. / Heaven too is promis'd only to the Valiant' (1.2.14). Caled's religiously justified cruelty reaches its apogee in a climactic encounter with Phocyas, in which he threatens to seek out Eudocia during the invasion of the city and force Phocyas to watch her handed over for rape by another Mahometan invader. While Caled's religion seems to license his aggression, Daran is in it – as he says – 'For War and plunder' (1.2.14). The Muslims have all the initiative in the play, as the weak and divided Damascene leaders are shown as largely unwilling to take the fight to the aggressors. But significantly, both Caled and Daran die in the campaign against Damascus and the Arab leader left victorious at the close is the humane and rational Abudah, Caled's deputy, who masterminds the final victory by coming to a gentleman's agreement with Phocyas. While the Christians have been humiliated and their hero, Phocyas, is dead, Abudah leaves the stage militarily triumphant and with honour intact. His moral superiority is acknowledged by Eumenes, the Christian leader, in a very suggestive final exchange:

> *Eum.* Still just and brave! Thy Virtues wou'd adorn
> A purer Faith! Thou better than thy Sect,
> That dar'st decline from that to Acts of Mercy!
> Pardon, *Abudah*, if thy honest Heart

---

[32] See Simms, *Three Victories and a Defeat*, 135–157, and N. A. M. Rodger, *The Command of the Ocean: A Naval History of Britain 1649–1815* (New York: Norton, 2004), 227–240.

Figure 1.   *Portrait of Mr Sowdon in the Character of Caled in* The Siege of Damascus.
Mezzotint. Artists John Fredrick Lewis and Andrew Miller. No date. Courtesy the
Victoria and Albert Museum, London

> Makes us ev'n with thee ours.
> *Abu.* (*Aside.*) O Power Supreme
> That mad'st my Heart, and know'st its inmost Frame!
> If yet I err, O lead me into Truth,
> Or pardon unknown Error! ——— Now, *Eumenes*,
> Friends as we may be, let us part in peace. (5.2.67)

Abudah's expression of the doubt prompted by Eumenes's claim of spiritual kinship is expressed in an address to the deity in terms of deliberate vagueness. Thoroughly ambiguous, the speech could suggest an awakening to Christianity or an articulation of deistic belief, genuine spiritual conviction oriented towards the single divine creator.

While the Muslims are on a roll in this play, the tragedy derives from the various difficulties in which Phocyas finds himself as result of failures in Christian conduct. In his Eulogy to Hughes (who died the night of the play's premiere) in *The Theatre*, Richard Steele described the moment at which Phocyas is 'admonished by a Tyrant to expect no mercy, but is left alone to consider with himself, whether he will comply with the terms he offers him, to wit, changing the Christian Religion for the Mahometan Idolatry, or die'.[33] The soliloquy in which Phocyas considers and rejects Caled's offer was, Steele writes, 'attended to with the greatest and most solemn instance of approbation, an aweful silence' (Number 15, February 20, 1720). The hero finds himself in this position because Eumenes, acting tyrannically in relation to his daughter, and mindful of his friend Herbis's poisoned advice, has refused her marriage to Phocyas. Phocyas's initial alienation from the Damascene patriarchy is followed by Eudocia's rejection of him as a traitor to religion and city when she discovers he has guided the Muslims. In both cases the spectator is likely to feel that Christian inhumanity, a lack of the sympathy so plentifully displayed by Abudah, has produced Phocyas's agonizing dilemmas. Overtly orthodox, and full of lurid invocations of Islamic cruelty as it is, as the action unfolds it is hard not to see the play subjecting the two competing faith communities to an equally critical gaze.

This view is legible in contemporary responses to the play. In a Preface to a posthumous collection of Hughes's poems published in 1735, his editor (and brother-in-law) William Duncombe ventriloquizes the complaints of anonymous commentators who (we are told) regard the 'Plan' as faulty. 'There does not appear (say some, who are esteem'd Persons of very

---

[33] Sir Richard Steele, *The Theatre 1720*, ed. John Loftis (Oxford: Clarendon, 1962). All quotations are from this edition and are cited in the text by page number.

good Taste and Judgement) a sufficient Ground and Foundation for the Distress in the fourth and fifth Acts. For what is *Phocyas's* crime? ... What is there in all this that a virtuous Man might not have done for the Good of his Country?' Duncombe goes on to suggest that Phocyas's undermotivated remorse and communal condemnation were originally generated by real (if temporary) apostasy and that in the first draft of the play Phocyas actually kissed the Alcoran as a sign of conversion. But the managers of Drury-Lane (who would still have included Steele at that point) insisted 'that he could not be a Heroe if he changed his Religion, and that the Audience would not bear the sight of him after it'. Hughes was persuaded to excise a scene that was exceptionally 'tender and rationally passionate' only in order to ensure the production went ahead to benefit his relatives, as he already knew he was dying.[34]

Clearly scenes of forced conversion were potent and made effective theatre. Whatever their differences about natural religion and Islamic virtue, the point on which both a putative deist such as Hughes and a thoroughly orthodox Whig Anglican such as Steele could agree would be in regarding religious persecution as thoroughly evil. In Bayle's *Philosophical Commentary*, published in English in 1708, the recent violence against Catholics in France is anathematized in terms that anticipate Hughes's condemnation of 'spiritual dragooning' in the Prologue:

> We affirm, there is as much Barbarity in Dragooning, Dungeoning, Cloistering etc, the People of a contrary Religion, in such a civiliz'd, knowing, genteel Age as ours; as there was in executing 'em by the hands of the common Hangman, in Ages of Ignorance and Brutality, before People had purg'd off the Manners of their Ancestors.[35]

Where *The Siege of Damascus* parts company from Steele's conventional hostility to 'Persecution' is in its implicit levelling of the Christian and Islamic communities and admiration for the latter's tolerance. In this regard, Hughes follows Bayle, who believed that in contrast to Catholic Christianity Islam justified forcible conversion theoretically but had largely avoided it in practice.[36]

Obviously most English people who were hostile to Catholicism did not share the philo-Islamism of certain radical philosophes and scholars. Why then might Hughes have thought he could modify the conventional Islamophobia of his audiences? The answer may lie in the particular

---

[34] See *Poems on Several Occasions* ... , 2 vols., ed. William Duncombe (London: J. Tonson and J. Watts, 1735), 1:xxvii.

[35] Quoted in Marshall, *John Locke*, 621.   [36] See Marshall, *John Locke*, 613.

strategic circumstances of the late 1710s. Nabil Matar has pointed out that the Nine Years' War and the War of the Spanish Succession demanded cooperation and considerable bribery of the Islamic powers of North Africa in order to keep Gibraltar and the Mediterranean fleets supplied.[37] The War of the Quadruple Alliance, coincident with the writing and production of Hughes's play, demanded no less. Imperial interest required treaties and trade with Morocco and the Algerines, to enable British action against the Spanish, against whom feeling would have been especially inflamed after the Ormonde invasion attempt. While reflecting something of Shaftesbury's universalist conviction that our natural affections 'are founded in Love, Complacency, Goodwill, and in a Sympathy for the Kind or Species' rather than limited to those born on the same 'dust and clay', Hughes's depiction of a humane Muslim succouring unwise and unkind Christians echoed the broader strategic circumstances of the Mediterranean war.[38] Further, the British and the North Africans were in de facto alliance against the leading contemporary exemplars of 'spiritual dragooning', namely the Spanish. Even for leading proponents of toleration such as Locke, emancipating Catholics was more problematic that allowing liberty of conscience to Jews and Muslims precisely because Catholics were presumed to be incapable of practicing toleration themselves. Caled's and Daran's fanatic and rapacious brutality thus prefigures the black legend of Spanish cruelty, conforming with stereotypes of Muslim imposture and conquest but also suggesting that contemporary Islam may be better embodied in the actions of the ethical and humane Abudah. It is the Catholics – especially the Spanish – who have inherited the mantle of sword and crescent.

Hughes's tragedy held the stage until the 1780s, with the play appearing almost annually until the 1760s, suggesting a receptive audience for the play's tolerationist ethos as well as the text's attractions to performers such as Elizabeth Younge (1744–1797), who won plaudits as Eudocia. Further, Georgina Lock has recently revealed that *The Siege of Damascus* also had an important afterlife in the dramatic pedagogy of Newcome's School at Hackney, being repeatedly performed by the pupil players of this academy. Newcombe's students included later clerical men of literature such as John Hoadley, who played Phocyas in the school's production and would complete James Miller's *Mahomet*; and important politicians such as

---

[37] Nabil Matar, 'Islam in Britain, 1689–1750', *Journal of British Studies* 47.2 (2008): 284–300.
[38] Anthony Ashley Cooper, Earl of Shaftesbury, *Characteristics of Men, Manners, Opinions, Times,* ed. Lawrence E. Klein (Cambridge: Cambridge University Press, 1999), 48.

Charles Yorke (1722–1770), who served as Lord Chancellor, and Augustus
Fitzroy, Third Duke of Grafton and British Prime Minister from 1768 to
1770. [39] Lock notes that Hughes's play was attractive to the schoolmaster
because it offered roles for extras as soldiers, exotic settings and an exciting
plot, but as Earl Cowper's verses *To the Memory of Mr Hughes* suggest, its
'glorious lessons' lay also in its presentation of inspiring exemplars:

> How does thy *Phocyas* warm *Britannia's* Youth, –
> In Arms to Glory and in love with Truth!
> Then Youths renowned for many a Field well fought,
> Shall own the glorious Lessons thou hast taught.[40]

While his patron stressed the successful didacticism of *The Siege of Damascus*, its specifically masculine appeal to patriotic and military honour, in
her own elegy 'To the Memory of Mr Hughes', Cowper's daughter Judith
emphasized the tragedy's softer and more sentimental effects:

> Virtue distress'd, thy happy lines disclose,
> With more of triumph than a Conqu'ror knows;
> Touch'd by thy hand, our stubborn tempers bend,
> And flowing tears the well-wrought scene attend. (51–54)

In a gesture echoed by other eulogists, she characterizes Hughes as a model
of patient resignation: 'Free from the bigot's fears or Stoic's pride, / Calm
as our Christian Hero liv'd, he died' (70–71).[41] The references to bigotry
and stoicism, against which extremes Hughes is contrasted, invoke the
fanaticism he condemns in *The Siege* on the one hand, while defending
him from the charge of freethinking associated with attacks on religion per
se on the other. While Judith Cowper's poem seeks to dismiss the taint of
apostacy, a Prologue written for a Newcombe School performance
acknowledges the issue does occur in the text:

> . . . this Night we break our Bounds
> See us transported to Poetic Grounds
> To Eastern Climes, where Hughes attempts to raise
> Fair Virtue's Temple on Religion's Base
> . . .

---

[39] Georgina Lock, 'The Siege of Damascus, 1764, at Mr Newcome's School in Hackney' (paper,
    Paying the Piper: The Economies of Amateur Performance, University of Notre Dame, June
    28–29, 2014).
[40] Earl Cowper William, 'To the Memory of Mr Hughes', in *The Poetical Works of John Hughes*, 2
    vols. (Edinburgh: Apollo Press by the Martins, 1779), 1:xliii.
[41] *Poetical Works of John Hughes*, 1:xliv.

If Phoigas for a moment quits the Truth
Think him a soldier, & forgive his Youth.[42]

The high regard for the play endured, but its appeal altered, with the thematic injunction to maintain patriotic unity eventually supplanting 'pathetic pictures of persecution'. The latter phrase comes from a laudatory reviewer of *Memoirs of the Life and Writings of John Hughes* (1777), who praised the tragedy for 'the sublimity of the sentiment, the correctness of the language, the propriety of the characters, the pathetic pictures of persecution, and the judicious disposition of the whole piece'. The reviewer went on to remark on the play's longevity: 'It is worthy of observation, that very few plays have succeeded so well as this', for despite the author having been unable to provide direction, 'it was well-received' initially 'and has maintained its credit since'.[43] In the following decade, in the wake of the loss of the American War, the horrid parallel to a defeated and declining empire suggested by the play was uppermost in spectators' minds, and a newly minted Epilogue spoken by a Mr. Fector at his private theatre in Dover on March 13, 1785, was reprinted in more than one periodical:

Britons attend! Nor be for you in vain
Th'historian's page explor'd, the poet's strain;
And whilst you weep, to gen'rous impulse just,
O'er worldly greatness humbl'd in the dust,
From wars long past, oh turn the pitying eye,
A nearer sorrow claims a Briton's sigh;
O'er your own country's fate one tear bestow,
From what Byzantium was is Britain now.[44]

As the American War opened, the text for the times from *The Siege* was national unity, rather than toleration.

Opposition, Toleration and Islam

In the 1730s Aaron Hill and James Thomson also wrote plays that used Near Eastern settings to revisit issues of cultural and religious difference and toleration. If *The Siege of Damascus* seems informed by the theological

---

[42] Prologue to *The Siege of Damascus*, spoken by Master Leaves, Folger W.b.464, quoted by Lock, 'Siege of Damascus.'

[43] *Universal Magazine of Knowledge and Pleasure* 61.425 (October 1777): 169–173.

[44] See *The Gentleman's Magazine: and Historical Chronicle* 55.11 (November 1785): 909–910. The Epilogue also appeared in *The European Magazine* of the same year.

and political radicalism of Locke and Bayle, shaped to underscore the necessity of war against Spain, Hill's *Zara* (1735) and Thomson's *Edward and Eleonora* draw inspiration from Voltaire. Their critique of Catholic fanaticism was equally consonant with the Opposition's campaign to force Walpole into renewed war with Spain.[45] Like *The Siege of Damascus*, however, *Zara* outlived the immediate ideological pressures of its initial production and became a fixture in the late Georgian repertory, with over a hundred fifty performances in London before 1800, while *Edward and Eleonora*, an early victim of the Licensing Act, was first staged by Thomas Hull, again on the eve of the American Revolution. Denied production at the time of its composition, *Edward and Eleonora* nonetheless went quickly into a second edition and remained a well-regarded work in Thomson's oeuvre.

Hill was undoubtedly drawn to *Zara* because of its huge commercial success in Paris, but the play was multiply appealing to him. Following a trip to Constantinople in 1708, he published an account of his Levant travels that was widely read, if now known primarily for the scorn heaped upon it by Lady Mary Wortley Montagu. But unlike his fellow dramatists, Hill had lived in an Islamic society, a perspective that may have informed his sympathetic treatment of the religious contest at stake in the tragedy. As Christine Gerrard points out, Voltaire wrote *Zaire* during his greatest period of anglophilia and Hill shared the former's fascination with exotic locales and spectacle.[46] Further, he believed that Voltaire's text could serve as a model for a newly moving form of drama performed by actors and actresses who had not yet acquired the ranting habits of established performers. To this end he trained Susannah Cibber minutely, scoring her text with underlining to micromanage her delivery.[47] Whether owing to these directorial efforts or her own native talent, Cibber emerged from *Zara* as a rising star and the part remained central to her career until her death.

Voltaire's prefaces to *Zaire* (1732) stress his interest in contrasting the 'moeurs' or manners of the Turks and Christians, but Hill's translation is more notable for the way it dramatizes the agonizing effects of interreligious strife and fanaticism. Set in thirteenth-century Jerusalem, the play's

---

[45] See Gerrard, *Patriot Opposition to Walpole*; and Kathleen Wilson, *The Sense of the People: Politics, Culture and Imperialism in England, 1715–1785* (Cambridge: Cambridge University Press, 1998) for discussions of Tudor-themed plays that become popular in the 1730s.

[46] Gerrard, *Patriot Opposition to Walpole*, 176–180.

[47] See Dorothy Brewster, *Aaron Hill: Poet, Dramatist, Projector* (New York: AMS Press, 1966), 142; and Gerrard, *Patriot Opposition to Walpole*, 178.

action is focused on Zara, a Christian captured by the Saracens when the city fell and brought up in ignorance of her parentage. We learn that she is to marry Osman, the Sultan of Jerusalem, but her joyful anticipation of her marriage is shattered when Nerestan, another Christian slave who has been given leave by Osman, returns from France with the means to ransom ten prisoners, including the heroine. When the Christian leader Lusignan is brought up from his cell, he recognized Zara and Nerestan as his own lost children. Acknowledging her Christian faith, Zara agrees to defer marriage to Osman, who mistakes her desperate confusion for infatuation with Nerestan. Driven beyond endurance by his jealousy, Osman stabs Zara: on hearing the truth, he kills himself.

Such recent commentary as there is on the play has noted the eighteenth-century debate over the degree to which the play is characteristically English or French, a question given point by whether – as Colley Cibber claimed in its Prologue – Osman should be read as an Othello figure, created by Voltaire under the influence of Shakespearean dramaturgy:

> From *English* Plays, *Zara's French* Author fir'd,
> Confes'd his Muse, beyond herself, inspir'd;
> From rack'd *Othello's* Rage, he rais'd his Style,
> And snatch'd the Brand, that lights his tragick Pile.[48]

Cibber's chauvinistic assertion is in ironic counterpoint to the play's own markedly relativist treatment of religious and cultural mores, in which fanatic adherence to creed and nation serves as the origin of the tragedy.[49] The historic cause of Zara's and Osman's dilemma is the conflict over Jerusalem, the ongoing crusader and Islamic zeal articulated by the minor characters, Nerestan, Orasmin and Selima.[50] The central couple are both willing to compromise their values: Osman declares his willingness to

[48] Colley Cibber, 'The Prologue', in *The Tragedy of Zara* (London: J. Watts, 1736), n.p. All quotations are from this edition and are cited in the text by act, scene and page numbers. For the best overall critical commentary, see Gerrard, *Aaron Hill: The Muses' Projector 1685–1750* (Oxford: Oxford University Press, 2003), 172–180.

[49] Angelina Del Balzo has also recently published an excellent discussion of the workings of sympathy in *Zara*, using a Humean formulation of spectatorial relations to explore the play's structures of sentiment. See 'The Sultan's Tears in Zara, an Oriental Tragedy', *SEL* 55.3 (Summer 2015): 501–521.

[50] Hill does not appear to have consulted alternative historical sources in shaping his translation. Voltaire seems to have drawn on Claude Fleury's *Histoire Ecclesiastique* (1691–1738) and the Jeseuit Louis Maimbourg's *Histoire des croisades pour la deliverance de la Terre* (1684–1685). According to Voltaire's most recent editors, his characters and actions have historical analogues, but he has freely reshaped the sources. See *The Complete Works of Voltaire* (Oxford: Voltaire Foundation, Taylor Institution, 1989), 8:296–302.

practice monogamy in his marriage with Zara, abandoning the seraglio. Like other theatrical Ottomans tamed by Christian beauties, he seems halfway to conversion of a different gender order, telling his minister Orasmin, 'The Sultans, my great Ancestors, bequeath'd / Their Empire to me, but their Taste they gave not; / Their Laws, their Lives, their Loves, delight not me' (1.2.5), for 'Passion, like mine, disdains my Country's Customs' (1.2.6). Zara wants to believe that she can marry Osman despite her change of faith, desperately telling Selima she believes that Saladin 'Drew Birth, tho' *Syrian* from a Christian Mother' (4.1.29) and pleading that as Osman's consort, she could help the Christian population. But she is forced to recognize no-one will let her choose both – 'I see my Country, and my Race, condemn me; / I see that, spite of all, I still love *Osman*.' Destroyed by the fanatic obduracy of those who surround them, Osman's and Zara's willingness to compromise suggests a rejection of all-encompassing modes of identity grounded in birth, blood or religion:

> What am I? What am I about to be?
> Daughter to Lusignan? Or Wife to Osman?
> Am I a Lover, most? Or, most, a Christian? (4.3.35)

Hill's version of Voltaire's play carries over the latter's well-known hostility to religious intolerance. Many of *Zara*'s spectators would have believed that Voltaire's admiration for toleration (and its positive social and economic consequences) was learned, like his intermittent appreciation for lively drama, from the English. As he put it in his *Letter of the Church of England*, 'England is truly the country of sectaries, (*in my father's house there are many mansions.*) An Englishman, in virtue of his Liberty, goes to heaven his own way.'[51] English audiences could presumably have felt comfortably superior to both the fanatic parties in conflict in the play – Catholics and Muslims – as well as being reminded of the need for constant vigilance against the Spanish.

Hill's aim was not simply to shore up chauvinist presumptions of cultural superiority, however. Consonant with his extended campaign to revive British tragedy, he saw Voltaire's text as a means to involve the audience in the protagonist's dilemma as profoundly as possible, stressing in the verse Dedication to Prince Fredrick his desire that the stage 'Teach a languid *People* how to feel', hoping that 'her full Soul shall *Tragic Pow'r* impart, / And reach *Three Kingdoms* in their *Prince's Heart*!' (n.p.).

---

[51] *The Works of M. de Voltaire*, vol. 13, trans. T. Smollett, T. Francklin, et al. (London: J. Newbest et al., 1762), 58.

Figure 2. *Mr Garrick and Miss Younge in the Characters of Lusignan and Zara.* Engraving. Artist Edwards, Engraver Joseph Colleyer II. London, 1777. Courtesy the Victoria and Albert Museum, London

Thomson believed he would succeed, commenting, 'I deeply feel the Difference betwixt Mr Voltaire and Mr Hill. The more generous Warmth in your Heart more animates the Scene, raises the dear Tumult in the Breast, and moves me much more.'[52] The play's persistent success was in part owing to its successful evocation of distress: after seeing Garrick's production in London in 1766, Rousseau himself, no friend to Voltaire, confessed that the tragedy had made him weep: 'I have cried all through your Tragedy, and laughed all through your Comedy, without being at all able to understand the language.'[53]

Zara's secure place in the repertory suggests that the long-term success of the dramatic sympathy first developed as national feeling in the she-tragedies but rapidly adapted to include communities as apparently alien as Amerindians and Muslims. The increasing valorization of pathos in eighteenth-century drama was often linked, as in William Guthrie's 1757 *Essay upon English Tragedy*, to an increasingly hagiographic view of Shakespeare and contempt for gallic-inspired neoclassicism.[54] But for practitioners such as Hughes, Hill and Thomson, the power to move audiences was not simply a question of producing shared national senti-ments. As we have seen, while Scottish thinkers such as Hume and Smith tended to characterize sympathy as an affect generated initially at least through contiguity, Shaftesbury had figured our 'moral sense' in cosmo-politan rather than local terms. As Brett Wilson has also observed, plays that argue for intercultural and interreligious tolerance had a particularly strong investment in their ability to generate dramatic sympathy both across national, ethnic and religious boundaries and to characters caught right on the borders.[55]

Critics of sentiment have been inclined to see such sympathetic per-formances of variously different 'Others' as acts of affective appropri-ation.[56] But in *Zara*, what is so moving about the heroine is the extent to which the agony of her *situation* is conveyed: as she says to remarkable effect towards the end of the final act, 'My only perfect Sense, is that of Pain' (5.3.42). In answering her existential query – 'Who am I?' – Zara

---

[52] Quoted in Gerrard, *Aaron Hill*, 177.

[53] From *Literary and Miscellaneous Memoirs* (London, 1826–1828), 1:206, quoted in Fred L. Bergman, 'Garrick's *Zara*', *MLA* 74.3 (June 1959): 225–232.

[54] See Guthrie, *Essay upon English Tragedy*. For modern commentary, see Michael Dobson, *Making of the National Poet: Shakespeare, Adaptation and Authorship* (Oxford: Clarendon, 1992); and Jean I. Marsden, *Re-imagined Text: Shakespeare, Adaptation and Eighteenth-Century Literary Theory* (Lexington: University Press of Kentucky, 1995).

[55] See Wilson, *Sense of the People*, esp. 63–69.   [56] Festa, *Sentimental Figures of Empire*, 7.

provides duelling answers that define her only in relation to men – her father or her would-be husband – rather than in terms of autonomous identity. For all its relish in deploying the topoi of stage orientalism and Crusader fanaticism, *Zara*'s interrogation of the inescapably customary nature of selfhood provides an extremely wide-ranging critique of conventional modes of identity formation. As the Epilogue's wry commentary on English gender relations suggests, such a critique extends to gendered as well as religious or national subjects.

Zara held the stage for decades, significantly in the form of Garrick's redaction, which cut Osman's rant but also his complexity, reducing Voltaire's and Hill's stress on his goodness and revising him as a conventional sultanic tyrant.[57] But while (as Christine Gerrard has noted) Hill's theatrical magazine *The Prompter* was accused of deistic sympathies, accusations of heterodoxy were more strongly attached to Thomson and his Crusader play, *Edward and Eleonora*.[58] When the text was published, a hostile reviewer in *The Gazetteer* wrote that Thomson put

> into the mouths of all his Characters, *Christians* and *Mohometan*, the favorite phrases that have been invented within these very *few Years*, to avoid the Expressions of *Jehovah, Lord,* God, *or* Jesus, which savour too strongly of *old Religion,* and too much countenance the Doctrine of *Revelation,* to be used by Professors of the *new Divinity,* the Friends of the *Essay on Man,* or the *devout Repeaters* of the *Philosophick Prayer.*[59]

The latter was by Matthew Tindal, a leading deist. But the censorship of *Edward and Eleonora* – it was the notorious second victim to the Stage Licensing Act – has been attributed previously solely to the play's admiring depiction of Prince Edward as heir to the throne and the characterization of the offstage Henry III as a weak figure dominated by suspect counsellors – providing too obvious a parallel with Opposition perceptions of relations between Prince Fredrick and George II to be producible.[60] While the salience of this motive for the play's suppression is undeniable, it has foreclosed analysis of Thomson's contribution to the ongoing theatrical revision of the dramatic tropes governing representations of Islamic rule, Christian mission and imperial adventurism.

Although Thomson's choice of subject is not as novel as Hughes's or Voltaire's, his treatment of the episode he selects was informed by the recent Protestant historiography of Rapin and other critics of the Crusades.

---

[57] See Bergman, 'Garrick's *Zara*', 225–232.   [58] Gerrard, *Aaron Hill*, 236.
[59] Quoted in James Sambrook, *James Thomson, 1700–1748: A Life* (Oxford: Clarendon, 1991), 197.
[60] Sambrook, *James Thomson*, 195.

A Huguenot refugee who fought for William, Rapin rejected divine action in history and was caustic at the expense of religion's barbarism. In writing *Edward and Eleonora*, Thomson focused on an episode discussed but rejected by Rapin as apocryphal, namely the story found in Thomas Baker's old-fashioned *Chronicle* in which Edward is saved from death at the hands of an assassin by Eleonora sucking the poison from his wound. In Thomson's inventive dramatization, Eleonora's own consequent death is prevented by the saving intervention of the Saracen leader Selim, who comes to the English camp in disguise, seeking to negate the shame generated by the Muslim zealot's treacherous mission by providing an antidote. While Edward is sunk in despair, Selim determines the unfolding of the play's happy climax, when Eleonora appears as from the dead to be reunited with her chastened husband. Selim's recuperation of Saracen honour underscores the illegitimacy of the Crusade itself, a project subject to unremitting critique from Edward's trusted advisor Gloster. In the course of the action we also see Theald, a churchman who is initially an enthusiastic proponent of the war, change his mind in the course of his interaction with Selim and Daraxa, Selim's beautiful betrothed who is held hostage by the Christians.

In a marked departure from his previous rather chilly neoclassical dramaturgy, Thomson (like Hughes and Hill) deliberately shapes his treatment of cultural and religious conflict in markedly pathetic terms. As early as 1730, Thomson had expressed the conviction that he needed more warmth: 'I think of attempting another Tragedy, and on a story more addressed to common Passions than that of *Sophonisba*. People nowadays must have something of themselves, and a public-spirited Monster can never concern them.'[61] Confirming his success in this regard, after reading three acts of play, Pope wrote to Aaron Hill that *Edward and Eleonora* 'excels in the Pathetick' rather than 'the Dignity of Sentiment and Grandeur of Character'.[62]

By focusing on the passionate spousal relationship of Edward and Eleonora (and deliberately downplaying Edward's response to his father's death), Thomson revises very considerably the honourable, filio-pious and calculating figure portrayed by historians. Obviously these changes offer complements to Frederick and Augusta and acknowledge the dissension

---

[61] James Thomson, *James Thomson: Letters and Documents*, ed. Alan Dugald McKillop (Lawrence: University Press of Kansas, 1958), 165.
[62] Alexander Pope, *Correspondence of Alexander Pope*, 5 vols., ed. George Sherburne (Oxford: Clarendon, 1955), 3:233.

between the Prince of Wales and the King. But the passion with which Thomson invests both characters and action does more than enliven the political allegory. While the warmth of the spousal relationship is celebrated, Edward's intensity of feeling for his wife is very deliberately paralleled with the mistaken Christian zeal of Christian and Islamic 'bigots' both. At one level the Crusades stand as an emblem of mistaken and imprudent policy, an exemplary failure of governance that wise heads such as Gloster condemn as a legally dubious waste of resources. As the action unfolds, however, Edward's intemperance stands in increasing contrast with the rational virtue of the honourable Islamic characters, Daraxa and Selim. The destructive potential of Edward's grieving rage is very precisely identified with the mad religious zeal animating both the assassin and the fanatic Christians who initiated the Crusade.

In the very first speech of the opening scene, Edward tells his counsellors Archdeacon Theald and Gloster of his decision to abandon the siege of Jaffa, concluding that 'Rash fruitless War, from wanton Glory wag'd / Is only splendid Murder' (1.1.2). Theald demurs but Gloster agrees, saying, 'I was never a Friend / To this Crusado' (1.1.2) but confining his arguments to the necessity of returning to England to support Henry III. In the next scene, however, Theald and Gloster return to the dispute, with Theald justifying the war as the repulsion of 'brute Force by Force' after the 'barbarous Torrent' from the Arabian deserts have swept down upon Asia and Africa (1.2.6). Gloster however views 'such Wars the fruit / Of idle Courage or mistaken Zeal / Sometimes of Rapine and religious Rage' (1.2.6), and he goes on to tell Theald that he views the Arabian empire, though raised on 'Rage and Zeal' (1.2.7) as theirs by 'some settled Ages of Possession, as good a right as most; further, 'I think these Wars / A kind of Persecution ... That most absurd and cruel of all Vices' (1.2.7).

As the play progresses, Gloster's view is systematically reinforced. The assassin is described by Theald as 'an unhuman Bigot / Who deem'd himself a Martyr in their Cause', language recalling Gloster's distaste for zealotry. Theald is converted to tolerance not so much by Gloster's argumentation as by the principled revulsion for the assassination attempt shown by the virtuous Daraxa, Selim's betrothed. Daraxa's rational forbearance is matched only by Selim himself, whose language from his first appearance suggests his tolerance, when he explains: 'A holy man's Humanity shall cancel / The savage Fury of an impious Bigot' (4.3.41). When Selim bravely confronts the raging and abusive Edward, who accuses the Saracens of being 'a shameless Race of People / Harden'd in Arts of Cruelty and Blood' (5.3.55), Selim keeps his cool, explains the assassin came from the Old Man of the Mountain and not him, suggests Edward be 'more humane and just' and that it was Christian bigotry which brought the English hither. While Selim undoubtedly wins the argument, it's only Eleonora's reappearance that finally persuades Edward to be reasonable. The latter ends with a big mea culpa:

> ... Once more Sultan,
> Forgive me, pardon my mistaken Zeal,
> That left my Country, cross'd the stormy Seas,
> To war with thee, brave Prince, to war with Honour. (5.4.64)

Selim closes the play, summarizing its message of tolerant ecumenism: 'Let holy rage, let persecution cease; / Let the Head argue, but the Heart be Peace' (5.4.64).

Like *The Siege of Damascus* and *Zara*, *Edward and Eleonora*'s perhaps surprising arguments against religiously motivated persecution and war, its defence of Islamic sovereignty in the Holy Land through conquest and settlement and its insistence on the rational humanity of Muslims are consonant with the historiographical, philosophical and theological arguments of early Enlightenment politico-theological thinkers such as Rapin, Locke and Bayle. To invest his action with the humane concern it demanded, Thomson drew on the pathetic forms of intercultural tragedy, modelled by Hughes, Voltaire and Hill, departing from the affectively and ideologically distant modes of oriental heroic drama. By yoking his critique of bigotry to an implicit indictment of Spain, the Patriots' current Catholic bugbear, Thomson also contributed to the process by which British tolerationist exceptionalism repeatedly justified colonial war. But it must have been the tolerationist rather than colonialist implications of the text that drew Lessing, like Thomson a freemason, to produce the play while acting as dramaturg.

A Tragedy of Fanaticism?

In 1744 James Miller returned to Voltaire's most explosive critique of fanaticism, *Mahomet*. Although at least one of Voltaire's main sources, Henri de Boulainvilliers's *La vie de Mahomed* (1731) was an enthusiastic account of the prophet, Voltaire shaped his material as a swingeing critique of extreme bigotry.[63] This was variously interpreted; Lord Chesterfield

---

[63] Melanie Ruthven, *Voltaire's Fanaticism, or Mahomet the Prophet: A New Translation* (Sacramento, CA: Litwin Books, 2013), 9.

thought the play an onslaught on Christianity as much as Islam, while other commentators believed Voltaire had sought Pope Benedict XIV's approval for the tragedy because the latter saw the drama as an attack on French Jansenists, to whom he was opposed. Christian fanaticism was not the only target however, as the play was also read as a critique of political tyranny, French absolutism specifically.[64] Although the Ottoman Ambassador to France famously complained about the play's depiction of Mahomet, Voltaire himself was not uniformly antagonistic to Islam and became increasingly positive about the religion in the later decades of his life.[65] Allegorical purposes notwithstanding, however, *Mahomet* recurs to the wholly negative views of Islam's founder widespread in Europe in the seventeenth century, depicting him as cruel, lustful, ambitious and, above all, hypocritical.

James Miller Englished the tragedy for production in the months that the young Pretender was first threatening to invade Britain. As Elaine McGirr points out, the English play was intended to be read as a denunciation of Catholicism quite as much as Islam, with the hapless parricide Zaphna, tricked into killing his own father, intended as a parallel for Charles Edward Stuart, in this account a puppet of Louis XV and the Pope.[66] It is surely right that contemporary spectators made this connection, but McGirr's characterization of the play as 'heroic farce' rather than tragedy does not fully account for affective and ideological dimensions of the Islamic vehicle. As Paula O'Brien points out, the Prologue indicates that Miller saw the play 'as an attack on 'Bigots' in the priesthood', by no means only the French.[67] A staunch member of the Opposition, who contributed to the satiric attacks on the Prime Minister, Miller was in orders and found ecclesiastical promotion blocked after being rebuked for his theatrical engagements by Walpole ally Edmund Gibson, Bishop of London. While critical of Handel's Italian operas, Miller admired the sacred oratorios and wrote the successful libretto for *Joseph and His Brethren* (1744). Like John Hoadley (who completed *Mahomet*), Henry Brooke (who authored another version of the play), John 'Estimate' Brown, Edward Young and others, Miller regarded his clerical role as fully consonant with dramatic authorship. From this perspective, the hostility to

---

[64] For a summary of responses, see Hanna Burton, 'Introduction: The Play in Historical Context', in Ruthven, *Voltaire's Fanaticism*, 13–20.

[65] Ruthven, *Voltaire's Fanaticism*, 9.   [66] McGirr, *Heroic Mode and Political Crisis*, 167–204.

[67] Paula O'Brien, 'Miller, James (1704–1744)', in *Oxford Dictionary of National Biography*, www.oxforddnb.com.

theatricality manifested by the English church hierarchy was itself a sign of the priestly prejudice attacked in the text.

In Miller's Prologue a contrast is drawn between French deafness to Voltaire's articulation of the 'blasphemies imposture dare advance' and English responsiveness to his message: 'Religion here bids persecution cease, / Without all order, and within all peace.' The usual self-congratulatory Whig link is made between the British constitution and its consequences for belief: 'Religion, to be sacred, must be free; / Men will suspect, when bigots keep the key.'[68] If the play's critique was widely understood to be the evil effects of clerical power enforced by tyranny, Miller's play certainly served as a text for the times in the context of the second Jacobite uprising. The malign effects of Mahomet's imposture are concentrated on the two children of Alcanor, a virtuous, vaguely Zoror-astian and Catonic figure, leader of Mecca's senate and the city's spiritual and military resistance to Islam. Alcanor's children, Zaphna and Palmira, were captured by Mahomet as children and have been brought up by him as enthusiastic devotees. They are drawn together by intense affection although Mahomet plans to marry Palmira. Their parentage is revealed to them only after Zaphna has murdered his father, reluctantly, at Maho-met's insistence.

The situation obviously echoes that in *Zara*, where the Christian siblings have been brought up in an Islamic court, their captor suspects them of an illicit amour and their reunion with their father and the final revelation of their parentage produces great mental agony. While the play depicts Mahomet as utterly monstrous and Islam as completely factitious, Zaphna and Palmira are presented as naturally virtuous characters, whose instinctive revulsion from their master's murderous commands indicts the deliberate creation and manipulation of 'enthusiastic Bigotry' by means of highly sympathetic characters. The parallels between Alcanor and Cato, last-ditch defenders of liberty against an overwhelming and unjust enemy, suggest that while perverted monotheism is Miller's target virtuous pagan-ism is not. Zaphna and Palmira speak the language of humanity and Alcanor that of civic humanism: although they all fall, their fates are tragic – it is Mahomet, disarmed by his alarmed followers and prevented from killing himself at the last, who appears farcical.

As befits a Machiavel in religion, it is Mahomet himself who best criticizes his own policy, remarking to this henchman Mirvan when he hears the 'Boy-Bigot' Zaphna has killed Alcanor 'What a reasonless

---

[68] James Miller, *Mahomet the Imposter* (London: John Bell, 1795), n.p.

Machine / Can Superstition make the Reason'r Man!' (5.1.60).[69] A thoroughgoing environmentalist, Mahomet tells Mirvan that 'those partial Ties of Blood, and Kindred, / Are but th'illusive Taints of Education: / What we call Nature is mere Habit' (4.1.45). These assumptions are disproved by the children's instinctive revulsion from their orders and by the careful distinction their speeches make between Mahomet as (false) prophet and the deity. As Zaphna asks in the next scene:

> How can Assassination be a Virtue?
> How can the gracious Parent of Mankind
> Delight in Mankind's sufferings? Mayn't this Prophet,
> This great Announcer of his heav'nly Will,
> Mistake it once? (4.2.46)

In the next scene Alcanor is revealed within a Pagan Temple, where he addresses his gods with dignified prayers for Mecca's protection. Suggestively, his final appeal is that, should the gods for their own reasons permit the imposter to take Mecca, they allow him to die in his children's arms. This is what follows, suggesting that the action has a divine sanction, consonant with Alcanor's patriotic piety. Asking in his final words that his murdered body be shown to the populace to unmask Mahomet, he asks rhetorically, 'What Patriot, or Parent, but would wish / In so divine a Cause to fall a Martyr!' (4.3.59).

By voicing sceptical arguments through Mahomet, and distinguishing Zaphna's, Palmira's and Alcoran's instinctive piety (whether pagan or monotheistic) from the former's perverted duplicity, Miller ensures that his play's celebration of British liberty of conscience would not be mistaken for a debunking of religion per se. This was a danger, as the notorious atheistical tract of *The Three Imposters*, circulating in print in Britain after 1719, not only suggested parallels between Jesus, Moses and Muhammad but attacked the political use of religion and the credulity of the people.[70] Both these theses are underscored in Miller's play, as in the final act resistance to Mahomet collapses when the Meccans are persuaded that Zaphna's death is not murder by poison but a sign from God of his guilt. While in libertine discourse such plebeian imbecility was understood

---

[69] James Miller, *Mahomet the Imposter. A Tragedy* (London: J. Watts and W. Dodds, 1744), 1:60. All quotations are from this edition and are cited in the text by act, scene and page numbers.

[70] For an acute reading of Mahomet that addresses his characterization in terms of misleading performance and imposture, see Ballaster, *Fabulous Orients*, 52–54.

as an attack on religion tout court as priestcraft, Miller's Prologue underscores the positive role of Britain's clergy should play in providing proper
guidance: 'No Clergy here usurp the free-born Mind, / Ordain'd to teach,
not to enslave Mankind.'[71]

While Miller's treatment of Islam marks a reversal of the more
admiring depictions legible in Hughes's, Hill's and Thomson's texts, it
shares with them a fascination with the potentially malign psychological
and political effects of any extreme religious affiliation. The fact that
bigotry is here identified with Catholicism/Islam serves the immediate
political purpose identified by McGirr, but the play does more than
ridicule (Jacobite/Papist) imposture. Zaphna and Palmira are attractive
characters whose struggles to align instinctive, proper feeling and religious doxa universalize rather than particularize their situation.
Although the text specifically attacks arguments from 'custom' and
intimates the existence of Providence and revelation, Alcanor's heroic
willingness to die for his city and his gods provides the only model of
virtue. His essentially pagan nobility is based on unswerving loyalty to
inherited traditions, suggesting he would be as resistant to Christianity
as to Islam. Through Alcanor the play leaves open the possibility that
belief systems congruent with practice of virtue might even be as valid as
those claiming divine inspiration.

The depiction of Islam in the four plays discussed above all is informed
by the authors' awareness of the debates over religious belief that characterized the early Enlightenment. It is highly suggestive that no further
plays making robust arguments for religious toleration were written for the
English stage for many decades: 1750 is also the year after which it is
generally agreed that deism ceases to be an urgent issue in English religious
and intellectual life. The restrictive effects of the Licensing Act cannot be
discounted of course, especially given the fact that Thomson's *Edward and
Eleonora* was itself an early, exemplary victim of the new censorship
regime. But *The Siege of Damascus*, *Zara* and *Mahomet* all retained a secure
place in the repertory, while *Edward and Eleonora* made a belated entry in
1776, suggesting their varying attacks on fanaticism retained ideological
heft as well as performative attraction.

---

[71] For a discussion of *Traité des trois imposteurs*, see Jacques Revel, 'The Uses of Comparison: Religions
in Early Eighteenth Century Culture', in *Bernard Picart and the First Global Vision of Religion*, ed.
Lynn Hunt, Margaret Jacob and Wijnand Mijnhardt (Los Angeles: Getty Research Institute, 2010),
331–347.

Anglo-Irish Ambivalence: Imposture, Conversion and Tolerance in 'West Britain'

A final belated and unperformed version of *Mahomet* does however appear in 1778, when a volume of Henry Brooke's poems and plays were published. Brooke (1703–1783) is best known now for his sprawling sentimental novel *The Fool of Quality* (1766–1770), *Gustavus Vasa* (1739), first victim of the Licensing Act, and *Universal Beauty* (1735), the long scientific ode that influenced Erasmus Darwin and made his literary reputation. Brooke had deist sympathies in his youth but became an enthusiastic churchgoer, showing growing sympathy for Methodism.[72] Politically, he was renowned first for his adherence to Patriot Opposition principles and later, after a politic retreat to Ireland, for his enthusiastic West British Whiggery. The latter was most obviously on show in the six vehemently anti-Catholic *Farmer's Letters to the Protestants of Ireland* (1745), which he wrote during the second Jacobite uprising, warning of the danger of a repetition of the Catholic rebellion and Protestant massacre in 1641, and which were followed by another anti-Catholic tract, *The Spirit of Party*, published in 1754.

In 1762, however, Brooke published a lengthy text titled *The Tryal of the Roman Catholics of Ireland* in which he staged a case between a 'Sergeant Statute' arguing for the necessity of the penal laws and a tolerant 'Mr Candour' who urged their repeal. In the 'Account of the Author's Life' that prefaced the second edition of his collected works published by his daughter Charlotte in 1792, his volte-face in relation to his Catholic countrymen is identified as a virtue: 'if, wrongly informed, he injured the innocent, the moment he found his error, he exerted himself with ten-fold zeal to clear and redress them'.[73] Although Charlotte stresses that 'the leading features of his mind were benevolence, meekness, and faith; for his country, patriotism to excess; and for humankind, that ever wakeful regard to the interests of religion and morality' (1:xvi), the patriotic affiliations of a hyper-Whiggish West Briton were not obviously reconcilable with the tolerant sympathies of a resident of a largely Catholic Irish countryside. Rather than simply being weak-minded, as his biographer Joep Leerssen

---

[72] For biographical accounts, see Helen Margaret Scurr, 'Henry Brooke' (PhD diss., University of Minnesota, 1922); and Joep Leerssen, 'Henry Brooke', in *Oxford Dictionary of National Biography*, www.oxforddnb.com. Scurr argues that Brooke's deism is evident in *Universal Beauty* and not incompatible with his enthusiastic Anglicanism.

[73] Henry Brooke, *Poems and Plays by Henry Brooke, Esq., with the Life of the Author*, 4 vols. (London: John Sewell, 1790), 1:xvi.

implies, or venal (Margaret Scurr's view), Brooke's change of heart and pen in relation to his Catholic and Gaelic countrymen suggests a belated attempt to bring his Whig principles of tolerance and liberty to bear on his immediate social and political circumstances.

Brooke clearly became preoccupied by the challenges to Whig orthodoxy presented by living in a colonial society that oppressed its majority faith group, not least through curtailing property rights. In addition to his version of *Mahomet*, he wrote a version of *The Indian Emperor* called *Montezuma* (1778): like *The Imposter,* this play was unperformed but its unsparing condemnation of colonial oppression extrapolates an analogy between the British treatment of Ireland and the Spanish Conquest in the Americas invoked by radical patriot Charles Lucas, for whom Brooke acted as propagandist. In *A Nineteenth Address to the Free-Citizens and Free-Holders of the City of Dublin* (1749), Lucas, an enthusiastic country Whig, thunders, 'I shew from the best authority that this nation has not been better treated by some of the ancient English governors than the Peruvians or Mexicans by the Spaniards.'[74] Anti-Catholic arguments in several of his earlier tracts have meant, as Sean J. Murphy argues, that Lucas's radical patriotism has been seriously underestimated in Irish historiography. During his parliamentary campaign in 1749 Lucas rearticulated arguments made by William Molyneux that claimed Irish sovereignty made the nation separate and equal to England: 'We owe [the British Parliament] no *Subjection* or *Obedience*'(*Nineteenth Address* 17).[75] Decades later, the lord lieutenant of Ireland, Viscount Townshend, would refer to Lucas as 'Ireland's Wilkes', although in fact Lucas softened his anti-Catholicism, if not his conviction that liberty was a global birthright: 'I have reminded the *Public*, that *Liberty* was not inherent to any particular Soil nor Climate; that it had taken its Revolution through the Globe' (*Nineteenth Address* 17). In his *The Political Constitutions of Great Britain and Ireland* (1751), a collection of his electioneering tracts, Lucas argues that all subjects, 'whether Papist or Protestant, Jew or Gentile', should have the 'full protection and benefit of the law'.[76]

Lucas's forceful articulation of the issues of liberty and toleration suggests that Brooke's ambivalence about Catholicism, his reversal in relation to the justice of the penal laws and his awareness that British

---

[74] Charles Lucas, *A Nineteenth Address to the Free-Citizens and Free-Holders of the City of Dublin* (Dublin, 1749), 18.

[75] Sean J. Murphy, 'Charles Lucas', in *Oxford Dictionary of National Biography*, www.oxforddnb .com.

[76] Charles Lucas, *The Political Constitutions of Great Britain and Ireland* (London, 1751), 443–444.

liberties were confined to the English metropolis, spurring negative comparisons with peninsular empire, developed in response to political and cultural developments within the larger Anglo-Irish community. Jacqueline Hill's brilliant delineation of the contours and limits of Lucas's patriotism serves as a reminder that Lucas never seriously envisaged extending the political nation beyond its traditional sectarian bounds, but he did expand popular participation in urban politics and his attacks on entrenched interests and corruption had a ripple effect.[77] Brooke's dramaturgy, both onstage and in the closet, is similarly engaged in critique of tyranny and bigotry from a self-consciously West British / Anglo-Irish and Patriot perspective, but his obsessive focus on the issues and texts in which unjust religious and colonial oppression are most in evidence is surely symptomatic of dis-ease with the British ordering of Ireland.

Brooke's first dramatic piece for Lucas, a comic opera called *Jack the Giant Killer* (1749), was ordered to cease playing by the government after its first performance, while the collapse of his friendship with Garrick would have put paid to hopes for London productions of his plays. In such challenging circumstances, it seems extraordinary that Brooke wrote another version of Miller's play, for Thomas Sheridan's production of *Mahomet* at Smock Alley in 1754 resulted in riots that destroyed much of the playhouse and drove Sheridan himself from Ireland. The riots are still the subject of scholarly contention, with Helen Burke arguing in her authoritative study of the eighteenth-century Irish playhouse that the audience 'identified the tyrant Mahomet with the viceroy and the 'English Interest' in Ireland' and thereby turned the dominant ideological calculus of the play (as outlined by McGirr) on its head.[78] Conrad Brunstrom has recently attempted to rescue Sheridan from the role of colonial lackey, suggesting instead that the manager naively miscalculated (believing that a fine play could be appreciated without factional interpretation) and thus was tragically misunderstood.[79] While Sheridan may not have functioned simply as a conduit for 'Court' preferences, Brunstrom's argument implies that Sheridan was willing to impose his own perspective of a highly contentious text on a profoundly divided audience, and as such he seems

---

[77] Jacqueline R. Hill, *From Patriots to Unionists: Dublin Civic Politics and Irish Protestant Patriotism, 1660–1840* (Oxford: Clarendon, 1997).

[78] Helen Burke, *Riotous Performances: The Struggle for Hegemony in the Irish Theater, 1712–1784* (Notre Dame, IN: University of Notre Dame Press, 2003), 272.

[79] Conrad Brunstrom, *Thomas Sheridan's Career and Influence: An Actor in Earnest* (Lewisburg, PA: Bucknell University Press, 2011), 41–42.

to have exhibited a degree of blind entitlement or arrogance that suggests a clear sense of cultural superiority.

Although Brooke's role in the complex politics of the Dublin stage has begun to receive attention, it remains opaque. After noting the myriad ways in which *Jack the Giant Killer* yoked a broad Catholic and native Irish critique to the more limited Lucasian patriot message, Burke suggests Brooke's inclusion of such subversive material was 'unwitting' (198). In a discussion focused primarily on the same text however, Kevin Donovan analyses the comic opera as a deliberate amalgam of (West) British drama and specifically Irish characterization that created a hybrid text with dual affiliations.[80] This claim is all the more convincing in light of the anthologizing activities of Brooke's daughter Charlotte, who in 1789 published a collection called *Reliques of Ancient Irish Poetry*, a foundational work of antiquarian assemblage of Gaelic literature. As Leith Davis has already shown, Brooke's father was engaged in collecting Gaelic materials along with his daughter, an unusually early engagement with indigenous culture by an Anglo-Irishman.[81]

Although it is uncertain exactly when Brooke wrote *The Imposter*, it was certainly well after the second Jacobite rising. The text expresses a profound hostility to bigotry and the manipulation of religious conviction, consonant with the sentiments expressed in the Epigraph to *The Tryal of the Roman Catholics*: 'Wherever Truth and Interest shall embrace, / Let Passion cool, and Prejudice give Place.'[82] *The Tryal* offers a clear account of Brooke's later public views on belief: as the 'case' gets under way, the Catholics' defender Mr Candour argues that good government by any faith group (specifically including Islam) should guarantee security and prosperity to all:

> Men, compared to Men, are, as Man to himself, a Compound of Vice and Virtue, a Balance of Propensities to Good and Evil. Complexion and Climate may make some Alteration; Education, Religion, Custom will have their Influence, more or less; but Nature is almost the same in All, It cannot be overcome, It cannot wholly be converted to Benevolence or Malevolence, to Good or Evil. And we have seen Christians and Mahometans

---

[80] Kevin Joseph Donovan, 'The Giant Queller and the Poor Old Woman: Henry Brooke and the Two Cultures of Eighteenth-Century Ireland', *New Hibernia Review* 17.2 (Summer 2003): 103–120.

[81] Leith Davis, 'Charlotte Brooke's Reliques of Irish Poetry; Eighteenth-Century 'Irish Song' and the Politics of Remediation', in *United Islands? The Languages of Resistance*, ed. John Kirk, Andrew Noble and Michael Brown (London: Pickering & Chatto, 2012), 95–108.

[82] Henry Brooke, *The Tryal of the Roman Catholics of Ireland*, 2nd ed. (London: T. Davies, 1764). All quotations are from this edition and are cited in the text by page number.

exchange Principles, as it were by mutual Consent; These inviting their Fellow-Creatures, tho' of an adverse Religion, to share the Blessings of Peace and Plenty under their Government; and those driving their Countrymen and Fellow Christians from the common Participation of Earth and Air. (17)

Continuing his rebuttal of Sergeant Statute's prejudiced account of the Catholic role in recent Irish history, Mr Candour points out that the historiography on which the former depends was created by 'Pencils' from 'Protestant or, rather, Puritan Hands' and thus 'inclined to shade and to blacken, without one charitable Teint' (18). And he goes on to condemn the fact that under the early Stuarts Irish Catholics 'were compelled, under the Pains of Fine and Imprisonment, to conform to a Religion that was contrary to their Conscience; a Grievance rarely imposed by the severest Tyrants, and what no Government on Earth can have a Right to enjoin' (20). In addition to this spiritual oppression, he notes that 'in the beginning of the Reign of *James* I, the Roman-Catholic Natives of *Ireland* were seized of most of the Lands of that Kingdom' (20), compounding the injustice under which they suffered.

The Henry Brooke who wrote the *Farmer's Letters* shared the fear of absolutist Papists identifiable in Miller's *Mahomet*, embodied in the monstrous figure of the 'Imposter' himself. But reflecting the sympathetic and less partial historical perspective on Catholicism visible in *The Tryal*, Brooke's rewriting of Miller's play as *The Imposter* provides an extensive analysis of the ways sectarian differences divide families and communities, threatening individual integrity and social bonds. Mahomet himself is still portrayed as a wicked hypocrite, but the process of conversion is presented in a more nuanced fashion, as Sopheian, Mecca's leader, is depicted as a Christian convert. By contrast, Miller depicted the Meccan leader Alcanor as a loyal pagan, whose adherence to his beliefs is a measure of his virtue. In Brooke's version, Sopheian is still the father of Daphnia, lost as a child and brought up by Mahomet but his estranged brother Joseph is the father of Palmyra, similarly fostered by Mahomet. The main action still turns on Mahomet's attempts to persuade Zaphna to kill his father in violation of his instinctive feelings of filial piety, but the plot is complicated by the more elaborate backstory. Mahomet almost succeeds in killing Zaphna with a slow-acting poison but is prevented by Hercides, one of his adherents, later revealed as a former member of Sopheian's household. Mahomet is stabbed instead of Sopheian by Zaphna, and in the final scene Hercides reveals that he was responsible for fomenting discord between Sopheian and Joseph at Mahomet's behest. Overcome by guilt and revulsion from Mahomet's murderous plans, Hercides prevents Zaphna's death by dashing the poisoned cup from his lips, and his repentance enables the reconciliation of the brothers Sopheian and Joseph and their recovery of their respective children. In contrast to the earlier treatments of interfaith conflict, the young hero and heroine are revealed to be cousins rather than siblings and are clearly intended to marry.

While Brooke had an undeniable tendency to add, digress and exfoliate his texts, his extension and alteration of *Mahomet* is tied to his thematic and argumentative investments. In Christianizing Sopheian and presenting Daphnia in the process of conversion, he voices his own enthusiastic but ecumenical piety, articulated at the play's close by Zaphna's final exchange with Palmyra. The negative effects of conversion to erroneous beliefs are exemplified by Hercides, whose early adherence to Mahomet all but destroyed Sopheian's family through ruthless emotional manipulation and by abducting the children. Yet Hercides's revulsion from Mahomet's worst actions creates the possibility of redemption, as we hear from Caled/Joseph:

> Heaven, art thou mighty and confess'd in this!
> With what an arm, through what a mortal maze,
> Hast thou led forth thy servants? – Rise, HERCIDES!
> Errors that meet reluctance in the will,
> Give place for reformation – (V.91).

Signs of goodness, despite apostasy, are recuperative in this text. The final exchange in the play shows Zaphna reassuring Palmyra, who says of herself that her 'life hath been one error' (V.92), that she has nothing to fear because divine illumination is universal, particular creed notwithstanding:

> Untutor'd as I am, and new to learn,
> Where, or to whom, revealing Heaven hath sent
> His outward lumination, sure I am
> His inward is to all men. Is it reason?
> No – 'tis the Bosom'd God, the Living Sense,
> That feels, not argues upon guilt or goodness.
> 'Tis our Internal Chymist, skill'd to try
> The bullion'd dross, or gold, of every faith. (V.92)

If Hercides embodies all those who knowingly embraced Mahomet's faith through conversion, and furthered his plans deliberately, Palmyra represents innocent adherents brought up knowing no better, guiltless believers in error. Both groups receive absolution in the final scene, when Caled and Zaphna point to the intrinsic human goodness – 'the native sense of goodness' (V.92) – that unites all human beings:

In vain we would The Eternal Unit part –
One in the Heavens, and in the feeling heart!
His laws to his impressions must be kin:
Where GOD without, he speaks to GOD within. (V.92).

The Imposter's recuperation of Muslims through the reverse conversions of the noble characters depends on an appeal to a broad human capacity for benevolence whose vague universality suggests deism and whose fervency seems Methodist. Also important however, although occupying only one scene, is the play's depiction of plebeian conversion. This scene suggests human benevolence operates not just horizontally, across different cultures and creeds but vertically, being found more reliably in peasants than in elites. In Act 2, Scene 2, a 'mob' of peasants are questioned by a Meccan doctor about their interest in Mahomet. Only a single member of the mob is individuated, one 'Dolt', and although he does ask the Doctor and another educated figure, one Master Gubbins about 'doctrine', the dialogue is dominated by the Doctor's emphasis on kindness. The Doctor elaborates a comparison between religion and a suit of clothes, suggesting to the mob that their belief is something they 'wear' unconsciously as they go about productive and charitable lives. He draws a contrast between their singular and useful conviction and the 'religion of your betters ... that is cut out and prank'd into infinite disguises', serving lawyers, merchants and politicians 'for the hiding of deformities' (2.2.26). Patronizing as the Doctor's lessons appear, he is emphatic as to the mob's religious virtues, 'the weakness of your poor hearts, that keep a foolish kindness for your neighbours; a bit for the hungry, and a tear for the afflicted', and he contrasts this generosity with the violence and rapacity of Mahomet (2.2.26). The latter, he claims, 'teaches you to cut throats, plunder houses, ravish maidens, sack towns, waste provinces; and when you are perfect in all these virtues, he leads you to his own paradise, where you are to rant, and drink, and whore, for ever' (2.2.28).

Dolt's response to the Doctor's account of Mahometan doctrine suggests the instinctive revulsion from evil that motivates Hercides's eventual resiling from his Prophet: 'Whoy! – Heaven may be vast koind in all this to be sure; but it goes against the grain of us poor sinners' (2.2.28). Here, Brooke is not just arguing for a fundamental goodness in even (or especially) the 'simplest' human beings but more specifically in the Roman Catholic peasantry of Ireland. *The Imposter* is unusually emphatic about the abuse of religion within implicitly Christian societies even as it uses Islam as a whipping boy for the extremities of fanaticism. The play cannot be read as an attack on Catholic priestcraft per se, not just because it seems likely to have been written after Brooke's revisionist account of 1641 in *The Tryal* but because both the active worldly programme (of conquest and rapine) offered by Mahomet and the fantasy of sensual paradise are specifically marked as Islamic. Even so, however, Brooke's citation of the many historic instances of communal tolerance between Muslims and Christians in *The Tryal* suggests that he wanted to represent Mahomet as an individual instance of the manipulative use of religion equally identifiable among (Christian) lawyers, merchants and politicians and to avoid condemning Muslims as a group.

Brooke is a fascinating instance of a figure caught in the crux of contradiction: his enthusiastic if unorthodox piety and patriotism appears to have brought him up against the limits of Whig commitments to liberty and tolerance once he was living permanently in Ireland. Always highly sensitive to literary and theatrical fashion, it is no accident that he chose dramatic vehicles ranging from ballad opera to black legend and 'Imposture' plays to explore and resolve his anxieties. But as we see from *The Imposter*, the implicitly deist enthusiasm he invokes as a solvent of religious difference cannot prevent his recognition of the persistence of political, professional and mercenary manipulations of faith. However sublime Zaphna's final panegyric, *The Imposture* leaves the questions at stake in the play open.

The Other Enlightenment on Stage

Many of the most successful and long-lived plays about Islam on the English stage in the eighteenth century were implicitly or explicitly tolerationist. But unsurprisingly, given the power of conservative Anglicanism, other Turk plays produced during the first half century of deist controversy were equally committed to religious orthodoxy. Unconcerned with presenting a clash of societies with competing claims to religious truth and civil order, both Eliza Haywood and Samuel Johnson focused on the situation of the 'fair captive' in the harem to test and in the latter case, reassert the power of Christian masculinity. Fascinated and in Johnson's case perturbed by the attractions of Islam, both writers used oriental scenarios to reiterate European gender dominance just where it seemed most vulnerable.

While the most celebrated Turk plays featuring Christian heroines held captive by enraptured sultans dealt with high politics within the Ottoman state and England, Haywood's text followed Joseph Trapp's *Abra-mule* (1704) in emphasizing the private experience of the woman imprisoned in the harem. Scholars have begun to explore the increasingly widespread depiction of such encounters, particularly in autobiographical slave narratives, novellas and romances.[83] In a survey of these narratives, Khalid Bekkaoui argues that contrary to the dominant assumptions of their culture, these texts often show British women actively choosing to remain with Islamic spouses, preferring a life of comfort, security and pleasure to their previous precarious existences.[84] While the Islamic captivity narratives used tropes of oriental wealth, sensuality and tyranny, they also undermined axiomatic presumptions of Western superiority in religion, polity and gender order. By contrast, Ros Ballaster has provided a compelling account of the way fictional narratives by women represented female agency as instrumental in establishing 'a progressive and modern state which triumphs over the stasis and control associated with the oriental despot'.[85]

The dramatic representation of oriental captivity in the early Georgian period has been relatively neglected. From the 1760s on – unsurprisingly concurrent with the growing scandals in the East India Company – comedies and farces that theatricalize the seraglio proliferate. Recent scholarship has shown the extent to which these dramatic scenarios of Eastern imprisonment served as screens onto which Britain's own despotic and corrupt governance could be projected and to some extent disowned or recuperated.[86] Although neither Haywood's play nor Samuel Johnson's *Irene* (1749) secured a place in the repertory, their revised stagings of Christian captivity serve as a vital bridge between the heroic dramas of state, eroticized she-tragedies and the often-humorous harem plays of the late eighteenth century. In both these dramas Christian male actors within the palace or even the seraglio assume much more aggressive roles than in previous Turk plays, modelling resistance to the seductions and violence of Ottoman power to vulnerable women.

In Davenant's *Siege of Rhodes* (1656) and Orrery's *Mustapha* (1667), the heroine's release from Ottoman captivity is enabled by her ability to awaken the sultan's admiration for her virtue, calling forth an answering

---

[83] See Joe Snader, *Caught between Worlds: British Captivity Narratives in Fact and Fiction* (Lexington: University Press of Kentucky, 2000); and Linda Colley, *The Ordeal of Elizabeth Marsh* (New York: Pantheon, 2007).

[84] Khalid Bekkaoui, 'White Women and Moorish Fancy in Eighteenth-Century Literature', in *The Arabian Nights in Historical Context: Between East and West,* ed. Saree Makdisi and Felicity Nussbaum (Oxford: Oxford University Press, 2008), 131–166. For an authoritative overview, see Ballaster, *Fabulous Orients,* 59–192.

[85] Ballaster, *Fabulous Orients,* 136.

[86] See esp. O'Quinn, *Staging Governance,* 15–26 and 125–163.

display of honourable conduct. The male Christian characters are unable to display any real degree of agency, with purely symbolic victories gained by steadfast female chastity. In *The Fair Captive* the action is inflected rather differently. In the absence of the sick and aging Sultan, power is held by the Grand Vizier Mustapha, married to Irene, the Sultan's daughter. Mustapha has seduced Daraxa, who haunts the seraglio disguised as a eunuch seeking revenge while Irene suffers torments of jealousy over Mustapha's infatuation with the Christian captive, Isabella. The noble Ozmin and Achmat, head of the janizzaries, are hoping to depose the tyrannical Mustapha.

While this scenario is conventional, novelty in the plan is evident from the first scene, in which Alphonso, a Spanish noble, discusses with his attendant Pedro his hitherto unsuccessful efforts to recover Isabella by paying ransom. His complaints about the ineffectiveness of the 'trading wretches' he has hired 'to treat for Isabella' are accompanied by boasts of his preference for using 'force' in her rescue, but as Pedro points out, faced with her immurement in the seraglio he has no option but to use 'policy' and intermediaries, such as a Jew and Haly, the Chief Eunuch.[87] Nonetheless eager to meet with Isabella, he imprudently enters the seraglio in disguise and is captured, tried and imprisoned for his trespass. An accidental beneficiary of the putsch against the Vizier, reluctant to accede to what he sees as Ozmin's dishonourable attempts to persuade him to assassinate Mustapha, Alfonso vocalizes resistance to various forms of Ottoman power. In a climactic scene in Act 3, when he is being tried by a court of Bashaws for having intruded into the seraglio, and in a speech echoing Oroonoko's defiance to his captors, Alonso asserts his integrity:

> In vain you wou'd make free-born Souls your Slaves;
> You've chain'd this Body but my Mind is free,
> Your boasted Pow'r does not extend so far,
> As to make that your Slave: King of myself,
> I'm great, and free, as your proud Emperor. (3.2.34)

At the opening of the next act we hear him soliloquizing piously over the Bible, before the desperate Isabella visits him. Although he dissuades her from suicide, his frantic suspicions of her ability to withstand seduction cause her to faint. Fearing for her honour, he orders her to avoid Mustapha, and on seeing her disordered after an interview with the Vizier in

---

[87] Eliza Haywood, *The Fair Captive. A Tragedy* (London: T. Jauncey and H. Cole, 1721). All citations are from this edition and are cited in the text by act, scene and page numbers.

which she had offered to exchange her life for Alfonso's, he condemns her as criminal in the most wounding language. Deaf to her explanations, it is only when the dying Mustapha confirms her account that he believes her chaste.

The Fair Captive shifts the register of Ottoman plays in two significant ways. By underscoring the fact that recovering high-status captives was habitually a matter of ransoms and bribery brokered by mercantile, Jewish and local intermediaries, the text acknowledges some of the basic mechanisms at work in the real traffic in Christian prisoners and slaves.[88] By inserting Alphonso and Pedro into the action, as aggressive but ineffectual allies to the noble Turks, the play intimates broader possibilities of mutual interest between Constantinople and Christian powers. At the same time, however, the erotic charge of the harem is diminished by introducing a European monitor.[89] The embodiment of masculine Christian authority, Alphonso's presence in the play is as much concerned with policing Isabella's encounters with her Ottoman captor as it is with rescuing her – and by extension, policing audience response. For in addition to controlling the Christian heroine, Alphonso also serves as a surrogate for spectators, modelling and (ideally) directing their reactions to the varied attractions and terrors of the Ottoman court. In this scenario, Isabella's private relationship to Alphonso is all-important, lacking the public and political importance of Queen Isabella's in *The Siege of Rhodes*, and underlining the developing importance of a specifically domestic role for women in private life.

However ineffectual Alfonso proves as an agent, his moral authority in *The Fair Captive* is unrivalled. Notably, this is not simply a question of honour – for Ozmin is presented as nobly motivated and conducted – but of belief. Alphonso is depicted drawing strength from scripture and his condemnation of Isabella when he believes her 'guilty' is biblically grounded:

> Thy Disobedience and Self-Conceit,
> That very Crime that damn'd thy Grandame *Eve*,
> Has ruin'd thee, I knew thee better than
> Thou knews't thyself! I knew thee very Woman. (5.2.72)

---

[88] For an account stressing the vulnerability of English traders in the Ottoman Empire, see James Mather, *Pashas: Traders and Travellers in the Islamic World* (New Haven, CT: Yale University Press, 2009), 105–178.

[89] The most extensive analysis of the sultan's absolute sexual power is in Grosrichard, *Sultan's Court*.

Although his misogyny is proved unfounded, despite having pushed Isabella once more to the brink of suicide, Alphonso is never upbraided for his mistaken rage, nor does he express contrition. But through her soliloquies, the audience is conscious of Isabella's continuous good faith and her uncertainty over approaching Mahomet as a choice inflected only by honourable considerations. The play ends therefore with Alphonso's highly traditional presumption of female sexual weakness and deceit unchallenged verbally if disproved in the event. That Alphonso's closing speech adverts to the danger of overweening passion – a moral that could be applied as readily to his own suspicions as much as to Isabella's propensity for despair – suggests that Haywood wanted her spectators to consider that the irrational jealousy of the bigoted male might be as dangerously irrational as female fear and desire.

Faith, chastity and apostasy are also at the heart of Johnson's *Irene*. In what remains one of the richest analyses of the play, Bertrand Bronson examines the sources, manuscript and biographical circumstances of the text's production in turn, to provide a compelling account of the tragedy.[90] Bronson shows it is highly likely that Johnson used aspects of all the previous dramatizations of the *Irene* story: he also argues that it is likely Aspasia's character was shaped with reference to the sad tale of a virtuous Greek woman called Manto, whose death at the hands of an irrationally jealous husband is the only prominent feminocentric narrative in Knolles other than those of Irene and Roxana. For Bronson, Johnson's investment in the scenario arises from his desire to administer the Christian instruction preached by Aspasia to Irene: animated by fear in the weakness of his own belief, and grateful to the strengthening presence of his wife, Johnson seized on the Irene/Manto plot to demonstrate faith overcoming apostasy.

As Johnson reconstructs the action, the patriotic Greeks Leontius and Demetrius are hoping to rescue their countrywomen Irene and Aspasia from the emperor Mahomet. To do so, they cabal with Cali Bassa, a statesman hostile to the aggressive young Sultan. The Greeks want to save both the captives and their homeland, while Cali claims to want the Turks to retreat from Europe in order to secure Ottoman stability. Cali is much more critical of the Ottoman polity than Haywood's Ozmin, echoing Paul Rycaut in lamenting 'the Woes when arbitrary Pow'r, / And lawless Passion, hold the Sword of Justice' and fantasizing about a land 'Where

---

[90] Bertrand H. Bronson, *Johnson and Boswell: Three Essays* (Berkeley: University of California Press, 1944).

common Laws retrain the Prince and Subject' (1.1.8).[91] By contrast, Mustapha articulates every familiar trope of Ottoman ambition, reminding his Bassa that 'Our warlike Prophet loves an active Faith', and instructing him 'With wonted Zeal pursue the Talk of War, / Till every Nation reverence the *Koran*, / And ev'ry Suppliant lift his Eyes to *Mecca*' (1.5.16). He is equally ambitious for universal monarchy, with 'vast Designs' and 'Plans of boundless Pow'r' (1.5.16).

Although the tragedy was not performed until 1749, Johnson composed *Irene* during the Austro-Russian-Turkish War (1735–1739), so it is not surprising that the play depicts a highly aggressive Sultan. Mahomet boasts that

> I rouse to War, and conquer for *Irene*
> Then shall the *Rhodian* mourn his sinking Tow'rs,
> And *Buda* fall, and proud *Vienna* tremble,
> Then shall *Venetia* feel the *Turkish* Pow'r,
> And subject Seas roar round their Queen in vain. (4.5.60)

While these lines would have been resonant of Turkish threat in 1739, the play finishes with Mahomet's arrogance humbled as the 'Band of Greeks' (5.13.86) escapes with Aspasia. Although he has avoided assassination, the sultan has been betrayed by his chief adviser and his beloved Irene has been strangled. While they do not succeed in killing Mahomet, or even in fighting for their women, the Greeks leave with their prize intact to fight another day while the Ottomans have been deprived, disappointed and humiliated. In contrast to the purely political and sensual intrigues pre-occupying the Turks, the Christians are engaged in moral warfare, as Irene and Aspasia succumb to and resist temptation respectively, under the watchful gaze of Demetrius, whose role is primarily that of guide, both moral and physical.

For Bronson, Demetrius is secondary to Johnson's creation of a com-pellingly attractive and morally authoritative heroine in Aspasia, whose firm belief sets Irene's seduction by the temptations of luxury and power into shocking relief. But as Chela Livingston argued in an early feminist account of the play, Aspasia is in many ways a passive figure while Irene can be construed as positively Amazonian in her pursuit of power.[92] Their differences notwithstanding, both these readings concur in recognizing

---

[91] Samuel Johnson, *Irene: A Tragedy* (London: R. Dodsley, 1749), 1.1.8. All quotations are from this edition and are cited in the text by act, scene and page numbers.

[92] Chela Livingston, 'Johnson and the Independent Woman: A Reading of Irene', *Age of Johnson: A Scholarly Annual* 2 (1979): 212–234.

that it was crucial for Johnson to externalize the conflict faced by Irene in previous redactions, creating an ideal figure of virtue who heroically resists Islam but obeys her Christian lover implicitly, and who stands in contrast with a female apostate.[93] Also critical to this strategy is a darkened characterization of Mahomet as tyrannical and violent, without the greatness of soul depicted in earlier versions of the story.

The cost of reforming and controlling the captivity scenario in this way was dramatic tedium. Characters who are exemplary or venal cannot generate much interest, and Aspasia and Irene are so much under Demetrius's surveillance that both their moral stature and their agency seem doubly constrained. The fantastic nature of Johnson's scenario – and by extension, all such attempts to heroicize captivity – is amusingly laid bare in an astute contemporary pamphlet analysing the fundamental implausibility of the setting and action. The anonymous author of *A Criticism on Mahomet and Irene* (1749) begins by pointing out the problems with Johnson's 'Scene': 'the Seraglio being a Place so guarded by Slaves, and kept sacred to the Sultan's Pleasures, how should it be possible two strange *Turks* (suppose they were really so) durst appear, dress'd in all the Magnificence of eastern State, in the most retir'd Walks of the Palace Garden, and never be enquir'd after?'[94] He follows the objection up by pointing out the improbability of a galley (for escape) being directly accessible from the seraglio garden, before switching to characterization, making mock of Johnson's clumsy ascription of Cali's admiration for a law-bound polity to an Ottoman statesman, as well as the rapidity with which Mahomet switches his preference from the resistant Aspasia to the compliant Irene. Mahomet's wooing also comes in for criticism, 'for instead of Flattery, and other gay Delusions to engage Affections, generally made use of by an eager Lover, he courts her out of the *Al-coran*; or, as my Lord *Foppington* says, seems to think a Woman shou'd fall in Love with him, for his endeavouring to perswade her she has not one single Virtue in the whole Composition of her Body and Soul –' (14).

The critic finishes by implying that Irene's execution, even by strangling offstage, rendered the whole play ridiculous, by reminding spectators that in the original story Mahomet beheaded her with a single stroke of his scimitar – 'which, when perform'd to the Height of Expectation, cou'd

[93] For a truly radical rereading of the play, in which the female strength of character is treated as an aspect of Johnson's reiteration of Habesha discourse, see Belcher's stimulating *Abyssinia's Samuel Johnson*, 131–169.

[94] *A Criticism on Mahomet and Irene. In a Letter to the Author* (London: W. Reeve and A. Dodd, 1749), 7. Other quotations are cited in the text by page number.

have been but a Pantomime Trick, and beneath the Dignity of a Tragedy; unless you cou'd suppose, the Hero was bred a Butcher. – As to the Trick, perhaps, some of our tender hearted Countrymen, wou'd have eas'd that Objection, by having her Head cut off in good Earnest, and so have had the Pleasure of a new *Irene* every Night' (17).

The complaints articulated here suggest that Johnson's attempt to reform the captivity scenario, however serious in intent, was vulnerable to parody. As we have seen, disapproving arbiters of taste such as Steele regarded female wits as the most opportunistic exploiters of these 'luscious' plots. When Johnson followed Haywood's lead by expanding the role of Christian men as putative guides and rescuers, both their disapproving gaze and their impotence made the heightened tropes of Ottoman sensuality and violence seem brutal if not absurd, rather than erotic. Sharing something of Johnson's wish to police female desire, the critic's hostility to the Epilogue's comic voicing of women's attraction to the Turk suggests revulsion from the practice of staging the seduction of Christian womanhood by Muslims tout court. In common with almost every Turk play, the Epilogue is spoken by an actress who denounces aspects of Islamic gender relations, especially polygamy and female seclusion. These epilogues' constantly reiterated insistence on the superiority of life for women in Britain seems intended as a disavowal of the seductiveness of harem life as depicted in the main piece. In *Irene*, however, the seraglio's attractions are consistently undercut by Demetrius's reminders of Christian duty and Christian gallantry. This reduces the erotic effect of the performance both by puncturing the fantasy of vulnerability to the omnipotent and singular male and by externalizing the woman's internal conflict: instead of their desire and fear being heightened by isolation, Irene and Aspasia have to answer to embodiments of masculine authority from their own culture.

While *Irene* sank without revival, Hughes's and Hill's very different depictions of Christian captivity flourished. The reason for the latters' success lies in the emotionally engaging situation of the protagonists that continued to be salient in changing circumstances, even as cosmopolitan and deistic sympathies waned. As one late eighteenth-century critic put it, *Irene* is 'colder than *Cato*. There is not, throughout the play, a single situation to excite curiosity and raise a conflict of passions'.[95] In both *The Siege of Damascus* and *Zara*, however, the hero/heroine are never tempted by the worldly allurements of Islam but do suffer the agonies of negotiating

[95] Robert Anderson, *The Life of Samuel Johnson, LLD, with Critical Observations on His Works* (Edinburgh: J. & A. Arch, 1795), 241.

competing but honourable affective claims. Although subject to external pressures, Phocyas and Zara are tested most effectively by their own divided loyalties and judgments, in scenarios whose relatively sympathetic characterization of Islam heightens, rather than simplifies their dilemmas.

A Patriot Sultan

In his hugely successful *History of the Rise and Progress of Poetry* (1764), John 'Estimate' Brown identifies the origins of drama in the triumphant celebrations of 'savages' (of whom North Americans were living exemplars) and stresses the legislative function of poets and dramatists among the early Greeks.[96] Although his enthusiasm for dramaturgy alienated him from his patron Bishop William Warburton (who may have been jealous of his protégé's success), Brown was emphatic as to the religious, political and moral functions of tragedy which he regarded as a common inheritance of the species. Writing from a thoroughly orthodox Whig and Anglican position, Brown used his Algerian setting in *Barbarossa* (1754) to create a model of conservative Enlightenment dramaturgy, one in which cultural difference is almost entirely subsumed by the projection of universality legible in his poetics. At the same time that *Barbarossa* abandons the more obvious semiotics of orientalist dramaturgy, however, his tragedy reveals the shaping influence of Shakespeare, increasingly hailed by the British as not just an English but a universal genius.

New tragedies of all kinds were rare in the 1750s and successful ones even fewer, in a decade of crisis for serious plays. Among these, however, Brown's *Barbarossa* (1754) opened to immediate acclaim and remained in the repertory.[97] Chiming with other filially focused tragedies produced in this decade, in *Barbarossa*, Brown borrows from *Zara* a heroine agonized by the opposing claims of lover and father, together with a parallel plot showing a mother and son tested by absence and reunion. While eighteenth-century commentators were agreed in condemning Johnson's plot and characterization, *Barbarossa* was generally if not universally commended for its plan, with Thomas Davies remarking: 'The plot of *Barbarossa* is founded on the strongest of all human connections, filial and

---

[96] John Brown, *The History of the Rise and Progress of Poetry through Its Several Species* (Newcastle: J. White and T. Saint for L. Davis and C. Reymers, 1764), 14. All quotations are cited in the text from this edition.

[97] John Brown, *Barbarossa. A Tragedy* (London: J. and R. Tonson, 1755). All quotations are from this edition and are cited in the text by act and page numbers.

maternal affection; a son made known to a mother who had supposed him to be dead, and had long since deplored his loss, is a fable on which several of our most affecting modern tragedies are founded.'[98]

Barbarossa's plot thus shares a maternal focus consonant with its near contemporary, John Home's *Douglas* (1756). The central role of mothers in these midcentury tragedies is more than a hangover from earlier forms of civic tragedy. By the 1750s the cult of maternity that both idealized and reduced women to the maternal function was gaining cultural traction.[99] In *Barbarossa* the female characters are tested primarily for filial piety, maternal tenderness and conjugal loyalty; the hero Selim is also tempted to subdue honour to filial feeling but political power is his primary aim. Suggestively, the play almost entirely eschews a Crescent/Cross dichotomy, for while Selim has taken refuge from Barbarossa's regime with the Spanish court at Oran, all the characters in the play, presenting the full panoply of behaviours, are Algerian. The effect is to generalize the play's claims as to the proper ordering of gender relations and political and religious institutions: attacking the play's originality, the most hostile of the tragedy's early reviewers suggested its characterization and plot were derivative of Greek models: 'This princess (Zaphira) appears a copy of Andromache, Merope, and Creusa; as the circumstances of the son concealed, bear too near a resemblance of Dorillus and Ilyssusum; nor can we easily forget Poliphontes while we see *Barbarossa*.'[100]

As the dramatic offspring of 'Estimate Brown', who shortly thereafter authored the wildly successful attack on contemporary luxury, one might expect a denunciation of oriental excess coding contemporary British corruption. Brown does use his North African setting to spectacularize the Whig and Anglican message of his widely praised sermons on *The Mutual Connexion between Religious Truth and Civil Freedom; Between Superstition, Tyranny, Irreligion, and Licentiousness* (1746) preached in Carlisle during the Assizes held for the trial of Jacobite rebels. The sermons exemplify Pocockian conservative Anglican Enlightenment: taking as his text the assurance 'that the Truth shall make us free!' Brown argues that liberty is natural to mankind and that political slavery is imposed only through the imposition of fraudulent superstition.[101] The sermons warn

---

[98] Davies, *Memoirs of the Life*, 1:197.

[99] For discussion of this issue at midcentury, see Toni Bowers, *The Politics of Motherhood: British Writing and Culture, 1680–1760* (Cambridge: Cambridge University Press, 1996), 153–160.

[100] *Covent Garden Monthly Review and Literary Journal*, 1752–1825 (January 12, 1755): 47.

[101] John Brown, *The Mutual Connexion between Religious Truth and Civil Freedom; Between Superstition, Tyranny, Irreligion, and Licentiousness: Considered in Two Sermons* (London: R. Dodsley, 1746), 6. All quotations are from this text.

against the dangers of Catholic-backed Jacobitism in the context of rebellion: *Barbarossa* is a dramatic spectacle of tyrannic superstition and licentiousness triumphant, a nightmarish evocation of unmitigated despotism,
replete with rack, chains and torture, a sexually predatory usurper, tormented lovers and persecuted heirs. In its un-Islamic dependence on
tolling bells as plot markers however (noted disapprovingly by the *Covent
Garden Monthly Review*), *Barbarossa's* Algiers is as much akin to a Gothic
castle as a Moorish court.[102]

In Brown's dramatization, Selim, son of the murdered ruler of Algiers,
returns disguised as Achmet, to lead a revolt against the usurper Barbarossa. Unfortunately meeting Barbarossa's daughter Irene, whom he has
earlier rescued from being sold into slavery at Oran, Selim is captured by
Barbarossa's men, after a charged encounter with his mother in which he
retained his disguise while reassuring her that rumours of his death are
false. Barbarossa is killed by Selim's ally Othman in a melee during the
uprising, thus freeing his mother from Barbarossa's hated advances and
enabling his marriage to the virtuous Irene. While the theme of an exiled
prince returning in disguise to claim his throne might have seemed
provocative, just eight years after Charles Edward Stuart's invasion, no
such parallels were mooted by reviewers: when Thomas Davies noted some
likenesses between Barbarossa and the Bajazet of Rowe's *Tamerlane* (the
latter a panegyric to William III), his remarks underscore the intended
likely parallel between 1688 rather than 1745.[103]

Everything in *Barbarossa's* mise-en-scène is directed to evoking the dark
oppression Brown associates with Jacobite/Catholic/absolutist threat. The
play's action unfolds at night, in gloomy courtyards and corridors in a
shadowed city more reminiscent of Elsinore in *Hamlet* than the scenes of
Turkish plays. Brown was careful to observe the unities and thus the entire
action is shrouded in a darkness symbolic of the religious, political and
moral corruption under which Algiers suffers. The initial scene shows the
plotters dressed in cloaks meeting late in the evening; the midnight bell
tolls and the revolution is primed to begin when the watch strikes two.
Characters describe their spiritual condition in terms of darkness and light

---

[102] The *CG* Monthly reviewer was roundly critical, pointing out that 'if what travelers assure us to be
true, the bell is the most unlucky piece of machinery the author could possibly have introduced in
a scene laid in a mahometan country, where bells are said to be prohibited'. *Covent Garden Monthly
Review* (52). The reviewer is equally caustic about the fable, condemning it as 'a romantick and
shallow plot, more worthy the invention of female novelists than of a tragic poet' (48).
[103] Davies, *Memoirs*, 197.

and the eventual downfall of the tyrant is figured as a return to daylight. The closing scene is drenched in pious references to Heaven, as Barbarossa repents, Selim forgives him and Zaphira praises divine justice. In celebrating Barbarossa's fall and repentance, Selim closes the action by announcing 'That Heav'n but tries our Virtue by Affliction; / That oft the Cloud which wraps the present Hour, / Serves but the brighten all our future days!' (5.1.80). As the virtuous characters reiterate the power of a monotheistic deity in terms that seem entirely familiar to the Christian audience, Brown seems to sever the distinction between North Africans and Britons, united in revulsion from tyrannic oppression. In this version of the Enlightenment Magrib, even the feared Algerians could be good Whigs and create reformed community.

Tolerance and 'Outlandish Englishmen'

The tradition to which Hughes, Voltaire, Hill, Thomson, Miller and Brooke belong reaches its apotheosis in Lessing's *Nathan the Wise* (1779). Ironically but not surprisingly, Lessing, a German freemason, deist and enthusiastic reader, translator and adapter of English plays, notably those of fellow freemason George Lillo, made less impact on the late Georgian stage than Kotzebue. His masterpiece of tolerationist drama was first translated into English in 1781 by Rudolph Eric Raspe, the disgraced but highly accomplished German scholar, now best known for his tales of Baron Munchausen, then in exile in England.[104] The play was not produced. English resistance to the play's truly radical resolution of the problem of interfaith difference is legible in responses to a new translation published in 1807, which several critics dismissed simply as 'superlatively foolish', objecting to Nathan because 'this honest Jew appears something of a mongrel, between a Christian and a Jew, a Deist and a Turk'.[105]

In *Nathan the Wise*, the competing truth claims of Islam, Christianity and Judaism are resolved by the eponymous hero through a fable.[106] Ordered by the Sultan of Jerusalem, a generous but capricious character, to adjudicate the matter, Nathan tells the story of a man who was unable to choose an heir among his three beloved sons. To express his love for all his sons, he has two extra copies made of the original ring that signified his

---

[104] For Raspe's extraordinary career, see John Carswell, *The Romantic Rogue: Being the Singular Life and Adventures of Rudolph Eric Raspe, Creator of Baron Munuchausen* (New York: Dutton, 1950).
[105] See *La Belle assemble: or, Court and Fashionable Magazine* 1.10 (December 1806): 15.
[106] The first English translation is *Nathan the Wise. A Philosophical Drama ... Translated from the German by R.E. Raspe* (London: J. Fielding, 1781).

own inherited power and authority and gives one to each. The story neatly explains why each faith community believes itself to be 'chosen', and even more radically it suggests that the truth claims of at least two groups are entirely factitious. But no one can ever know which faith is 'real' and which is a facsimile.

Nathan's brilliant resolution of the dilemma of competing faiths is embedded within a plot reminiscent of the preceding Enlightenment treatments of this topic. He has adopted an orphaned daughter with Christian parentage who is rescued from death by a characteristically angry anti-Semitic and Islamaphobic Crusader. The two young people are found (like Nerestan and Zara) to be siblings and the Sultan's threatened wrath turns to benignant patronage. Unperformed in Lessing's lifetime, this remarkable play has had an extremely active afterlife in the twentieth and twenty-first centuries, being repeatedly performed in places where the religious differences it negotiates are violently legible.[107]

It is hardly surprising that *Nathan the Wise* was not produced on the late Georgian stage. There were a number of reviews when a new translation appeared in 1805, most of them hostile. The most extended and respectful, in *The Annual Register* and *The Edinburgh Review*, respectively, both identified the ecumenical tendency of the play with disapproval.

> The purpose of the play is obvious. Lessing's writings had raised an outcry against him for infidelity, and this was written in favour of toleration. The purport was good, but the writer has too openly displayed the unfairness of a partisan. All his characters are philosophers of his own school, all indifferentists, except the old woman and the patriarch, who is made a villain: and he most unphilosophically represents the three religions as equally favourable to the happiness of mankind, in defiance of history and experience.[108]

The assessment in *The Edinburgh Review* was not greatly different, although it places more stress on the Germanic background to Lessing's deism:

> Its moral, we are informed, is to inculcate the moral of mutual indulgence in religious opinions; and truly, it must be confessed that it does this in a very radical and effectual way, by urging, in a very confident manner, the extreme insignificance of all peculiar systems of faith, or rather, the strong presumption against any of them being worth attending to, or in any respect better than another. The author's whole secret, for reconciling Jews, Mahometans, and Christians to each other, is to persuade them all to

---

[107] See Urban, 'Lessing's Nathan the Wise'.
[108] *The Annual Register and History of Literature* 4 (January 1805): 639.

renounce their peculiar tenets, and to rest satisfied with a kind of philo-sophical deism, in which they may all agree.[109]

When playwrights turned again to the issue of religious prejudice in the last decades of the eighteenth century, they did in very different terms from dramatists shaped by the early Enlightenment. Michael Ragussis has documented the plethora of anti-Semitic *and* philo-Semitic depictions of Jews on stage during the 1770s, 1780s and 1790s, a 'complicated, multi-valenced, contradictory group of representations' that he argues prepared the British nation for the long route to Jewish emancipation in the 1830s, after the public clamour over the Jewish Naturalization Act (1753).[110] In an argument with implications for the effects of abolitionist drama, Jean Marsden has recently suggested that Richard Cumberland's use of a recuperative sentimental dramaturgy in *The Jew* served more ominously as a means of assuring British spectators of their own (nationally marked) benevolent humanity, rather than enjoining real empathy and reformist action.[111]

What seems striking in a comparison between the early and mid-Georgian dramatic denunciations of fanaticism and advocacy for tolerance is the domestication and individuation of the issue in evolving forms of sentimental drama, as well as a reorientation away from Islam to Judaism. Hughes, Hill and Thomson create sympathetic Islamic protagonists, but their plays all use episodes of crucial importance in the centuries-long history of conflict between Crescent and Cross. In plays such as *The Siege of Damascus* and *Zara*, the Muslim individuals are embedded in commu-nities of faith in which their own cultural and political mores are signalled by costume, gesture and scene. However much explicit or implicit framing in metatextual materials such as prologues and epilogues orients spectators towards a Eurocentric reading of the action, these plays present Christian and Islamic societies as broadly comparable, genuinely competitive in military, political and religious terms. Later in the eighteenth century this is much less the case: new plays about the Ottomans introduce hitherto almost unimaginable scenes of farce, as in Charles Dibdin's *The Seraglio* (1776) and Isaac Bickerstaff's *The Sultan* (1781), while a thinly disguised John Howard tours Sumatran prisons and lectures the Sultan on his

---

[109] *The Edinburgh Review*, ed. Francis Jeffrey, 8 (April 15, 1806): 148–154.
[110] Ragussis, *Theatrical Nation*, 92.
[111] Jean Marsden, 'Richard Cumberland's *The Jew* and the Benevolence of the Audience: Performance and Religious Tolerance', *Eighteenth-Century Studies* 48.4 (Summer 2015): 457–477.

oppressive cruelty in Elizabeth Inchbald's *Such Things Are* (1788). As Daniel O'Quinn has shown, in the last three decades of the eighteenth century, these very different theatricalizations of Asian courts become preoccupied with managing the anxieties that resulted from British imperial rule in India and defeat in America, as 'Asian despotism' looked increasingly less like a comforting contrast to and more like a mirror of British rule.

In the tolerationist plays of the earlier period, plots in which characters are always discovering a natal origin at odds with their customary identity suggest that cultural and religious differences are not essential but accidental and malleable. Tragedy is generated by those who believe otherwise. Islamic and Christian characters share a syncretic, deist rhetoric that implicitly suggests what *Nathan the Wise* makes plain: the three monotheistic faiths overlap, none can claim the monopoly on truth but equally, the different histories and traditions of the creeds are the shaping inheritance of each community. Each should be valued by its adherents without denigrating or seeking to convert others. By contrast, Cumberland's *The Jew* suggests that an excoriated minority figure be recognized as 'same': that under his trappings of Jewishness, Sheva is really Christian, a common trope of implied conversion identified by Ragussis. By setting his scene in contemporary London, Cumberland renders the reverse passage from Christianity to Judaism unthinkable: 'passing' goes only one way.

The Jew suggests that late eighteenth-century stagings of toleration reduce the religious other to an object of (convertible) pathos. This radical delimitation of tolerationist argument is symptomatic of the concurrent emergence of Evangelical enthusiasm, generally antagonistic to deism and radically hostile to comparativist attempts to justify non-Christian beliefs. While European unbelievers were very keen to find 'a pure ethical code in a non-Christian society', Evangelists were equally anxious to 'have done with this groundless commendation of natural law ... ; examine its influence over the pagans of our own times, over the sensual inhabitants of Otaheite, over the cannibals of New Zealand, or the remorseless savages of America'.[112] As the eighteenth century came to a close, civilizing mission and conversion assumed a new urgency in imperial policy and on the stage.

---

[112] P. J. Marshall (ed.), *The British Discovery of India* (Cambridge: Cambridge University Press, 1970), Introduction, 28; R. Watson, *An Apology for Christianity*, 2nd ed. (Cambridge, 1777), 212. For a general account of the growth of Evangelistic hostility to non-Christians, see R. N. Stromberg, *Religious Liberalism in Eighteenth-Century England* (Oxford: Clarendon, 1954).

CHAPTER 3

The Black Legend, Noble Savagery and Indigenous Voice

> This tradition tells us further, that he had afterwards a sight of those dismal habitations which are the portion of ill men after death; and mentions several molten seas of gold, in which were plunged the souls of barbarous Europeans, who put to the sword so many thousands of poor Indians for the sake of that precious metal.
>
> —Joseph Addison, 'The Vision of Marraton', *The Spectator*,
> No. 56, May 4, 1711.

In an essay inspired by the visit of four sachems to London in 1710, Joseph Addison wrote an account of the Amerindian afterlife supposedly provided by one of the 'kings'' interpreters. The delightful prospects that greet the Native American after death are interrupted only by the miserable fate provided for the cruel and avaricious Europeans, who have done so much to turn the Americas themselves into a living hell for their original inhabitants.[1] What Samuel Johnson was to call 'European oppression in America' was already a well-ventilated topic among early eighteenth-century Whig ideologues such as Addison and Steele, to whom the notion that fanatic Catholicism served as a cover for brutal avarice was an *idée reçue*. Much more radical critics of religious intolerance, commercial society, political hierarchy and imperial expansion also saw rich rhetorical possibilities in the staging of new world encounter and the dialogues in which they depicted debates between European and indigene became classics of Enlightenment writing.[2] Less well-known are the eighteenth-century plays that go beyond voicing a debate between noble savages and

---

[1] Joseph Addison, *The Works of Joseph Addison with notes by Richard Hurd*, 6 vols., ed. Henry G. Bohn (London: George Bell & Sons, 1901), 2:335–339.

[2] For a recent, rich account, see Muthu, *Enlightenment Against Empire*, esp. 11–66. Muthu argues it is only in the late Enlightenment that European philosophers developed the capacity to recognize European cultures as humanely equal if culturally incommensurable. For Anthony Pagden's sceptical view of Lahontan (and Montezuma), see 'The Savage Critic: Some European Images of the Primitive', in *The Uncertainties of Empire: Essays in Iberian and Ibero-American Intellectual History* (Aldershot: Variorum, 1994), 39–42.

Westerners by staging theatrical representations of the military conflict, sexual predation and cultural and religious contestation generated by European invasions in the new world. Throughout the eighteenth century London spectators could go to the theatre to watch noble Amerindians and Caribs, Aztecs and Incas resisting, allying themselves with or succumbing to European invaders. John Dennis's Canadian play *Liberty Asserted* appeared in 1704, with Gay's West Indian *Polly* being written and published in 1729, followed by James Miller's *Art and Nature* (1738) and Cleland's *Tombo-Chicqui* in 1758. Plays about the Spanish Conquest of the new world, of which Dryden's *The Indian Emperor* was the *locus classicus*, were frequently performed: in 1718 Sir Thomas Moore, Milton's nephew, had a tragedy set in Paraguay, called *Mangora, King of the Timbusians*, produced (if only for one night); a new version of *The Indian Emperor* was performed in 1728; in 1736 Aaron Hill adapted Voltaire's huge Peruvian hit *Alzire* and Arthur Murphy provided another tragedy of Andean conquest in 1773. In the 1790s, a plethora of new world plays appeared, beginning with Morton's *Columbus* (1792) and reaching a climax with Sheridan's outstandingly successful *Pizarro* (1799).

Written and produced over many decades in differing political and cultural circumstances, these new world texts served varying commercial and ideological purposes.[3] Broadly speaking, however, British playwrights and spectators presumed that plays about New Spain would reiterate, even if they modified, the black legend of Spanish Conquest, while theatre about Caribbean indigenes and Northern Amerindians always participated in the discourse of noble savagery.[4] The black legend developed in

---

[3] Understandably, Gay's *Polly* has received much more critical attention than any of the rest of these plays, with the exclusion of Dryden's *Indian Emperor*. For recent articles with a transatlanticist perspective, see Rob Canfield, 'Something's Mizzen: Anne Bonny, Mary Read, Polly and the Female Counter-Roles on the Imperialist Stage', *South Atlantic Review* 66.2 (Spring 2001): 45–63; 'John Gay's *Polly*: Unmasking Pirates and Fortune Hunters in the West Indies', *Eighteenth-Century Studies* 34.4 (Summer 2001): 539–557; 'Conquer or Die: Staging Circum-Atlantic Revolt in *Polly* and *Three-Finger'd Jack*', *Theatre Journal* 59.2 (May 2007): 241–258; and John Richardson, 'John Gay and Slavery', *Modern Language Review* 97.1 (January 2002): 15–25.

[4] Most of the commentary on the literary dimensions of the black legend focuses on the Renaissance, rather than the eighteenth century. See William S. Maltby, *The Black Legend in England: The Development of Anti-Spanish Sentiment, 1558–1660* (Durham, NC: Duke University Press, 1971) and Margaret Rich Greer, Walter D. Mignolo, and Maureen Quilligan (eds.), *Rereading the Black Legend: The Discourses of Religious and Racial Difference in the Renaissance Empires* (Chicago: University of Chicago Press, 2007). Classic essays on noble savagery appear in Edward J. Dudley and Maximillian E. Novak (eds.), *The Wild Man Within: An Image in Western Thought from the Renaissance to Romanticism* (Pittsburgh: University of Pittsburgh Press, 1973). See also Anthony Pagden, *European Encounters with the New World: From Renaissance to Romanticism* (New Haven, CT: Yale University Press, 1993). In *The Myth of the Noble Savage* (Berkeley: University of

north-west Europe in the aftermath of Spanish colonization in the Americas, drawing on critical accounts of the process such as that provided by Bartolomeo Las Casas in *The Tears of the Indians*, to represent Hispanic conquest as exceptionally violent, oppressive and exploitative. Although encoding critiques of European colonization, religious intolerance, social relations and institutions, black legendry and noble savagism have generally been seen as forms of colonial discourse. The black legend alibied (Protestant, liberal, commercial) British imperialism, a form presumed superior to the Spanish cross-and-booty model, while noble savagism identified indigenes as relative primitives whose natural virtues and capacities were inferior to those of (Christian) Europeans.[5] In certain of the plays discussed below, however, dramatizations of colonial competition in Canada, and the Spanish invasion of the Andes cannot be reduced to iterations of noble savagery or black legendry. Revisiting both the pretexts by which plays such as *Liberty Asserted, Alvira* and *Alzuma* are shaped opens up the possibility that these texts, in performance, actually incorporate, rather than simply ventriloquize, indigenous critique.

In recent revisionary discussion of the noble savage, Robert Stam and Ella Shohat argue that far from being a pure projection of European fantasies, ventriloquizing European critiques of their own cultures, dialogues spoken by new world natives and Western interlocutors constitute a 'discourse of radical indigeneity'.[6] Stam and Shohat argue that from the Renaissance on, encounters with Amerindians were the catalyst that enabled Europeans to articulate the critiques of monarchy, of hierarchical society and of empire that we associate with Enlightenment and out of which, via Marxism and liberalism, anti-colonialism tout court emerged. From this 'Red Atlantic' perspective, the Enlightenment is less an originary source of radicalism than an arena of contestation characterized by 'critical acts of interlocution' between indigenous Americans and Europeans (376). Protesting the 'vanishing' of indigenes and the negation of their cultural and intellectual agency, Stam and Shohat argue that the figure of the noble

California Press, 2001), Terry Jay Ellingson argues the figure disappears during most of the seventeenth and eighteenth centuries.

[5] For a discussion of the competing imperial modes as they were dramatized in the Restoration, see Bridget Orr, *Empire on the English Stage, 1660–1714* (Cambridge: Cambridge University Press, 2001). For a recent, trenchant account of the noble savage as cultural critic, see Doris L. Garraway, 'Of Speaking Natives and Hybrid Philosophers: Lahontan, Diderot, and the French Enlightenment Critique of Colonialism', in *The Postcolonial Enlightenment: Eighteenth-Century Colonialism and Postcolonial Theory*, ed. Daniel Carey and Lynn Festa (Oxford: Oxford University Press, 2009), 207–239.

[6] Stam and Shohat, 'Where and Whither Postcolonial Theory', 376.

savage should be reconceived as more than a purely projective figure, so that we recognize Montaigne's *Des Cannibales* as produced through his encounter with the three Tupinama who visited King Charles IX's court in 1562 (374).

Chiming with Wendy Belcher's claim that Samuel Johnson's writing can be read as 'energumen', or discourse of an Other, this argument is provocative in the context of eighteenth-century British stagings of new world societies, opening up the question of the extent to which theatrical reenactments of early conflicts with European colonizers may be shaped by indigenous perspectives. Because El Inca Garcilaso de la Vega, a Peruvian mestizo, published the authoritative account of preconquest Inca society and the Spanish invasion, his role as an influence over the Andean plays that drew on the *Royal Commentaries* is beyond dispute, although the extent to which the redactions of his narrative reiterate his account needs extensive amplification.[7] On the other hand, the role of Northern Amerindians in dramatizations of their presence in the English metropolis and the colonization of their territories has never been seen as other than projective noble savagery, on those rare occasions it has been noticed at all.[8] This occludes the fact that the publication of Amerindian voices or the actual presence of native North Americans preceded the production of plays depicting Hurons, Iroquois or Caribs. *Liberty Asserted* was written out of Lahontan's *New Travels in North America* (1703), and Miller's *Art and Nature* was written in the wake of a well-publicized visit by Creek leader Tomochichi to London, during which he and his entourage met the King and the Archbishop of Canterbury as well as attending the theatre on several dozen occasions.

Reading Dennis's *Liberty Asserted* against Lahontan's *New Voyages in North America* provides a model for the complex process by which new world encounter ends up as theatrical representation, revealing how inter-cultural locution rewritten as Enlightenment critique gets incorporated

---

[7] See Merle E. Perkins, 'The Documentation of Voltaire's *Alzire*', *Modern Language Quarterly* 4 (1943): 433–436. Michelle Buchanan suggests 'Nothing in *Alzire* suggests a Peruvian background', in 'Savages, Noble and Otherwise, and the French Enlightenment', *Studies on Eighteenth-Century Culture* 15 (1986): 105. There is a useful overview of Garcilaso's influence on Voltaire in the critical edition of *Alzire, ou les Americains* by T. E. D. Braun, in *Complete Works of Voltaire*, 14:6–27.

[8] For a recent discussion of 'breeding' and its relation to social norms in James Miller's sentimental comedy *Art and Nature*, see Freeman, *Character's Theater*, 200–204. For a still-unsurpassed survey of eighteenth-century British literature about native North Americans, see Benjamin Bissell, *The American Indian in English Literature* (New Haven, CT: Yale University Press, 1925).

into an emphatically patriotic and Whig play.[9] *Liberty Asserted* is set in Canada and was performed the year after Lahontan's famous account of his travels among the North American tribes was published in English in London. Notwithstanding their expectations that a serious play would contribute to ongoing political debate, spectators would have expected the text to be broadly consonant with its sources, in this case the rather novel and fascinating *New Voyages*. And so among other features, *Liberty Asserted* has Indian characters with names drawn from the brief glossary provided by Lahontan at the end of his second volume. 'A Short Dictionary of the Most Universal Language of the Savages' reveals that the protagonist's mother Sakia means love (and the character's previous name, Nisakia, means 'I love').[10] The heroine Irene is a version of Irini, which means nation, or people; the Iroquois warrior Arimat means a thing of value; Okiwa, confidant of Irene, means 'leader' and the protagonist Ulumar's name means 'red powder', much esteemed by the Indians. Head of the Iroquois, 'Zephario', is presumably a nod to Adario, Lahontan's famous 'savage' interlocutor. The play's action depends on the much-noted Iroquois practice of adoption, as the plot turns on the consequences of the absorption of a Huron child Ulumar into the Iroquois people. Ulumar's mother Sakia shows an 'external conformity' and underlying resistance to this absorption, a common response charted in detail by Daniel K. Reichter.[11] Sakia's strength of character is characteristic of stature of women in matrilineal Huron society, in which councils of mothers were responsible for appointing and dismissing (male) leaders. Beyond these traces of Indian language and practice, Dennis's apparently fantastic conclusion, in which the French Viceroy Frontenac rebels against Louis XIV, actually bears witness to the Governor's long-standing disputes with Louis XIV and Colbert over his extension of political freedom in New France and Ulumar's betrayal by one party of the French, and the final Iroquoian agreement with Frontenac, provide a lapidary version of the

---

[9] Dennis's only successful play has not received much critical attention. See however a Lockean reading in Loftis, *Politics of Drama*, 42–43. Ellison's *Cato's Tears* focuses on the unresolvable agonies of Ulumar, the hero; Bridget Orr argues the play encodes a specifically Whig theory of empire (*Empire on the English Stage*, 277–278), and in *Race of Female Patriots* Brett D. Wilson argues the play suggests sentimental union can encompass people of different culture and political affiliation (72). For commentary on the use of Lahontan, see Nicholas von Maltzahn, '"Acts of Kind Service" and the Patriot Literature of Empire', in *Milton and the Imperial Vision*, ed. Balachandra Rajan and Elizabeth Sauer (Pittsburgh: Duquesne University Press, 1999).

[10] Lahontan, *New Voyages to North America*, vol. 2. All quotations are from this edition and are cited in the text by page number.

[11] Daniel K. Richter, *The Ordeal of the Longhouse: The People of the Iroquois League in the Era of European Colonization* (Chapel Hill: University of North Carolina Press, 1982), 72.

Governor's longer engagement with the nation. After his recall from Canada, Frontenac's replacement betrayed an agreement with the Iroquois, took fifty sachems prisoner and sent them to the galleys in Marseilles. Before taking up his second and final term as Governor, Frontenac found thirteen of the still surviving chiefs and took them with him to Canada when he returned.[12]

Dennis used Lahontan's *New Voyages* for a great deal more than a novel exotic setting, however. The most celebrated section of Lahontan's *Voyage* was the in-set *Dialogue*, 'Between the Author and *Adario*, A Noted Man among the Savages', the latter apparently based on his friend and interlocutor, a prominent Huron called Kondiaronk, nicknamed 'Le Rat' by the French, then and now a controversial text.[13]

In his Preface to the English translation of the *New Voyages*, Lahontan lays out the complex process of cultural transmission and adaptation that led to the publication of the *Dialogue*. Explaining that while an earlier version of his book was being printed in Holland, he visited England and was asked by several English gentlemen to expand his text:

> [They wanted] a more ample Relation of the Manners and Customs of the People of that Continent, whom we call by the name of Savages. This obliged me to communicate to these Gentlemen, the substance of the several Conferences I had in that Country with a certain Huron, whom the *French* call *Rat*. While I stayed at that *American's* Village I employed my time very agreeably in making a careful Collection of all his Arguments and Opinions; and as soon as I return'd from my Voyage upon the Lakes of *Canada* I shew'd my Manuscript to Count *Frontenac*, who was so pleas'd with it, he took the pains to assist me in the digesting of the Dialogues, and bringing them into the order they now appear in: For before that, they were abrupt Conferences without Connexion. Upon the Solicitation of these *English* Gentlemen, I put these Dialogues into the hands of the Person who translated my Letters and Memoir: And if it had not been for their pressing Instancies, they had never seen the light; for there are but few in the World that will judge impartially, and without prepossession, of some things contain'd in 'em.

---

[12] For Frontenac's biography, see W. J. Eccles, *Frontenac: The Courtier Governor* (Toronto: McClelland and Stewart, 1965); for a recent account of the Canadian wars, see Michael G. Laramie, *The European Invasion of North America: Colonial Conflict along the Hudson-Champlain Corridor, 1609–1760* (Santa Barbara, CA: Praeger/ABC, 2012).

[13] The other source Dennis mentions but uses much less extensively is Louis Hennepin, *A New Discovery of a Vast Country in America, Extending above Four Thousand Miles between New France and New Mexico, with a Description of the Great Lakes, Cataracts, Rivers, Plants and Animals: Also the Manners, Customs, and Languages of the Several Native Indians and the Advantage of Commerce with Those Different Nations* (London: T. Bentley et al., 1698).

Lahontan's English Preface seeks to authorize a heterodox text through a rich variety of rhetorical gestures. What Anthony Pagden has described as a fundamental mode of new world discourse, autopsy or eyewitnessing, is the basis of his narrative authority, but his depiction of his exchanges with Kondiaronk as a dialogue draws on and amplifies the very different genre of the Lucianic dialogue of the dead, a satiric and critical form that flourishes in times of social upheaval.[14] Fontenelle had published his famous *New Dialogues of the Dead* in 1683, closing his text with an exchange between Fernando Cortez and Montezuma, in which the latter convincingly demolishes the Spaniard's claims of European intellectual and ethical superiority and new world sovereignty. The dialogue would become a favourite Enlightenment genre for the staging of cross-cultural dispute, as in Diderot's *Supplement au voyage de Bougainville*, but the invasion and colonization of the new world also appears in Lyttleton's *Dialogues of the Dead* (pitting William Penn against Cortez), while Thomas Tyers's *Conversations Political and Familiar* (1782) presents Thomas More arguing with Sir Francis Drake. These dialogues are characteristically tilted in favour of the conquered, so that the boastful *alazon* generally loses the debate with the simpler *eiron*. The rhetorical process thus reverses the conqueror's historic triumph with a rhetorical loss at the hands of a defeated enemy who is revealed as the victor's ethical and intellectual superior.

Rhetorical superiority might seem a poor substitute for historic agency, but the dialogue's naturalization of imperial processes is seriously qualified by its form, depending as it does on the ventriloquism of an intellectually commanding, speaking subject. In an acute recent essay, Doris Garraway argues that Lahontan's and Bougainville's ventriloquism of the native critic parodies the trope of the enlightened native, as their fictionalized colonial subjects are imagined finally consenting to a rationally reformed Eurocentric global order. But although she recognizes that Lahontan's critique is shaped by 'the author's experience in colonial Canada', her final dismissal of 'Adario' as a fully fictitious mimic erases the Huron contribution to the

---

[14] See Pagden, *European Encounters*, 51–87. Pagden discusses the way in which autopsy developed to supplement the older form of discursive legitimation, the reference to authoritative texts, in a new world context in which no such precedents existed. For the standard account of the dialogue of the dead, see Fredrick M. Keener, *English Dialogues of the Dead: A Critical History, an Anthology, and a Check-List* (New York: Columbia University Press, 1973). Kevin L. Cope (ed.), *Compendious Conversation: The Method of Dialogue in the Early Enlightenment* (Frankfurt: Peter Lang, 1992) contains a number of essays outlining the ideological uses of the dialogue, notably (in this context) David McNeil, 'Dialogues on Military Affairs', 129–137.

text, which ends up as a rearticulation of purely European thought, a prelude to a new form of colonial discourse.[15]

Should Adario's perspective be dismissed in this fashion? The semi-dramatic mode of the dialogue certainly establishes that the reader is encountering a rhetorical performance, not authentic voices. 'I would not have the Reader to take it amiss, that the thoughts of Savages are laid out in *European* dress' (Preface). While 'Lahontan' speaks in his own name, the difference in perspective between the parody of orthodoxy he espouses in the exchange and the more philo-Indian account he provides in the enclosing narrative, suggests that we treat 'Lahontan's' views as strategic, in the same way 'Adario,' renamed with classicizing if not archaizing grace, is necessarily at some distance from his narrative avatar 'Rat.' But does this self-conscious staging necessarily imply that Adario is simply a mouthpiece? Wendat-Huron scholar Georges Sioui argues that the views the Huron articulates were indeed those of the Wendat, making the point, affirmed by Bruce Trigger that 'Lahontan's authenticity is also attested to by Lafitau and earlier Jesuit writers, who frequently confirm Lahontan in matters of fact, although their attitude to native cultures was radically different from his.'[16] One of the most striking testimonies to Adario's eloquence comes from Charlevoix, who writes of Kondiaronk that he was always verbally commanding on public occasions:

> He was no less brilliant in private conversations, and we often took pleasure in irritating him, so as to hear his retorts, which were always lively, full of wit, and generally irrefutable. On that score, he was the only man in *Canada* able to stand up to the *Comte de Frontenac*, who often invited him to his table to procure the pleasure of his officers.[17]

In the fullest recent historical analysis of Lahontan's veracity, Gordon Sayre comes to the conclusion that the *Dialogue* is a hybrid, that Adario is best understood as a 'synthesis of Indian culture and European deism'.[18] Sayre suggests that Lahontan's alienation from French society – begun by his family's social and financial bankruptcy and ending with his disastrous quarrel with the commander of a Newfoundland fort – along with his extensive hunting trips with Hurons, made him sympathetic to Amerindian values and lifeways. Sayre concludes that 'the deism and

---

[15] Garraway, 'Of Speaking Natives and Hybrid Philosophers.'
[16] See Georges Sioui, *For an Amerindian Autohistory: An Essay on the Foundations of a Social Ethic*, trans. Sheila Fischman (Montreal: McGill-Queens University Press, 1992), xii.
[17] Pierre F. X. de Charlevoix, *Histoire et Description Generale de la Nouvelle-France* (Paris, 1744), cited in Maurice Roelens *Avec un Sauvage* (Montreal: Lemeac, 1974), 45.
[18] Gordon M. Sayre, *Les Sauvages Americains: Representations of Native Americans in French and English Colonial Literature* (Chapel Hill: University of North Carolina Press, 1997), 38.

primitivism [Lahontan] is often accused of imposing on the Amerindians, of placing in the mouth of the Huron character Adario ... were in fact learned from the Indians as much as imposed on them' (31).

Rightly conscious of the likely scepticism of his readership, in his English Preface, Lahontan produces as his first supplementary witness none other than Frontenac himself, suggesting that the Governor has in effect edited his text, inventing nothing but improving its presentation and by implication authenticating its claims to voice Huron opinion. The plausibility of this claim is increased by Charlevoix's testimony of Frontenac's own friendship with Kondiaronk/Adario. Lahontan's final claim is that he was induced to publish the translation of the *Dialogue* solicitation of some unnamed English gentlemen. Whether or not Dennis was among these gentlemen is unknown, but the ideological affiliations Lahontan announces in the Preface were consonant with his own enthusiastic commitment to the Revolution Settlement. In an ingratiating panegyric to precisely the kind of English exceptionalism Dennis trumpets, Lahontan voices his dual affiliation with the North American and the English:

> I envy the State of the poor Savage, who tramples upon Laws, and pays Homage to no Sceptre. I wish I could spend the rest of my Life in his Hutt, and so be no longer expos'd to the chagrin of bending the knee to a set of Men, that sacrifice the publick Good to their private Interest, and are born to plague honest Men.
>
> But after all my Misfortunes, I have this to solace me, that I enjoy in *England*, a sort of Liberty that is not met with elsewhere: For one may justly say, that of all the Countries inhabited by civiliz'd People, this alone affords the greatest Perfection of Liberty. Nay, I do not except the Liberty of Mind, for I am convinc'd, that the *English* maintain it with a great deal of tenderness: so true it is, that all degrees of Slavery are abhorred by this People, who shew their Wisdom by the Precautions they take to prevent their sinking into a fatal Servitude. (Preface)

Lahontan's identification of Liberty as the defining characteristic of both American Indian and English society is Dennis's great theme in *Liberty Asserted*, motivating the alliance between the Iroquois and the English and generating his characters' obloquy for the perfidious and servile conduct of the French. 'The design of this Tragedy is to make Men in love with Liberty, by shewing them that nothing can be more according to Nature', he remarks in the Preface.[19] Dennis's claim would have been stimulated by Adario's characterization of Huron fraternity: 'We content ourselves in

---

[19] John Dennis, *Liberty Asserted. A Tragedy* (London: George Strahan et al., 1704), Preface, n.p. All other citations are from this edition and are quoted by act, scene and page numbers.

denying all manner of Dependency, except upon the great Spirit; as being born free and joint Brethren, who are all equally Masters; whereas you are all Slaves of one Man' (*New Voyages*, 2:124). Further, Adario's condemnation of France as a realm dominated by tyrannical private ends – he hopes 'that at last you'll abhor that thing call'd Interest which occasions all the Mischief *Europe* groans under' (*New Voyages*, 2:138) – is echoed in *Liberty Asserted*'s trial of the Iroquian Ulumar's integrity. As Brett Wilson has argued, the central action of Dennis's play requires Ulumar to learn the necessity of subduing private, family concerns (in the heart-wrenching form of his Huron mother Sakia's threats of suicide) to the good of his tribe, in this case maintaining hostility to the French and remaining allied with the English.[20] Dennis dramatizes this quintessentially Whig contest between private interest and public good through the Iroquois practice of adoption: Ulumar's contented absorption into the tribe is consonant with the practice of naturalization, the process by which the English were enriching their human capital at the expense of persecutory Catholic regimes. If the adopted/naturalized subject remains loyal, the nation is empowered through its heterogeneity: Sakia's stubborn adherence to her original loyalties figures the internal threat to the state when an immigrant retains alien affiliations.[21]

Wilson is right to stress the emotional register in which Dennis makes his argument in *Liberty Asserted*, characteristic as it is of emergent Whig dramaturgy of sentimental union. In stressing the importance of benevolent feeling as a model of political unity however, Dennis is again indebted to his Amerindian source, in which Adario contrasts both the filial piety and the harmony of Huron society with French dissension: 'We are all of one Mind; our Wills, Opinions and Sentiments we observe in exact Conformity; and thus we spend our Lives with such a good Understanding, that no Disputes or Suits can take place among us' (2:147). In his Preface, Dennis claims that the love of liberty is a natural corollary of 'that most Tender of all Sentiments which Nature has implanted in the Minds of Men, that is, the Love of their Children', a point reiterated in the Epilogue:

> The fiercest Creatures that the Woods contain
> What they bring forth, with pleasing Love maintain.

[20] Wilson, *Race of Female Patriots*, 70–93.
[21] For a discussion of Whig enthusiasm for demographic heterogeneity, see Schmidgen, *Exquisite Mixture*.

> That Love the Lyon softens, and the Bear,
> The World's supported by that tender Care,
> All Savages but Men, their Off-spring share.
> But Man, grown blind, by Lust of Pow'r or Pelf,
> Will fell his darling Off-spring and Himself.

While the Amerindians in Dennis's play display both familial love and a deep attachment to political autonomy, *Liberty Asserted* warns against the corrupting effects of power and pelf visible among Europeans. The play is also deeply concerned with the threat posed by false religion. Dennis found in Lahontan – and even more Adario – a deep hostility to the Catholic priesthood. 'Notwithstanding the Veneration I have for the Clergy, I impute to them all the Mischief the Iroquese have done to the French Colonies, in the Course of a War, which had never been undertaken, if it had not been for the Counsels of these pious Church-men' (The Preface). Adario's critique of the Jesuits was unsparing, a perspective that Dennis, whose first successful publication was *The Danger of Priestcraft to Religion and Government,* published in 1702, doubtless found congenial. Buttressing *Liberty Asserted*'s secular reconstitution of Indian subjects as sentimental Whigs is a constant drumbeat of anti-Catholic deist rhetoric that underscores the indigenes' readiness for conversion to Protestantism. Sakia is an early critic of Catholic bigotry, explaining to Ulumar that clerical disapproval of her marriage to his French father forced the couple apart. She is however now ready to covert, telling Miramont, 'By my Conferences here with Beaufort, / My Son and I both strongly are inclin'd / T'embrace the *Christian* Faith' (1.5.14). Both Sakia and Ulumar are advocates of natural religion, swearing oaths 'by that awful, that all-seeing Mind' (1.5.11). Reflecting Adario's practice in the *Dialogue*, the Indian characters frequently invoke 'th'Almighty Mind' (2.4.23 – Irene); 'th'Eternal Mind' (2.2.15 – Sakia) and regard the law of nature, understood as the manifestation of the Great Spirit as their guide (*New Voyages*, 1:92–108). Ulumar is as notable for his (natural) piety as his patriotism: 'When e'er I cease to hearken to the Dictates, / Of the World's Ruler and his Servant Nature, / I shall deserve to be a thing accurst', he tells Sakia (2.2.17) and in trying to decide how to respond to her suicide threats, he prays to 'th'Eternal Mind, / Master of Life, great Mover of all Spirits, / O guide my Will by thy unerring Light!' (3.2.32). His primitive monotheism leads Ulumar to the impeccably monogenesist conclusion ''Tis true we were created Brothers all, / And are descended from one eternal Sire' (2.2.17).

It is striking that when the French delegation make their case with Ulumar, it is manners rather than Catholicism that they claim as cultural mission. All of *Liberty Asserted*'s Indian characters are religious but anti-Catholic, buttressing the process by which the play naturalizes Protestant Whiggism. Exorbitating Lahontan's anti-clericalism and political anglophilia, Dennis's theatrical Canada is thus characterized by primitive religion, adherence to the law of nature and pre-state political practices that anticipate, if they do not fully coincide with, Revolution principles. Dennis's construction of Iroquoian society as an early version of England can be seen to imply inferiority, insofar as Adario's rhetorical triumph over Lahontan in the *Dialogue* seems to be reversed by Dennis's reduction of the indigenous world to precursor, a relation most strikingly figured by Ulumar's tutelage to Beaufort. But the process by which the play reconstructs the *New Voyages* also suggests that the Whig and broadly Enlightenment principles of political liberty and religious toleration are propped on, as much as projected onto, indigenous practice and belief. The confidence to claim values are universal depends on finding and incorporating cross-cultural instances, contemporaneously as well as historically, and it is suggestive that Dennis's rapid appropriation of Lahontan produced his only really successful play.

Traces of Indian practice, belief and language may not now be easily legible to contemporary readers, but as Matthew Duques has shown, they structure Dennis's text as surely as his much more obvious Whig verities.[22] Moreover, while the play might look as if it was speaking only to an English political class whose support for the War of the Spanish Succession needed firming, England's struggle with France had intercontinental dimensions. Allied to the English during King Billy's War, the Iroquois sat out Queen Anne's, but in 1710 three Mohawk leaders and an Algonquian Mahican came to London to discuss military aid for use against the French and Protestant missionaries to offset the success of the Jesuits. Not just Whig myth, Dennis's play lays out the ideological grounds for the kind of political and confessional alliance at stake in the visit of the 'Indian Kings' some seven years later, as a living example of how 'patrocinium', the Whig model of federalist empire, might actually work.[23] For although the

---

[22] Matthew E. Duques, 'John Dennis's Dramatis Personae', *Notes and Queries* 62.262 (2015): 271–273.

[23] For a full empirical account, see Richard P. Bond in *Queen Anne's American Kings* (Oxford: Clarendon, 1952), and for a rich commentary of the cultural implications of the visit, see Roach, *Cities of the Dead*, 119–178. For more on patrocinium, see David Armitage, *Ideological Origins of English Empire* (Cambridge: Cambridge University Press, 1998).

play proliferates intercultural homosocial and heterosexual alliances, its decisive actions coincide with Lahontan's entirely unsentimental assessment of the ways in which the northern nations made strategic decisions in order to ensure communal self-preservation. 'I have intimated already several times, that their respect for the *English*, is tacked to the occasion they have to make use of 'em' (*New Voyages*, 2:271).[24]

Black Legend?

Liberty Asserted and the comedies of noble savagery that follow Dennis's play all dramatize the North American or West Indian territories with which the English were directly concerned. The other major new world scene was that of Latin America, the site of the British commercial aspiration and the black legend. But while conflict with Spain might provide an opportunity for the production of new world plays, their meanings were by no means determined by their moment of production. In the case of Hill's *Alzira* and Murphy's *Alzuma*, in fact, the texts are demonstrably shaped by their source in the *Royal Commentaries* of 'El Inca', Garcilaso de la Vega, in ways that extend beyond the provision of exotic colour. The interaction between the *Royal Commentaries* and the dramatic texts it shaped can be seen as exemplary of the process by which early Enlightenment writers refigured, incorporated and explored forms and texts beyond Europe to address, not simply repress, other cultures and civilizations. In his widely read *Essai sur l'empire des Incas*, Algarotti cites Garcilaso as his source for a panegyric on the political and technological superiority of the Incas, an opinion he shared with Sir William Temple, writing in the *Essay on Heroic Virtue*.[25] His works translated into several European languages from the original Spanish, Garcilaso also became known to Anglophone readers through the translation of the *Royal Commentaries* published by Paul Rycaut in 1688. Rycaut's translation was a characteristically cross-cultural venture: most famous for his *Present State of the Ottoman Empire*, he had also published histories of the papacy and the Eastern church, as well as translating Lorenzo Gracian's *The Critick*, itself a reworking of ibn Tufal's *Hayy bin Yaqqzan,* widely regarded as an inspiration for Locke's *Essay on Human Understanding* and Defoe's *Robinson Crusoe.*

[24] See Lahontan, *New Voyages to North America*, 2:270–273, for a comparison of French and English interests and Indian policies.
[25] Francisco Algarotti, 'An Essay on the Empire of the Incas', in *Letters from Count Algarotti to Lord Hervey and the Marquis Scipio Maffei* (Glasgow: Robert Ure, 1770).

The *Royal Commentaries'* account of precontact Andean history and the Spanish Conquest became the preeminent eighteenth-century source for educated English opinion on the early history of Peru and its conquerors.[26] One of the most suggestive aspects of this historiographic and proto-ethnographic authority is the fact that Garcilaso, as is highlighted in the first sentence of Rycaut's Translator's Letter to the Reader, was a mestizo, the child of a union between the daughter of the Inca princess (palla) Ocllo Chimpu and a Spanish conquistador, Sebastian Garcilaso de la Vega. Although he goes on to stress that his work is constituted by previous histories by Spanish writers, the author is emphatic that his indigenous perspective places him in an authoritative position, able to judge and correct the earlier colonial accounts. He explains that he was raised an Indian for twenty years and that he learned his nation's history from his family and as an eyewitness. Thus he asserts that 'those stories . . . which in my youth I received from the relation of my mother and my uncles . . . will certainly be more authentick and satisfactory than any account we can receive from other Authors' (Garcilaso, 1:11).[27] In addition to the memories he retains from youth, however, El Inca tells us that 'as soon as I took a Resolution to write this History, I acquainted my School-fellows, such as were taught the Art of Grammar, of this my Intention, desiring them to search into the Archives and Registers of their Countries, and to send me the various successes of them; the which purpose of mine they so well approved, that every one readily contributed to this Work, sending me the History of the Exploits and Actions of their respective Incas' (1:16). By structuring his work as a commentary, Garcilaso mobilizes the ancient legitimating rhetoric of reference to authority, while his biography provides autoptic claims to truth.[28] But in the chapter aptly titled 'Wherein the Author Alledges the Authority he Hath for the Truth of This History' he pushes his claims even further, characterizing his text as the expression of the Inca community, an account whose revisionary articulation of Andean history draws its legitimacy from all who remain of the indigenous elite.

---

[26] Bissell, *American Indian in English Literature*. Bissell speculates that the eighteenth-century popularity of the *Royal Commentaries* stemmed from the ease with which El Inca could be construed as a deist recording the operations of natural law (18–33).

[27] Garcilaso de la Vega, *Royal Commentaries of Peru*, ed. Paul Rycaut (London, 1688), pt. 1, 11. All other quotations are from this edition and are cited in the text by page number.

[28] I refer here to the competing modes of discursive authority discussed by Pagden in *European Encounters*.

Garcilaso's text is of great importance in Andean studies, not least because (unlike the case in Mexico) almost no written sources describing precolonial society exist, with historians relying instead on material heritage and European accounts.[29] Anticipating Stam's and Shahat's claims, he has been described as 'one of the prime inventors of the noble savage', although the same writer stresses 'he used his facts with care'.[30] He has been well-served by recent Renaissance scholars, notably Margarita Zamora and Barbara Fuchs, both of whom have provided sophisticated accounts of his most famous project. Zamora reads the *Royal Commentaries* as an attempt by Garcilaso to combine a celebration of Incan history with the Spanish Conquest, in pursuit of a characteristically early modern humanist ideal of *harmonia*.[31] Fuchs extends her analysis to Garcilaso's posthumous *Historia general del Peru* (1617) and locates in his texts less success in the attempt to do justice to both Inca and Spanish empire, documenting the multiplying contradictions in his narrative and authorial posture.[32] Current assessments of his work are perhaps less sympathetic: Aurora Fiengo-Varn argues that Garcilaso was primarily a Spanish apologist, whose anxieties over his mestizo heritage led him to depict Incan history and the Spanish Conquest in positive, Augustinian terms as the unfolding of Providentialist design in a fashion that denigrated indigenes.[33] In assessing the influence of the *Royal Commentaries* beyond Latin America and Spain, Fernanda Macchi sees Garcilaso's work as contributing to the black legend, with French adapters using the work for anti-Spanish purposes and romanticizing Andeans.[34]

In the depictions of the Spanish Conquest in Peru on the English stage in the eighteenth century, anti-Catholicism and anti-Spanish sentiment is indubitably important. But what has been largely occluded is the full extent to which the Incan voice of the *Commentaries*, however

[29] For an overview of recent perspectives on this period of Peruvian history, see Kenneth J. Andrien, 'The Invention of Colonial Andean Worlds', *Latin American Research Review* 46.1 (2011): 217–226.

[30] Augustin de Zarate, *The Discovery and Conquest of Peru*, trans. and ed. J. M. Cohen (Harmondsworth: Penguin, 1968), 9.

[31] Margarita Zamora, *Language, Authority and Indigenous History in the* Commentarios reales de los Incas (Cambridge: Cambridge University Press, 1988).

[32] Barbara Fuchs, *Mimesis and Empire: The New World, Islam, and European Identities* (Cambridge: Cambridge University Press, 2001), 72–85.

[33] Aurora Fiengo-Varn, 'Reconciling the Divided Self: Inca Garcilaso de la Vega's *Royal Commentaries* and His Platonic View of the Conquest of Peru', *Revista de Filologia y Linguistica de Universidad de Costa Rica* 29.1 (2003).

[34] Fernanda Macchi, *Inas Illustrados:reconstrucciones imperiales en la primera mitad del siglo XVIII* (Madrid: Iboamericana-Veruet, 2009).

remodulated by Rycaut and the various dramatic adapters, informed both French and English performances of Spanish Conquest. By contrast with Augustin de Zarate's *History of the Discovery and Conquest of the Province of Peru*, the other source used by dramatists, Garcilaso's text is Inca-centric. He begins by describing precontact Peru and ends his account of the conquest not with the final establishment of royal authority, like Zarate but with the death of the last Inca. His text is shaped to emphasize both the technological sophistication of Inca civilization and the rationality of their religious beliefs. Assertions of Incan civility, as consonant with deist beliefs in a general human capacity for Enlightenment as they were to Augustinian Providentialism, rendered the *Commentaries* attractive material to Voltaire, and Richard A. Brooks has demonstrated how Voltaire used elements of the *Royal Commentaries* to create 'the outlines of a deistic, enlightened, scientifically-oriented state' in *Candide.*[35] But what has not been noticed is the fact that all of the dramas of Spanish Conquest, *Alzire*, *Alzira* and *Alzuma*, have plots structured by Garcilaso's account of the crucial role of exploitative sexual alliance in enabling the Spanish Conquest, a topic scarcely mentioned by Zarate. Enlightenment dramas about Peru extrapolate the *Royal Commentaries'* record of elite female resistance to marriage with Spaniards and highlight protests made by Indian women as the Spaniards sought to eradicate all male descendants of the Incas – including their own mestizo sons – as they appropriated the bodies and properties of the female heirs to Andean lands.

Rycaut's version of *Royal Commentaries of Peru* subsumes the second part under the one title, but the work remains divided into two volumes, the first describing the Incan conquest of the Andean peoples and the civilization they created, and the second focused on the post-Conquest period during which Incan rule was finally extirpated. Peter Gose has argued that the process by which Spanish rule was established depended on indigenous collaboration, as both Incas but particularly disaffected Andeans identified the Spanish as ancestral figures called *viracochas*, descended from the Sun, and hence recognizable as kin. Gose suggests that the Spaniards accepted indigenous incorporation – which included extensive intermarriage – as the easiest route to ascendency, while Andeans saw the newcomers' dominance as a means to regain pre-Incan sovereignty. When the Spanish eventually repudiated their putative ancestral status, Andeans challenged colonial governance and extraction, reinventing their communities as Christian, egalitarian and republican and beginning the process of decolonization.[36]

Although it departs radically from the philo-Incan perspective of the *Commentaries*, Gose's revisionary account both is dependent on and bears out the importance of sexual and marital alliance in the Spanish ascension. Commenting on the early years of the Conquest, Garcilaso remarks,

> In the beginning of those times, when an *Indian* Woman had brought a Child to a *Spaniard*, all the Family of the Woman were devoted and swore themselves slaves and servants to that *Spaniard*, worshipping and adoring him as their Idol, because he had entered into an affinity with them; and hereby they became very useful to the *Spaniards* in their Conquest of the *Indies*. (491)

This posture of indigenous devotion does not last long, however, for the story of the latter part of the *Commentaries* is what de la Vega calls the 'Tragedy' of Inca decimation, begun with massacres perpetrated by the usurping Atahualpa, assisted to power by the Spanish presence and continued by the Spaniards themselves. After each new round of killing, it is Inca women who lament the dead and accuse the murderers. After the Battle of Huarina, one Donna Maria Calderon protested,

> [She] vented many opprobrious speeches against *Picarro*; saying, that the time would come when his tyrannies would have their end, like those of more powerful Governments, such as the *Greeks* and *Romans* of which were all brought to destruction: and so violently did she express herself, without any discretion, fear, or wit, that *Carvajal* caused her to be strangled, and afterwards hanged out at a Window looking to the Street. (814)

Shortly after this incident, Garcilaso explains that in the wake of the civil wars between the Spanish and their various allies, the Governor decided to marry the widows of rebels with large estates to trusted subordinates. One such was a daughter of Inca Huayan Capac. Holding an extensive estate in her own right, she was outraged to be forced to marry a man whom it was rumoured had once been a tailor, resisting the pleas of the Bishop of Cusco and many other 'Persons of Quality.' Only her brother, who warned her that a continued refusal 'would so disoblige the *Spaniards* that for ever after they would become mortal enemies to their Royal Family and Lineage' (856), was able to persuade her to submit. Garcilaso's view of the rectitude

---

[36] Peter Gose, *Invaders as Ancestors: On the Intercultural Making and Unmaking of Spanish Colonialism in the Andes* (Toronto: University of Toronto Press, 2008). Gose begins his account with a polemic against what he sees as the annihilation of indigenous agency in current, poststructurally inflected postcolonial theory.

of these proceedings can be heard in his conclusion: 'Many other Marriages like these, were contracted all over the Empire, being designed to give Estates to Pretenders, and satisfie them with the goods of other Men' (856).

The protests of trafficked women resound at the murderous climax of the *Commentaries*, the death of the last Inca ruler, Tupac Amaru. Concerned least the last Incas, who retreated to the inaccessible mountain redoubt of Villcapampa, might serve as a focus for resistance, the Spanish viceroy Martin Garcia de Loyola persuaded first the Inca Manco and then Tupac Amaru to place themselves in Spanish hands. After Manco died, as Tupac Amaru refused Garcia's call to come to Los Reyes (later Lima), all the remaining Incan princesses were forced into marriages with Spaniards. When Tupac continued to resist, Garcia (himself married to an Incan princess) indicted all male mestizos over twenty, imprisoning the sons of Spaniards born to Indian women, torturing some of them to uncover evidence of rebellion and planning to kill them all. An Indian woman took to the streets in vocal protest:

> Amidst this mad Rage, and Tyrannical Proceedings by Imprisonment, and Torture, an *Indian* Woman, whose Son was condemned to Question upon the Rack, came to the Prison, and in a loud Voice cryed out, *Son, since thou are sentenced to the Torment, suffer it bravely like a Man of Honour; accuse no Man falsely and God will enable thee to bear it, and reward thee for the Hazards and Labours which thy Father and his Companions have sustained to make this Country Christian, and engraft the Natives whereof into the Bosom of the Church. You brave Sons of Conquerors, how excellently have your Fathers been rewarded for gaining this Country, when a Halter is the only Recompense and Inheritance provided for their Children! . . . And if the Fate of them be determined (said she) and that they must dye, let them also kill the Mothers, who had the Sin upon them, to bring them forth; and who were so culpable as to deny their own Country and Relations, for the Sake of those Conquerors, and joined with them in the Design of making this Empire subject to the* Spaniards.

Remarkably, Garcilaso tells us, Garcia was so disturbed by her indictment that he released the imprisoned mestizos of Incan blood, although by sending them into exile, he killed them just the same.

Female protest (and its dignified suppression by Tupac Amaru) frames the final scene of the *Commentaries*, in which the last Inca is executed. While the scenes of maternal lamentation are the most vivid and affecting, the text is full of mordant judgments on the colonizers. In Part 1, chapter 7, for example, acknowledging there are two perspectives on the purported benefits of the American conquest, Garcilaso makes it clear he shares the view that the riches gained by Spain were corrupting (425). Elsewhere, in his critique of other chroniclers, he asserts that the Spanish historians habitually occlude their countrymen's 'cruel and unjustifiable proceedings' (458). For all Garcilaso's foregrounding of the Providential logic of conquest, and the benefits of Christianization, later generations of Andeans would respond to the text's celebration of Inca civilization and its indictment of Spanish usurpation and cruelty. In 1780–1781, when Tupac Amaru II led a rebellion against the Spanish, the *Commentaries* were suppressed, as the authorities believed they provided intellectual inspiration and succour for the rebels. The text remained unpublished in Latin America until 1918.

Garcilaso's text, published in Lisbon, necessarily conformed to both ideological and rhetorical conventions of its scene of production. But rather than simply collaborating with the conquest, the *Commentaries* speak in the sometimes ironic, sometimes elegiac but always distinctive voice of an Incan elite that has had to come to terms with external power. Postcolonial critique offers various ways of characterizing such discourse, notably Homi Bhabha's formulations of sly civility and hybridity. In much of Garcilaso's text, and particularly in his reportage of female Indian protest, however, direct indictment of the Spaniards' strategic sexual predation, territorial appropriation and racially motivated filicide is voiced with startling directness.

In the case of the widely circulated *Commentaries*, it is easier to make the case for Garcilaso as an indigenous producer of recalcitrant, extra-European knowledge, shaping a cosmopolitan Enlightenment that included the Andes as well as the West. His text was important initially to intellectuals and men of affairs such as Rycaut, but when its subject was dramatized, its resistant voices were embodied and revivified among a much larger public, both French and English.[37] Although (as we have noted in the previous chapter) Islamic and Asian polities made their own shaping contribution to the Enlightenment critique of organized religion, the new world indigenous denunciation of Christian fanaticism and hypocrisy was certainly as significant as the questioning of political and ecclesiastical authority. The *loci classici* for the rational questioning of revealed religion are the dramatic scenes and dialogues featuring

---

[37] See Russell Goulbourne, 'Voltaire's Masks: Theatre and Theatricality', in *The Cambridge Companion to Voltaire*, ed. Nicholas Cronk (Cambridge: Cambridge University Press, 2009). This essay provides a brilliant overview of Voltaire's work as a dramatist and reminds us that to his contemporaries, he was known primarily as a writer for the stage.

Montezuma, Atahualpa and Lahontan's Adario.[38] Further, the *Royal Commentaries'* extended and repeated critique of the forced traffic in women that facilitated European incursion can be seen to anticipate contemporary feminist and postcolonial critique. While the Pocahontas *topos* is familiar and has been extensively analysed, an important trope of new world colonial appropriation, Garcilaso's analysis of and ventriloquism of female Incan protest at such processes, and its subsequent dramatization in new world plays, has been ignored.

Alzire

The circumstances of Voltaire's production of *Alzire*, Aaron Hill's model for *Alzira*, are well-documented. Attempting to rehabilitate himself in the face of clerically inspired government hostility, Voltaire wrote a play that sought to condemn fanatic Catholicism as well as the errors of paganism, both of which could be readily (and positively) distinguished from the Gallicanism of the French regime.[39] Not all his clerical opponents were persuaded, but the play was hugely successful and deflected official disapprobation for a period. In his *Discours preliminaire* to *Alzire,* however, Voltaire also stressed his interest in dramatizing the contrast of *moeurs* between the Peruvians and the Spaniards, and he took a keen interest in trying to see these cultural differences sustained through scenery and costume. As important as these philosophical or even ideological considerations, however, was the way the lessons in tolerance were conveyed through sympathetic identification with (or disgusted antipathy to) the characters who embodied the various positions. The action was intended to persuade audiences through sentiment and there was general agreement that it succeeded – as Gresset wrote in 'Sur la Tragedie d'Alzire', 'Si mon esprit contr'elle a des objections, / Mon Coeur a des larmes pour elle; / Les pleurs decident mieux que les reflexions' ('If my mind opposed her objections / My heart wept for her / The tears were stronger than the arguments') (quoted in Voltaire, 14, 47, author's translation).

Although the sources on which Voltaire drew had been available for years, it seems likely that his interest in the Andean subject was provoked

---

[38] Indigenous discourse is more than critical: Garcilaso's description of Pachacamac, the creator of the universe, as an impersonal being who did not require formal worship or sacrificial rites, but only personal adoration, can be seen not only as an example of but as shaping force in the creation of Voltaire's deism.

[39] For a good introduction to the play, see *Alzire, ou les Americains*, ed. T. E. D. Braun, in *Complete Works of Voltaire*, vol. 14.

in part by the departure of La Condamine in 1735 for Quito to measure the earth at its equator. Public interest in Peru would have been stimulated by this event and in the previous fifteen years, as Braun points out, there had been numerous – but mostly comic – depictions of the new world on the Paris stage (Voltaire, 14, 5). In considering the Andean template that Voltaire created, it is important to note that his presentation of the natural virtue and intelligence of the Indians was not simply motivated by the necessities of his tolerationist argument but conformed with his new world sources. Garcilaso was insistent about the practical rationality of the Indians, poised for Christianization through the Incan establishment of civilization: God decided, he tells us, 'to issue out the light of his Divine Rays on these poor Idolators, that they might be found more docile, and easily disposed to receive the principles of the Christian faith ... those whom the *Inca* had subjected, and reduced to some Terms of Humanity and Political Government, were much better and easier to receive the Evangelical Doctrine presented unto them, than those ignorant wretches who lived in their natural stupidity' (*Royal Commentaries*, 11). Later he reiterates that 'these [were] a people who were inclined to live according to their Laws which the Light of Nature dictated' (*Royal Commentaries*, 51).

Alzire's plot replicates the pattern of indigenous virtue and Christian perfidy legible in Garcilaso, but strikingly Voltaire chooses to focus his condemnation of Christian hypocrisy not on a traduced and humiliated emperor – as in Dryden's *The Indian Emperor* – but on the agonies of an Incan princess forced into precisely the kind of politic marriage to a Spaniard presented in the *Commentaries*.[40] In identifying sources for *Alzire*, scholars have focused on the differing perspectives on Incan religion and technology to be found in Zarate and Garcilaso, entirely ignoring the latter's stress on indigenous female experience.[41] *Alzire* exorbitates the series of female protests voiced in the *Commentaries*, whose inclusion may owe something to the experience of Garcilaso's mother, herself partnered with a Spaniard.[42] Although the way in which the elite women of a conquered nation respond to their violent or seductive appropriation by alien victors has been an important dramatic subject since the Greeks, Garcilaso's *Commentaries* provided an unprecedented historical record of

---

[40] Understandably, there have been claims that Dryden's influence on *Alzire* was strong: for an overview of the discussion, see Braun, *Alzire, ou les Americains*, 13–19.

[41] See Perkins, 'Documentation of Voltaire's *Alzire*.' More recently, Michelle Buchanan denies there is anything specifically Peruvian about the play. See 'Savages, Noble and Otherwise', 105.

[42] For a speculative account of this relationship, see the biography of Garcilaso by John Grier Varner, *El Inca: The Life and Times of Garcilaso de la Vega* (Austin: University of Texas Press, 1968).

such responses in the new world context. Already interested in the position of women divided by the claims of religion, nation and passion, Voltaire used the mestizo source to rearticulate the accommodation and resistance spoken and enacted by Inca women and men. What is strikingly different from *Zaire*, in fact, is the weight assigned to the woman's role as protector of her people. In *Zaire*, the heroine's argument that as the sultan's wife she would act as a shield for the Christian community is roundly dismissed by her father and brother: in *Alzire* that responsibility is presented as utterly compelling.

Alzira

The play's relocation to England necessarily involved more than verbal translation. Hill was keen to repeat his recent great success with the Voltairean *Zara* (1734), but *Alzire* appealed for a variety of noncommercial reasons. Hill was as interested as Voltaire in a new scenography and costuming that would create much richer and more precise visualizations of exotic locales than was currently the case: *Alzire* was designed as a model for such new practices. The play's celebrated sentimentality was also critical to Hill, for whom the theatre was a school of national virtue: in his lengthy Dedication of the play to Prince Fredrick, he argues,

> When *Tragedies* are strong in *Sentiment*, they will be *Touchstones* to their Hearer's *Hearts*. The Narrow, and Inhumane, will be unattentive, or unmov'd: while Princely Spirits like your Royal Highness's, (impell'd by their own conscious Tendency) shew us an Example, in their generous Sensibility, how *Great Thoughts* should be *receiv'd*, by Those, who can *think Greatly*.
>   . . . -Your Royal Highness, but *persisting* to keep Reason and Nature in Countenance at the Theatres, will universally *establish*, what you so generously and openly *avow*. For, if where Men *love*, they will *imitate*, Your Example must be *copied*, *by Millions:* till the Influence of your Attraction shall have *planted* your Taste; and *overspread Three Kingdoms with Laurels.*[43]

Hill stresses that the stage has an 'incredible Influence, upon the Spirits, and Passions, of a People' (vii) and goes on to cite Bacon's conviction that 'The *Stage* is an Instrument, in the Hands of the *Poet*, as capable of giving *Modulation* and *Tone* to the HEART; – as the *Bow*, to the VIOLIN, in the Hands of a *Musician*' (vii).

---

[43] Dedication, iv–v in Aaron Hill, *Alzira. A Tragedy* (London: John Osborn, 1737). All quotations are from this edition and are cited in the text by act, scene and page numbers.

In the Dedication, Hill dwells on Fredrick's function as the exemplary sentimental spectator, inspiring others to a disinterested humanity, wisdom and virtue by his performance of 'discerning delicacy' (Dedication, v). Fredrick, as patron of Opposition politicians, would be convinced that theatre had a special place in the 'political Affection of Princes' (Dedication, vi), supporting such anti-Walpolean tragedies as *Mustapha*. While Mallet's Ottoman palace tragedy criticized the King and his prime minister, Fredrick was equally supportive of plays that encouraged the Opposition's anti-Spanish obsession. From the late twenties, opinion 'out-of-doors' had been inflamed by reports of Spanish reprisals against British shipmen interloping in the Spanish Americas and colonial officials were concerned about British America's encirclement by Catholic powers. The French navy was expanding, and despite disarray in the Spanish royal household, its alliance with France produced huge anxiety in Britain. Brendan Simms argues that the popular anti-Spanish hysteria of the 1730s became compelling to large numbers of the political elite because control of new world colonies came to be seen to be central to the power and security of any European state, essential to Britain's ability to hold her own in the continental state system. Those who were opposed to war with Spain – English merchants engaged in trade with Old Spain – were marginal: Jews, Irish and English Catholics, Jacobites without parliamentary representation. Although Walpole was never enthusiastic about entering into hostilities with the Spanish, the popular attractions of regime change in the new world are sardonically summarized by Simms: 'One British seaman predicted that "Millions of miserable people would bless their deliverers; their hearts and their mines [*sic*] would be open to us". The reference to 'mines' for 'minds' was surely a Freudian slip, revealing as it did the synergy between liberation and resource extraction.'[44]

Kathleen Wilson and Christine Gerrard have shown that the anti-Spanish feeling that became more and more widespread through the thirties was actively encouraged by the Patriot Opposition and inspired theatrical celebrations of Elizabethan naval heroes and London merchants.[45] In addition to the performance of new plays on these themes,

[44] Simms, *Three Victories and a Defeat*, 259. The standard Anglophone comparative history of the two empires is J. H. Elliott, *Empires of the Atlantic World: Britain and Spain in America, 1492–1830* (New Haven, CT: Yale University Press, 2007). It is also worth bearing in mind that as David Weber points out, up to the end of the eighteenth century almost half of the southern cone was in indigenous hands. See *Barbaros: The Spanish and Their Savages in the Age of Enlightenment* (New Haven, CT: Yale University Press, 2005).

[45] See Gerrard, *Patriot Opposition to Walpole* and Wilson, *Sense of the People*.

the extant repertory was consulted for apposite texts and Dryden's *Indian Emperor* and his 'protestant play' *The Spanish Fryar* were both revived repeatedly through the thirties and early forties. Despite its suspicious French provenance (ameliorated by Voltaire's well-known admiration for English tolerance and modernity), *Alzira* was readily identifiable as a black legend play and thus a highly attractive candidate for production. Donald Schier's close comparison of the two texts makes it clear that Hill expands this aspect of the play, ramping up the anti-Spanish critique of religious fanaticism, and making a much more explicit connection between Spanish cruelty and their religious beliefs. More dubiously, Schier also suggests that the deist dimension of the text was less important to Hill, who converts Zamor, Alzira's rebel lover.[46]

As we have seen in relation to plays about Islam, early eighteenth-century dramatizations of Christian fanaticism habitually code it as implicit or explicit Spanish Catholicism. Hill was not unsympathetic to deism so the politically expedient anti-Catholicism of *Alzira* was congruent with his beliefs.[47] But as is the case with *Alzire, Alzira* can be read as a dramatization of the conflicts generated among the indigenous elite over the best survival strategy in the face of colonization, not just as anti-Spanish propaganda or deist advocacy. In Hill's play, the scene opens with a discussion between Don Alvarez, former governor of Peru, and his son and successor, Don Carlos. Alvarez pleads with his son to spare the lives of a group of wandering Indians who have been imprisoned, and are to be executed by the suspicious Carlos, arguing the Spaniards should show humanity to the conquered Americans. Carlos agrees, on condition the Indians convert, and asks his father to use his influence with her father Ezmont to persuade the reluctant Inca princess Alzira to accept his suit. Alvarez is willing because, he says, the alliance would secure the conquest peacefully:

> *Alzira* governs a whole *People's* Minds:
> Each *Indian* reads her studied Eye,
> And to *Her* silent *Heart* conforms his own.
> Your Marriage shall unite two distant *Worlds*;
> For, when the stern Repiner at our Law

---

[46] Donald Schier, 'Aaron Hill's Translation of Voltaire's *Alzire*', in *Studies on Voltaire and the Eighteenth Century*, vol. 67 (Geneva: Institut et Musee Voltaire, 1969), 45–58.

[47] In her definitive account of Hill's life, Christine Gerrard suggests that while Hill was for most of his life an orthodox Anglican, the *Prompter* defended the freethinker Matthew Tindal from attack, and in 1746 Hill published a deistic poem, 'Free Thoughts upon Faith; or, The Religion of Reason.' See Gerrard, *Aaron Hill*, 236–237.

Sees, in your Arms, the Daughter of his King,
With humbler Spirit, and with Heart less fierce,
His willing Neck shall *court* the Yoke he scorn'd. (1.1.19)

As a tribute to Alvarez's Christian mercy, Ezmont agrees to give Alzira to
Carlos, 'And with her, all *Potosi* and *Peru*' (1.2.20). (Potosi was the most
famous mine in the world.) When Ezmont tells Alzira of his decision, she
characterizes the marriage as a 'frightful sacrifice' particularly ill-timed
'When the rais'd Sword of this all-murd'ring Lover / Hangs o'er my
People's Heads, with threat'ning Sway' (1.3.21). Still mourning her Inca
lover Zamor, whom she believes died a year previously, she reproaches her
father for demanding that she 'nobly lose *[My]self,* to save a *State*' (1.3.22).
The act closes with Carlos and Alzira quarrelling over her continuing love
for Zamor and the governor's determination that he will take her hand by
force.

This first act tells us that *Alzira* will explore the conflict between what
the heroine calls the 'Public Duty' of intermarriage or concubinage to a
conquistador and 'our *private* Truth' (1.3.22), namely revulsion from a
brutal invader and continuing love for a fellow Inca. Each character speaks
to the motives for such alliances, with Ezmont echoing Garcilaso's stress
on the utility Indians initially saw in such relationships, Alvarez regarding
marriage as a means of securing Spanish rule and Carlos viewing Alzira as
the fruit of conquest. Although Alzira does not complain of Carlos's birth,
her resistance to the marriage recalls that of Donna Maria Calderon, who
tried to refuse the man to whom she was assigned by Pizarro, and had to be
persuaded to accept by her brother, for fear the Spaniards would turn
against the Incas. Alzira's sense that her personal integrity, her 'private
Truth', is threatened by the marriage echoes the lament of the Indian
woman who cried out that the mothers of the imprisoned mestizos were
culpable because they had denied 'their own Country and Relations, for
the Sake of those Conquerors, and joined with them in the Design of
making this Empire subject to the Spaniards' (Garcilaso, 638). Alzira's
circumstances further parallel those of the Indian mother because her
engagement with Carlos is backgrounded by the presence of the
imprisoned, rebellious and threatened Indians, who recall the mestizo
men tortured and condemned by the paranoid Garcia.

The next act focuses on the differing responses of Incan men to the
Spanish invasion. Ezmont/Zamor suggest an anagram of Montezuma, the
ruler conquered, tortured and killed by the Spaniards in Mexico. The older
Ezmont argues for alliance and assimilation via Christian conversion, while

Figure 3.   *Act 3, Scene 1, Alzira.* Engraving. Artist William Hamilton. Engraver James Heath. London, 1791. Courtesy the Victoria and Albert Museum, London

Zamor speaks for resistance, revolt and freedom. Ezmont articulates the Providentialist argument legible in Garcilaso, while Zamor condemns the 'pilfering Zealots, who usurp thy Throne / And would convert thy Daughter to a *Slave*' (2.1.31), from a perspective also available in the *Commentaries*. Neither strategy would command immediate support from an English audience, to whom the idea of capitulation by freedom-loving patriots to Spanish invasion was anathema, especially in the late 1730s. Peaceable conversion from pagan, bloodthirsty polytheism was putatively desirable but not perhaps if the monotheism was of the idolatrous, Roman kind.

The second act leaves the strategic question open but helps explain Alzira's capitulation. While the two Inca men argue over policies and action, Alzira performs and embodies the subjection enjoined on her by her father and her ruler. Having married Carlos, her regret for Zamor expresses itself in her concern for the imprisoned Indians, whom she believes her husband is about to murder. Again, her lamentation echoes that of the Inca mother in Garcilaso:

> Have I for *This*, in vain, betray'd my *Peace*?
> *Dares* the dire *Husband*, recent from the *Altar*,
> New to my forc'd *Consent*, – and scarce, yet *Lord*,
> Of my repenting *Hand*; so *soon*, let loose
> His recommission'd *Murders*! Must my Nuptials
> Serve, as the *Prelude*, to my People's *Blood*! (3.1.35)

In the meeting with Zamor that follows his being freed at Alvarez's request, Alzira's agony reaches a climax as she confesses the name of 'the dreadful husband' she 'owes' to her father. When Alvarez and Carlos enter to greet the former's rescuer, Zamor upbraids Carlos with having 'basely' tortured him. As Carlos prepares to kill Zamor, news comes of a well-organized Indian attack and the Inca prince is bundled offstage.

Although this act is filled with Alzira's reproaches to her father Ezmont, he is notable for his absence. The paternal figure supervising the action is her 'new' father Alvarez, who also regards Zamor as a son. Ezmont's position as Incan patriarch is negated as Alvarez assumes paternal authority over both the Incan heirs. Although legible as a mode of proper Christian patronage of new and potential converts (Alvarez has been identified with Las Casas, famous defender of the Indians), Alvarez's fatherly role is more than symbolic: by casting Alzira and Zamont as siblings, he places an insuperable barrier between them and ensures the Spaniards succeed in a genetic appropriation of Alzira's royal status. The scene drives home the fact that the sexual reproduction of Incan power has been negated by Spanish intervention, as Alvarez's final speech makes clear:

> I feel the Pity of a Father, for thee.
> I mourn afflicted *Zamor*; I will *guard* him:
> I will protect you, both, unhappy Lovers!
> Yet, ah! Be mindful of the *Marriage Tye*,
> *Thou* art no longer *Thine*, my mournful Daughter. (3.2.43)

Lost to herself, Alzira does indeed resemble the 'slave' Zamor names her.

In the next scene, Alvarez and Alzira try to prevent Carlos from killing Zamor. This act intensifies invocations of tropes of savagery on the one hand and cruelty, tyranny and illegitimacy on the other, as Carlos and Alzira bandy insults. Carlos complains that 'I reduce my Hopes, beneath a *Savage* / And poorly envy such a Wretch as *Zamor*' (4.1.45), so illiterate of polished ways that he would 'hardly, in our courts, be judg'd a MAN' (4.1.45). Alzira responds by upbraiding him not only for cruel hypocrisy, the 'civiliz'd Assent, of social *Murder*!' but for political illegitimacy:

> Mark the proud, *partial*, Guilt of these *vain* Men!
> *Ours*, but a Country, *held*, to yield *Them*, SLAVES;
> Who reign, our *Kings*, by Right of *diff'rent Clime*!
> *Zamor*, mean while, by Birth, *true* Sovereign here,
> Weighs but a *Rebel*, in *their* righteous Scale! (4.1.47)

Alzira's insistence on Zamor's sovereignty recalls the last ambiguous line of the *Commentaries*, in which Garcilaso also emphasizes Incan authority: 'I hope I have as well done Justice, and Right to the *Spaniards*, who have conquered this *Empire*, as to the *Incas*, who were tho true Lords and Possessors of it' (1019).

The conclusion of the action seems to bear out Garcilaso's suggestion that Spanish usurpation recoiled upon itself. Remarking on the fact that Garcia, murderer of Tupac Amaru, would-be killer of all the other Incan heirs and husband of the 'Incan Infanta' died at the hands of rebel Indians in Chile, El Inca comments, 'it was confessed, that *Providence* had so ordered these matters, that the Death of the late *Inca* should in this manner be revenged on the *Spaniards* by the Hands of his own vassals' (1017). Likewise, in *Alzira* Don Carlos is Governor of Peru, married to the Inca infant and eager to torture and extirpate all Indians he perceives as rebels. In the end, however, he dies at the rebel Zamor's hand, and the Incas survive, confirmed in possession of their 'conquer'd States' (5.1.60). Even Carlos's last minute forgiveness of Zamor and Alzira has its counterpart in Garcia's revocation of his death sentences on the Incan heirs, although there is nothing in the *Commentaries* to suggest that Garcia died a model of Christian mercy, as Carlos does. However implausible both Carlos's belated charity and Zamor's admiring response, the conversion of the elite Incans is consistent with the historical record and Garcilaso's invocation of a larger Christian framework for his narration.

The Christian triumphalism of *Alzire*'s conclusion did not persuade all of Voltaire's clerical opponents that he had abandoned heterodoxy and similar doubts persist in relation to *Alzira*'s depiction of a reformed Spanish ascendency. Presumably Hill's audience saw in Don Carlos's belated (and undermotivated) realization of the need to recognize the Peruvians as 'subjects not slaves' an endorsement of their own, British and putatively more liberal colonial policies, beliefs that animate the liberatory rhetoric identified by Simms. But the play is irreducible to such schematic black legendism: notionally Christianized, the politically unappeased Incas survive and are confirmed as owners of their lands, allies rather than enslaved and defeated enemies. The wish fulfilment we see at *Alzira*'s conclusion seems closer to the compromise-formations of the *Royal Commentaries* than Bolingbroke theatricalized.

Alzuma

In an influential recent argument, Christopher Miller has read *Alzire* as a text that implicitly condoned, rather than effectively critiqued, chattel slavery: like other critics, he occludes the play's reiteration of the *Royal Commentaries* and their articulation of indigenous protest, resistance and accommodation, all aspects of colonial conflict quite distinct from the trade in slaves.[48] Although I do not believe that Voltaire's primary aim in *Alzire* was an engagement with the slave trade, it is certainly the case that at least one contemporary saw a parallel between the dramatic treatments of enslaved Africans and invaded and imprisoned Indians. In his *Advertisement* to his own new world play, *Alzuma* (1773), after suggesting that Voltaire was influenced by Dryden's *Indian Emperor*, Arthur Murphy argues that '*Oroonoko*, from some striking points of situation, and some

---

[48] Miller, *French Atlantic Triangle*. Miller stresses the gap between the *philosophes'* unremitting hostility to political slavery and indifference to chattel slavery, pointing out that Voltaire for one invested in the slave trade and had a slave ship named after him. He further argues that the progressive agenda of a putatively anti-slavery play like *Alzire* was utterly ineffective because it was actually performed on a slave ship at Goree (71–77). *Alzire*'s ineffectiveness as an anti-slavery vehicle can also be understood if the play's religious and political aims are characterized not as displaced critiques of slavery but as arguments for toleration and indigenous sovereignty.

features of character, may not unfairly be supposed to have furnished the GREAT POET of FRANCE with many useful hints.'[49] The parallels in the situation include the captive condition of Alzire/Zamore, politically unfree if not reduced to chattel slavery, like Oroonoko and Imoinda. Oroonoko and Zamore share a radical anti-Christian scepticism, and like Alzire they are royal personages chafing against degradation. Alzire's preference for rebellion echoes Imoinda's, as does her resistance to a sexual alliance with a captor. What Murphy may be registering is the erasure of the previously sharp distinction between political slavery – a concept inherited from Aristotle – and chattel slavery, which became widespread in north European possessions in the early eighteenth century. Although the difference was still often implicit in public discourse, influenced by Shaftesburian benevolism, Francis Hutcheson effectively demolished the philosophical grounds of the distinction in 1733, although his argument was published only in 1755.[50]

An equally important point of similitude is the sentiment that animates the two plays; both *Oroonoko* and *Alzire* were regarded as strikingly pathetic. Pathos is a rhetorical device also employed by Garcilaso, who not infrequently characterizes the Andean natives and Indians in general (including himself) as simple figures who should inspire sympathy in Europeans, whether invaders or readers. But in the *Royal Commentaries* the topos exists in tension with distinctly heroic depictions of Incas and so assumes a degree of instability, much as it does in *Oroonoko*, where the implications of the protagonist's dual status as royal rebel and slave remain contested. While current criticism has focused on the dehumanization and reduced agency identified with sentimental objects (women, Indians, slaves, lascars, etc.), both Oroonoko and Alzira address their audience in much more complex ways than invoking affective patronage. Alzira and Zamor are fiercely patriotic, rebellious, eloquent and sceptical: demanding admiration as much as pity, they model forms of ideological and political resistance.

Murphy's Seven Years' War

It seems likely that Murphy's interest in repeatedly dramatizing the effects imperial conflict was shaped by the fact he composed his most of his

---

[49] *Advertisement to Alzuma: A Tragedy* (1773), reprinted in *The Plays of Arthur Murphy*, ed. Richard B. Schwartz (New York: Garland, 1979), 1:314. All quotations are from this edition and are cited in the text by act, scene and page numbers.
[50] See the discussion in Sypher, *Guinea's Captive Kings*, 89.

tragedies during or in the wake of the Seven Years' War, often described as the first truly global conflict. With campaigns in South Asia, the Caribbean and North America as well as Europe, the war was imperial in scope, and Britain emerged from the struggle in a newly dominant position.[51] Murphy linked his composition of *Alzuma* to the contemporaneous conflict with the Spanish imperial state. In his other tragedies of empire he followed theatrical precedent by avoiding the depiction of episodes from Britain's own colonial past, instead availing himself of the extensive repertoire of dramatic and narrative representations of imperial conflict familiar to him from ancient sources. Strikingly, however, this learned classicist went beyond Greek and Roman history to draw on subjects from the much less familiar but equally venerable civilizations of China and Peru.[52]

Dramatic engagement aside, Murphy's own role in the Seven Years' War was that of publicist for the hated Earl of Bute, who as George III's favourite had wrested control of government from the much more popular Pitt. Bute spent much of 1762 and the first months of the next year negotiating peace with France along somewhat less punitive terms than those desired by the commercial and financial interests who supported Pitt. Tobias Smollett's *The Briton* tried but failed signally to soften public opinion towards Bute's peace policy, and in June 1762 Murphy took up the cudgels, using a new journal called *The Auditor* to attack Pitt and generate enthusiasm for peace on Tory terms. Murphy was no more successful than Smollett and his theatrical career suffered as a result of his unpopular, if apparently sincere, political journalism. The most effective attack on him was made by Wilkes and Churchill, who like the rest of Bute's enemies were strongly hostile to returning Havana in exchange for Florida.[53] In December 1762, aware of the strength of feeling on this topic, Murphy published an anonymous letter he had received purporting to come from one 'Viator', claiming that Florida was a desirable colony whose rich peat or turf resources could form a useful trade with those Caribbean colonies in need of fuel.[54] Almost immediately, attacks on the

[51] For a recent overview, see Simms, *Three Victories and a Defeat*.

[52] For modern accounts of Murphy's career, see Howard Hunter Dunbar, *The Dramatic Career of Arthur Murphy* (London: Modern Languages Association and Oxford University Press, 1946) and John Pike Emory, *Arthur Murphy, an Eminent Dramatist of the Eighteenth Century* (Philadelphia: University of Pennsylvania Press, 1946).

[53] A full account of this episode can be found in Conrad Brumstrom and Declan Kavanagh, 'Authur Murphy and Florida Peat: *The Gray's Inn Journal* and Versions of the Apolitical', *Eighteenth-Century Ireland/Iris an du culture* 27 (2013): 123–141.

[54] *The Auditor*, June 1762, 153–154.

absurdity of the claims came raining down, not just from the predictably hostile Whiggish *St James Chronicle* but from *The Chronicle* and even the more conservative *Gentleman's Magazine*. The concluding blow came, unsurprisingly, from Number 35 of *The North Briton*, likely source of the spurious Letter from 'Viator.' Beginning by mocking Murphy's credulity in arguing for the '*commercial advantages*' of 'the *Florida Turf*, that fine, rich vein of trade, just opened by our AUDITOR, to give, as he says, *comfortable fires* to our cold, frozen *West-Indian* islands', the paper amplifies the joke by linking Murphy's enthusiasm for the 'Peet Trade' to his ethnicity.[55] 'This wonderful genius, the AUDITOR', we are reminded, emerged 'from his native bog of Allen', and as an Irishman, it is suggested he would 'be ready to bargain for his dear *natale solum*, and would not more scruple to *sell his country* than to sell himself' (*NB*, 228). Turf, land, territory, nation – each homologous entity is rendered vendible by the slavish, mercenary and treacherous Irish, *The North Briton* suggests. The attack climaxes in a suggestion that Murphy would find congenial company among the Floridians because 'it is well-known that *Florida* has been chiefly peopled by *convicts* from *New-Spain*' (*NB*, 228). Thus 'our disciple of *St Omer's* . . . would surpass in perfidy and fraud the most refined Jesuit, who is to *tolerated* in these new conquests – possibly to read mass to this good *Irish Catholic*' (*NB*, 229). Concluding with a dig at Murphy's theatrical career, *The North Briton* sneers, 'If no untimely end prevents the dullest *play-wright* of our times, he may then at last present us with a woeful *Tragedy*, both new and *interesting*, but drawn not from fable and invention, but founded on his own real adventures, and *hair-breadth escapes*' (*NB*, 229).

Ironically, the last offensive comment is richly suggestive, notwithstanding its reiteration of a much-repeated accusation of plagiarism. Like many if not most of his peers, Murphy certainly rifled other texts in search of usable scenarios and in his prologue to *Zenobia*, he used an aggressively patriotic nautical metaphor to justify, indeed glorify, his literary plundering:

> Yet think not that we mean to mock the eye
> With pilfer'd colours of a foreign dye.
> Not to translate our bard his pen doth dip;
> He takes a play, as Britons take a ship;
> They heave her down; – with many a sturdy stroke,
> Repair her well, and build with Heart of Oak.

<hr>

55 *The North Briton* 35 (July 1762): 228.

To ev'ry breeze set Britain's streamers free,
New-man her, and away again to sea.[56]

Despite the aggressive rhetoric of maritime appropriation invoked here, however, Murphy showed a distinct preference for theatrical vehicles that voiced the suffering and protests of those victimized by national and imperial conflicts, frequently shifting towards or expanding a specifically feminine perspective on war. Contemporary critics often commented on the Sophoclean and Aeschylean echoes in his texts, unsurprising from a writer steeped in the Western classics.[57] But Murphy did not rearticulate the scenarios he adapted as facile patriotism along the lines suggested in the prologue to *Zenobia*: he did in fact use them, as *The North Briton* suggested sardonically, to articulate 'his own real adventures', as a Catholic Irishman making his way in a strange and hostile metropolis. Forced to abandon the devotional affiliation he inherited from his adored mother, Murphy's dramaturgy suggests an unresolved ambivalence over the religious, political and subjective abjuration enjoined by colonial domination and a strong degree of identification with those on the defeated side of imperial conflict.

After his father's death at sea when he was a child, Murphy's education at the Jesuit College at St Omer was sponsored by his aunt, with whom he lived in Boulogne before commencing his studies. A much-repeated highlight of his school career was his recitation of Virgil's *Aeneid* on his graduation day, testament to his extraordinary classical learning. When he returned to London after completing his schooling, a period he later described as 'the happiest in my life', his faith was attacked brutally by his uncle, who had charge of establishing him in business. The former called Catholicism 'a mean, beggarly, blackguard religion', but although 'my Mother desired me not to mind his violent advice ... my brother, who was educated at Westminster school, spoke strongly in support of my uncle's opinion, and he never gave up the point till he succeeded to his utmost wish'.[58] His older sibling shared Murphy's literary and theatrical interests, so it is unsurprising that his persistent but amiable suasion appears to have led to the younger brother's conversion to an undemonstrative Anglicanism. In considering *Alzuma*'s treatment of the issue, however, it's worth bearing in mind that Murphy was deeply and persistently attached to his mother, who retained her faith. On the other hand,

---

[56] Arthur Murphy, *Zenobia. A Tragedy* (London: W. Griffin, 1768), n.p..
[57] For modern accounts of his education and career, see Dunbar, *Dramatic Career of Arthur Murphy* and Emory, *Arthur Murphy*.
[58] Jesse Foot, *The Life of the late Arthur Murphy Esq.* (London, 1812).

his uncle, who disinherited him after Murphy refused to travel from Cork to Jamaica to take up another clerical post, embodied a bigoted form of Protestantism, a dictatorial attitude to his dependents and a contempt for a career outside commerce. A decade later, the social heft of his uncle's prejudice would be confirmed by the pejorative characterizations of Murphy's nationality and education not just in *The Auditor* but by Charles Churchill in *The Rosciad*, in which he characterized Murphy as a latter-day Shadwell: 'Bred at *St Omer's* to the shuffling trade, / The hopeful youth a Jesuit might have made, / With various readings stor'd his empty skull / Learn'd without sense, and venerably dull.'[59] It is suggestive that in eschewing journalistic work, Murphy cited the example of Sir Richard Steele, who also suffered from xenophobic attacks focused on his Anglo-Irish origins.

Despite the libels, like Steele, Murphy remained loyal to his original affiliations, most conspicuously by taking a prominent role in opposing the Gordon riots. He also openly saluted Pope's adherence to Catholicism, devoting one Letter in the *Gray's Inn Journal* to publishing an epistle from Pope to Racine, in which the former responded to French perceptions of the *Essay on Man* as deistic by declaring his devotion to the doctrines of Pascal and the Archbishop of Combray and his detestation of Spinoza and Leibnitz.[60] In general, however, *The Gray's Inn Journal* suggests that Murphy was a serious advocate of toleration. In Letter 84 of the *Journal*, Murphy uses an oriental tale to argue against attempts at religious conversion, using a divine messenger to instruct an ambitious proselytizer that 'it will better behove thee to pay submission to the established Forms of Worship of thy Country, than to disturb the Peace of the faithful', pointing out that the result of throwing off 'settled Forms of Devotion' is to see those unmoored from their traditional beliefs as 'immersed in all manner of vicious Practices. Uncontrouled they invade each other's Rights; they make War to satisfy their Ambition.'[61] His support of toleration extended to the Jewish Naturalization Bill and for that he was mocked by *The North Briton* (*NB*, 141). Acutely aware of the violence of religious

---

[59] Charles Churchill, *The Rosciad*, 6th ed. (London, 1766), 29. There was also an extended attack on Murphy in the anonymous *The Murphiad. A Mock Heroic Poem* by 'Philim Mocolloch' (London: J. Williams, 1761). This poem focused on Murphy's supposed birth in the bog of Allen and the goddess of mud's prophesies as to his future in the theatre, emphasizing his Irish birth, his 'popish zeal' (18) and his pretentions to classical learning – 'Grecian rules' (13).

[60] Arthur Murphy, *The Gray's Inn Journal*, 2 vols. (Dublin: William Sleater, 1756), vol. 2, Letter 69, 96–100.

[61] *The Gray's Inn Journal*, vol. 2, Letter 84, 181–185.

bigotry and racism from his own familial and professional experiences of anti-Catholic and anti-Irish prejudice, Murphy became a forceful proponent of tolerance, that most critical Enlightenment virtue, not just in his periodical writing but in his dramaturgy.

Alzuma

Murphy's tragedy *Alzuma* was written 'in the year 1762, [when] the British forces were then actually doing at the HAVANNAH, what ALZUMA prays for in the third act'. Towards the end of the Seven Years' War, which produced a high water mark of imperial hubris, hostilities were declared with Spain. The British rapidly achieved successes in the Caribbean and in the Pacific, taking Havana in August and Manila in October. It therefore seemed to Murphy an obvious time to dust down the black legend and recast 'the story of a people massacred because they abounded in gold-mines, and had not heard the important truths of the Christian religion, [which] seemed of all others the fittest for the English stage, as it tended in a strong degree to that pathetic distress, and that vigour of sentiment, which constitute the essential beauty of tragedy'.[62]

Although Murphy stressed in his *Advertisement* that he did not follow Voltaire (the model for Hill), and the plot does diverge from *Alzire* and *Alzira*, this version of the end of Incan rule shares the focus they drew from Garcilaso de la Vega on the central role of Inca women in the Spanish Conquest: intermarriage, concubinage and the eradication of Incan male nobles in securing Spanish land ownership and rule are the critical issues. In both the *Commentaries* and the plays drawn from this account, Incan noblewomen are the most vociferous protesters against Spanish oppression. *Alzuma* is even more feminocentric than *Alzira*. In Murphy's play, Orellana's father is dead and her mother has married his murderer, Pizarro. *Alzuma* is shaped to contrast Orazia's and Orellana's antithetical responses to the invaders: Orazia chooses conversion, cultural assimilation and marriage while Orellana is a model of political, religious and sexual resistance. Although Alzuma is the eponymous hero, Orellana is the more compelling figure. Alzuma brings about the climax, but for most of the play he is markedly impotent, helplessly imprisoned and saved from death only by the repeated interventions of his female relatives (an aspect of the plot drawn from de la Vega). In *Alzira*, Zamor represented a real challenge

---

[62] Arthur Murphy, *Alzuma. A Tragedy* (London: T. Lowndes, 1773), advertisement, n.p. All quotations are from this edition and are cited in the text by act and scene number.

to the Spaniards, not just because he was a militarily threatening claimant to the throne but because his alliance with Alzira would have guaranteed the sexual and political reproduction of the Inca regime. By making Alzuma the heroine's brother rather her lover, and eradicating her father from the text, Murphy's text radically reduces the agency of male indigenes. In *Alzira*, the friendship between Don Alvarez and Ezmont and their joint enthusiasm for their children's marriage created an impression of alliance and patriarchal mutuality: in *Alzuma*, indigenous patriarchy is already defeated and the chief Inca woman is already traduced.

The Prologue to *Alzuma* deftly charts the play's appeal to British sensibilities by condemning 'the bigot rage and avarice' of the Conquistadors, appealing to the supposedly tolerant audience for a sympathetic hearing for the 'voice suppress'd 'of 'the FEATHER'D CHIEFS'. While the latter may be 'in error blind', Bennett exhorted his audience 'Against the pow'r that would opinion bind, / Assert the freedom of the human mind', drawing a contrast with the 'fierce religious zeal' that produces 'dread calamities'. Throughout the Prologue, Murphy's own position oscillates; described at one point as an 'advent'er', implicitly comparing him to the Spanish, in the closing six lines he is aligned with the Indians, hoping the audience will demonstrate 'moderate principles' and 'toleration' as opposed to the 'persecuting spirit' of Rome.

The rhetorical fluidity of the authorial posture in the Prologue encapsulates Murphy's multiple allegiances; as an unenthusiastic convert from Catholicism, and an Irishman who sought professional success in the imperial capital, he had himself occupied the position both of supposed bigots, and persecuted indigenes. While attempting to interpellate his audience as above all tolerant and merciful, *Alzuma*'s characteristic effect, noted by several critics, was that of horror: the nightmare of forced conversion, sexual predation and cultural genocide. In an early speech that encapsulates these horrors, Orellana describes a prophetic dream to her attendant Emira:

> -   Methought Pizarro
> With fury dragg'd me to the altar's foot;
> There urg'd imperious to renounce my gods,
> And wed Don Carlos; with apostate zeal
> My mother join'd her aid; – conspir'd against me;
> When, oh! Distracting sight! My brother, rushing
> To save a sister from the vile dishonor,
> Receiv'd Pizarro's dagger in his heart.
> The altar smoak'd with gore; – the cruel Spaniard

> Look'd a grim joy to see the only hope
> Of desolate Peru, – a Prince descended
> From a long race of Kings, ignobly fall
> And welter in his blood before him. (2.3)

But while Orellana does come under great pressure from her mother to marry 'the cruel Spaniard', the play actually concludes with the indigenous royalty alive, while viceroy Pizzaro is dead and his fanatic son is dying. The play closes however with intimations that Carlos's last minute renunciation of 'mistaken zeal' and consequent forgiveness of his father's death has finally convinced Orellana and Alzuma of the rectitude of Christianity. Somewhat bizarrely, it is 'the cruel Spaniard' who closes the play with a paean to toleration:

> Enlighten'd hence, ye rulers of each state
> Learn to extinguish fierce religious hate; (5.70)

The contemporary response to *Alzuma* suggests that for portions of the audience at least, the anti-Spanish dimension of the text was itself a sign of prejudice: one reviewer inquired with obvious scepticism 'whether it be required in times of peace, that an odium should be cast on the Spanish for acts that have long been execrated among themselves.'[63] Dismissing the play with a familiar accusation of plagiarism, the *St James Chronicle* reworks the merchant-adventurer trope with venom:

> If Murphy steal his tasteless tragick Hash,
> Like Shakespeare's thief, he surely steals but Trash,
> Have we not late the Graecian seen him roam,
> Nor yet one grain of Attick salt bring home?
> And now the rich Peru the Bard will travel
> But what does he bring home? A load of gravel.[64]

Suggesting Murphy was persuasive in his overt aims, however, there was a good deal of agreement that the primary aim of the play was indeed the indictment of forced conversion: 'The question between the Spaniard and the American is, whether any man has a right to compel another to be of his opinions, or else to put him to the sword?'[65] There was also a degree of consensus on the elevated nature of Orellana's role in bearing this theme: 'The spirit of her character shows itself in a prayer to the Sun, which she

---

[63] 'An Account of *Alzuma*, a New Tragedy, Now Acting at Covent-Garden Theatre', *Universal Magazine of Knowledge and Pleasure, June 1747–Dec. 1803* 52.361 (March 1773).

[64] *St James Chronicle* Number 1850, March 6, 1773.

[65] 'Plan of the Tragedy of *Alzuma*', *Sentimental Magazine, or General Assemblage of Science, Taste and Entertainment* 5 (March 1775): 26–27.

Figure 4.   Frontispiece to Arthur Murphy, *Alzuma: A Tragedy, as Performed at the Theatre-Royal in Covent-Garden: 'I Am, I Am, Alzuma!'* Artist Charles Taylor. London, 1773. By permission of the Houghton Library, Harvard University

concludes with a vow never to join the enemies of her country' (*Plan*, 27). Her mother is clearly seen as in negative contrast: 'Orazia, who was the wife of the last Peruvian emperor, and is now married to Pizarro, has embraced the Spaniard's religion and the cruelty of his principles' (*Plan*, 26). Another reviewer similarly stressed the contrast between Orellana and her mother: 'On the advance of Pizarro, Orazia, etc. candour and bigotry are strikingly contrasted, and the sentiments of Carlos, and the simplicity and firmness of Orellana, do honour to the Author.'[66]

Commendations of patriotic loyalty to inherited belief and religious toleration are familiar topoi in eighteenth-century discourse: what is striking here is their application to a play by an Irishman educated by the Jesuits. As is invariably the case, Murphy's decision to write a black legend play is caulked on the outbreak of hostilities with Spain in the new world. But just as *Alzuma*'s reiteration of de la Vega's anti-conquest discourse problematizes a reading of the text in which 'noble savages' are simply mouthpieces for anti-Spanish propaganda, so too Murphy's own experience of the politics of conversion and the midcentury development of West British patriotism suggests the tragedy encodes a critique of 'bigotry' and colonialism that is more complex than first appears.

The Black Legend and Irish Patriot Drama

Murphy's shaping of *Alzuma* was surely informed by his own experience of the pressures to convert within a colonial society, but he was not alone in recognizing the salience of the black legend in characterizing the relationship between the English and the Irish. As we have noticed above, from the midcentury at least comparisons between Ireland and Spain's new world colonies were being made in Irish patriot discourse, notably in Charles Lucas's attacks on 'English governors.' Henry Brooke, Lucas's dramatic ally in the production of *Jack the Giant Killer*, was also the author of *Montezuma*, a text that has never been performed but was published in 1778. We know nothing about the immediate circumstances that provoked Brooke to write *Montezuma*, a tragedy that revisits *The Indian Emperor*. While incorporating much of Dryden's text, *Montezuma* presents the Conquest as an event in which indigenous agency – and competition and disarray – play a much more significant role than in the original play. In Brooke's version, the lust, avarice and cruelty of the Spaniards are less

---

[66] '*Alzuma, A Tragedy* as Performed at the Theatre Royal in Covent-Garden', *Monthly Review; or Literary Journal, 1752–1825* 48 (March 1773): 212–215.

vividly depicted while the internal conflict between Traxallans and Aztecs is highlighted. Montezuma himself, a figure of dignified and stoic but largely passive resistance in *The Indian Emperor*, is presented in Brooke's tragedy as active and forceful and the notorious scene in which he is racked is notable for its absence. He appears after being tortured, upright if supported by his children, rather than being shown as a spectacular victim of priestly cruelty.

Brooke's play thus underscores the importance of indigenous politics and religious conviction in colonial conflict, suggesting internal division rather than superior force produces imperial victory. Although the text includes familiar references to human sacrifice, the extended depiction of the Mexicans extends their figuration beyond the terms of noble savagery (and romance) that govern Dryden's characterization. *Montezuma*'s alterations in plot and character provide a reading of the Conquest in which Spanish triumph seems much more contingent and much less certainly authorized by Providence, technology and civilizational superiority. This relative levelling of the two sides makes an emphatic case for the necessity of patriotic unity in the face of imperial power along with a less strenuous argument for toleration. The arraignment of Catholicism is more muted than in Dryden, presumably because Brooke wished to create the possibility of Irish readers and spectators (whether Catholic or Protestant) being able to interpret the Mexicans as fellow sufferers of imperial oppression.

Brooke's play develops the Lucasian analogy between England and Spain in regard to Ireland by rehumanizing the Mexicans, exorbitating their agency and complexity, arguing for patriotic unity in the face of oppression. Murphy's reworking of the black legend also focuses on the colonized, those reckoning with invaders violently insistent on conversion. In a scenario that echoed his own personal history, *Alzuma* presents women as the bearers of traditional religion, sources of social as well as sexual reproduction. The affective and physical violence with which conversion is associated through the figure of Don Carlos does relatively little to indict Catholicism specifically – as the reviewer points out, that was an ancient *canard*. But the tragedy does most severely condemn attempts to enforce religious uniformity in a subordinate territory, a policy still pursued to the detriment of Murphy's fellow countrymen and former co-religionists across the Irish Sea.

Serious drama from the beginning to the end of the eighteenth century presented indigenous peoples from North and South America protesting against and actively resisting the colonization of their lands by Europeans. The Wendat, Mexican and Incan characters on stage from *Liberty Asserted* to Sheridan's *Pizarro*, rearticulated indigenous speech recorded and circulated by witnesses, such as Charlevoix and Lahontan, and native informants, such as Garcilaso de la Vega, to attack the physical and ideological violence of imperial invasion. Rather than serving as noble savage mimic men or women in the service of metropolitan critique or self-interested black legendry, characters such as Alzira and Alzuma need to be recognized speaking an Other discourse. The extensive Irish investment in representing such anti-colonial rhetoric, by writers whose affiliations varied from West Patriot to lapsed Catholic, underscores the compelling authority of this dissonant speech to members of the United Kingdom's most oppressed and subject nation.

CHAPTER 4

The Masonic Invention of Domestic Tragedy

On May 16, 1747, a procession of freemasons accompanied the new Grand Master of their order to Drury Lane. One of the plays they watched together was a two-act farce called *The Double Disappointment* and was written by one of their own, a certain Moses Mendez (1690–1755). Mendez, the first Jewish writer to be published in England, was a friend of James Thomson and Paul Whitehead, made a fortune as a stockjobber and then turned to poetry, writing three more pieces for the stage, all of which were produced at Drury Lane. Ironically perhaps, *The Double Disappointment* turned on a plot revealing the means by which by Irish and French outsiders attempted to pass as genteel Englishmen, thus satirizing a process of reidentification in which, as a Christian convert married to a Gentile, Mendez was himself involved.[1] Not all his texts were boundary marking however: it seems likely that Mendez was also the author of the libretto for Handel's *Solomon*, a composition that can be read as a paeon not just to Patriot values but to the religious eclecticism at the heart of freemasonry.[2] Although prominent, Mendez was by no means the only Jewish freemason; the first public mention of an initiation was recorded in the *Daily Post* on Monday, September 22, 1732, in an article that reveals Jews were already active in the craft:

> On Sunday, about two in the afternoon, was held a Lodge of Free and Accepted Masons, at the Rose Tavern in Cheapside, where in the presence of several Brethren of Distinction, as well Jews as Christians, Mr. Ed. Rose

---

[1] See Ragussis, *Theatrical Nation*, 52. For an account of the attractions exerted by freemasonry to Jews in this period, see John M. Shaftesley, 'Jews in English Regular Freemasonry, 1787–1860', *Transactions of the Jewish Historical Society of England* 25 (1973–1975): 150–209. Shaftesley explains that the first Jewish name appears in the records of the Lodge of Antiquity in 1723 and that Lodge 84, founded December 23, 1731, contained six Jewish members (154). He also notes that some lodges did exclude Jewish members (102).

[2] Pink, 'Musical Culture of Free-Masonry', London), 255. This splendid dissertation is the best extant account of theatre and freemasonry in London.

was admitted of the Fraternity by Mr Dan. Delvalle, an eminent Jew Snuff Merchant, the Master, Capt. Wilmott, Etc., who were entertained very handsomely, and the evening was spent in a manner not infringing on the Christian Sabbath.[3]

The masons' theatrical outing to Mendez's play was part of a regular pattern occurring annually, as the Brothers supported their new Grand Master on a public visit to the playhouse following his inauguration. From 1728 to 1747 or so, Andrew Pink explains, the masons processed together through the West End from one of a number of taverns and then sat together in a reserved block in the pit, before a 'bespoke' performance. Although the plays chosen represent a cross-section of the repertory, the main piece was framed by a special masonic Prologue and Epilogue and masonic actors would sing masonic songs at regular points through the evening. In addition to these annual visits (which ceased after anti-masonic demonstrations at the end of the 1740s), there were at least twenty-one bespoke performances of a less formal kind that functioned as benefits for masons involved with the theatre.[4] In a typical instance, the minutes of a Grand Lodge meeting on December 27, 1728, record that 'the Grand Master proposed going to the Old Play House on the next Monday night and desired as many of the Brethren as could conveniently go to accompany him; that he had bespoke a Play and had ordered a new Prologue and Epilogue to be made, which was to be spoken that Night on the Stage in Honour of Masonry'.[5] The minutes for the Grand Lodge meeting of December 13, 1733, close with 'the Grand Master recommend[ing] to the Brethren Br. Theobald's Play, and desir[ing] they would all come clothed'[6]; and on January 27, 1729, at the anniversary feast of the Ancient and Honourable Fraternity, after dinner the Grand Master 'bespoke the Tragedy of the Sequel to Henry IV with the Humours of Sir John Falstaff, etc. to be acted on the 12th day of February following, at the Theatre Royal in Drury Lane, for the Entertainment of the Society'.[7] The theatre itself would be adjusted for the masons' presence, with the *Daily Post* recording, 'For the Convenience of the Brethren, four Rows of the Pit will be laid to the Boxes, and kept for the Masons only.'[8]

---

[3] *Daily Post*, September 22, 1732, 30.   [4] Pink, 'Musical Culture of Free-Masonry', 202–223.
[5] From *The Minutes of the Grand Lodge of Freemasons of England, 1723–1739, Quatuor Coronatorum Antigrapha* (Masonic Reprints of the Quatuor Coronati, vol. 10, Lodge 2076, London), quoted in A. M. Broadley, *The Craft, the Drama and Drury Lane* (London: Freemason Printing Works, 1887), 96–97.
[6] *Minutes of the Grand Lodge of Freemasons*, 237.   [7] *Minutes of the Grand Lodge of Freemasons*, 96.
[8] *Daily Post*, April 24 and 28, 1731.

Freemasons were not simply prominent and distinctive patrons of the drama, however, for they were equally as populous onstage as performers and offstage as managers, prompters and scene painters. Among the better-known masonic actors were James Quin, Dennis Delane, Theophilus Cibber, John Cory, Barton Booth and Robert Wilks, while the theatre managers included Sir Richard Steele, Cibber Junior, Charles Fleetwood, Henry Giffard, Thomas Odel and John Potts. And in addition to theatrical professionals involved in performance and production were the dramatists: William Rufus Chetwood, who authored a play called *The Generous Freemason* (1749), not only was prompter at Drury Lane for some twenty years but wrote the celebrated *General History of the Stage* (1749). Sir Richard Steele aside, the playwrights included Charles Johnson, Lewis Theobald (the recipient of a benefit, as above), Edward Moore and George Lillo. Theatrical lodges proliferated: the Bear and Harrow Lodge, which met in Butchers Row, had a strongly dramatic cast, as did the Shakespeare Lodge No. 131, and the charmingly titled Lodge of the Nine Muses, No. 330 and the Apollo Lodge of Harmony.[9]

The connections between freemasonry and the stage were powerful in London from shortly after the establishment of the British Grand Lodge in 1717. When the movement spread to the Continent, actors become associated with the craft both in France and the Netherlands: Margaret Jacob has highlighted the fact that the first lodge to admit women, the Dutch Loge de Juste was established in 1751 with a female membership consisting almost entirely of members of the Comedie Francaise in the Hague.[10] And European dramatists were equally important members of freemasonry, with both Voltaire and Lessing being celebrated Brothers.

What is at stake in the interconnection of speculative freemasonry and Georgian theatre? Jacob's account of the craft as an Enlightenment practice is highly suggestive as regards the broad social and ideological attractions of freemasonry in the central decades of the eighteenth century. Within the walls of the lodge, she argues, freemasonry created a society that was governed constitutionally and relatively democratically; while the content of members' beliefs might vary considerably, their proceedings enacted a form of republicanism that would remain a utopian dream in the external

[9] See Henry William Pedicord, 'George Lillo and Speculative Masonry', *Philological Quarterly* 53.3 (Summer 1974): 403.

[10] Jacob, *Living the Enlightenment*, 120–142. The undoubted modern authority on freemasonry, Jacobs nonetheless builds on older work identifying speculative masonry with Enlightenment idealism, such as Bernard Fay's *Revolution and Freemasonry 1680–1800* (Boston: Little, Brown, 1935).

world for decades if not centuries. Masonic constitutionalism was derived from the English classical republican tradition: excoriated by (royalist and clerical) opponents as Cromwellian, it was in truth better understood in terms of mainstream Whig ideology.[11] But any constitutionalism was threatening to the defenders of absolutism, and in addition lodges included those of low class status, Jews, men of colour and even, in some cases, women, thus modelling a society of radical egalitarianism.[12] Masonic lodges can thus be seen as microcosmic utopias, in which enlightened men and eventually occasionally some women of widely varying ranks, races and beliefs could meet in amity and equality.[13] Stressing their social inclusiveness, an account published in 1766 proclaimed that the craft 'has been countenanced by the Wise and Great in all Ages and Nations; Emperors, Kings and Nobles have at all Times honoured this Society with their peculiar Patronage, and thought it no Disgrace to call the meanest Members, *Brethren and Fellows.*'[14] Margaret Jacob's classic account summarizes the myriad ways in which the lodges modelled and inculcated practical Enlightenment:

> The importance of the lodges lay in their ability to teach men identified by their support how to integrate enlightened values with the habits of governance. The lodges sought to criticize, to teach manners and decorum, to augment the order and harmony of civil society. They taught men to speak in public, to keep records, to pay 'taxes,' to be tolerant, to debate freely, to vote, to moderate their feeling, and to give devotion to other citizens of their order.[15]

Stressing the pacific toleration of masonry, a rejoinder to the slanderous Gormagons put it, 'Although a Lodge is no theological school, the Brethren are, nonetheless, instructed in the great Principles of its ancient Religion, its Morality, its Humility and its Friendship, namely, to avoid all Persecution, and to be peaceful Citizens of the Realm wherever they

---

[11] See Jacob, *Living the Enlightenment*, esp. introduction and chap. 1.

[12] Jacob, *Living the Enlightenment*, 3–4.

[13] The masonic exclusion of women has generated critiques of Jacob's work as over-idealizing. For a careful account of women's role in relation to eighteenth-century English freemasonry, see Robert Peter, '"The Fair Sex" in a "Male Sect": Gendering the Role of Women in Eighteenth-Century English Freemasonry', in *Gender and Fraternal Orders in Europe 1300–2000*, ed. Maire Fedelman Cross (London: Palgrave Macmillan, 2010), 133–155.

[14] *Hiram; or, The Grand-Master Key to the Door of Both Ancient and Modern Free-Masonry by a Member of the Royal Arch* (London: W. Griffin, 1766), 1.

[15] Margaret C. Jacob, *The Origins of Freemasonry: Facts and Fictions* (Philadelphia: University of Pennsylvania Press, 2007), 243.

may be present.'[16] The masons' fraternal responsibilities explicitly included the duty to assist foreign Brethren, with *Hiram* recording the obligation 'that every Mason receive and cherish strange Fellows, when they come from other Countries, and set them to work; if they will as the Manner is; that is to say, if they have mould stones in their purse; or else he shall refresh him with Money unto the next Lodge'.[17]

The religious toleration and vocal cosmopolitanism of the lodges were highly attractive to many participants and equally sinister to absolutist and clerical opponents. Proscribed by the papacy in 1738, lodges included deists as well as harbouring Catholics, Jews and Dissenters: the leading figure in the reestablished British Grand Lodge, John Desauguliers, was the son of a Huguenot refugee, but the Grand Lodge was also at one point led by Lord Petrie, leader of England's Catholics. Masonic discourse was clearly influenced by England's new science, with the characterization of the deity as the Grand Architect invoking a Newtonian idea of cosmic design. *Hiram* records that 'the Form of the Entered Apprentice's Oath differs in many Lodges ... and in some Societies, instead of saying 'In the presence of Almighty God', it runs thus: 'I promise before the Great Architect of the Universe' etc.'[18] While the content of Masonic belief proved assimilable by a huge range of adherents, published material makes it clear that religious toleration and a universalist humanism were central aspects of communal identity. As it was expressed in the founding *Constitutions* (1723–1738), the craft created 'a centre of union and means of conciliating true friendship among Persons that must have remain'd at a perpetual distance', a sentiment echoed some fifty years later by William Preston: 'The distant Chinese, the wild Arab, or the American Savage, will embrace a Brother Briton; and he will know, that, besides the common ties of Humanity, there is a still stronger obligation to engage him to kind and friendly actions.'[19]

The Brotherhood was active in recruitment, establishing lodges not just within Britain but in Spain, Turkey, India and various American territories. A lodge was established in Calcutta in 1728–1729, in Bombay in 1764 and in Madras in 1767, the same year in which a lodge was set up in Canton. In 1730 Randolph Took was established as Grand Master for South America, and Provincial Grand Masters were appointed to Antigua

---

[16] Quoted in Michael Baigent and Richard Leigh, *The Temple and the Lodge* (Jonathan Cape: London, 1989), 57.

[17] *Hiram*, 10.   [18] *Hiram*, 21.

[19] William Preston, *Illustrations of Masonry* (London: William Preston, 1772), 75–76.

in 1738, Jamaica in 1739 and Barbados in 1740. The 1730s also saw
Provincial Grand Masters appointed to Gambia, the Cape Coast and the
Coast of Africa. Although the membership of the overseas lodges was
dominated by merchants, trading company men and military personnel,
indigenous allies of British such as the Mohawk Thayendanegea, also
known as Joseph Brant, became freemasons, and in 1775 the Nabob of
the Carnatic, Orudat-ul-Omrah, was initiated.[20] The lodges track the
rapid expansion of imperial power through this period, so it is hardly
surprising that Jessica Harland-Jacobs sees empire itself as a masonic
project.[21]

But as Harland-Jacobs also makes clear, freemasonry was not only a
version of imperial soft power, the cultural extension of British ideology.
The craft was highly attractive to Native Americans over a lengthy period
and incorporated the prime movers of colonial revolution, Toussaint
L'Ouverture and Jean-Jacques Dessalines.[22] While the masonic rituals
are susceptible to marxisant and Freudian analysis, records by individuals
(including actors) suggest the persistent valuation of a 'highly personal
inner journey, undertaken within the warm embrace of the lodge', a
nondenominational spirituality that proved attractive across profound
cultural divides.[23] With the notable exception of Revolutionary North
America, where in Boston and elsewhere lodges of whites refused to admit
applicants of African descent, for much of the eighteenth century freemasonry offered the promise of intercultural integration on terms of
equality, with Brothers joined in quasi-familial relations of loyalty and
harmony. Formally opposed to cultural, social, religious, ethnic and racial
hierarchies, the craft was thus potentially subversive of imperial hierarchies.
As imperial governance became more oppressive and racialized, however,
anti-colonial activists in South Asia especially pressed at its increasingly
specious promise of equality.

---

[20] See John Hamill, *The History of English Freemasonry* (London: Lewis Masonic, 1994), for a
chronology of establishments.

[21] See Jessica L. Harland-Jacobs, *Builders of Empire: Freemasonry and British Imperialism, 1717–1927*
(Chapel Hill: University of North Carolina Press, 2007). Harland-Jacobs provides a compelling
account of the way in which masonry was spread regimentally, with travelling warrants enabling
lodges to move with military units. She is also astute in analysing the ways in which the colonized
used the masonic promise of inclusion to test actual, increasingly racialized boundaries.

[22] For a very thoroughgoing account of Amerindian involvement in freemasonry, see Joy Porter,
Native American Freemasonry: Associationalism and Performance in America (Lincoln: University of
Nebraska Press, 2011). While taking Harland-Jacobs's more instrumental view seriously, Porter
stresses the spiritual and communitarian attractions of freemasonry to different Amerindian societies
and individuals.

[23] See Porter, *Native American Freemasonry*, 133.

Dramatic Masons in North America

The intimate connections between freemasonry and theatre in Britain and Europe were equally powerful in the new world, with masonic managers running theatres and companies from Jamaica to Philadelphia. Thomas Wignell, a Jamaican freemason, was manager of the American Company of Comedians and Alexander Reinagle, an enthusiastic freemason, ran the Chestnut Street Theatre in Philadelphia. The first theatre built in Philadelphia, the Southwark, was constructed in 1766–1767 by a freemason, Douglas and masons were later active in the repeal of Philadelphia's anti-theatrical ordinances. In 1789 construction of the Chestnut Theatre began with masonic ceremonies, and the Company there sought out and performed plays by masonic authors, such as *The Generous Free-Mason*, performed in 1800.

American freemasons also continued to patronize theatre in a highly public way, well after the practice had ceased in Britain. On May 28, 1737, the *South Carolina Gazette* records that '*The Recruiting Officer* was acted for the entertainment of the Honorable and Ancient Society of Free and Accepted Masons, who came to the playhouse about seven o'clock in the usual manner, and made a very decent and solemn appearance … A proper prologue and epilogue were spoken and the Entered Apprentice's and Master's song sung upon the Stage, which were joined *in chorus* by the Masons in the Pit, to the satisfaction and entertainment of the whole Audience. After the play, the Masons returned to the lodge at Mr Shepherd's in the same order observed in coming to the Play-house.'[24] In Charleston, on December 27, 1754, masons processed to church, ate dinner at Mr Gordon's tavern and then went together to the New Theatre to see *The Distressed Mother*.[25] Masonic authors Steele and Moore were particularly popular for American bespoke performances preceded by public procession. Steele's *The Conscious Lovers* was requested by and presented before the masons at the Nassau Street Theatre, the *Mercury* records on December 31, 1753, and *The Tender Husband* was revived at the John Street Theatre (New York) in 1769. Moore's *The Gamester* was also produced in New York, in 1761 'by particular Desire and for the Entertainment of the Masters, Wardens and the rest of the Brethren of the Antient and Honorable Society of Free and Accepted Masons.'[26] While

---

[24] *South Carolina Gazette*, May 28, 1737, quoted by Richardson Wright, *Masonic Contacts with the Early American Theatre A.L.C.*, vol. 2, no. 2, 164.
[25] Wright, *Masonic Contacts*, 164.   [26] Wright, *Masonic Contacts*, 178.

theatrical performances served to celebrate and unite the masonic community, and served charitable purposes as benefits for performers or fundraising for the victims of conflict, American freemasons also believed in the culturally uplifting effects of drama. Commenting on a recent production of Elizabeth Inchbald's tribute to prison reformer and international activist John Howard, *Such Things Are*, the *Columbian Herald* of March 23, 1795, remarked that 'Mr Chambers ... selected the play for that evening's performance as abounding with universal benevolence and philanthropy, congenial with the principles of Masonry.' Popular with other American masonic spectators, Inchbald's celebration of philanthropic heroism, embedded in a not-too-veiled critique of absolutist monarchy, provided a flattering portrait of masonic masculinity embedded in a larger celebration of communal good fellowship and civic virtue.

Performing Freemasonry

Early Georgian theatrical professionals were social rather than religious or cultural outsiders, but masonry presented special attractions for them also: in a clubbable age the lodge offered an unusually egalitarian space for socially marginal men. For professional actors from the early eighteenth century forward, the fact that the masonic journey, as enacted in the first three degrees of Entered Apprentice, Fellow Craft and Master Mason, involved highly ritualized performance, may also have increased the craft's appeal. In a culture in which professional theatricality was frequently the target of savage denunciation, the communal veneration of and commitment to ritual role-playing was surely compelling, while the assistance of theatrical professionals was presumably an advantage to unpractised performers. Admission to each of the three first degrees of masonry required the candidate to engage in a complex ritual drama. The first stage involved admission as an Entered Apprentice, in which the candidate appeared before the Brethren with a bare leg below his right knee, a slipper on his left foot, a halter round his neck and a hood over his head.

QUESTION: How was you prepared, Brother?
ANSWER: I was neither naked nor cloaked; barefoot nor shod; despised of all Mankind; hoodwinked, with a Cable of Tow about my Neck, was I led to the Door of a Lodge by the Hand of a Friend. (*Hiram*, 23)

The lines in the dialogue that accompany the candidate's admission require his acknowledgement that he enters the Lodge in ignorance, guilt and vulnerability, to be saved by generous, enlightened and forgiving Friends. The role the Entered Apprentice plays here is redolent both of a sinner seeking admission to a spiritual community and a felon approaching punishment: in a later part of the dialogue the candidate tells his questioner, 'If I had recanted, and ran out in the street, the People would have said I was mad; but if a Brother had seen me, he would have brought me back, and seen Justice done me' (*Hiram*, 28). The second level of masonry, that of Fellow Craft, stresses the requirements of fraternity and included an oath that 'I will keep all my Brother's Secrets as my own, that shall be entrusted to me as such, Murder and Treason only excepted' (*Hiram*, 32–33). The third level, that of Master-Mason, involves a symbolic reenactment of the murder of Hiram, whose building of Solymon's Temple stands at the origins of the masonic narrative. In the masonic account, when the Temple was almost finished, three of the fifteen masons working on the structure killed Hiram while twelve held back. The three guilty men were taken to Solymon with blood on their hands while the unspotted aprons and hands of the others revealed their innocence (*Hiram*, 40), thus explaining the white aprons and gloves that signify masonic adherence. In some reenactment of the murder, gauges, squares and gavels are wielded against the candidate.

These identities and the dramas through which they are achieved can be understood in terms of the desire for a spiritual selfhood of a familiar yet radically unsectarian kind, enormously attractive in a secularizing society. Equally important is the masonic framing of relationship in terms that mimic the familial, without the accidental or authoritarian contingency that shapes genetic domestic relations. A third equally important aspect of the fraternity of masonry is the emotional and material shelter it provided from the ravages of early capitalism. Each of these elements will reemerge in Georgian domestic tragedy.

The record of masonic Prologues and Epilogues in Stephen Jones's *Masonic Miscellanies* (1800) suggests a further critical juncture with Georgian drama of a more overt kind. The active virtues accompanying the masonic veneration for order and harmony were not just tolerance but benevolence and charity and the masons were renowned for the support they offered to their own fraternity and their dependents. The edition of the *Constitutions* (1721) republished in 1756 with additional material records that 'much time was spent in receiving and bestowing Charity', that in 1731, for instance, 'the Grand Lodge ordered fifteen pounds for the Payment of the Debts of one Brother, and for releasing him from Prison: As also several other sums for the further relief of distress'd

Brethren.'[27] Charity extended abroad, with twenty pounds being extended to 'a Brother, who had been cruelly treated by the Inquisition at Florence, on the sole account of his being a Mason' (*Constitutions*, 229) and money flowed in from overseas; 'Brother Rigby from Bengall ... brought from thence twenty Guineas for the Charity' (*Constitutions*, 219). As we have noted, theatrical professionals were frequently supported by the masonic patronage of benefit performances. Increasingly however, benevolence extended beyond individuals: especially after the 1750s, the masons began creating institutions for the support of the dependents of their Brethren, including schools for boys and girls.

In the first three decades after the Grand Lodge's establishment, London freemasons celebrated themselves publically through frequent and elaborate processions that culminated in theatrical attendance and feasting. They courted publicity, not just through their processional exhibitionism but through their theatrical patronage, signalled by the specially composed Prologues and Epilogues. The many masonic Prologues are self-congratulatory, but they spell out the craft's commitments to tolerance, cosmopolitanism and benevolence, values they shared with much Whiggish dramaturgy. A characteristic example occurs in Prologue VIII, recorded in the *Masonic Miscellanies* (1800). Here the speaker has put on a Gyges ring of invisibility to spy on a masonic meeting, describing the scene as follows:

> Friendship on wing aethereal flying round
> Stretch'd out her arm, and blest the hallow'd ground.
> Humanity well-pleas'd there took her stand,
> Holding her Daughter Pity in her hand:
> There Charity, which soothes the widow's sigh,
> And wipes the dew-drop from the orphan's eye;
> There stood Benevolence, whose large embrace,
> Uncircumscrib'd, took in the human race;
> She saw each narrow tie, each private end,
> Indignant, Virtue's universal friend;
> Scorning each frantic zealot, bigot fool,
> She stampt on every breast her golden rule.[28]

The roll call of personifications summarizes the masonic ideals of friendship, humanity, pity, charity, human solidarity and tolerance. An earlier Prologue celebrates the virtues more discursively, as a father explains to his

[27] *The Constitutions of the Ancient and Honorable Fraternity of Free and Accepted Masons* (London: Brother J. Scott, 1756), 208 and 212.
[28] Stephen Jones, *Masonic Miscellanies, in Poetry and Prose* (Dublin: Brother Joseph Hill, 1800), 172.

daughter the masonic belief in equality – 'All children of one gracious
Father are, / To whom no ranks of rich and poor appear.' The masonic
egalitarianism extends to race and religion:

> Fa: Who'er belives in the Almighty cause,
> And strict obedience pays to moral laws,
> Of whatsoever faith or clime he be,
> He shall receive a Brother's love from me.
> 'For modes of faith let graceless zealots fight,
> We know he can't be wrong whose life is right.'[29]

The many songs, cantatas, catches, oratorios, anthems, eulogies and odes
recorded in the *Miscellanies* celebrate fraternity but more as good fellowship than equality: social harmony is praised but generally within the lodge
rather than as a more general virtue. But the masonic Prologues, though
doubtless written for performances patronized by members of the frater-
nities, are more oriented towards explaining and promulgating masonic
values in a context open to 'cowans' (non-masons) also known as the
profane. Sensitive to its context therefore, and foregrounding the shared
values of sentimental drama and masonry, verses such as Prologue VII is
structured by an extended parallel between masonic virtues and the proper
workings of the stage. The poem begins by celebrating the origins of
tragedy:

> In earliest times, as man with man combin'd,
> And Science taught them, and the arts refin'd,
> The tragic muse arose, and o'er the stage,
> Wept with feign'd grief, or rav'd with mimic rage;
> . . .
> T'was her's beside, by strokes of magic art,
> To raise the feelings, and expand the heart;
> To touch those secret springs within that move
> The tender sympathy of social love.

This thoroughly Whig history of tragedy is sutured onto a celebration of
the freemasons' commitment to fraternity, pity and benevolence, as 'Here,
to assist the Muses' great design, / With smiles the sons of Masonry may
join.'[30] Tragedy teaches its spectators sympathy but freemasonry ensures
they act on such feelings, the poem suggests.

---

[29] 'Prologue IV, Delivered before the Union Lodge, Exeter', in Jones, *Masonic Miscellanies*, 166.
[30] 'Prolgue VII', in Jones, *Masonic Miscellanies*, 170–171.

The Generous Freemason

As the Prologues' frequent address to excluded women suggests, while masons were keen to publicize their values and virtues they maintained secrecy in their meetings, rendering their activities a problematic, if not impossible, subject of representation. Their insistence that they avoided politics and religious disputation was equally a bar to the depiction of masonic action.[31] One of the few dramas thematizing masonry directly, Chetwood's *Generous Freemason* is valuable because it reveals the contemporary popular understanding of freemasonry written by someone who may have been a member of the craft. *The Generous Freemason; or, The Constant Lady* was first presented in the summer of 1730 at Oates and Fielding's Great Theatrical Booth during Bartholomew Fair. After transferring to a Booth at Southwark Fair, the opera was produced at the Haymarket over the New Year; at Drury Lane on a benefit night (May 3, 1731); at Lincoln's Inn Fields for another benefit on June 16, 1739, and finally at the New Wells Theatre in Clerkenwell, following fourteen performances at Lee and Woodward's Booth at the Tottenham Court Fair in August 1741.[32] All in all *The Generous Freemason* was performed for a more than respectable 156 times. Along with a farcical low plot of forced marriage, which includes some broad satire on masonry's occult ritualism, the opera has a potentially tragic action focused on Sebastian and Maria, who run away to Spain (where Sebastian's uncle is Consul) to escape her tyrannical father. They are captured by the Tunisian Admiral Mirza en route and in Tunis the King falls in love with Maria and his consort with Sebastian. They are freed however by Mirza, who turns out to be not just a Christian Englishman turned Tunisian admiral but a mason.

While Mirza's revelation of his religion and nationality obviates the effect to some extent, the opera emphasizes the same themes of tolerance, cosmopolitanism and sympathy laid out in the Prologues. When persuading Maria to leave for Spain, Sebastian tells her 'But yet one Pang I feel, thro' all my Joy / That from my noble Brethren I must part',[33] although he

---

[31] See Jacob, *Living the Enlightenment*, 47.

[32] See Harry William Pedicord, 'Masonic Theatre Pieces in London, 1730–1780', *Theatre Survey: The American Journal of Theatre History*, 25.2 (November 1984): 153–166, for details of texts and productions. See also Henry Pedicord's 'White Gloves at Five: Fraternal Patronage of London Theatres in the Eighteenth Century', *Philological Quarterly* 45.1 (January 1966): 270–288.

[33] William Rufus Chetwood, *The Generous Freemason: or, The Constant Lady. With the Humours of Squire Noodle and his Man Doodle* (London: J. Roberts, 1731), 1.1.3. All other quotations are cited in the text by act, scene and page numbers.

goes on to console himself of their ubiquity – 'But yet all Climes the Brotherhood adorn' (1.1.3). When the Tunisians approach, Sebastian announces that 'a *Briton* and a Mason cannot fear' (2.1.16) despite being overcome. His valour and his staunch refusal to convert to Islam inspire Mirza with pity and admiration and lead to the revelation that Mirza too is a mason.

The scene in which their mutual masonic identities are revealed is however suggestively ambiguous. Sebastian shows Mirza a masonic badge that leads the latter to embrace his prisoner, revealing himself to be 'a Brother, and a Friend' (3.1.32). Sebastian is initially incredulous, questioning whether 'in this barbarous Clime . . . Our antient, noble, and most glorious Craft . . . Shou'd find Reception in a *Moorish* Breast' (3.1.32). To this bigoted query, Mirza responds with ambiguity: 'No, no, my Brother! So Divine an Art / Cannot subsist but with Humanity' (3.1.32). Does he mean freemasonry is indeed universal among men or that it can be found only among the (implicitly European, Christian) humane? Sebastian's next query suggests that he at least believes masonry to be cross-creed, when he 'grieve(s) to think my Friend has lost his Faith' (3.1.33). Mirza is able to reassure Sebastian that he is not an apostate Moslem but a Christian Englishman who was rescued from the previous Tunisian king's conversion efforts by regime change. Mirza's belated revelation of his nationality and religion thus allows us to imagine (briefly) that masonry *is* universal before discovering that its adherents are (despite appearances) Christian Englishmen after all.

The Generous Freemason deploys its high plot of voyaging, captivity and escape to suggest that the apparently subversive commitment to masonry can coexist harmoniously with patriotic (British) and Christian affiliation – in Mirza's case, in fact, his masonry serves as the route back to the resumption of his natal identity. Sebastian's flight from England and Maria's tyrannical father to his own putatively more generous uncle in Spain is not only risky but insubordinate, an action undertaken in defiance of patriarchal authority. The lovers' capture by pirates suggests their insubordination has invited disaster but their trial and escape through Mirza recuperates their disobedience, implying that the fraternal bond of masonry offers a complementary model of loyalty to that of the absolutist patriarchal family. But the voyaging motif also allows Chetwood to harmonize the relation between imperial expansion, trade and voyaging and masonic cosmopolitanism. The serious action concludes with the two heroes and Maria celebrating their imminent return to England. Their moral triumph is underlined by the last Air, sung by Neptune and a

Chorus of Tritons, which celebrates the geographic reach of the brother-hood: 'All Climates are their Native Home' (3.7.51). Neptune's appear-ance amplifies the parallelism of Briton and mason, first invoked by Sebastian in Act 2, insofar as the ocean was itself increasingly figured as British: as masters of the waves, Britons could be at home anywhere, just as masonry promised that strangers everywhere were really brothers. As Briton and Tunisian, Sebastian and Mirza are enemies locked in violent competition for power and resources: as masons, they discover identity. *The Generous Freemason* displays a certain scepticism about the dangers of voyaging we will notice elsewhere in related drama, but it is also revealing of the limits of masonic cosmopolitanism.

The Generous Freemason suggests that the fraternity functions not just as a cross-class, cross-creed, cosmopolitan utopia but as a refuge, a source of security in a frightening and unpredictable world threatened by absolutist patriarchs or absolute monarchs. Voyaging through the expanding empire of commerce, even if simply to a consulate in Spain, could bring disaster: disaster averted by the discovery of masonic fraternity. It is my contention that it is out of this nexus of imagined masonic security, where the individual participates in a model *socius* of constitutionally governed equals who provide shelter from the storm of economic turbulence, that domestic tragedy emerges.[34]

Domestic Tragedy

Both the two tragedies that can claim precedence to Lillo's creation of domestic tragedy in *The London Merchant; or, The History of George Barnwell* are focused on the effects of economic disaster, and the authors of both were probably masons. Charles Johnson's *Caelia*, the play that inspired *Clarissa*, has a female protagonist whose fate is driven by her penury. Johnson claims a masonic affiliation in his lengthy Dedication of his 1723 *Love in a Forest* 'To the Worshipful Society of Free-Masons', published by none other than W. Chetwood.[35] More to our purposes here

---

[34] For the best recent collection of essays on domestic tragedy, see Julie Carlson, 'Like Me: An Introduction to Domestic/Tragedy', *South Atlantic Quarterly* 98.3 (Summer 1999): 331–624. The essay by Tom McCall, 'Liquid Politics: Towards a Theorization of 'Bourgeois' Tragic Drama', offers a particularly acute account of sensibility and the form (593–622).

[35] Charles Johnson, *Love in a Forest. A Comedy.* (London: W. Chetwood, 1723). Johnson strikes the familiar note of cosmopolitan tolerance: 'You have taught all Nations one Idiom, which, at the same Time that it gives a mutual Understanding, inspires a mutual Benevolence, removes every Prejudice of a distant Sun and Soil, and no Man can be a Foreigner who is a Brother' (vi).

however is *The Fatal Extravagance* (1721), supposedly authored by Joseph Mitchell. Although Mitchell does not appear in the lists of London lodges, his father was a stonecutter and thus highly likely to have been a mason, increasing the probability of his son following suit.[36] *The Fatal Extravagance* was written in 1721, in the wake of the collapse of the South Sea Bubble, when enormous amounts of money were first made and then lost as shares in the South Sea Company became hugely inflated and then collapsed. The company was created in 1711 to take advantage of Britain's acquisition of the *asiento*, or the trade in slaves to Latin America, at the conclusion of the War of the Spanish Succession, and it was so profitable that it was mooted as a rival to the Bank of England, servicing the national debt.[37] Mitchell's contemporaneous tragedy focused on a new kind of protagonist, already proposed by Richard Steele – a person 'not exalted above the common level' who has lost all his money, first by gambling and then, fatally, by investing in South Sea stocks. Distraught at the prospect of ruin, Bellmour tries to kill himself and all his family but is suspected by his wife's uncle and prevented from poisoning his wife and family and succeeds only in stabbing himself. The horror of his death is intensified by the last-minute discovery that his long lost brother 'Returning Rich, from the remotest East, / Dy'd but in sight of Land, and has bequeath'd / His whole, heap'd wealth, to *Bellmour*.'[38]

It seems likely that much of *The Fatal Extravagance* was actually composed by Aaron Hill, whose Prologue lays out with great precision the aims of the new model domestic drama.[39] Although Hill does not appear in the records of a lodge, Ronald Paulson assumes his membership because of Hill's attack on the supposed lowering of standards in masonic admissions. If Mitchell and Hill were both masons, the latter's willingness to sacrifice the ownership of *The Fatal Extravagance* to a needy Brother provides a neat exemplum of the drama's moral.

---

[36] See Robert Shiells, *The Lives of the Poets of Great Britain and Ireland to the Time of Dean Swift*, 5 vols. (London: R. Griffiths, 1753), 4:349.

[37] For the standard historical account of this disaster, see John Carswell, *The South Sea Bubble* (London: Cressett Press, 1960). The first critical account linking the text to the South Sea Bubble is found in Bernbaum, *Drama of Sensibility*.

[38] Joseph Mitchell, *The Fatal Extravagance. A Tragedy* (London: T. J. Jauncey, 1721), 3.42.

[39] The story appears in Shiells, *Lives of the Poets*, 4:349–350: 'Once, when Mr Mitchell was in distress, Mr Hill, who could not perhaps relieve him by pecuniary assistance, gave him a higher instance of friendship, than could be shewn by money. He wrote a beautiful dramatic piece in two Acts, called The Fatal Extravagance, which exposed the hideous Vice of Gaming ... This Play met the Success it deserved, and contributed to relieve Mr Mitchell's difficulties, who had honour enough to undeceive the world.'

Hill does of course appear as the author of the Prologue, celebrating the tragedy as an expression of dramatic union and Scottish cultural regeneration: acknowledging Caledonian bravery, he goes on to suggest that Scottish playwright Mitchell's tragic prowess shows the Scots have rejected the repressive censoriousness of the Kirk and embraced the 'rising Arts' to which they've been exposed by their civilizing union with England. The tragic action is equally timely, showing how 'rash, believing Avarice gulls a State; / What private Sorrows from wild Hazards flow.' Hill goes on to reiterate a maxim of Steele's, suggesting the disasters of the mighty are much less moving than those of ordinary people: 'To Ills, remote from our Domestic Fears, / We lend our Wonder, but with-hold our Tears.' *Fatal Extravagance* thus exemplifies Steele's belief in the culturally unifying effects of tragic sympathy, while taking a much darker view of the effects of the economic developments brought about by the trading companies and the expansion of credit than is visible in *The Conscious Lovers*. *Fatal Extravagance* not only shows Bellmour driven to suicide (and the attempted murder of his family) through imperial speculation but depicts the invasion of his house by his manipulative creditor Bargrave. Here the traditional landed estate is literally taken possession of by one of the 'new gentry' created by the growth of a credit economy fuelled by colonial trade.

The fact that Bellmour's family are absent or impotent, that assistance can be requested only from friends, underscores the weakness of the traditional family and hints at the need for new forms of emotional and material support. Bellmour's situation is carefully characterized as exemplary; until he kills Bargrave, his crime – his 'fatal extravagance' – is precisely financial. He falls victim to new modes of consumption, new instruments of credit, new forms of investment and ultimately, a new source of wealth will rescue his family from poverty. His own constant recourse to a discourse of honour only underscores the inadequacy of such a code in a market society with global reach. In this new context, the traditional family (represented here by his father and uncle) is unable to assist him, while his brother, as an Indies merchant the sole productive participant in the new economy, is too distant to help. With family absent or impotent, it is peers who supply real succour; as Bellmour cries in Act 1, 'yet Friends sometimes / Are more than Fathers! A Father cannot be / More than a Friend!' (1.1.6). And as the play shows, the man who has helped Bellmour most selflessly is his exceptionally loyal friend Woodly, who is almost ruined on his account.

While we lack definitive evidence that Mitchell (or Hill) were freemasons, Quin, who played the protagonist Bellmour, certainly was.

While Mitchell may have depended on a Scots support network, it is still striking that his Preface pays such pointed thanks to those 'Friends' who provided support during the play's production, the most important of whom was the emphatically English Aaron Hill.[40] 'Friendship' is as central to Mitchell's account of the writing and performance of the play as it is thematically: hardly surprising given his potentially isolated position as a Scot in London. While the play's analysis of the weakening role of family and expanding dependence on friends may well have been inflected by Mitchell's own position, his situation as a displaced Scot trying to make his way in the Grub Street in the newly constituted capital is itself symptomatic of broader socioeconomic trends. The lodge, in such circumstances, may well have appeared as a haven, a community whose egalitarian and supportive practices might not just supplement but provoke a reimagining of the traditional family itself. This seems all the more likely given the pervasiveness of familial metaphors in masonic self-description.

The London Merchant

The formal novelty of *The Fatal Extravagance* suggests that the dramatization of fraternal bonds, which emerged in tandem with the expanding imperial economy, shaped the striking refashioning of domestic tragedy in the early Georgian theatre. Henry Pedicord first argued that Lillo's *The London Merchant;* should be read as a masonic text many years ago. His claim is based both on external evidence (that several if not all the original members of the first production were masons and the play was transferred to a rival but masonically managed theatre for a further run) and on his belief that the panegyrics to merchants given by Thorowgood to Barnwell in the first act are close to transcriptions of masonic self-description. But Pedicord was not able to state definitively that Lillo was a mason, and he does not address the relationship between masonic values and the generic novelty of the play, which is generally accounted the origin of modern European domestic tragedy.

There is no doubt that Lillo was in fact a mason, as the records of the Freemasons Library in London reveal.[41] Recent critics have been more

---

[40] For an account of these friendship networks, see Stana Nenadic (ed.), *Scots in London in the Eighteenth Century* (Lewisburg, PA: Bucknell University Press, 2010), esp. 13–48.

[41] There are two records, kindly provided to me by Mr Martin Cherry, librarian at the Freemasons Library, London. The Wonnocott Index lists George Lillo, jeweller, in attendance at a meeting at

attentive to the play's imperial, sentimental and homosocial dimensions, noting that it celebrates the putatively productive activities of London's merchants while mobilizing a timely anti-Spanish sentiment in the form of Millwood's self-description of herself as a conquistador. Kathleen Wilson and Christine Gerrard have pointed to the implicit support this offered to the Patriot Opposition's enthusiasm for a war with Spain, and indeed other plays in Lillo's oeuvre suggest such an affiliation.[42] Although Andrew Pink argues persuasively that Prince Fredrick's induction into masonry firmed up alliances between freemasons and the Opposition, *The London Merchant* seems not to have registered as partisan commentary: on October 28, 1731, George II and Queen Caroline commanded a performance and the play became rapidly institutionalized as a didactic piece of improvement for apprentices.[43]

Like its generic predecessor *The Fatal Extravagance* and its masonic contemporary *The Generous Freemason,* Lillo's tragedy is responsive to the pressures of the emergent imperial market. But while *The London Merchant* looks like a paeon to the capital's merchants, Barnwell's fall does not simply show us a sexual and moral naïf traduced by appetites generated by a sophisticated metropolis. More than an idealized version of bourgeois values per se, Thorowgood's household is one governed by the masonic commitment to fraternal support and benevolence.[44] This operates in different registers, but all are designed to suggest the productive (rather than subversive) imbrication of masonry, patriotism and domestic order.

The first, public instance is Thorowgood's boast that his brother merchants and he were able to thwart the Spanish invasion by appealing to their peers in Genoa.

> [Elizabeth] sent Walsingham, her wise and faithful secretary, to consult the merchants of this loyal city; who all agreed to direct their several agents to influence, if possible, the Genoese to break their contract with the Spanish court. 'Tis done. The state and bank of Genoa having maturely weighed, and rightly judged of their true interest, prefer the friendship of the

---

the Sun in Fleet Street, April 12, 1732, and at the Oxford Arms, Ludgate Street, June 29, 1732. The full list of Brothers present at these meetings is recorded in W. J. Songhurst (ed.), 'Quatuor Coronatorum Antigrapha: Masonic Reprints of the Quatuor Coronati Lodge No. 2076, London', vol. 10, in *The Minutes of the Grand Lodge of Free-Masons of England, 1723–1739* (Margate: W. J. Parrott, 1913), 190 and 191.

[42] See Gerrard, *Patriot Opposition to Walpole* and Wilson, *Sense of the People.*

[43] See Pink, 'Musical Culture of Free-Masonry', 244.

[44] For an important discussion of the role of fraternity and homosocial relations in relationship to apprenticeship, see Lucinda Cole, '*The London Merchant* and the Institution of Apprenticeship', *Criticism* 37.1 (Winter 1995): 57 –70.

merchants of London to that of the monarch, who proudly stiles himself king of both Indies.[45]

While this passage is often cited as foregrounding the new assertiveness of the London's monied interest, the text makes it clear that the cooperation extends beyond the mercantile community in Genoa – that the Genovese 'state' as well as the bank were responsive to the Londoners' plea. This suggests a collusion of aristocratic and mercantile interests most likely to be found, at this time, among masons. Thorowgood's initial, negative characterization of the Spanish as tyrannical, aggressive and exploitative is extrapolated through Millwood, who famously tells Barnwell, 'I would have my conquests complete, like those of the Spaniards in the New World, who first plundered the natives of all the wealth they had and then condemned the wretches to the mines for life to work for more' (1.3.24–27). But the rhetorical antithesis Thorowgood attempts to establish between *doux* (British) *commerce* and Peninsular rapine is undermined by Barnwell's invocation of a specifically mercantile language of ruin to declare his fall:

> I would not – yet must on –
> Reluctant thus the merchant quits his ease,
> And trusts to rocks, and sands, and stormy seas;
> In hopes some unknown, golden coast to find,
> Commits himself, though doubtful, to the wind. (1.8.24–29)

The trope that Barnwell uses to figure his seduction by Millwood suggests not so much that he has been conquered but that he has been transformed into a merchant adventurer – as proves to be the case, when he goes on to thieve and murder. Rather than being a secure and virtuous identity, Barnwell's language, as much as his experience, underlines the extent to which the merchant's role is 'doubtful', vulnerable to both internal and external pressures. These include the relatively straightforward exigencies of climatic catastrophe (storms and shipwrecks), the more challenging order of political threat (despotism, onerous taxation, invasion) and the internal household problems caused by the corruption of valued servants and, most disastrously, one's own moral weakness.

How is such vulnerability to be defended? If the opening scene sketches out the merchant/mason's patriotically useful role as a financial agent

---

[45] George Lillo, *The London Merchant; or, The History of George Barnwell*, ed. William McBurney (Lincoln: University of Nebraska Press, 1965), 1.1.34–43. All other quotations are from this edition and are cited in the text by act, scene and line numbers.

whose cosmopolitan affiliations help safeguard the state, the bulk of the action is spent exploring the implications of a household governed by the masonic tenets of sympathy, benevolence and fraternity. Within Thorowgood's family these virtues are pervasive, rendering the family (considered in its contemporary form as the unit including servants and apprentices) a model of masonic kindness. As has often been noted, all the characters who compose Thorowgood's household display a highly developed sense of compassion. Barnwell himself is in a sense the victim of his own sympathy, responding as he does to Millwood's pleas for money at the end of Act 2: feeling love and pity but without the means to act on his feelings honestly, he is driven to the final murder. Thorowgood himself demonstrates a remarkable degree of compassion in response to Barnwell's misconduct in staying out overnight: sympathetically recalling the impulsiveness of youth, he forgives Barnwell and refuses to hear his confession as to the reason.

Thorowgood's daughter Maria, who secretly loves Barnwell, is also moved by pity to replace money he has stolen in order to save him from exposure and later, in full knowledge of his criminal connection with Millwood, she visits him in prison to express her compassion. The most suggestive embodiment of fraternal feeling is however the relation between the protagonist and Trueman, Barnwell's fellow apprentice. In the discussion of love into which Barnwell is led by Millwood on the evening of his seduction, he announces his commitment to universal benevolence and fraternity very distinctly: 'if you mean the general love we owe to mankind, I think no one has more of it in his temper than myself. I do not know that person in the world whose happiness I do not wish, and would not promote, were it in my power. In an especial manner, I love my uncle, and my master; but above all, my friend' (1.2.33–38). This privileging of the horizontal, fraternal relationship over the familial and the horizontal duty of loyal to a master is consonant with the masonic commitment to the Brethren.

While Barnwell will go on to betray all of these particular loyalties, he is not so betrayed himself. As we have seen, Thorowgood's first impulse is to compassionate and forgive him and Maria and Trueman both do everything they can to save Barnwell from the consequences of his crimes. It is striking however that when Barnwell arrives back from his night with Millwood, the first person he sees and with whom he has the longest and most painful interview is Trueman. The exchange between them is intense, running a gamut of reproach, guilt, accusation, defensive hostility, self-recrimination and forgiveness, more akin to a lovers' quarrel and reconciliation than an exhibition of male friendship. But Trueman betrays no jealousy of Maria, even when they collude together to shield Barnwell from the effects of his theft, instead praising her compassion: 'Will you save a helpless wretch from ruin? – Oh, it were an act worthy such exalted virtue as Maria's! Sure Heaven, in mercy to my friend, inspired the generous thought' (3.3.50–53).

Trueman is never tempted to conceal Barnwell's fault through an extension of the fraud, characterizing Maria's intervention as Christian mercy, presumably because she provides the missing funds from her own supplies. The solidarity Thorowgood's household displays to Barnwell never falters, forming the bulk of the final act as the merchant, Trueman and Maria each visit him in prison in turn to offer solace. Although the scene builds towards the contrasted depictions of Maria's virtuous passion and Millwood's despairing refusal of comfort, the greatest intimacy and physical closeness occurs between Trueman and Barnwell. 'We have not yet embraced, and may be interrupted', Trueman says, 'Come to my arms.' 'Never, never will I taste such joys on earth; never will I so soothe my just remorse', replies Barnwell, before relenting and embracing his friend (5.5.30–33). The embrace is accompanied by Barnwell's clearest expression of comfort:

> Since you propose an intercourse of woe, pour all your griefs into my breast, and in exchange take mine. [Embracing.] Where's now the anguish that we promised? You have taken mine, and made me no return. Sure peace and comfort dwell within these arms, and sorrow cannot approach me while I am here. (5.5.46–51)

Although Thorowgood and Maria also offer Barnwell loving compassion, it is only within the physical enclosure of his union with Trueman that the protagonist finds peace and security. Trueman is the person he actually wishes to see, asking Thorowgood to arrange the interview: their homo-social bond is reenacted, and in that process Barnwell recovers a sense of himself. By contrast, the meetings with Thorowgood and Maria highlight and extend his sense of guilt, despite their forgiveness.

The most intense and functional relationship in *The London Merchant* is finally the fraternal bond shared by Trueman and Barnwell. Like free-masonry, it is predicated on the radical equality of friends who are pledged to assist each other unstintingly. While all the members of Thorowgood's household display the humanity and compassion idealized in masonry, the hierarchical nature of his master's authority on the one hand and gender protocol on the other ensure that Barnwell is kept at a certain distance from his other two friends. Critics have puzzled over Trueman's willingness to hide Barnwell's theft from Thorowgood, but in fact this can be seen as the fulfillment of the oath made by the masonic Fellow Craft, never to betray a fellow mason, 'murder and treason only excepted'. Trueman's loyalty is tested, but unlike his friend he is not found wanting. As a predatory, avowedly immoral enemy to society in general and men in particular, the Hobbist Millwood is the very embodiment of 'profane' temptation and danger, a figure whose specifically sexual power unravels the mercantile/masonic utopia of Thorowgood's family. But even Millwood can be recuperated by Trueman – importantly, the character who closes the play. Echoing masonic Prologue VII's conviction that tragedy's ability 'to melt us to compassion's softest mood, / And rouse the slumb'ring soul to active good' paralleled freemasonry's production of 'social love', Trueman cites her as the necessary negative avatar:

> In vain
> With bleeding hearts, and weeping eyes, we show,
> A humane, gen'rous sense of other's woe;
> Unless we mark what drew to ruin on,
> And by avoiding that – prevent our own. (5.9.11–15)

Metonymically identified with the whole range of dangers facing the civic subject, ranging from Spanish invasion to erotic temptation, Millwood also embodies every absolutist, Catholic element of the profane world that threatened masonic fraternity.

The final element to suggest a masonic crafting of Lillo's action is the nature of the Barnwell's appearance in the last scene. As noted above, in the drama of initiation through which an Entered Apprentice is inducted into the first Degree of the fraternity, the candidate enters partially naked to the waist, hooded and with a rope around his neck. In the original version of the final scene of *The London Merchant*, Barnwell makes his last appearance at the gallows, thus echoing the condition of the masonic apprentice in the ritual of initiation.[46] While the masonic process presages a new identity and community on earth, given his remorse and spiritual renewal, Barnwell's imminent death by hanging – a literalization of the symbolic death of the 'old' man figured by the masonic rope – suggests an ultimately joyful passage to rebirth as a purified soul in Heaven. It may even be that Barnwell's murder of his uncle has a masonic resonance, for the initiation into the third degree or status of Master Mason, involving a

---

[46] See Porter, *Native American Freemasonry*, 134.

Figure 5.   *Mr Bereton in the Character of Barnwell.* Engraving. Artist Robert Dighton the Elder. London, 1776. Courtesy of the Victoria and Albert Museum, London

reenactment of the murder of Hiram. The murder of Barnwell's uncle presents him as presciently foreboding of death but also resolved and hopeful of the life thereafter. This echoes the spiritual scenario of entry to Master status, reenacting a process of murderous betrayal by a subordinate and a rebirth into a new degree of mastery. It is striking that Lillo's dramatization of an apprentice's murder and death by hanging, leading to a transformed and purified selfhood, while scarcely susceptible to exact allegorical reading, is so close to his first recorded attendance at a masonic lodge in 1731.

Fatal Curiosity

Lillo produced another important domestic drama, along with more conventional dramas of state signalling his Patriot sympathies. Five years after his success with *The London Merchant*, his *Fatal Curiosity* (1736) was produced at the Little Theatre in the Haymarket under Henry Fielding's management. Fielding was firmly of the view that *Fatal Curiosity* was the greatest tragedy of the age. Although literary historians have agreed with Fielding about *Fatal Curiosity*'s dramatic brilliance, it is striking that it never achieved the same success as *The London Merchant*. In an influential discussion of the play published in 1780, 'Hermes' Harris identifies the characteristic effect of the play as one of tragic horror – rather than pity – and William McBurney's account of its eighteenth-century production history suggests that this contributed to its unpopularity with audiences. The tragedy climaxes in an act of filicide, and on one occasion the audience was so horrified by this prospect that they flooded onstage to prevent the murder.

While the sheer revulsion felt by spectators may indeed explain the play's limited performance life, the tragedy must have been disturbing for other reasons.[47] The action consists of Young Wilmot, the scion of a ruined Cornish gentry family who has been sent to the Indies to repair his parents' fortunes, being shipwrecked on the coast three miles from his native Penrhyn. Disguised by his sun-burnt countenance and Indian habit, he reveals himself to his selfless sweetheart Charlotte, who has ruined herself while supporting Wilmot's parents during his absence abroad. Wishing to intensify the joyful effects of reunion with his father and mother, he takes shelter at their house, still in disguise, and after telling

---

[47] For an account that shares my view of the play's anti-colonialist aspects, see Dominick M. Grace, 'Fatal Curiosity, Fatal Colonialism', *English Studies in Canada* 28.3 (September 2002): 385–411.

them his adventures, entrusts his mother Agnes with a casket containing valuable jewels and retires to bed. Lady Macbeth–like, Agnes urges Old Wilmot on to murder the 'stranger' for his jewels. When Charlotte and their faithful servant Randal reveal Young Wilmot's identity, the guilt-stricken father kills himself and his wife.

Fatal Curiosity's relative failure seems the more surprising in that like *The London Merchant* the play deals with the issues of overseas trade and patriotism, set like the earlier play during the Elizabethan period and first performed in the 1730s when anti-Spanish feeling was at its most inflamed. But while the tribulations of colonial trade and imperial competition inform both plays, in *The London Merchant* the 'social love' that Millwood has exploited in Barnwell serves in the end to suture up the divisions she has caused. In *Fatal Curiosity*, by contrast, sympathy is not only implicated directly in the tragic denouement but fails to mend the tattered family and social relations presented. And while *The London Merchant* explores the peculiar vulnerabilities of mercantile existence, in *Fatal Curiosity* colonial trade seems to breed, rather than recuperate, metropolitan corruption, crime and violence. Brief panegyrics to the 'prolific ocean' notwithstanding, this play brings the drama of domestic disaster caused by the globalizing market to a devastating climax.

Both *The London Merchant* and *Fatal Curiosity* begin with allusions to the Elizabethan contest with Spain. But while in the first play Thorowgood rejoices at the successful arrival of a ship that has escaped Spanish attack, in *Fatal Curiosity* Old Wilmore receives much darker news from his servant Randal: following a dreadful storm, 'A noble ship from India / Ent'ring in the harbor, run upon a rock / And was there lost.'[48] This reminder of the often fatal hazards of the Indies trade is followed by an even more ominous account:

> But I've heard news much stranger than this shipwreck
> Here in Cornwall. The brave Sir Walter Raleigh,
> Being arrived at Plymouth from Guiana,
> A most unhappy voyage, has been betrayed
> By base Sir Lewis Stukely, his own kinsman,
> And seiz'd on by an order from the Court,
> And 'tis reported he must lose his head
> To satisfy the Spaniards. (1.1.29–36)

---

[48] George Lillo, *Fatal Curiosity: A Tragedy*, ed. William H. MacBurney (Lincoln: University of Nebraska Press, 1968), 1.1.22–24. All other quotations are from this edition and are cited in the text by act, scene and line numbers.

This passage obviously foreshadows Young Wilmot's fate – like Raleigh, he is a colonial adventurer who returns home not to a hero's welcome but to mortal betrayal by his family. But the tale of Raleigh's courageous but fruitless voyage frames an action in which maritime adventuring and trade seem pervasively associated with luxury, corruption, violence, degradation and death.

Although Young Wilmot appears in the second act as a successful adventurer and tells his companion Eustace only that 'the sinking fortune of our ancient house / Which time and various accidents had wasted, / Compelled me young to leave my native country' (1.3.62–64), his mother's final and most effective argument in her attempt to persuade his father to kill him, is ironically, her accusation that Old Wilmot's self-indulgence forced their son to go abroad:

> Barbarous man!
> Whose wasteful riots ruined our estate
> And drove our son, 'ere the first down had spread
> His rosy cheeks, spite of my sad presages,
> Earnest entreaties, agonies and tears,
> To seek his bread 'mongst strangers, and to perish
> In some remote, inhospitable land! (3.1.120–126)

While Agnes is accusatory here, her own appearance in Act 2 in 'faded dress, unfashionably fine' (2.2.98) suggests that her own expensive appetence has contributed to the family's ruin – that both the elder Wilmots have contributed to their fatal extravagance. The point is underlined when Old Wilmot turns loyal Randal away from his service because (as was the case with his son) he can no longer support him. Randal's resolution to go to sea to make his fortune mirrors that of Young Wilmot:

> Poor! Poor! And friendless! Whither shall I wander?
> And to what point direct my views and hopes?
> . . .
> I would aspire to something more and better.
> Turn thy eyes then to the prolific ocean
> Whose spacious bosom opens to thy view.
> There deathless honour and unenvied wealth
> Have often crowned the brave adventurer's toils.
> This is the native uncontested right,
> The fair inheritance of ev'ry Briton. (2.2.1–2, 8–14)

The repetition of the process by which a virtuous youth is forced abroad to a dangerous future by feckless seniors figures Britain not as the home of liberty and enterprise but as a land of wasteful rentiers, unable to sustain, let alone increase, the wealth of their own households. Oceanic adventure is not here so much Randal's source of 'unenvied wealth' as the desperate expedient of the destitute, ruined by others' extravagance.

The play suggests that the dangers to such adventurers are moral as well as physical. The shipwreck with which the action begins is the third that Young Wilmot has endured, and his other sufferings have included robbery and enslavement:

> At sea twice shipwrecked, and as oft the prey
> Of lawless pirates; by the Arabs thrice
> Surprised and robbed on shore; And once reduced
> To worse than these, the sum of all distress
> That the most wretched feel on this side Hell –
> Ev'n slavery itself. (2.3.79–85)

And the danger that the shipwrecked mariner will be betrayed rather than succoured by savage shore dwellers is not confined to the coasts of Araby and Africa; as Young Wilmot points out to Eustace on their first appearance, they've been 'deliver'd twice: first from the sea, / And then from savage men who, more remorseless, / Prey on shipwrecked wretches ...' (1.3.2–4). The wreckers and salvagers' violation of the laws of hospitality, echoed and intensified by the Wilmots' murderous actions, implicitly collapses distinctions between Indies and British civility. The wealth generated by colonial trade has produced its own violent and parasitical service industry, while the temptations of Indian jewels prove too much for the weak and corrupted Wilmots.

While Young Wilmot appears initially as a victim rather than a perpetrator of cruelty, his very appearance – 'in Indian habit', with a 'marred complexion', so that he looks 'more like a sun-burnt Indian / Than a Briton' – suggests that he may have been irrevocably altered by his exotic experiences. Further, his deliberate refusal to adopt English garb and his unwillingness to reveal himself immediately, either to Charlot, Randal or his parents, suggests a mistrustfulness and a desire to manipulate others' ignorance and emotional vulnerability that verges on the sadistic. Randal, a figure of unimpeachable integrity, certainly thinks so, and he links Young Wilmot's affective experimentation to both his colonial adventuring and his family's moral weakness, telling him roundly: 'You grow luxurious in your mental pleasures ... To say true, I ever thought / Your boundless curiosity a weakness' (2.2.76–79).

Randal's accusation is a serious one, echoing the titular implication that Young Wilmot's desire to extend the effect of his recognition scenes was – as much as his mother's greedy curiosity about the contents of the casket – the cause of the tragedy. Wilmot's voyaging to strange lands is one form of curiosity that the play suggests is likely to prove mortal, but his luxurious indulgence in affective experimentation – a corruption that links him to his dissolute parents – is another. Unwilling to reveal his true identity and shorten his lover's and his parents' agonies, he prefers to play on their sensibilities while vaunting his exotic persona and wealth – a form of moral extravagance as fatal as penury.

The Gamester

The last really successful domestic tragedy, Edward Moore's *The Gamester* (1753), was also composed by a freemason who seems to have been considerably assisted by aristocratic and masonic patrons in shaping a literary career after failing as an entrepreneur. Moore enjoyed considerable patronage from Lords Lyttleton and Chesterfield and wrote the libretto for Boyce's oratorio on the masonic subject of Solomon. *The Gamester* became well established in the repertory and was successful on the Continent: Diderot adapted the play, and it was influential in Germany. Moore drew on *The Fatal Extravagance* in composing his text: both gamblers, Bellmour and Beverley, are led to ruin by characters adept at legal and financial chicanery and in both plays, the much-loved but hopelessly flawed protagonist is riven by guilt at the prospect of his family's degradation and kills himself with poison before hearing that a relative's fortune would have rescued him from ruin.

In *The Gamester* the role of friendship is even more important than in the source text. Moore's play is structured round a contest between Beverley's true and false friends, Lewson and Stukely, respectively. Having known each other since their childhood, each is well positioned to influence Beverley, the somewhat naive protagonist. Like Millwood, Stukely is linked to sexual temptation, as we learn his motivation for ruining Beverley is not only envy of the latter's attractive disposition and wealth but desire for his wife. Symmetrically, the virtuous true friend Lewson is engaged to Beverley's shrewd and spirited sister Charlotte, and wants nothing more than to be fully a 'brother' to the destitute gambler. Stukely however is more astute at manipulating the discourse of friendship to manage Beverley as he desires. When pretending to be destitute after lending Beverley money, he leads his gull on to offer his wife's jewels: 'She shall yield up all. My friend demands it' (2.2.678). When Beverley hesitates about handing over her property, Stukely feigns distress saying, 'Lead me to a prison; it is the reward of friendship' (2.1.678). Beverley naturally replies that he won't be 'callous to a friend's distress' (2.1.678) and flagellates himself after receiving a lying message from Stukely, that his companion has been 'Ruined by friendship!' (2.2.680).

The false friendship (and destructive sympathy) of gamblers – one a gull, the other predator – figures as an implicit counterpoint to the compassionate, practical loyalty of true friendship. Like its source text, *The Gamester* uses gambling to figure the cultural and moral problems generated by larger economic processes. Invoking the language used by Barnwell to describe his ruin, Beverley characterizes their gambling to Stukely as imprudent adventurism: 'We have been companions in a rash voyage, and the same storm has wrecked us both' (2.1.678). Although Beverley is preoccupied by his own evil waste of 'plenty', other crucial moments of the play raise questions about the potentially corrupt means by which wealth is produced, as well as consumed. At the opening of the play, Mrs Beverley tells Charlotte that she is reconciled to poverty, even for her son: 'Why, want shall teach him industry. From his father's mistakes he shall learn prudence, and from his mother's resignation, patience. Poverty has no such terrors as you imagine. There is no condition of life, sickness and pain excepted, where happiness is excluded. The husband-man, who rises early to his labour, enjoys more welcome rest at night from it. His bread is sweeter to him, his home happier, his family dearer, his enjoyments surer' (1.1.673). This panegyric to honest labour and the simple life is ironically counterpointed by her husband's first speech in the Gambling House where he first appears in Act 2:

> Why, what a world is this! The slave, that digs for gold, receives his daily pittance, and sleeps contented; while those, for whom he labours, convert their good to mischief, making abundance the means of want. (2.1.677)

Mrs Beverley evokes a rustic if not arcadian vision of contentment whose pastoral language suggests her convictions are profoundly nostalgic, if not entirely illusory while her husband's characterization of the laborious life as enslavement is more contemporary but equally fantastic, envisaging its oppression and privation as contentment.

Their ignorance is a measure of their distance from any form of productive labour and economic reality and stands in contrast to the sinister familiarity with financial and legal manoeuvres demonstrated by Stukely and his minions Dawson and Bates. Their manipulation of instruments of credit creates the danger that Beverley's uncle's estate could fall to Stukeley through reversion, suggesting a thoroughly improper appropriation of a landed estate by the immoral and financially astute. Among the genteel characters, only Charlotte and Lewson exhibit a properly prudential if still disinterested relation to money, and it is their alliance that would provide Beverley with a proper friend and 'brother', reconstructing his kinship group in terms of mutual assistance, loyalty and prudence – the values central to freemasonry. Including men who worked as craftsmen as well as affluent elites, membership of a lodge demanded that a Brother pay fees and contribute to charity, ensuring that at least on entering members were financially prudent. The frequent dispersal of charity recognized the dangers of economic life, especially for the less wealthy, but gambling could be seen as antipathetic to the masonic stress on personal and financial probity.

The contest for Beverley's allegiance is echoed among the minor characters: Beverley is assisted by an ancient servant called Jarvis, while Stukeley's expects his off-siders Bates and Dawson to murder as well as deceive. But as in *The London Merchant*, the villain's assistants take a lesson in morality from the action unfolding before them, and tiring of their roles as accessories, resign their parts as conspirators. The diffusion of ethical struggle to minor, less-than-genteel characters, who emerge from the play as ethical subjects with a complexity distinct from Jarvis, a stereotypical loyal retainer, is reminiscent of the inclusiveness of the lodge, where Brothers of every varying degree take their turn as the protagonist and then the spectator of a series of dramas.

There is nothing about *The Gamester* to suggest an occult meaning legible to its masonic spectators but like other domestic tragedies, the play depicts protagonists tested by the peculiar exigencies of the emergent market economy, without familial support and dependent upon friends for compassion and charity, the moral and material insurance exemplified by freemasonry. All five of the plays discussed here are shaped by the particular economic possibilities and demands of the expanding imperial market. Each dramatizes a scenario in which trading wealth, a source of interstate competition, presents mortal temptation and objective danger to British subjects who lack any claim to traditional tragic status. In Chetwood's opera and in *The London Merchant*, the moral and material risks of the new economic environment are contained by masonic aid and the assertion of masonic values, which offer a peculiarly intense form of the ideological and affective bonds imagined capable of overcoming the impersonal catastrophes contingent on colonial and commerce. In *The Fatal Extravagance*, *Fatal Curiosity* and *The Gamester*, however, 'friendship' proves ineffectual. These plays identify affective and financial excess – extravagance – as a systemic social ill, one that is imbricated in morally and materially dubious colonial exploitation. Although friends attempt to assist the protagonists of these plays, the fraternal bonds of 'social love' are shown to be ineffective against the particular subjective corruptions and external contingencies of the imperial market.

Domestic tragedy emerges, paradoxically, not just in the decades in which a mercantile elite was becoming more culturally assertive but in response to the increasing opportunities and dangers presented by overseas empire. The genre's early imbrication with masonry is hardly surprising, given the mixture of anxiety and expansive optimism identifiable in the dramatic treatment of colonial commerce. Freemasonry offered a positively utopian vision of cosmopolitan cooperation and a material safety net: although subject to suspicion by continental states and the Catholic Church, membership was regarded as consonant with an active British patriotism. But fraternity could go only so far, and as the production history of *Fatal Curiosity* demonstrates, the critical possibilities of domestic tragedy were too fertile to be ignored as the crises of empire deepened.

In 1781, in the wake of Harris's praise of Lillo's tragedy in his *Philological Inquiries*, both George Colman Senior and Henry McKenzie revised *Fatal Curiosity* for production. Colman's version, pared down and even swifter than the original, was the more successful, in that it gradually supplanted Lillo's own version in the compendia of British drama in which it was habitually included. While Colman's version hews to what Harris saw as its neoclassic evocation of a stark archetypal scenario, McKenzie's version introduces pathos (through the addition of an orphaned Wilmot grandson) and extends the anti-colonial dimension of the play to a more pointed critique of slavery.

While *Fatal Curiosity* is sharply critical of Young Wilmot's indulgence of luxuriant sympathy, McKenzie's Advertisement explains that he believed there needed to be 'a better apology for Wilmot's commission of the crime' and that the charming boy Charles was introduced to provide 'somewhat more Pity into the calamities of the Wilmot family'.[49] The revision includes not only Charles, the Wilmots' grandson by a dead daughter, but the introduction of a treacherous attorney and former Steward called Sewell. Both these alterations recall *Fatal Extravagance* and *The Gamester* in both of which the protagonist is tortured by the

---

[49] Henry McKenzie, *The Shipwreck: or, Fatal Curiosity. A Tragedy. Altered from Lillo* (London: T. Cadell, 1784), 5. All quotations are from this edition and are cited in the text by act, scene and page numbers.

thought that his children and their descendants will be reduced to beggary or prostitution and in which the crisis of his affairs is brought about by an envious rival who has plotted his ruin using legal chicanery.

McKenzie's text thus disperses culpability, by rendering the older Wilmots more sympathetic both as concerned grandparents and as victims of financial entrapment. Expanding the pathos of the older Wilmots' situation, this version of the play thus diminishes the critique of affective self-indulgence that is so striking in Lillo. McKenzie's embrace of sentiment in fact extends to a more distinct and focused critique of slavery, which serves here as a synecdoche for overseas enterprise generally. Young Wilmot's possession of the diamonds is interpreted as the fruit of wicked exploitation by Agnes in both texts, but here it is linked explicitly to the evils of the slave trade, rather than overseas enterprise generally. We first hear of Young Wilmot's enslavement from Maria, who reports it to her mistress Charlotte:

> The savage nation, who, like beasts of prey,
> Prowl on the desert beach, and seize whate're
> The storm has spar'd, dragg'd him and his companions,
> The weakest to a miserable death,
> The rest to slavery. (2.1.24)

The narrative is taken up by 'Roberts' (Young Wilmot) who reiterates he was 'Yes, a slave, / Doom'd, at the bidding of his savage lord, / To toil and sweat beneath the burning sun' (3.1.27). The account is graphically amplified by Maria's plea for imaginative sympathy:

> ... Had you seen him bend
> Beneath the burdens of his tawny master,
> While the sun darted fierce on his head,
> And scorched the sand beneath him; whilst the wounds
> That wanton cruelty at times inflicted
> The fiery poison of a thousand insects (3.1.28)

Pointing a very timely moral during a period of abolitionist campaigning, Roberts/Wilmot declares,

> Let them think of that
> Whose avarice first made traffic of their kind
> And taught those sultry shores that impious trade
> That desolates creation! (3.1.29)

Returning to his own story however, Wilmot recurs to the much iterated topic of his changed complexion:

> His various toils beneath the burning zone,
> Where one eternal sultry summer reigns,
> Have marr'd the native hue of his complexion,
> And chac'd its bloom – (3.1.31)

Young Wilmot repeats his tale to his parents, but his sufferings prove no match in the face of Agnes's fears for her grandson, her suspicion of Wilmot and her own need. She begins her suasion by bemoaning that 'meagre penury / Hang, like a blight, upon our innocent boy' (5.1.58). Old Wilmot's Hobbesian conviction that 'In ev'ry state ... man preys on man' (5.1.62) provokes Agnes to denounce her the stranger:

> 'Tis so – these very diamonds
> Were dug by wretches, whom
> Their masters chain'd
> To miserable life, to whom to die
> Had been a blessing! Nay, tis probable
> This stranger won them from their first possessors
> By rapine or by murder – (5.1.62)

These attempts at justification are given even greater urgency by their grandson Charles appearing with the news that Sewell is on the point of arresting them both for debt and seizing their house.

Although McKenzie's adaptation was not revived, his attempt to amplify the play's treatment of colonial corruption underscores its capacity to critique imperial trade and degeneration. At the same time, *The Shipwreck* follows *The Fatal Extravagance* in attempting to project such corruption onto an identifiable group, financially and legally manipulative and socially upstart men of business, thereby partially recuperating the profligate landed gentry and suggesting the corruption depicted is less than general. It is suggestive that while McKenzie's version was markedly less successful than Colman's, another adaptation called *Preservation*, by the American John Brown Williamson, did do well on stage in the late 1790s.[50] *Preservation* extends McKenzie's alterations, adding the impoverished wife of an old friend of Young Wilmot's and her son to the cast. Living in a hut on the seashore, they exemplify the depths to which the genteel can sink. The older Wilmots are however recuperated to some degree: persecuted by 'Malign', an evil relative, they avoid killing their son and all ends happily.

Pioneered in England, domestic tragedy was a genre that emerged in tandem with the marketization of the British economy and the expansion

---

[50] J. B. Williamson, *Preservation: or, The Hovel of the Rocks: A Play in Five Acts. Interspers'd with Lillo's Drama, in Three Acts, call'd 'Fatal Curiosity'* (London, 1800).

of overseas trade. These developments shape the plots as well as the novel kinds of characters depicted in Mitchell's and Lillo's plays, all of whom are vulnerable to the vicissitudes of colonial commerce and mercantile adventure. Less evident but equally important is these texts' implicit embrace of masonic ideals of benevolent fraternity. The lodge provided a model of supportive, ecumenical, cross-cultural cooperation, close to the ideal version of trade often characterized as *doux commerce*. Within its walls, absolutism, fanaticism, envy and need were to be excluded, as men practiced novel forms of social and quasi-political equality. Translating this model to the stage shows men of no great rank tested by the vicissitudes and temptations of the profane world, and offered succour by 'friends'. The ultimate failure of friendly benevolence to rescue the victims of the modernizing economy confirms the distance between the utopian space of the lodge and the society from which it formed a refuge.

CHAPTER 5

Local Savagery
The Enlightenment Countryside on Stage

The default Enlightenment subject is the citizen, whether of the Republic of Letters, or the World. Generally speaking, although the philosophes interrogated human relations to the natural world, explored it with vigour and withdrew to its solitudes, they were not countrywomen or men. The Habermasian framework that has dominated recent analyses of early eighteenth-century English culture focuses on the developing public sphere, a series of essentially urban spaces in which Enlightenment citizens are bred. The 'postal principle' helped reproduce such citizens beyond the metropolis as various forms of print such as newspapers and novels extended participation in the formation of public opinion beyond the metropolises and provincial seats.[1] As we have seen, however, enlightened discourse on such topics as religion and the state, toleration and empire, both drew from an extensive range of non-European sources and recirculated such discourse in what Habermas called 'the market of culture products' in which theatre held a prized position.[2] The most prestigious theatres were very much part of the 'Town', but like fashion magazines, modish plays made their way everywhere, in the slow circuits of strolling players, in barns and fields, in amateur productions as well as in the ever-increasing numbers of provincial playhouses.[3] But in the course of the eighteenth century, rural England not only recycled opinion and critique through reading and spectating but became itself an object of unprecedented attention on stage. This was driven in some instances by party

---

[1] Guillory, 'Enlightening Mediation', 37–63.

[2] I am drawing here on Russell's *Women, Sociability and Theatre*, where she mounts a compelling argument for the importance of the 'culture market' (8–9) in the later Georgian period.

[3] The foundational work here is Sybil Rosenfeld's *Strolling Players & Drama in the Provinces, 1660–1765* (1937; repr., New York: Octogon Books, 1970). See also her *Temples of Thespis: Some Private Theatres and Theatricals in England and Wales, 1700–1820* (London: Society for Theatre Research, 1978) and *The York Theatre* (London: Society for Theatre Research, 2001). For a more recent survey, see Brewer, *Pleasures of the Imagination*.

political competition for the (English) nation's symbolic heart, identified with its shires and counties; in others, by a more radical desire to use a labourer's or yeoman's voice to critique the social and political order at large. As the century progressed, the clowns and clods who traditionally performed the role of indigenous wild man or savage became less stable as foils to upper-rank or civil subjects. Whether voiced by a 'natural genius' such as the former footman turned bookselling entrepreneur Robert Dodsley or radical Tory Irishman Oliver Goldsmith, the complaints and challenges of labouring-class countrymen were articulated with a novel sophistication and authority. Their criticisms extended beyond an articulation of the country interest to attack local tyranny, environmental degradation and imperial war.

Until recently, the importance of setting or 'scene' in Aristotelean terms was relatively neglected by theatre and drama historians. Following Steven Mullaney's pioneering work in *The Place of the Stage* (1988), which started to map theatre's role in shaping a rhetoric of space in early modern London, scholars of early modern drama have shown how Jacobean playwrights provided new ways of comprehending a fast-evolving and expanding urban environment of unprecedented size and complexity.[4] There is no comparable work on the spatial rhetoric of late seventeenth-century and eighteenth-century plays, although Richard H. Perkinson has provided a survey of the several dozen seventeenth-century texts whose titles signal their focus on a particular locale. Dismissing the notion that these 'topographical' plays invoked locales for anything other than fabular convenience, Perkinson discounts the way these comedies use specific scenes to shape and identify particular places and groups within London, both before and after the Restoration. Thus he records without analysing one of the great innovations of the Restoration stage, the extension of comic scenes beyond London (or the continent) to contemporary English towns such as Epsom, Tunbridge and Bury, as well as the northern countryside.[5]

The representation of specific, non-metropolitan spaces in Restoration and eighteenth-century plays carries over the relatively new practice of using highly particular settings from Jacobean antecedents, but these texts and performances also employ new discourses and new technologies.

---

[4] Steven Mullaney, *The Place of the Stage: License, Play and Power in Renaissance England* (Chicago: University of Chicago Press, 1988) and Douglas Bruster, *Drama and the Market in the Age of Shakespeare* (Cambridge: Cambridge University Press, 1992).
[5] See Richard H. Perkinson, 'Topographical Comedy in the Seventeenth Century', *English Literary History* 3 (1936): 270–290.

Recent scholars have argued that the early modern period saw a paradigm shift in ideas of place and space, in that Galilean astronomy and Cartesian geometry generated ideas of unbounded, undefined space against which local and specific topographical knowledges could be defined.[6] Examples of just such authoritative place making abound in late sixteenth- and seventeenth-century Britain, in the development of both cartography and chorography, the latter being the description of natural and social environments in prose. The late seventeenth century was an extremely active period for such knowledge generation, with antiquarians publishing local histories of most English counties by 1700.[7] Such antiquarian activity provides a paradigmatic instance of Michel de Certeau's argument that *lieux* (or places) are characteristically constructed by the 'strategies' of dominant groups who use techniques such as mapping, planning and inscription to stabilize the meanings of particular locations, thereby asserting the primacy of place over time.[8] By contrast, in practices like graffiti or flashmobbing, subordinate 'others' deploy unpredictable, unscripted, ephemeral 'tactics' to subvert the dominating place making of the powerful. In theatre, the play script might be seen as a *lieu*, but in performance such texts were and remain subject to the exigencies of space, as they are appropriated and reshaped by performers and spectators. Further, even within the play script, topographical comedies set in historically novel environments (such as spas) stage contests between dominant understandings of place and the attempts of a variety of subordinate groups to undermine such meanings. Often staging conflicts between the town (or London) and the country, courtiers and polite urbanites and bumpkins, such plays often show characters who rely on conventional and authoritative discourses of place outwitted by those who mime such strategic language for their own highly individual, often improper or subversive purposes.

Enthusiastic exploiters of new spatial technologies, Restoration and eighteenth-century theatre managers rendered their houses sites of ever-more specific dramatizations of exotic and provincial locales.[9] Increasingly

---

[6] Edward S. Casey, *The Fate of Place: A Philosophical History* (Berkeley: University of California Press, 1997).

[7] See Graham Parry, *The Trophies of Time: English Antiquarians of the Seventeenth Century* (Oxford: Oxford University Press, 1995).

[8] Michel de Certeau, *The Practice of Everyday Life* (Berkeley: University of California Press, 1984), 117.

[9] The classic study of Restoration theatre scenery is Richard Southerne, *Changeable Scenery: Its Origin and Development in the British Theatre* (London: Faber and Faber, 1952). For the uses of exotic scenery, see Orr, *Empire on the English Stage*.

sophisticated moveable scenes and flats was employed to evoke locations both far and near and slowly such scenery began to modify the practices of earlier theatre, in which, as Alan Dessen has shown, the speech, appearance and conduct of characters were sufficient to signal location.[10] The use of such scenery not only developed spatial rhetorics of the Ottoman Empire, China, India and the Americas but also enabled the exploration of new psycho-geographies in market towns and distant counties. The most innovative and influential creator of such new scenes was Thomas Shadwell, whose provincial and resort-town plays were enormously popular. Constructing his authorial identity through a claimed affiliation with Jonson – a great predecessor in mapping London locales – Shadwell transformed space into place, while staging threats to and contests over localized terrains. Depicting highly vested locales such as spas (catering to commercialized leisure) and Lancashire (divided between the nonconformist south-east and the Catholic north-west), he explored the new social tensions and enacted the political, religious and representational struggles that were convulsing the nation at large.

Beyond Booby and Prue

The first two decades of the eighteenth century saw a decisive change in the nature and frequency of dramatic depictions of the countryside. While there were more precedents to Farquhar's *The Recruiting Officer* (1706) than is generally realized, the play's celebratory invocation of a provincial and rural setting marks the beginning of a dramaturgical descent upon the shires. Many of these plays serve factional purposes, as Whig dramatists of various stripes move to construe the countryside as the true home of ancient constitutionalism and moderation, the site of resistance to Jacobitism and the refuge of patriots.[11] But such politically mainstream representations are joined by plays that voice much more radical critiques of social and political hierarchy. Farquhar's depiction of a countryside shaped by the demands of imperial war provided models for radical rural drama

---

[10] Alan Dessen, *Elizabethan Stage Conventions and Modern Interpreters* (Cambridge: Cambridge University Press, 1984), 95.

[11] The framework within which Whig, Tory and later Country Whig and Court Whig ideologies are understood has been provided by Isaac Kramnick, *Bolingbroke and His Circle: The Politics of Nostalgia in the Age of Walpole* (Ithaca, NY: Cornell University Press, 1992); Pocock's *Virtue, Commerce and History.* Christine Gerrard's account of the opposition's dramatic contributions to the campaign against Walpole remains seminal: see her *Patriot Opposition to Walpole* and Wilson, *Sense of the People.*

from Charles Dodsley to Burgoyne. Party political plays set in the country reveal an unwillingness by Whigs to cede the symbolic ground of national identity to the Tory squirearchy. Much recent scholarship on georgic and pastoral poetry and landscape art has revealed the extent to which the countryside was the site of aesthetic contestation, but with the crucial exception of John Loftis's *Comedy and Society from Congreve to Fielding* (1959), the theatrical dimension of such ideological conflict has been occluded.[12] The countryside was the site of intense class warfare, as improving agriculturalists enclosed ever more common land and stripped labouring-class people of their rights to hunt and forage.[13] Plays set in the countryside engage with these conflicts also, and reveal an increasing tendency to destabilize the traditional class hierarchy of gentry, yeomanry and peasantry. This process is accompanied and to some extent preceded by the reversal of the city/country dichotomy, in which the rural characters are inevitably less intelligent, if not less wellborn, than their city bred counterparts. These developments were shaped by a reaction against perceptions of urban corruption following the financial crises of the 1720s, by growing beliefs in human equality and by a renovation in the category of 'savagery' in relation to the Enlightenment citizen.

The 'wild man' has an extensive lineage in Western culture and his intellectual history has been decisively delineated in *The Wild Man Within*,

[12] Loftis's characteristically incisive study – *Comedy and Society from Congreve to Fielding* (Stanford, CA: Stanford University Press, 1959) – does note the increasingly genial dramatic treatment of the countryside in the first half of the century. The critical discussion of georgic's role in mystifying the negative effects of enclosure and agricultural improvement (following Raymond Williams's seminal work) is rich and extensive. See Raymond Williams, *The Country and the City* (Cambridge: Cambridge University Press, 1973), esp. 61, 106. In addition, see Robert Irwin, on agriculture as a primary form of commercial activity, in 'Labour and Commerce in Locke and Early Eighteenth-Century English Georgic', *ELH* 76.4 (2009): 963–988; Karen O'Brien on agrarian capitalism in 'Imperial Georgic, 1660–1789', in *The Country and the City Revisited: England and the Politics of Culture, 1550–1850*, ed. Gerald MacLean, Donna Landry, Joseph P. Ward and Jo Ward (Cambridge: Cambridge University Press, 1999), 160–179; Rachel Crawford on the cultural occlusion of agricultural labour in 'English Georgic and British Nationhood', *ELH* 65.1 (1998): 123–156; and another classic work, John Barrell's *The Dark Side of the Landscape: The Rural Poor in English Poetry* (Cambridge: Cambridge University Press, 1980), esp. 1–16. For an important revision of the positions held above, see Michael Genovese's 'An Organic Commerce: Sociable Selfhood in Eighteenth-Century Georgic', *Eighteenth-Century Studies* 46.2 (Winter 2013): 197–221. Genovese argues that georgic nostalgia actually offers an emancipatory critique, not just a mystification of rural conflict, redirecting self-interest towards a productive cooperative whole that works to create profit through sympathy rather than coercion.

[13] See K. D. M. Snell, *Annals of the Labouring Poor: Social Change and Agrarian England, 1660–1900* (Cambridge: Cambridge University Press, 1985) and for a more radical perspective on rural resistance, E. P. Thompson, *Whigs and Hunters: The Origin of the Black Act* (New York: Pantheon, 1975).

edited by Edward J. Dudley and Maximillian E. Novak.[14] In a more recent account, Richard Nash attempts to systematize various instances of wild men as the alter ego of Enlightenment culture, arguing that three kinds of 'other' enabled the definition of the social and rational subject as 'human'. In Nash's schema, passionate solitaries such as castaways and exiles, passionately sociable but brutish indigenes and solitary creatures of passion like feral children were characterized as marginally if not emphatically subhuman, thus securing the fully human identity of the sociably rational citizen.[15] He also however acknowledges that the real or discursive presence or invocation of wild men put pressure on the ideal citizen-subject, as Swift employed Yahoos and Houynanams to mock English pretensions to civility and Defoe explored the travails of the shipwrecked. More concerned with tracking the role of wild men in contemporary political debate over English expansionism, Kate Fullagar explores responses to a series of new world visitors to reveal how their characterization was governed by polemics between defenders of the new mercantile order and its Tory, country Whig and Patriot Opposition. In her account, 'savages' can be idealized or vilified according to the ideological need of the moment; their representation is always fluid and interested, rather than expressive of essential meaning.[16]

Rural plays depict England's own savages and wild men, those bred and thriving far from the great urban centre of empire, which was increasingly understood as a locus of politeness, civility and fashionable consumption. Charles Macklin claimed that in the midcentury all countrymen were instantly recognizable:

> The manners of the town and country, he said, were very distinct at that period, to what they were at the close of the last century. A countryman in town was instantly known by his dress as well as his manners; the almost uniform habit being a complete suit of light grey cloth or drab colour, with a slouched hat, and lank hair.[17]

Country characters were as recognizable onstage, playing 'Hodge', Yorkshiremen, booby squires and naive ingenues ripe for seduction. But the depiction of rustics, like that of new world savages, was much more mobile and polemical than first appears, providing the opportunity not just for

[14] Dudley and Novak's is still a classic study: see *Wild Man Within*.
[15] Richard Nash, *Wild Enlightenment: The Borders of Human Identity in the Eighteenth Century* (Charlottesville: University of Virginia Press, 2003), 3–8.
[16] Fullagar, *Savage Visit*.
[17] William Cooke, *Memoirs of Charles Macklin* ... (London: James Asperne, 1806), 71.

party polemic but for more fundamental forms of social criticism. Most Restoration comedies are extremely hostile to the countryside, characterizing it as the tedious antithesis to the scintillating town. Just as the social geography of London defined fashionable West End wits or parvenu cits, rural characters of all ranks were identified with their country origins and hence, metonymically, with the earth itself. This proximity to nature explained the untrammelled desire expressed by 'country wives' like Wycherley's Miss Prue, just as the unpolished qualities of country gentlemen were presumed to stem from their keeping company with their brutish social inferiors.

But as Sir Roger de Coverley's immense popularity suggests, the countryman's presumed naivety also had powerful attractions. Both Tories and country Whigs pointed to the shires as the origin of England's social and constitutional order, while the economic integration of country, city and empire was repeatedly celebrated in georgic. The countryside was also the site of extensive antiquarian investigation, with county histories being produced apace. As Rosemary Sweet explains, antiquarianism was a learned discourse of peculiar importance to the gentry, as it took as its object the disposition of manorial boundaries, thus supporting the squirearchy's claims to be the most ancient inhabitants of the nation.[18] Some very successful early eighteenth-century plays, such as *Tunbridge Walks* (1703) include figures like the 'Yeoman of Kent', chiefly notable for the strength of their county loyalty.

The theatricalization of rustic life was further complicated by the emergence of playwrights such as Dodsley, who were of low provincial origin.[19] The idealization of rusticity available in the pastoral was given new impetus by the increasing valorization of local forms of noble savagery, fascination with which motivated Pope's friend Spence in his pursuit of 'natural Genius'.[20] Fashionable patronage of unlettered labouring-class writers created opportunities that Dodsley in particular

---

[18] Rosemary Sweet, *Antiquaries: The Discovery of the Past in Eighteenth-Century Britain* (London: Hambledon, 2004).

[19] Dodsley's remarkable ascendance from provincial poverty to a pivotal position in British culture is documented in Harry M. Solomon's excellent *The Rise of Robert Dodsley: Creating the New Age of Print* (Carbondale: Southern Illinois University Press, 1996). For a more recent account of his status as embodiment of genteel taste, see George Justice, *The Manufacturers of Literature: Writing and the Literary Marketplace in Eighteenth-Century England* (Newark: University of Delaware Press, 2002), 125–131.

[20] See James M. Osborn, 'Spence, Natural Genius, and Pope', *Philological Quarterly* 45 (January 1966): 123–137. Osborn describes the craze among the learned in the 1730s for identifying examples of untutored intellectual brilliance among the labouring classes, of whom Stephan Duck is probably the best known.

exploited.[21] His hits *The King and the Millar of Mansfield* and *Sir John Cockle at Court* provided effective critique of Walpole but also included unusually full and sympathetic characterizations of labouring-class and yeoman characters.

As a genre, the 'pastoral' ballad operas developed in London by opposition writers such as Gay, Lillo and Dodsley condemned the state of the Robinocracy but also included much more systemic critiques of class and gender hierarchies. Both ballad opera and rural comedies frequently used the trope of the disguised maiden of high birth in their courtship plots but they also began to depict socially disparate marriages. Clearly the country locales were crucial for this development, providing settings in which the true nature of character would be legible, not to mention uncorrupted, and intrinsic nobility could be recognized. Ultimately ballad opera failed to flourish however, precisely because, Suzanne Aspden argues, its 'low' nature was at odds with the pretensions of mid-Georgian theatre.[22] Certainly, when Isaac Bickerstaff began rewriting ballad opera as comic opera in *Love in a Village* some thirty years later, he produced an apparently inoffensive celebration of a traditionally ordered village. But even this apparently anodyne drama was attacked for suspected Wilkite sympathy and its criticism of the tyrannical squire Woodcock encodes a reformist agenda that would be much more fully developed by John Burgoyne in his *Lord of the Manor*. The incremental revision of the country/city, savage/civil dichotomy is especially complex in Goldsmith's *She Stoops to Conquer*, in which the local knowledge and 'refin'd simplicity' of rural indigenes outwits polite invaders.

Restoration Anti-Idyll

Although there are Elizabethan and Jacobean plays set in rural or provincial settings, such plays never cohered into distinct urban genres such as city comedy or the comedy of manners. In the canonical Restoration comedies of manners, the countryside is generally characterized as brutish and boring. In *The Country Wife*, for example, the masculine desire to ensure absolute domination and property in a wife is exemplified by Pinchwife's marriage to the naive rustic Margery, a perfect example of

---

[21] The careers of labouring-class poets have received much new attention following Donna Landry's groundbreaking *The Muses of Resistance: Laboring-Class Women's Poetry in Britain, 1739–1796* (Cambridge: Cambridge University Press, 1990).

[22] Suzanne Aspden, 'Ballads and Britons: Imagined Community and the Contiguity of 'English' Opera', *Journal of the Royal Musical Association* 122.1 (1997): 24–51.

what Lady Sullen, in *The Beaux's Stratagem* (1707), refers to as a 'standing Maxim in conjugal Discipline, that when a Man wou'd enslave his Wife, he hurries her into the Country; and when a Lady wou'd be Arbitrary with a Husband, she wheedles her booby up to Town' (2.1.143–148). Plays actually set in the countryside were few and far between: one such, however, is John Lacy's *The Old Troop* (1672), which suggestively antici-pates Farquhar's scenario in *The Recruiting Officer* by presenting a group of soldiers encamped among villagers.[23] Here the rustics are figured as brutal in the extreme – reluctant to provide supplies, they claim to be without food until the exasperated officers demand they bring their children to be eaten. Even Raggou, the French cook, is taken aback when one woman takes them at their word and turns up proffering twin babies whose nursing costs are in arrears. The comic grotesquerie of this scene is proleptic of the way later plays use a military presence to depict the brutality of occupation and the demands of war while also suggesting the innate aggression of country life, with its habitual incorporation of vio-lence against the human and nonhuman alike.

By contrast, Robert Howard's and George Villiers's *The Country Gentle-man* (1670) presents an early defence of the country interest, in a comedy whose satire on Sir Cautious Trouble-all and Sir Gravity Empty opposes men of business to the decent, well-meaning Sir Richard Freeman, his daughters and their rural suitors Worthy and Lovetruth.[24] The satire on Londoners also takes in the vacuous beaux Vapid and Slander and the ambitious barber Trim whose daughters end up married to the bureau-crats. This is not a fate the women welcome, preferring husbands of their own rank but it underscores the promiscuous mingling of ranks and the breakdown of social hierarchy presumed characteristic of London that the play criticizes. Derek Hughes notes that William Cavendish's *The Tri-umphant Widow* (1677) provides another rare example of rural virtues and that in 1696 three plays with country locales appear.[25] In the most successful of these, Peter Motteux's *Love's a Jest* (1696), London compares badly to Hertfordshire while two years later, John Vanburgh's translated farce *The Country House* (1698) takes up a topic with a future by present-ing a successful lawyer whose expensive trophy estate is infested with parasitic hangers-on. The action turns on the protagonist's attempts to

---

[23] John Lacy, *The Old Troop; or, Monsieur Raggou* (London: William Crook and Thomas Dring, 1672).

[24] Sir Robert Howard and George Villiers, Duke of Buckingham, *The Country Gentleman*, ed. Arthur H. Scouten and Robert D. Hume (London: Dent, 1976).

[25] Derek Hughes, *English Drama, 1660–1700* (Oxford: Clarendon, 1996), 115.

rid himself of his fashionable encumbrance and its inhabitants. Antithetical therefore to the ideal of the country house as the decorative and fertile seat of time-hallowed social, political and cultural authority, Vanburgh's play reveals the acquisition of country estates as the result of parvenu social and economic adventurism.

The most complex dramatization of the contest between metropolitan corruption and rural virtue is however Vanburgh's earlier *The Relapse* (1696), a play that held the stage until the 1770s despite a dubious moral reputation. In his *Short Vindication of* The Relapse *and* The Provok'd Wife (1698), a reply to Collier's invective, the dramatist underscores the importance of place in the play. Arguing that his comedy can be seen as an illustration of the injunction in the Lord's Prayer 'to lead me not into temptation', Vanburgh writes, 'I saw but one danger in Solitude and Retirement and I saw a thousand in the Bustle of the World; I therefore in a moment determin'd for the Countrey, and suppos'd *Loveless* and *Amanda* gone out of Town'.[26] Reiterating the connection between the countryside and virtuous contentment, he continues, 'In Town, in short, they come, and Temptation's set at defiance' (65). After Loveless's fatal visit to the playhouse, where he sees Berinthia, Amanda is 'alarm'd at [his] story, and looks back to her Retirement' (66) but does so, of course, in vain.

Vanburgh's exegesis highlights the main plot's imbrication in a moralized characterization of country and city voiced within the play by Amanda, to whom her husband ascribes 'country principles': 'I confess I am not much [the town's] friend', she says, noting the widespread toleration of vicious and criminal conduct in urban society (2.1.199–200). But the subplot complicates the country/town distinction Vanburgh is at pains to draw in the *Vindication*. Young Fashion's successful scheme to appropriate his brother's intended bride, the rustic heiress Miss Hoyden, depends on a familiar presumption of rural stupidity in the girl, her father Sir Tunbelly and his household. As Coupler the matchmaker puts it, 'This plump partridge that I tell you of lives in the country, fifty miles off, with her honoured parents, in a lonely old house which nobody comes near; she never goes abroad, nor sees company at home; to prevent all misfortunes, she has her breeding within doors.' (1.3.295–300) Sir Tunbelly's enclosure of his daughter has produced a combination of ignorance and sensuality familiar in the characterization of Margery Pinchwife and Miss Prue, so that in contrast to Amanda's ability to fight off two sophisticated attempts on her

[26] John Vanburgh, *A Short Vindication of* The Relapse *and* The Provok'd Wife (London: N. Walwyn, 1698), 63. All quotations are from this edition and are cited in the text by page number.

virtue, Miss Hoyden is perfectly willing to take on two husbands. Further, while Sir Tunbelly's appearance on Young Fashion's arrival at his gate surrounded by servants armed with 'guns, clubs, pitchforks and scythes' (3.3.45) mockingly underlines the vulnerability of his household to less self-evident modes of encroachment, Amanda's invitation to her bewitching cousin Berinthia to stay in her lodgings echoes the squire's rustic ingenuousness. Although possibly able to maintain her own integrity, Amanda's exercise of the 'country principle' of unsuspicious hospitality proves as disastrous to her own familial interest (by facilitating her husband's intrigue with Berinthia) as Sir Tunbelly's deluded extension of welcome to Young Fashion. Whether ignorant or innocent, all the country folk of *The Relapse* are overset by an urban exploitation of their most characteristic virtue, hospitality.

Although Vanburgh's account of *The Relapse* in *A Short Vindication* simplifies his own text's effects for polemical purposes, in presenting himself as a proponent of the moral advantages of rural retirement he occupied (however implausibly), a time-honoured position. A compendium of this conventional wisdom appeared a year after *The Relapse* and *A Short Vindication* in the eighteen letters of *The Country Gentleman's Vade Mecum.*[27] The author asserts the superiority of country life through a thoroughgoing attack on the vice, folly and danger of the town. He tries to combat the diverse attractions of urban life, notably better 'Company, Diversion, and Education' (2), by stressing that the 'sickly, feeble, Pleasures of [the] Town' compare poorly with the 'hawking, hunting, fishing and fowling' which are 'free and open and deriv'd to you, as it were, from the general grant of *Nature*' (13), unlike the 'mercenary and base' town pleasures involving both 'charge and danger' (13). Such charges were not only the informal costs of theft and trickery but the informal expense of theft and trickery, not to mention the most important likelihood that one's estate will be robbed in one's absence by dishonest servants.

The Country Gentleman's Vade Mecum articulates a defence of the country interest through a reiteration of traditional tropes, heightened by hostility to the city as the seat of economic as well as political power and danger. The positive virtues of rural life are those of liberty, quiet, the ability to pursue musical, architectural and literary studies, as well as genteel sports while fulfilling one's social, economic and judicial

---

[27] Ed S----cy, *The Country Gentleman's Vade Mecum* (London: John Harris, 1699). All quotations are from this edition and are cited in the text by page number.

obligations as an estate holder. Our first glimpse of Amanda and Loveless suggests that domestic felicity can be added to this list but as in the *Vade Mecum*, the urban playhouse has a peculiarly powerful capacity to undo the country gentleman. After describing the degenerate urban characters of sots, beaux and gamesters, the *Vade Mecum* proceeds to the theatre, 'for thither I'm confident your Inclinations or Curiosity, or both together, will soon lead you' (38). In just this way, heedless of his own weakness, Loveless rushes to the playhouse, catches fatal sight of Berinthia and resumes his former (urban) identity as a rake. While the Restoration drama includes occasional defences of rusticity, even a text as critical of urban corruption as *The Relapse* depicts country characters and values as vulnerable to urban temptation.

Staging the Provinces: Shadwell

While the country/city division is an important element in *The Relapse*, Vanburgh doesn't specify precisely where Loveless and Amanda had retired and the action takes place in London. It was in fact Thomas Shadwell who preceded Farquhar in writing plays set in specific provincial locations, both by creating and exploiting new theatrical locales such as the spa town Epsom Wells and politically divided Lancashire while giving the familiar urban/rural rivalry a local habitation in his home town, Bury St Edmunds. While Shadwell did not always explain why he chose these settings, the cultural logic that informed the increasingly specific topographical aspects of city comedies must have shaped his scenic decisions. The very names of city comedies – Shirley's *Hyde Park* (1632), Shadwell's *The Squire of Alsatia* (1688), Jonson's *Bartholomew Fair* (1614) – signalled both physical and social setting, creating and reiterating generic expectations in spectators and readers. While the social, political and cultural tensions played out in these plays and the later comedies of manners have been fully analysed, very little such attention has been paid to the many 'scenes of provincial life' depicted on stage following Shadwell's early example.[28]

---

[28] For some of the more recent discussions of early modern drama and locale, see Andrew Hiscock, *The Uses of This World: Thinking Space in Shakespeare, Marlowe, Cary and Jonson* (Cardiff: University of Wales Press, 2004); Jean E. Howard, *Theater of a City: The Places of London Comedy, 1598–1642* (Philadelphia: University of Pennsylvania Press, 2007); Henry S. Turner, *The English Renaissance Stage: Geometry, Poetry, and the Practical Spatial Arts, 1580–1630* (Oxford: Oxford University Press, 2006); and James D. Mardock, *Our Scene Is London: Ben Jonson's City and the Space of the Author* (New York: Routledge, 2008).

There are three aspects of Shadwell's innovative scenic practice I wish to highlight here, noting how they bear on and helped shape English Enlightenment culture. First, in *Epsom Wells* (1672) the dramatist created the spa town play, successfully copied by Thomas Baker in *Tunbridge Walks* (1703) and by a host of later eighteenth-century playwrights, including, of course, Richard Brinsley Sheridan in *The Rivals* (1775). Spa towns began as places of royal recreation but rapidly became hubs of commerce and scandal, the latter circulated initially in ballads and pamphlets and then in newspapers.[29] Spas such as Bath, Tonbridge and Epsom were godsends to journalists (and eventually novelists) but as so often, playwrights seized on their possibilities first. Technically places for the recovery of health, spas were notorious for physical, sexual and social promiscuity: located in arcadian rural environments, they hummed with the corruptions of the town, as all sorts of parvenus, tricksters and sharpers sought to prey upon the more ingenuous gentry and people of fashion who also resided there. Shadwell's and Baker's spa town plays created and peopled the places of resort that figured from Tobias Smollett to Jane Austen as manageable, miniature versions of metropolitan life, plausibly concentrated enough to facilitate the resolution of plot but sufficiently varied to provoke rivalries, hostilities and intrigues of the kind which (when reported) sold newspapers.

The creation of spa town plays is an early instance of a general, national spread of commercialized leisure activities through England in the course of the eighteenth century documented by John Brewer in *The Pleasures of the Imagination* (1996). What Thomas Baker also seized on with particular verve were the dramatic possibilities offered by such settings to further particularize the country/city divide. In Baker's *Tunbridge Walks*, the Tory squire Woodcock is robbed of his daughter by the impoverished gentleman-adventurer Reynard.[30] Unlike a number of his rustic predecessors, Woodcock is no fool, easily able to see through Reynard's first ploy, an unconvincing mad act. He does however fall victim to an address by Reynard disguised as a fellow Kentish landowner. In *Epsom Wells,* this play and Shadwell's *Bury-Fair,* all the country gentlemen show themselves to be fiercely proud of their county, filled with the shibboleths of local history. In characterizing their identities in these particular terms, the dramatists

---

[29] Individual spas have their own histories, but for two overviews see Phyllis Henbury's *The English Spa: A Social History* (London: Athlone, 1990), and James Steven Curl's *Spas, Wells and Pleasure-Gardens of London* (London: Historical, 2010).

[30] Thomas Baker, *Tunbridge Walks; or, The Yeoman of Kent* (London: Bernard Lintott, 1703).

bear witness to the patronage practices of local gentry, who paid for most antiquarian research: focused on manorial, shire and county records, the rural gentry (rather than the aristocracy) were the group with most at stake in the antiquarian project. Unable to compete with the nobility at court or in the new modes of investment, the gentry had a vested interest in county identifications based on ancient landholding and local social and judicial power.[31] In *The Yeoman of Kent* (as Baker's play was subtitled) and *Bury-Fair*, plotting depends on precisely such powerful local feelings.

The third notable effect of Shadwell's provincial plays was their interest in unifying the spatially disparate identities they so carefully create. In the Letter to the Reader that prefaces *The Lancashire Witches*, Shadwell explains that he chose a provincial setting because comedy was being stifled by the 'unhappy division' of politics, which prevented any dramatist from satirizing 'any Humour of this time'.[32] Despite the rumours of 'dangerous reflections', primarily on Catholicism but also on the Anglican priesthood, which prompted close scrutiny by the Master of the Revels, the play wasn't censored and had a long afterlife as a pantomime – thanks to its aerial effects. In the letter, Shadwell stresses that he casts no aspersions on the North:

> Some of the worst Party of the Hissers were so malicious as to make People believe (because I had set the Scene in *Lancashire*) that I had reflected personally on some in that, and an adjoining County; which no Man will give himself leave to think, can do. And I do swear by the contrary, that it was never once in my thoughts to do so. (n.p.)

In fact, however, Lancashire (and Yorkshire) were noted for the strength of their Catholic communities, so Shadwell was exploiting a well-established association by setting his anti-Popish satire in this county.[33] But it is striking, that as the dramatis personae suggests, both the patriarchal Lancashire squire and the two genteel (Yorkshire) gallants who succeed in marrying the heroines are anything but clownish or fanatic. Sir Edward Hartfort is 'A worthy Hospitable true English Gentleman, of good understanding and honest Principles' and Bellfort and Doubty are 'Two *Yorkshire* Gentlemen of Good Estates, well-bred and of good Sense' (104).

[31] Sweet, *Antiquarians*, 1–20.

[32] References to *The Lancashire Witches* and *Bury-Fair* are drawn from Montagu Summers (ed.), *The Complete Works of Thomas Shadwell*, vol. 4 (London: Fortune Press, 1927). All references are to act, scene and page numbers.

[33] See John Richard Robinson, *Recusant Yeomen in the Counties of York and Lancaster: The Survival of a Catholic Farming Family* (Kirstead: Frontier, 2003); and J. C. H. Aveling, *Northern Catholics: The Catholic Recusants of the North Riding of Yorkshire, 1558–1790* (London: Chapman, 1966).

In the second act we learn that Sir Edward has completed the Grand Tour when he explains to the young men that 'I knew your Fathers well, we were in *Italy* together' (2.129). Travel has not corrupted his national loyalties however, as he boasts that 'all of us came home with our English Religion and our English Principles' (2.129) and that 'I wou'd endeavor to imitate the Life of our country Gentry before we were corrupted by the *French*' (2.129). But while Sir Edward and the other gentry are emphatically conforming Anglicans – and the young people are fashionable spa-goers – Shadwell does deploy Hartford's Lancashire household to figure the disruptive and corrupting effects of Popish plotting in the nation at large. The knavish chaplain Smerk and the other servants embody a plebeian credulity which enables even such a clumsy plotter as Teague to unsettle loyalties and allegiances in the 'lighter people', however immune the gentry remain to his lures. By locating the action on a single estate in a county with Catholic predilections, Shadwell presents Popery as a superstition akin to witchcraft whose adherents are all knaves, fools, clowns or plebs. In this context, Catholicism can be a butt of satire but not a serious national threat: even in England's Catholic heartlands, those who hold political and social authority are shown to be immune to Popery's blandishments and threats.

Shadwell's last provincial play, *Bury-Fair*, evokes the same atmosphere as the spas, as the annual fair suspends ordinary life and encourages an unusual degree of sexual and social traffic. Here however, Bury's exemplary parochialism is central to Shadwell's purpose. Late seventeenth-century Suffolk was politically quiescent but the county had been a rich source of parliamentary recruits during the Civil War.[34] Setting his scene in Bury allowed Shadwell to assert through provincial example the acquiescence of the nation as a whole to the recent Revolution. *Bury-Fair* demonstrates the variety of internal differences, signalled by the characters' attachments to town, county or metropolis, but all these competing loyalties are subsumed by shared pride in national identity of a peculiarly Whiggish cast. An exercise in exploring the possibilities of dramatic chorography, satiric potential in *Bury-Fair* arises from the extremity of the characters' spatial affiliations, with humour generated by too great or too little attachment to local habitation. Lady Fantast and her daughter Mrs Fantast are mocked for their Francophilia, their gimcrack imitation of Gallic manners and their

---

[34] See Clive Holmes, *The Eastern Association in the English Civil War* (Cambridge: Cambridge University Press, 1974), and Keith Lindley, *Fenland Riots and the English Revolution* (London: Heinneman, 1982).

inability to recognize that La Roche, a French wig maker, is a tradesman and not a count. At the other extreme, Sir Humphrey Noddy's excessive pride in Suffolk and townsman Trim's in Bury render them both ridiculous. The central male characters embody the quarrel between metropolitan and local loyalties in more sophisticated form and unusually, at the end the honours are even.

Shadwell and his early adopter Baker showed that 'scenes' beyond London had sophisticated dramatic possibilities. Even as country towns, country seats and country people were mocked, their increasingly particularized and sympathetic depiction extended and complicated the imaginary construction of England created in the London playhouse. Shadwell's commitment to this project suggests that from an early point, Whig playwrights were unwilling to cede the 'country' to a 'country interest' conceived of as Tory. In one of the most politically telling scenes of *Bury-Fair*, the heroine Belinda defends an (English) yeoman's right to strike a genteel opponent against the horrified protests of the Frenchman La Roche: 'Our Peasants have Quarter-staves; and if Gentlemen go to run 'em through, they will knock 'em down; and we commend 'em for't.' (2.1.327) The hero Wildish drives the Williamite point home, praising the English king 'who is a King of Men, and Free Men!' (2.1.328). The violence of the scene and its justification by the genteel characters hint at the older internecine broils of the mid-century but the resolution of the quarrel and the judgements passed upon it imply that the English now present a united front against external foes, an apt message from the Poet Laureate in the context of the Nine Years' War. The scene is proleptic of similar moments in the rural plays that follow Shadwell's in the next two decades. Farquhar's *The Recruiting Officer* (1707), Addison's *The Drummer* (1715) and Charles Johnson's *The Country Lasses* (1715) are all composed during periods of war. While *The Recruiting Officer* in particular treats war's effects ambivalently, it is striking that all three of these plays implicitly present the audience with more or less idealized images of England as a nation whose green heart is the countryside, not the counting house.

Rural Revisionism: Farquhar and Johnson

Although Farquhar's use of a provincial locale was not without antecedents, the play's initial and subsequent reception stressed the originality of the Shrewsbury setting. The generally perceived effect was celebratory, echoing the notes of good fellowship signalled in his Dedication, in which the play is pledged, not to a grandee, but 'To All Friends round the Wrekin' (the latter being a large hill near Shrewsbury and the emblem of Shropshire).[35] Farquhar is at pains to address and dismiss the local fear 'that, by the Example of some others, I would make the Town merry at the expense of the Country Gentlemen' (Dedication, 31–33), emphasizing that 'I have drawn the Justice and the Clown in their *puris Naturabilis*, the one an apprehensive, sturdy, brave Blockhead; and the other a worthy, honest, generous Gentleman, heart in his Country's Cause' (Dedication, 37–41). It is easy to see why Salopian audiences were mollified. Justice Balance is a markedly patriotic figure, continually nagging Plume to provide him with a firsthand account of the recent triumph at Blenheim, which the fluent Plume is unwilling to grant, hinting perhaps that such carnage is not a proper subject for comic discourse. Along with justice itself, the magistrate's name invokes the Whig commitment to England's vaunted international role as guarantor of the balance of power. The Justice's local benevolence is exemplified by the careful attention he pays to the soldiers' treatment of Rose, the daughter of his own daughter's nurse, for whom he feels a paternalistic concern. His daughter Silvia, who famously boasts she can 'gallop all Morning after the Hunting Horn, and all the Evening after a Fiddle; in short, . . . can do everything with my Father but drink and shoot flying' (1.2.42–46), is a tribute to her liberal upbringing and the physical prowess of the squirearchy. Sharing her father's sense of *noblesse oblige*, she sends money to a local woman said to have borne Plume a child in a gesture Plume describes as 'Noble and Generous, Manly Friendship' (1.1.366–367). Unlike the plebeians of urban plays who are generally servants intent on miming their betters or function as mere extensions of their masters' wills, Farquhar's rustics echo Silvia's unmodish freedom and agency. They may be clownish, but like Sir Humphrey Noddy's assailant they have a distinct sense of their status as freemen of property: 'Flesh, I'se keep on my Nab' says Thomas Appletree, and 'I'se scarcely doff mine for any Captain in *England*, my Vether's a Freeholder' asserts Coster Pearmain (2.3.65–68). The plebeian characters are not only verbally assertive – their treatment is crucial to the play's justification of local governance, justice and the ongoing continental and colonial wars.

---

[35] George Farquhar, *The Recruiting Officer and Other Plays*, ed. William Myers (Oxford: Clarendon, 1995), 161. All quotations are from this edition and are cited in the text by act, scene and line numbers.

The play's judgement of these matters is an undecided issue in current criticism. In a pair of essays, Derek Hughes has argued that the obsessive quantification of Farquhar's plays signifies the triumph of number over place, or (new) money over older, land-based social arrangements and that the way the dramatist refigures deformed or maimed bodies as economic indicators rather than moral signs bears witness to the new power of the corporeal disciplines of capitalism and technologically sophisticated war.[36] While refusing to characterize Farquhar as nostalgic, Hughes does imply the play bears critical witness to the dehumanizing processes enjoined by economic and political modernity. In another recent discussion however, Kevin Gardner argues that in *The Recruiting Officer* Farquhar succeeds in dispelling the anxieties attendant on the remodelling of England into a state with unprecedented military and fiscal capacities through a genial ironization of potentially explosive issues.[37]

For all the containing effects of Farquhar's geniality, the play's legibility as a critique of governance is undeniable. Certainly contemporary commentators such as Arthur Bedford, author of *The Evil and Danger of Stage Plays* (1706), believed so, arguing that in the aftermath of Marlborough's continental triumphs the unpatriotic stage sought to undermine the campaign at home: 'there was no Way to oblige the common Enemy, and prevent our further Successes, except by hindering *the Raising of Recruits*. According, there was lately published a *Comedy* call'd *(a) The Recruiting Officer*, *(b)* to render this Employment as odious as possible'.[38] While Arthur Bedford's objections to the play focus on its putative misrepresentations of officers and justices, and the consequent danger of undermining confidence in authority, accounts of the debates over the Recruiting Bills that authorized Plume's actions suggest that the scenarios Farquhar presents could have cut very close to the bone: As Tindal puts it succinctly, if with some partiality, 'The party in the House, who had been all along very cold and backward in the war, opposed this act with unusual vehemence, pretending zeal for the public liberty and freedom of persons, to which, By the Constitution they said, every Englishman had a right; which they thought could not be given away but by a legal judgement and for some crime. They thought this put a power into the hands of justices of the

---

[36] Derek Hughes, 'Body and Ritual in Farquhar', *Comparative Drama* 31.3 (1997): 414–435, and 'Who Counts in Farquhar?', *Comparative Drama* 31.1 (1997): 7–27.

[37] Kevin J. Gardner, 'George Farquhar's *The Recruiting Officer*: Warfare, Conscription, and the Disarming of Anxiety', *Eighteenth-Century Life* 25.3 (2001): 43–61.

[38] Arthur Bedford, *The Evil and Danger of Stage Plays, Showing Their Natural Tendency to Destroy Religion, and Introduce a General Corruption of Manners* (Bristol: W. Bonny, 1706).

peace which might be stretched and abused to bad purposes'. The objections in the Commons were echoed by many in the Lords who also complained that the rolls of the Justices had been stacked with Tories. Not only poachers but those with whom the magistrate had a private dispute might find themselves forcibly enlisted.[39]

In this context, it is not surprising that for all Plume's vaunting of his own reluctance to abandon Liberty and Ambition, to 'farewell Subsistence and welcome Taxes' (5.7.106–107) through his marriage to Silvia, his escape from the drudgery of recruiting and the danger of war is, as he finally acknowledges, a matter of thorough 'good fortune' (5.7.195). Highlighting the disruption to families and communities caused by war, Balance's fellow justices, Scale and Scruple, complain bitterly about the soldiery debauching local women and the illegal recruitment of men with professions and families. Balance defends the military's casual morality by arguing their sexual warmth stirs them up for battle, thus keeping English communities safe from 'French Dragoons . . . that wou'd leave us neither Liberty, Property, Wife, nor Daughter' (5.3.13–14). But Plume's singular flight into the Shropshire gentry throws the miserable fate of the skilled plebeian and yeoman whom he and Kite have recruited into relief. Further, for all his indifference to the human costs of war, Balance has his own, very concrete anxieties about the effect of a newly prominent military on the countryside. Expostulating against Plume as 'Heir to my Estate and Family' (2.2.28), he tells Silvia that 'all Captains have a mighty aversion to Timber, they can't endure to see Trees standing, then I shou'd have some Rogue of a Builder by the help of his damn'd Magick Art transform my noble Oaks and Elms into Cornices, Portals, Sashes, Birds, Beasts, Gods and Devils, to adorn some magotty, new-fashion'd Bauble upon the *Thames*; and then you shou'd have a Dog of a Gardner bring a *Habeus Corpus* for my *Terra Firma*, remove it to *Chelsea* or *Twitnam*, and clap it into Grass-plats and Gravel-walks' (2.2.37–48). Balance not only is fearful of a newly powerful professional caste usurping squirearchal place and property but fears for their transformative effects upon the land itself. In his nightmare scenario, his property's immemorial oaks and elms, traditional signifiers of English strength, longevity and endurance, are not even used in naval construction but are reduced to lumber useful in

---

[39] For accounts of hostile commentary on the local tyranny enabled by the innovative conscription acts (Mutiny Act of 1702 and Act for Raising Recruits of 1704), see Major R. E. Scouller, *The Armies of Queen Anne* (Oxford: Clarendon, 1966), 103–106, and George Macaulay Trevelyan, *England under Queen Anne*, 3 vols. (London: Longman, 1930), 1:224.

constructing the pretentious Palladian mansions of arriviste suburbanites. Under military ownership, he suggests, even the country's earth, literal ground of national identity and authority, may be changed into a mere decorative commodity, movable property drained of its ability to generate produce or support traditional social reproduction.

Farquhar's other great rural play, *The Beaux's Stratagem* (1707), is less obviously innovative although the circumstances of its heroes carry similar implications as to the enforced professionalization – most frequently military – of superfluous gentry – if Aimwell and Archer fail to gain wives, they plan to enlist. Both these plays were influential through the rest of the eighteenth century and *The Recruiting Officer* served as a model for Burgoyne's caustic treatment of recruitment in *The Lord of the Manor*. But an equally popular and influential alternative model to Farquhar's modern rusticity was provided some ten years later by Charles Johnson, in *The Country Lasses: or, The Custom of the Manor* (1715).[40] Continually reprinted and revived through the century, Johnson's play provides a celebratory vision of the countryside as the seat of the essential 'old Hospitable Genius of *England*' (1.1.15), marked by virtues of generosity and service, land-based wealth, innocence and freedom that would have sounded familiar to Howard's Country Gentleman, Sir Richard Plainbred.[41] The markedly partisan tone of the Dedication to Thomas Pelham, newly created Earl of Clare and fierce Whig, praised for his steadfast defence of the Constitution, reveals the extent to which this characterization of the countryside had become a cultural property claimable across party divides – and as such, a foundational aspect of the national imaginary.

Country House Ethos

Johnson's Dedication frames the comedy with a Whiggish panegyric to the national constitution and Britain's role as defender of liberty and holder of the balance of power in the Western world. But from that point on England, threatened by Jacobite rebellion and invasion, recedes, to be replaced not by a locale as specific as Shropshire but by 'A[ny] Country

---

[40] Charles Johnson, *The Country Lasses; or, The Custom of the Manor* (London: J. Tonson, 1715). All quotations are from this edition and are cited in the text by act, scene and page numbers.

[41] The last production of the play was in 1813. Two successful revisions in the later part of the century are William Kenricks's *The Lady of the Manor* (1778) and John Phillip Kemble's *The Farm House* (1789).

Village, about Forty Miles from *London*.[42] The main action concerns the courtship of Londoners Heartwell and Modely, who fall in love with Flora and Aura, ladies whom they meet dressed as, and take to be, rustics. Tested by the heiress Flora, Heartwell marries her believing her to be a farmer's daughter while Modely tries to rape Aura. Tricked into fighting a duel with Aura disguised as a boy, Modely is taken up for her putative murder to be sentenced by a model of traditional hospitality and local justice, Sir John English. The repentant Modely agrees to wait two years to marry Aura. The subplot turns on a plot by Sir John's nephew, the heavily indebted Lurcher, to abuse his uncle's famed hospitality by pretending to be the Duke of Gasconde and obtaining a considerable sum from his credulous relation while in that role. Lurcher repents however and the play closes with uncle and nephew reconciled.

While Sir Richard's cozening recalls Sir Tunbelly's similar vulnerability to the glamour of condescending nobility, the hospitality trope is here redeemed rather than abused when Lurcher has his change of heart. Further, while Sir John is the local most genteel embodiment of the trait, Heartwell and Modish are guests of the welcoming Freehold. While they take him to be a yeoman, Aura eventually reveals that her father was a gentleman of fortune, who much like Fielding's Wilson, ran through his money in town before retiring to a decent if modest life in the country. In the main action, the Londoners are tested and tricked by the country dwellers, in a reversal of the usual practice. In other revisions of the 'country girl' motif, whereby rustic naïfs such as Miss Prue are inducted into the town's linguistic and moral corruption, Flora insists on being courted in 'Plain English' rather than with florid metaphors. By assuming the role of farmer's daughter, she also succeeds in removing considerations of economic or status advancement from Heartwell's pursuit.

Unlike *The Recruiting Officer*, set in an identifiable location and provided with a plot and characterization driven by contemporary public issues, *The Country Lasses* constructs its nameless rural environment largely out of idealizing tropes: the benevolent and hospitable lord of the manor, the crusty but fiercely independent yeoman, the dull but faithful servants. Sir John is a Gentleman of 'right old-fashion'd Hospitality' (1.2.14) and with his niece, the Lady of the Manor, a young woman who 'uses no Face

---

[42] Johnson, *Country Lasses*, n.p. The phrase 'country house ethos' is the title of Virginia C. Kenny's excellent analysis of the cultural and political function of great rural houses in *The Country-House Ethos in English Literature, 1688–1750: Themes of Personal Retreat and National Expansion* (Brighton: Harvester, 1984). Her focus is primarily on poetry.

Physick' and 'looks like the Blooming Rose' (1.2.15), he extends a 'general good' over the whole neighbourhood. The former rake Freehold has turned his sword into a ploughshare and denounces all cosmopolitan town habits, telling Heartwell and Modely that he drinks no French wine, 'that Brewer of false Love and Politicks: We live upon *English* Beef and Beer, the Staple of our own Country' (1.1.14). By presenting these embodiments of national virtue on their own terms and their own ground, in the context of a novel plot where the urban lovers are reformed by innovative female leads, *The Country Lovers* depicts Sir John's manor as a specifically English utopia.

The play's scenic and performative effects form a crucial part of its everyday arcadianism, creating visualizations of the countryside as a fertile site of economic productivity and social harmony. In the opening scene, a country dance takes place in a field behind that is 'a Gentleman's Seat on a Hill, at the Foot of which is seen a Farm House' (1.1.1). Set against this idealized depiction of rural order, the dance celebrating the sheep-shearing enables the audience, as well as Heartwell and Modely, to observe the genteel Flora and Aura, dressed as countrywomen and wearing 'the garland of the green', as graceful embodiments of English fertility. The initiation of the action via a dance, a form in which bodies of persons from different social levels move as equals and as a unity, underscores the play's investment in questioning status hierarchies and asserting national identity. Johnson's additions to a traditional sheep-shearing ballad refigure this archetypal Doric idyll as a modern British scene:

> The Shepherd sheers his jolly Fleece
> How much richer than that which they say was in Greece
> 'Tis our Cloath and our Food,
> And our Politick Blood;
> 'Tis the Seat which our Nobles all sit on;
> 'Tis a Mine above Ground,
> Where our Treasure is found,
> 'Tis the Gold and the Silver of Britain. (1.1.4)

This patriotic celebration of sheep-farming baldly voices the imperial georgic of poems such as Dyer's *The Fleece* (1757). In the exchange that follows the dance, however, Aura decries the country and its inhabitants in familiar accents of metropolitan scorn, calling the shepherds 'Beings between Men and Beasts, and of an inferior Nature to People who grow in Cities', no better than 'Things' or 'Savages' (1.1.4). Deaf to Flora's responsive denunciation of urban ills, Aura will have to learn the value of 'the Innocent, Simple and Undisguised' value of rural life though her near escape from Modely's rape attempt (1.1.5).

Figure 6.   Frontispiece to Charles Johnson, *The Country Lasses; or, The Custom of the Manor.* Engraving. Artist and Engraver Louis Du Guernier. 1735. By permission of the Houghton Library, Harvard University

Johnson's achievement is to render his utopia concrete and amusing as its native inhabitants sometimes fall victim to but mostly successfully parry the mercenary and erotic assaults of the metropolitan invaders. In a moment characteristic of the text's general effect, one of Lurcher's parasitic creditors, the vintner Carbuncle, inquires scornfully, 'Is this your Land of *Canaan* that you talked of, that flow'd with Strong Beer and Chines of Beef?' (2.1.20). For all his scepticism, like the other hangers-on, Carbuncle will discover that Flora's manor is indeed a land of plenty, and having been sated with rural hospitality he will be sent home with his money restored to him, transfigured by Sir John's characteristically generous words to him into one of '*Falstaff's* followers' (5.2.71). This pervasive geniality is especially notable in the play's closing scene that focuses on the impending wedding celebration for Flora and Heartwell. But while the play stresses the ease with which all danger of moral and social disorder may be safely contained, it is unsurprising that even this apparently escapist text was read 'for an innocent allegory', with Lurcher/the Duke of Gasconde readily identified with the Old Pretender. As is the case with *Bury-Fair* and *The Recruiting Officer*, the fact that war provided the immediate background for the play's production presses the audience to read the often idealized rural or provincial scenes as the ultimate justification for contemporaneous military and political conflict. Appropriating a philo-rural discourse that might previously been seen as the preserve of 'the country interest', in moments of national crisis Whig dramatists attempted to persuade largely urban spectators that preserving *this* version of England was the stake at issue.

Addison's *The Drummer*, like Johnson's *Country Lasses*, was first produced during the Jacobite Rebellion and remained in the repertory through the whole century. The play was launched by Richard Steele at Drury Lane in 1715, and although there were only five initial performances and Thomas Tickell excluded it from his edition of Addison's complete works, the play was frequently republished and went on to a successful life in production. Steele's Preface to the first edition stresses two qualities in the comedy: 'the scenes were written very much after *Moliere's* manner, and that an easy and natural Vein of Humour ran through the whole.'[43] In addition, however, Steele mentions that 'My Brother-Sharers were of Opinion, on the first reading of it, that it was like a Picture in

---

[43] Joseph Addison, *The Drummer; or, The Haunted House. A Comedy* (London: Jacob Tonson, 1715), preface by Richard Steele, n.p. Quotations are from this edition and are cited in the text by act, scene and page numbers.

which the Strokes were not strong enough to appear to Advantage at a distance', although, he goes on to suggest, it succeeded on the stage. In the Dedication to Congreve that precedes his later edition of the text, Steele amplifies this characterization, drawing an analogy between Addison and his comedy, suggesting *The Drummer* showed that 'smiling Mirth, that delicate Satire, and genteel Raillery, which appeared in Mr Addison, when he was free among Intimates.'

The play is indeed unusual, not least for its setting in an old country 'Mansion-house' – referred to as an example of the '*Gothick* way of building' (1.1.12) by the fortune-hunting fop Tinsel – populated by simple rustics, a prosy but honest Steward and presided over by Lady Truman, recently widowed by the supposed death of her husband in the War of the Spanish Succession. As an allusion by Vellum in Act 2 reminds us, the situation recalls Penelope's besieging by suitors as she waits for Ulysses, because in fact the lord of the manor is not dead but has returned to observe his wife's conduct and chase out his two would-be successors. The more serious aspirant, an acquaintance called Fantome, has bribed Lady Truman's maid Abigail to enable him to haunt the house, disguised as Sir George and beating a drum to frighten off the vacuous Tinsel. Dressed as a conjurer to gain access to the house, Sir George allows Fantome to expel Tinsel, before appearing as himself and chasing off the would-be usurper.

Addison seems to have composed the play around the time he purchased a country estate, Bilton in Warwickshire, an eight-thousand-pound acquisition that cemented his claims to elevated social position. Although the property brought with it the title of Lord of the Manor, Addison drew on a much humbler story from his own rural childhood, as the source of the plot. In *Addisoniana* (1813) we learn, 'It was currently reported in the neighbourhood of Tadworth (not far from Amesbury) that the house of Mr Mompessim of that town was infested with a demon. Upon this story, related to him early in life, it is said Mr Addison imbibed the first idea of writing his play of "The Drummer, or the Haunted House"'.[44]

As is the case with *The Country Lasses*, the play is focused on celebrating the English manor house and its proper inhabitants at the expense of city vice. While gentle humour is generated by the cowardice, ignorance and naivety of the Butler, the Coachman and the Gardiner, and the Steward Vellum's verbosity is mocked, the real satire is directed at Tinsel, the London fortune hunter. Although we learn that Tinsel is well-born and

[44] Addison, *Addisoniana*, 1:47.

well-connected, he not only lacks an estate but is characterized by pretentious ignorance and greed. Addison specifies his foolishness very distinctly, in his initial conversation with Lady Truman about the mysterious drum. Contemptuous of the fears the apparition generates in the household, Tinsel claims to be a freethinker, disbelieving in spirits and souls and an adherent, as Lady Truman puts it, to 'your Doctrine to me in the Garden just now, that every thing we saw was made by Chance' (1.1.10). A confused adherent of Lucretian materialism, Tinsel tells her that after marriage 'I shall then have time to read you such Lectures of Motions, Atoms, and Nature – that you shall learn to think as Freely as the best of us, and be convinced in less than a Month, that all about us is Chance-work' (1.1.10).[45] Questioned further by an incredulous and disapproving Lady Truman, Tinsel eventually confesses that his freethinking is entirely superficial, a parodic version of enlightenment acquired secondhand:

> To tell you the Truth, I have not time to look into these dry Matters myself, but I am convinced by three or four learned Men, whom I sometimes over-hear at a Coffee-House I frequent, that our Fore-fathers were a Pack of Asses, that the World has been in an Error for some Thousands of Years, and all the People upon Earth, excepting those two or three worthy Gentlemen, are impos'd upon, bubbled, abus'd, bamboozl'd – (1.1.11)

This critique of such fundamental institutions of enlightened inquiry as coffeehouse conversation continues in Act 2, when Sir George explains that the misapprehension of his death was caused by an early instance of what will become a very familiar dramatic and narrative trope – inaccurate journalism. Vellum explains that 'Your name was, in all the News-papers, in the List of those that were slain' (2.1.15), when in fact Sir George was a prisoner of war.

The play is concerned to establish the resolutely rural Sir George and Lady Truman as the avatars of rational authority, superior both to Tinsel's absurd but fashionable atheism and their servants' ignorant credulity. Truman's conjurer's disguise amplifies our view of him as a classically educated soldier when his conversation with the rustics enables him to display his intimate knowledge of his household, his estate and the parish. Sir George thus appears as an ideal rural Whig – a gallant participant in

---

[45] Lucretius was more widely known in England in the seventeenth- and eighteenth-century Enlightenment than has been thought. See David Hopkins, 'The English Voices of Lucretius from Lucy Hutchinson to John Mason Good', 254–273, and Eric Baker, 'Lucretius in the European Enlightenment', 273–288, both in *The Cambridge Companion to Lucretius*, ed. Stuart Gillespie and Phillip Hardie (Cambridge: Cambridge University Press, 2007). See also Catherine Wilson, *Epicureanism at the Origins of Modernity* (Oxford: Clarendon, 2008), esp. 200–246.

Marlborough's war but an exemplary manorial patriarch, whose relict is equally committed to maintaining his estate. The second scene revealing the threat Tinsel embodies comes symmetrically with the first, in Act 4, prepared by Abigail's entirely accurate suspicion that should he marry Lady Truman, 'That young Rake-hell wou'd send all the old Servants a Grazing. You and I shou'd be discarded before the Honey Moon was at an end' (3.1.32–33). After rudely revealing his appropriative intentions to Vellum, Tinsel pursues his mockery of the Steward with Lady Truman. She is particularly offended by Tinsel's contempt for Vellum's piety, which precedes the suitor's extensive fantasy about the 'pretty Transformations' he would make in her house (4.1.40). Tinsel imagines plate turned into horses, plate turned into china; and plate turned into diamond buckles, as he has taken, as the widow caustically observes, 'a great Affection for my moveables' (4.1.41). As apprising of rent roll and timber as he is of gold caudle cups and large silver cisterns, Tinsel makes it clear that to him the estate consists of nothing but saleable property, echoing Justice Balance's anxieties that his grounds and woods might be similarly metamorphosed into fashionable commodities.

It is hardly surprising that Steele decided to premiere *The Drummer* in 1715, as the text must have seemed timely, with the patriotically/regally named Sir George beating off outlanders' feeble attempts at appropriating his little piece of England in the wake of the Old Pretender's campaign. The plot device of the mock drummer – literally a 'phantom' – suggests that the cleverer of the two pretenders to his estate can awaken irrational fears in clowns, women and fools but is no match for the real ruler of the estate/England. What authority the suspiciously Gallic sounding Fantome possesses, he borrows from his role model Sir George through disguise, and he loses it in the most humiliating circumstances. Tinsel is equally fraudulent but rather than seeking to usurp Sir George's position, he is indicted for the cultural threat offered by radical enlightenment and an urban society oriented towards consumption. By locating his defence of the Whig settlement in an ancient manor house, Addison takes his argument to Sir Roger de Coverley land, triangulating his bid for authority between the ghostly claims of the usurping Jacobites and the corrupt clamour of greedy men of fashion.

The Patriot Countryside

Addison's refusal to cede the symbolic ownership of the countryside to the Tory squires prefigures a crucial element in the country Whig position that valued the economic and political independence of the yeomanry and the landed gentry. As opposition to Walpole hardened, coalescing around the increasingly alienated figure of Prince Fredrick, theatrical critique of the Robinocracy was frequently couched in terms which celebrated rural life. Picking up on the romance trope of disguised gentility in Johnson's *Country Lasses*, George Lillo made his first foray into playwriting with *Silvia; or, The Country Burial* (1731), a ballad opera.[46] Although the production was not very successful, the template Lillo established would be developed by later dramatists such as Francis Waldron, author of *The Maid of Kent* (1778). *Silvia* uses its country setting to explore female oppression and plebeian ambition, developing Johnson's playful invocation of disproportionate marriage to raise sharper questions about the relations of virtue and birth.[47] Possibly drawing on a story by John Hughes published in *The Spectator* No. 375, the eponymous heroine is wooed by an avowed libertine, the good-natured Sir John Freeman, who wishes to set Silvia up as his mistress. When she refuses the proposal with disgust, he consoles himself with a village maiden called Lettice. Lettice's speeches reveal she is eager to avoid the dismal 'work, poverty and confinement' of a conventional marriage to another villager and she revels in her status as the temporary mistress of the manor (1.10.20). Silvia's father Welford becomes incensed when he discovers Sir John's perfidy and licentiousness but instead of taking physical revenge, as Silvia fears, he reveals the fact that Sir John is his own child and that Silvia is in fact the true heir to Freeman's estate. When Sir John displays true penitence, the way is cleared for the lovers to marry.

The play differs from urban comedies of intrigue or manners in which socially ambitious tricksters are unveiled and humiliated by providing a very clear rationale for the willingness of plebeian women to take wealthy lovers capable of removing them from lives of tedium and poverty. The eponymous 'country burial' of the subtitle is that of Lettice's mother Dolly, a woman genuinely mourned by her husband Timothy but characterized primarily by the other vicious village gossips as a shrew addicted to gin.

---

[46] James L. Steffensen (ed.), *The Dramatic Works of George Lillo*, including *Silvia*, ed. Richard Noble (Oxford: Clarendon, 1993). All quotations are from this edition and are cited in the text by act, scene and page numbers.

[47] Criticism on *Silvia* is sparse, but there is some discussion of the text's gender politics in Wolf Warner's 'Eighteenth-Century Sensibility and Its Ambivalent Position in the 'Herstory' of Gender Roles: Cibber's *The Careless Husband*; Lillo's *Silvia*; and Richardson's *Pamela*', in *Framing Women: Changing Frames of Representation from the Enlightenment to Postmodernism*, ed. Sandra Carroll, Birgit Pretzsch and Peter Wagner (Tübingen: Niemeyer, 2003), vi, 25–50.

Her unexpected return to life delights her husband but her alcoholism suggests to the audience just what desperate forms of self-oblivion Lettice is likely to pursue in the search for escape from her circumstances. Thoroughly resistant to marrying her suitor Ploughshare, after briefly revelling in her position as Freeman's mistress, Lettice is exposed to general condemnation. Sir John's previous conquest Betty takes a lesson from her rival's humiliation and decides to settle on marriage to a class-appropriate wooer called Jonathan. While she's at odds with the play's overt moral schema, it's hard not to sympathise with Lettice, for whom life as a labourer's wife would surely be as distinctly a 'country burial' as her mother's escape into alcoholic oblivion.

Silvia's unsentimental treatment of cross-class sexual exchange is matched by a similar clarity in its treatment of property. Relations between Sir John and all the other characters are inflected by their financial vulnerabilities. While the plebeian women see attachment to Sir John as a means to income and status, Welford, Silvia's yeoman father and a former soldier, is presented as relatively indifferent to his own economic fate. This independence of mind enables him to berate Sir John for his willingness to abandon his family estate to distant relatives, urging him to take responsibility for reproducing the social order presided over by the landed elite.

Radicalism in Arcadia

Plays about the countryside seem to appear in moments of crisis, often during years of impending or actual war. Writing from a complex perspective as a socially ascendant servant, Robert Dodsley, the poetic footman who became midcentury England's leading publisher, had an innovative rural play called *The King and the Miller of Mansfield* produced at Drury Lane in 1737. Dodsley came from an impoverished background, being apprenticed to a weaver before entering service in London, and his anger at the effects of social hierarchy are legible in his early poetry, which included such texts as *Servitude* (1729), *A Sketch of the Miseries of Poverty* (1731) and *The Muse in Livery* (1732).[48] Despite his criticism of social hierarchy, he was able to garner considerable aristocratic patronage for *The Muse in Livery* and Pope, who became a major patron, assisted by encouraging Rich to put on his first play, the very successful satirical farce *The Toy Shop* (1735). *The King and the Miller of Mansfield* also did extremely well,

---

[48] Solomon, *Rise of Robert Dodsley*, 120–125.

remaining in the repertory and encouraging Dodsley to produce a some-what less effective sequel set at court.

As a writer with a servile past, Dodsley both required and challenged traditional modes of patronage and cultural legitimation. He began his literary career at a moment when interest in unlearned talent was high and benefitted from the interest that Pope (himself unconventionally educated and from very middling circumstances) showed in such figures.[49] Under Pope's tutelage he rapidly became a player in the opposition conflict with the court, set up in deliberate competition with Stephan Duck, the thresher-poet patronized by the queen. In this game, Dodsley was cele-brated as an unlettered 'natural genius' whose untutored lucubrations happened to coincide with those of the opposition. But Dodsley was clearly well aware of the delicate cultural politics of his position and avoided being reduced to a poetic tool. He was extremely agile in man-oeuvring his way through the cultural terrain with integrity intact: although positioned as a rival, in his 'Epistle to Stephan Duck' he signals his respect for his peer. While *The Muse in Livery* as a whole was conceived of as an implicit challenge to Queen Caroline, the second poem was a tribute to her patronage of religious toleration. With Pope's assistance, Dodsley moved rapidly into the much safer and more lucrative business of bookselling but he also capitalized on his sudden celebrity to shape a career as a serious social critic whose analysis of England's political problems was considerably more radical than that of his opposition colleagues.

The King and the Miller of Mansfield is informed by the unusual perspective Dodsley brought to a consideration of proper governance. While Gay's 'Newgate pastoral' *The Beggar's Opera* suggested that 'great men' were indistinguishable from criminals, Dodsley's plays capitalize on his own humble backstory to power up the more traditional pastoral contrast between the supposed moral purity of the countryside and the court and city. But while the antithesis of court and country serves the critique of corruption, *The Miller* also functions as a panegyric to rural life and working people, in which the rustic locale and characters are deliber-ately expanded beyond their usual status as clownish if well-meaning foils for more intelligent and attractive gentry.

The 'Dramatick tale' is set in Sherwood Forest, itself a tribute by Dodsley to his native county, as he was born and bred in Mansfield, Nottinghamshire, a town located within the Forest. The action occurs during the Middle Ages, but while Sherwood Forest possesses strong

---

[49] Osborn, 'Spence, Natural Genius, and Pope', 123–137.

associations with popular resistance to tyranny through the Robin Hood legend, Dodsley chose to centre his action on Henry II. The choice did have implications for his critique of governance, however, as Henry was celebrated as a great administrative reformer, thus providing a pointed contrast with the widely despised George II. The plot turns on the trope of the disguised governor, familiar from its origins in the *Thousand and One Nights* through Chaucer and *Measure for Measure*. The king and his courtiers are lost in the woods, and after hearing a shot, Henry is taken into custody by the Miller, who also serves as a Keeper of the Forest. Henry decides to remain incognito and accepts the Miller's offer of hospitality. Another plot line is introduced when we learn that the Miller's son Dick, who has been absent in London, has lost his sweetheart to a wicked courtier called Lurewell, who has tricked and seduced his beloved Peggy. As the king is regaled with simple but hearty hospitality, he admires the Miller's integrity and wisdom. In the meantime, the other courtiers are rounded up by keepers and brought along to the Miller's on suspicion of poaching. On seeing Lurewell among them, Dick makes his accusation of deceit and seduction against him and the king's presence, now revealed, transforms the encounter into a trial. Henry is convinced by Dick's evidence and settles the matter by enjoining Lurewell to pay Peggy an annuity of three hundred pounds per annum. He knights the Miller and gives him a thousand marks.

An afterpiece, the 'tale' is happily anachronistic, as the king is initially shown disturbed by hearing a gunshot and Dick's satirical account of London includes attacks on the Royal Exchange, coffeehouses, Bedlam, theatre, opera and other metropolitan phenomena that characterized the contemporary but not the medieval capital. While the primary indictment is an attack on aristocratic corruption that articulates subaltern rage at sexual violence and exploitation, the invasion of a plebeian man's property through the predation of his potential partner, the play's inclusion of the king's voice allows for a top-down as well as a bottom-up perspective. Dodsley invokes the trope of the evil counsellor in characterizing the courtiers' self-interested advice to ignore Dick's complaints, thus using a folkloric register to make a very Bolingbrokian point about the need for a truly disinterested ruler – a Patriot King no less – able to unite all his disparate countrymen. The opposition discourse comes to a climax in the king's response to Lurewell, when the latter pleads that his rank should excuse his having to rectify matters by marrying Peggy:

> Your rank? My lord. Greatness that stoops to actions so base and low, deserts its rank, and pulls its honours down. What makes your lordship

great? Is it your gilded page and dress? Then put it on your meanest slave, for he's as great as you. Is it your riches or estate? A villain that should plunder you of all, would then be as great as you. No, my lord, he that acts greatly, is the truly great man. I therefore think you ought, in justice to marry her you thus have wronged.[50]

With the condemnation of 'greatness' being voiced by the king, the subversive edge of the speech is contained, although the attack on Walpole would have resonated. But the play is not only preoccupied with critical judgements on a predatory aristocracy. Dick, described by the king as a 'satirist', is a character with real force and agency: his relationship with Peggy is presented with much more pathos than is usual with servant amours and his judgements on both London and Lurewell stand without contradiction by his social superiors. In a remarkable attack on the falseness of great men, Dick tells his father that after several years of being 'tantaliz'd with hopes and expectations' he realized that 'so far from having it in his power to gain a place for me, that [the great man] has been all this while seeking a place for himself' (I.13). The conclusion Dick comes to is that if plain honesty is the recommendation a place seeker brings to court, 'I recommend you to become a footman, perhaps, but nothing further, indeed. If you look higher, you must arm yourself with other qualifications: You must learn to say ay, or no; to run, or stand; to fetch, or carry, jump over a stick at the word of command. You must be master of the arts of flattery, insinuation, dissimulation, and [Pointing to his palm] right application too, if you mean to succeed' (I.14).

Arguing that 'plain honesty' makes one fit only for a position as a footman, Dodsley undercuts the apparent meanness of that role by describing the courtier's 'qualifications' as even more servile, both physically and morally. The edge of this speech comes from Dodsley's knowledge that his audience would be aware of his own history as a servant: in placing great men below footmen, he amplifies the levelling challenge of his poetry. The challenge was noted by the numerous footmen in the upper galleries, who responded to *The King and the Miller* by becoming rowdier and more assertive during performances. The disturbances became so great, in fact, that on Monday, February 21, 1737, Westminster's magistrate read the Riot Act in an attempt to restore calm. But the overt displays of loyalty and the very distinct claims to yeoman virtue in *The King and the*

---

[50] Robert Dodsley, *The King and the Miller of Mansfield. A Dramatick Tale* (London: Printed for the Author at Tully's Head, 1737), 26. All quotations are from this edition and are cited in the text by act and page numbers.

Miller of Mansfield made it much harder to accuse the play of subversion than *The Beggar's Opera*. William Cooke reports that Sir John Fielding 'once told the late Hugh Kelly', on a successful run of *The Beggar's Opera* 'that he expected a fresh cargo of highwaymen in consequence at his office'; and upon Kelly's being surprised at this, Sir John assured him 'that ever since the first representation of this piece, there had been, on every successful run, a proportionate number of highwaymen brought to the office.'[51] But Dodsley retained Dick's caustic view of English politics: in his parodic *Chronicles of England* (1740), a riposte to Hervey's pro-ministry *Ancient and Modern Liberty* (1740), the lengthiest narrative is given over to Wat Tyler's rebellion. As Harry Solomon argues, the *Chronicle* differs from other opposition pamphlets that participate in this historiographic debate by characterizing 'George II as a symptom and kingship as the disease.'[52]

The King and the Miller of Mansfield had a theatrical existence well beyond its topical success in the mid-thirties, as it was performed in every year of Dodsley's life. Its enduring appeal surely lay in what a contemporary reviewer identified as 'a rural Simplicity ... which is excessively entertaining'[53] as well as its conformity to the canons of sentimental drama.[54] But the play's early capacity to provoke plebeian riot should disabuse us of the idea that sentimental plays necessarily contained rather than provoked radical protest, and remind us that opposition argument could be used to do more than deplore the regime of the great screen master. Dodsley's plays were the most culturally prominent reminder that the 'natural genius' that generated his extraordinary career was no respecter of a hierarchical social order.

Country Comic Opera

The next innovation in rural dramaturgy came in the penultimate year of the Seven Years' War, when Isaac Bickerstaff, the 'dramatic cobbler' who has scored an initial success with the patriotic *Thomas and Sally* (1761), reworked Charles Johnson's *Village Opera* (1729) as a comic opera. Johnson's text revisits the rural locale he created with such effect in *The Country Lasses*, setting the action in and around the estate of Sir Nicolas Wiseacre, a

---

[51] Cooke, *Memoirs of Charles Macklin*, 64. Cooke is emphatic about the ill effects on the 'lower orders' in watching the play and 'having [their] ambition whetted to rise in a superior style' (63).

[52] Solomon, *Rise of Robert Dodsley*, 86.

[53] *A View of the Edinburgh Theatre during the Summer Season, 1759* (London: A. Morley, 1760), 16.

[54] Solomon, *Rise of Robert Dodsley*, 55.

city merchant retired to the country who arbitrarily insists on his daughter Rosella's marriage with the son of his old friend Sir William Freeman.[55] Young Freeman is serving in the household as a gardener called Colin, having fallen in love with Rosella's chambermaid Betty, herself a gentlewoman in disguise and on the run from a forced marriage. The action is brought to a head by the plot hatched by two roguish footmen, Brush and File, for the former to impersonate Young Freeman and marry Rosella. Such tension as there is resides in the mutual attraction and uncertainty of the secretly genteel Betty and 'Colin', each troubled by their infatuation with a supposed social inferior. The nature of breeding is central to the play, with servants and gentlefolk using horticultural and livestock metaphors to define character and identity. Unsurprisingly, much of the language bestializes and commodifies the plebeian characters. In the third scene of the first act, we are shown a country 'mop' or fair at which servants present themselves to prospective employers. Lined up by sex in two rows to be inspected by their potential masters, the servants suggest nothing so much as the slave market depicted by Dryden in *Don Sebastian*, in which the hero of the comic subplot is assessed by a purchaser who talks about him as a jennet. The equine language used by Dryden recurs in *The Village Opera*, when two town gentlemen examine the young women for hire:

2ND GENT.   Hum! What pretty Filly is this?
1ST GENT.   Are you to be let or sold my beautiful little Pad?
2ND GENT.   She has an excellent Forehand.
1ST GENT.   Very well let down, and treads well upon her Pasterns. (1.3.20)

The young woman is vocal in her resentment of their verbal and physical abuse, which extends to the men, whom the gentlemen call 'the Beef and Pudding of the Land, well-manured' (1.3.20). Manure is a leitmotif – Margery, a girl rejected by her former lover Hobinol who is infatuated with Betty, tells him 'Thou art a piece of cold Clay, not to be enlivened by any manure' (2.4.41). By contrast with the demeaning language of soil, Betty says of Colin that 'there is Blood in him', and Lucas the gardener observes of his mistress Rosella that 'she looks to me to be a creature of a different make and kind, quite another species, from the noisy Squire (the disguised footman Brush) who is to be her husband' (3.1.58).

---

[55] Charles Johnson, *The Village Opera* (London: J. Watts, 1729). All quotations are from this edition and are cited in the text by act, scene and page numbers.

The language of cultivation, blood and breeding licensed by the rural setting, along with the structure of disguise, allows Johnson to question, before affirming, the naturalness of class distinctions. In an early conversation with the distracted Young Freeman, who has been neglecting his watering, the head gardener Lucas tells him, 'Come Colin, take thy Spade, turn the Gravel in yon Walk; prune those Nectarins, or roll the Terrace; don't let us idle away our lives like those Creatures they call Gentlefolks, who seem born only to eat, and drink, and sleep, and do nothing' (1.1.4). In a reversal of the usual rhetoric, Lucas here characterizes the gentry as bestial, idling their way through life in a purely sensual existence. The gardener's contrast between (gentry) being and (servant) doing establishes a broader implicit tension between the ownership of the estate and the labour required to maintain it. Young Freeman/Colin muses that his loving Betty is a folly, that he should reasonably be attached to Rosella, 'Daughter to Sir Nicholas Wiseacre, to whom all the Beeves, and Sheep, and Poultry, and Fields, and Men, and Women, round this Village, solely appertain; and to whom I ought to appertain' (1.1.3). While Colin/Young Freeman characterizes the entire community as an 'appurtenance' of Sir Nicholas, the closing sequence of the first act underlines the dependence of the estate owner on honest and productive servants, without whom there would be no beeves, sheep, poultry, fields or gardens. First the sightseeing two gentlemen meet an asset-stripping Steward and then the servants collectively celebrate their working identities in song. The Steward provides a succinct account of bad estate management, the antithesis of the country house ethos embodied in Addison's Vellum but reflective of the economic imperatives driving agricultural management:

> Why Sir, when any Gentleman is uneasy in his Affairs, I take his Estate into my Possession; I allow him a Pension out of it; I rack his Tennants, cheat his Creditors, steal his Timber, starve his Servants, and keep him constantly in Debt to me with his own Money, which I lend to him at 20% discount. (3.3.21)

By contrast, in the communal song and dance which closes the act, the servants proudly announce their particular expertise in the huge range of skills required to keep the estate running:

> I milk your cows, I clean your house,
> Your Linnen I wash, and I whiten.
> I plow and I mow; I reap and I sow,
> If your garden you take delight in,
> I prune and I plant ... (1.3.22)

The very fact that we are shown servants as labourers advertising their skills to a putatively diverse range of employers, rather than as members of a local tenantry, hints at a more dialectical relationship between master and servant than Colin seems able to imagine. The disturbance to his class prejudices created by his desire for Betty is ultimately resolved through the mutual uncovering of genteel birth, but the fact he shares his transgressive love for a chambermaid with almost all the young male villagers suggests commonalities of desire that are normally repressed by status hierarchy. It is suggestive that Sir Nicholas himself registers that Betty's effect on the estate is disruptive, interrupting as she does the usual sexual alliances that propel social reproduction among the labouring class villagers. Betty's toying with the male villagers seems as unpleasant in its way as the exchange between the maid for hire and the two gentlemen at the mop, a scene that highlights the exploitative nature of more conventional cross-class eroticism.

Like *The Country Lasses*, *The Village Opera* is intended to exhibit a model of the country estate but here the external threats to the rural utopia are even more limited. Making a last-minute satire on the 'Great', while begging for pity from a surprisingly merciful Sir Nicholas in the final scene, Brush compares himself and File to corrupt politicians:

> We are but the Mimicks,
> Of those vers'd in Chimicks,
> Who extract from the People their Riches;
> They empty their Pockets,
> While gaping at Blockheads
> For their Money, and are paid with fine Speeches. (3.2.64)

While primarily legible as a swipe at the Robinocracy, Brush's song actually indicts all parliamentarians, including members of the Opposition, supporters of the country party doing their political duty by sitting in the House. But Brush defends himself effectively by attacking mimicry, an easy scape-goat in a play wants to resolve itself by asserting the absolute nature of essential identities. Lucas's point about the gentry's uselessness is never really answered but it doesn't matter – only the labouring-class characters are interested in knowing what others can do – all the gentlefolk want to know is who they really are.

Planting Comic Opera

When Isaac Bickerstaff revised *The Village Opera* as *Love in a Village*, he retained the focus on the issue of disproportionate marriage characteristic of rural plays but addressed the perceived threat of unchecked local and national tyranny much more distinctly. The political dimension of the text has not been much discussed, although the huge success and importance of the production as the inaugural instance of comic opera as an English genre is acknowledged.[56] The sentimental, musical form Bickerstaff 'cobled' or 'tailored' together (the patronizing terms are contemporary) was to serve as a vehicle for popular reformism, as in Colman's *Inkle and Yarico*.[57] *Love in a Village* appeared in December 1762, at the end of a torrid year of success in war abroad and intense infighting among the political elite at home. By midsummer George III's favourite, the Scottish Lord Bute, was established as first minister, replacing Newcastle, who resigned in June. Bute was intensely unpopular among large swathes of the populace, and the radical opposition spearheaded by John Wilkes focused insistently on his family name (Stewart) in order to accuse him of absolutist quasi-Jacobite ambitions.[58] Although *Love in a Village* was praised for its 'simplicity and nature', the reviewer of the *St James Chronicle* noted disapprovingly, 'We are very sorry to see the spirit of party run so high, as to produce loud applause in the theatre, on Miss Brent's delivering the following words – "When Princes are oppressive in their government, subjects have a right to liberty"'.[59] The depth of anti-Bute/Scottish feeling was expressed at another performance of *Love in a Village* that James Boswell attended soon after his arrival in London. When two Highland officers came in just before the interval, fresh from duty in Havana, they were hissed and pelted with apples and shouts of 'No Scots' were heard: Boswell took it upon himself to save his national honour by leaping on the benches and shouting back.[60]

Anodyne as it might appear therefore, Bickerstaff's depiction of an English estate menaced by a tyrannical incomer was thoroughly topical. While reflecting Johnson's characterization of the cit turned squire Sir Nicholas, Bickerstaff's Justice Woodcock is shown extending his oppression beyond his daughter's marital choice to the community at large. Insensitive to local manners, he has to learn how to live in, rather than violently reshape, his habitus. Woodcock's authoritarianism can be read as

[56] See Peter A. Tasch, *The Dramatic Cobbler: The Life and Works of Isaac Bickerstaff* (Lewisburg, PA: Bucknell University Press, 1971), 43–65, for a useful overview of the initial production and reception. The opera equalled *The Beggar's Opera* in popularity, and a printed text went into eight editions within the year.

[57] Francis Gentleman called Bickerstaff a 'dramatic cobbler' (2, 470), and he was compared to a dramatic 'Taylor' in the *Theatrical Review* 1 (1771): 52–55, quoted in Tasch, *Dramatic Cobbler*, 58.

[58] Simms, *Three Victories and a Defeat*, 463–531.   [59] *St James Chronicle*, December 1762, 674.

[60] For a full account, see Ian McIntyre, *Garrick* (London: Allan Lane, 1999), 323.

an outsider's (Scot's) unfamiliarity with specifically English customs, manners and liberties. When his servant Hodge and his neighbour Hawthorne try to nudge him towards enjoying the fair for hiring servants, which Hodge describes as 'a nice shew', Woodcock responds contemptuously, threatening to close it down: 'No no, 'tis a very foolish piece of business; good for nothing but to promote idleness and the getting of bastards: but I shall take measures for preventing it another year, and I doubt whether I am not sufficiently authorized already: for by an act of parliament, *Anno, undecimo, Caroli primo,* which impowers a justice of the peace, who is lord of the manor –.'[61] Interrupted by Hawthorne, Woodcock is prevented from making further threats, but his invocation of legislation passed under Charles I underlines both his absolutist tendencies and his preference for formal law over local custom. The instructive contrast with Hawthorne continues when the two squires arrive at the fair. As he makes his way through the crowd, Woodcock announces, 'I'll put some of them in the stocks' and strikes a bystander. Hawthorne's disapproving response is telling:

HAW.   For shame, neighbor.

He then continues with a very pointed passage:

HAW.   Well, my lad, are you willing to serve the king?
COUNTRYMAN.   Why, can you list ma? Serve the king, master! No, no, I pay the king, that's enough for me, ho, ho, ho!
HAW.   Well said, sturdy-boots.
J. WOODCOCK.   Nay, if you talk to them, they'll answer you.
HAW.   I would have them do so, I like it that they should. (1.10.20)

The response to Hawthorne's query suggests the countryman shares the widespread popular hostility to Pitt's Militia Act (1757), believed by many to be 'yet another scheme' to force 'the poor . . . to defend the rich' and productive of severe rioting.[62] Hawthorne's question establishes his own patriotism but his good-humoured response to the countryman's riposte makes it clear he recognizes his interlocutor as a political subject with a right to his own opinions. The countryman's understanding of his relation with the monarch as contractual underlines both his independence of mind and his understanding of basic constitutional principle. The pleasure

---

[61] Isaac Bickerstaffe, *Love in a Village. A Comic Opera* (London: W. Griffin, 1763), 1.5.12. All other quotations are cited in the text by act, scene and page numbers.

[62] For a discussion of the militia in the context of popular imperialism, see Eliga H. Gould, *The Persistence of Empire: British Political Culture in the Age of the American Revolution* (Chapel Hill: University of North Carolina Press, 2000), 74.

that Hawthorne takes in the exchange, stressing as it does the depth of English liberty, distinguishes him from Woodcock, who talks of and treats his tenants with a violence that suggests feudal arrogance. The scene recalls that in Shadwell's *Bury-Fair*, when the false French Count La Roche is horrified by the physical resistance offered by a 'peasant' to an attack by a gentleman. The lesson here is a similar one: rank notwithstanding, all Englishmen are possessed of liberties discursively and in the disposition of their persons. The fair itself is a reminder of that, insofar as it offers the labourers not just the prospect of pleasure but the chance to enter a household away from their native village and its domineering estate owner. Woodcock's neighbour and informal mentor Hawthorne is one of Bickerstaff's most significant additions to Johnson's original text and his characterization sharpens the opera's political point. Covent Garden's manager John Beard took the role himself and the counterpoint between himself and Shuter as Woodcock was so successful that Zoffany painted several portraits of the two actors in role, one of which hangs at the National Theatre.[63] Hawthorne enters Woodcock's hall 'with a fowling piece in his hand, and a net with birds at his girdle' (1.5.10); a self-described sportsman, always up early, hunting and shooting, he is not wealthy but never sick. Unlike the booby hunter-squire presented in Mary Pix's *The Beau Defeated* (1706), Hawthorne is an embodiment of the country house ethos, humane, tolerant and shrewd, uninterested in the fashionable 'alterations' Woodcock is making to his estate by building a ha-ha and enclosing the park. Rather than trying to improve and profit from the landscape, Hawthorne responds to the countryside and its inhabitants in terms of its fertility and beauty; serially chucking servant girls under the chin, he exclaims, 'What health, what bloom! – This is nature's work; no art, no daubing' (1.10.21). His paternalistic pleasure in the young women's beauty is a contrast not only to the salacious manners of Johnson's two beaux in the same scene but also to Woodcock's hypocritical pursuit of Rosetta.

Woodcock is as blind to his daughter's desires as he is hypocritical about his own, and Bickerstaff uses Hawthorne to model benevolent management in regard to the family as well as the estate. Proper masculine assistance is requisite, the text suggests, because men are predatory. At the beginning of Act 2, Woodcock's daughter Lucinda compares women in love to Indians:

---

[63] See McIntyre, *Garrick*, 323.

> We women like weak Indians trade,
> Whose judgement, tinsel shew decoys:
> Dupes to our folly we are made,
> While artful man the gain enjoys: (2.1.26)

The similitude was noted and admired by Francis Gentleman, who remarked, 'her comparing women in love to weak Indians who barter intrinsic value for tinsel toys, conveys a sensible, instructive idea.'[64] While Lucinda's use of the topos underlines feminine/Indian vulnerability, her father's invocation of an Indian trope at the end of the scene works rather differently. Pretending he himself has no interest in 'romps' – the kind of sensual pleasure exemplified by the fair – Woodcock tries to stop Hawthorne's teasing questions about his meeting with Rosetta by announcing: 'I protest master *Hawthorne*, this is all *Indian*, all Cherokee language to me; I don't understand a word of it.' (2.9.43) By invoking Cherokee, Woodcock implies that Hawthorne's ribald observations are completely alien to his own civil identity, instances of a rustic preoccupation with sex that smacks of savagery.

For Bickerstaff's early audiences, however, the allusion would have done more than suggest a tired antithesis. In June 1762 a large party of Cherokee, led by a warrior called Ostenaco, arrived in Britain escorting the Virginian negotiator responsible for the treaty that ended the gruesome Anglo-Cherokee conflict of 1759–1761.[65] Capitalizing on the visit, Garrick put on a successful pantomime called *The Witches; or, Harlequin Cherokee* over the Christmas season. The highly visible role that Native Americans played in the Seven Years' War has led Troy Bickham to argue that from this visit forward, metropolitan Britons began to view Indians more pragmatically, as real actors in political and military conflicts, and less through the lens of noble (or ignoble) savagery.[66] Although it was well known that the Cherokees' interpreter had died at sea and communication was therefore limited, Woodcock's reference to Indian language would no longer simply signal incomprehension. The Cherokee presence confirmed the establishment of alliance, a community of interests overcoming manifest difference. He might claim ignorance of 'country matters', the untrammelled sensuality associated with rurality and the uncivil, but like the

---

[64] Francis Gentleman, *The Dramatic Censor; or, Critical Companion*, 2 vols. (London: J. Bell, 1770), 1:159.

[65] For astute commentary on this visit, see 'Ostenaco and the Losing of America', in Fullagar, *Savage Visit*, 88–109.

[66] Troy Bickham, *Savages within the Empire: Representations of American Indians in Eighteenth-Century Britain* (Oxford: Oxford University Press, 2005), 33, 67.

newly allied British and the Indians, Woodcock has been 'playing at romps'. His claim not to know Cherokee thus reveals itself as purely projective, a disavowal of lust onto the 'savage'.

This act's contrasting use of the Indian/Cherokee trope – signalling both the masculine exploitation of the feminine/indigene and masculine disavowal of such exploitation – gets plenty of rearticulation. Meditating on the cruelty shown by her servant admirer Hodge to his cast-off sweetheart Margery, Rosetta soliloquizes, 'The brutality of this fellow shocks me! – Oh man, man, – you are all alike. – A bumkin here, bred at the barn door! Had he been brought up at court, could he have been more fashionably vicious? Shew me the lord, "squire, colonel or captain of them all, that can out-do him" (2.12.51). Rather than acting Rosetta's patronizing advice to begin again as a 'good girl', however, Margery decides to take up the alternative option to marriage already presented by the fair by resolving to go to London to seek work:

> Air XXX
> Since Hodge proves ungrateful, no farther I'll seek,
> But go up to town in the wagon next week;
> A service in London is no such disgrace,
> And register's office will get me a place:
> Bet Blossom went there, and soon met with a friend,
> Folks say in her silks, she's now standing on end!
> Then why should I not the same maxim pursue?
> And better my fortune as other girls do. (2.13.52)

Citing the register office highlights the difference between Margery's work world in the countryside – where she is likely to be known by the limited range of local prospective employers – and the anonymity of London, governed by much more impersonal, bureaucratic processes. Her awareness that in 'town' she could re-create her identity and capitalize on her sexuality, rather than be shamed by it, underlines the conventional moral superiority of the countryside but leaves open the rather more subversive possibility that the city could allow Margery a 'better fortune'.

This scene, showing the resolution of Margery's fate through urban exile, is carefully placed just before the close of the second act, in which 'Daddy' Hawthorne (as he is known to Lucinda and Rosetta) brings news of the suitor who will resolve both their fortunes. The last line of the trio sung by Rosetta, Lucinda and Hawthorne underscores the difference from the genteel heroines and the open future awaiting Margery: 'Observe it ye fair in the choice of a mate; Remember 'tis wedlock determines your fate' (2.15.55). While this is emphatically the case for the upper-rank characters, Margery's decision may be potentially disastrous but (as is the case in Lillo's *Silvia)* taking your chances in town may well seem more attractive than a 'country burial'.

Although the recuperation of the country house ethos in *The Country Lasses, The Village Opera* and *Love in a Village* might seem profoundly conservative, these plays' topoi of genteel lovers disguised as servants provided a vehicle for exploring the possibility of disproportionate marriage, with all the implicit threat to traditional social hierarchy such relationships implied. In constructing *Pamela*, Richardson obviously found the rural scenarios of both *The Country Lasses* and *The Village Lovers* compelling because the country setting stresses the universality and 'naturalness' of human desire, highlighting the way attraction spreads beyond socially prescribed bounds. Although in *Love in a Village* Bickerstaff keeps the issue hypothetical, in Johnson's *The Country Lasses* Heartwell does in fact marry Flora, believing her to be a farmer's daughter. The disguise motif forces higher status lovers to perform identities in which they either love as or are wooed by servants. The confusion experienced by genteel lovers who believe they 'have fall[en] in love with a chambermaid!' (1.2.7), or who wish to 'hang the fellow for not being a gentleman' (1.3.7) have to consider the possibility that natural 'virtue' (like 'natural genius') might actually be found in the lower orders. Contemporary responses to the characters' dilemmas were sympathetic, with Gentleman writing that Rosetta's 'confession of her love for young Meadows, even in his servile condition, is ingenuous' (1, 167).

The disproportionate marriage plot had a long way to run on the English stage, with Bickerstaff returning to the topos in his very successful *Maid of the Mill* (1765), Kenrick's *The Lady of the Manor* and Waldron's *The Maid of Kent*, among others. Although most of these texts reveal the genteel (if impoverished) origins of their morganatic lovers, and tend therefore to suggest a conservative resolution of the social anxieties of which the plots are symptomatic, their very repetition suggests the need to reiterate an axiom under threat. While cities were conventionally understood to be locations in which identities could be refashioned and disguised, and status altered through new modes of accumulation and professional expertise, the country was by contrast assumed to demonstrate human hierarchy as natural, immemorial and unchanging. By pressing on the contradictions in ideas of 'nature' as both a universal and a guarantor of social distinction, however, low-born dramatists such as Johnson, Lillo and Bickerstaff all used the rural disproportionate marriage topos to open up the possibilities of cross-class social and sexual alliance, of relationships

pursued without reference to interest or wealth. As Miss Younger faux-
naively puts it in the Prologue to *The Country Lasses*, alluding to Congreve's intensely urban manners comedy in which love is most definitely
subject to negotiation, by contrast Johnson 'leads you to the Rural Scenes
to prove / The Country Bargain still is Love for Love' (n.p.).

Bickerstaff's success with *Love in a Village* was disturbing to David
Garrick, who found his own theatre eclipsed by the popularity of the
new mode. Attempting a riposte, Garrick commissioned a youthful
Charles Burney to produce an English version of Rousseau's huge hit *Le
Devin du Village* (1752) called *The Cunning Man* (1766). Despite its
impressive pedigree, *The Cunning Man* was not a success. It seems likely
that the failure arose from the adaptation's retention of Rousseau's very
simple, pro-pastoral fable, in which a restless shepherd and shepherdess are
convinced by the eponymous soothsayer to marry and stay in their native
village rather than seek an unknown destiny in the city. Garrick was
obviously drawn to the pastoral theme, which had been so central to
Bickerstaff's successful production, and Rousseau, whose *Social Contract*
was published in 1762 and who had taken refuge in England, was a well-
known and fashionable figure. But while *The Cunning Man* reiterated in
operatic form the Rousseauian conviction of the superiority of a retired
rural life, the mode of living most approximating savagery available to
contemporary Europeans, London audiences did not find the pastoral
entertaining.

Critics have suggested the contrast in the opera's continental success and
English failure arose from the simplicity of its fable and the unfamiliarity of
a pastoral form.[67] But the failure of *The Cunning Man* is not simply a
formal matter. English rural drama, whether comedy, arcadian interlude,
ballad or comic opera, was ideologically coded, its characters, plots and
motifs expressive of the most intense issues of patriotism, governance
and sexual and social identity. However fascinating English readers found
Rousseau's discursive denunciations of the extant social, political and
cultural order, his pastoral drama lacked the cross-class tensions and
specific political reference that characterized even as apparently placid a
text as *Love in a Village*.

---

[67] For a recent critique alert to Rousseau's treatment of gender in *Le Devin du Village*, see Rita
C. Manning, 'Rousseau's Other Woman: Colette in "Le Devin du Village"'. *Hypatia* 16.2 (Spring
2001): 27–42. For a useful introduction to the text and discussion of its English failure, see
Elizabeth Le Guin, 'Opera Review: Charles Burney and *The Cunning Man*', *Eighteenth-Century
Studies* 44.1 (Fall 2010): 113–116.

Celebrating the Remnants of 'Low Life'

In the first two decades of the eighteenth century, Farquhar and Johnson established contrasting templates for the depiction of rural England. Farquhar's vision may be genial to a degree but the countryside he shows in *The Recruiting Officer* is a specific place negotiating the pressures of economic and social change, not least of which is the human degradation involved in recruitment. But the concerns generated by impressment, enlistment and overseas war did not diminish: even Goldsmith's supremely genial *She Stoops to Conquer* (1773), the apotheosis of eighteenth-century rural drama, bears traces of anxieties about contemporary masculinity, imperial war and domestic oppression as it asserts the values of rural community against the incursion of polite and commercial culture. In Burgoyne's *The Lord of the Manor* (1781), the humiliated loser of Saratoga created a production whose radical attack on the Game Laws and recruitment practices registers a remarkable protest against those many who were wrongly excluded from the national estate.

Goldsmith's oeuvre is undergoing overdue reassessment in terms of his Irish origins and affiliations. Nigel Wood suggests that Goldsmith's experience of displacement shapes the melancholy rootlessness informing much of his writing, while Helen Burke has argued in detail that *She Stoops to Conquer* should be understood as a protest at the slow withering of the specifically Irish tradition of genteel hospitality.[68] The strength of Burke's argument arises from the detail with which she extrapolates the early account of the play's origin in an error committed by Goldsmith himself as a young man, when he himself mistook a private house for an inn. While the comedy may well have spoken to Irish audiences of disappearing lifeways, to English audiences the plot and characterization of *She Stoops to Conquer* would have been recognizable as an amalgam of earlier comedies.[69] Tony Lumpkin had antecedents in Humphrey Gubbin in Steele's *The Tender Husband* (1705), Jerry Blackmore in Wycherley's *The Plain Dealer* (1676) and Young Hartford in *The Lancashire Witches* (1681) among others, while the plot between the unwilling booby and the witty

---

[68] See Nigel Wood, 'Goldsmith's "English Malady"', *Studies in the Literary Imagination* 44.1 (Spring 2011): 63–85; and Helen Burke, '"Country Matters": Irish "Waggery" and the Irish and British Theatrical Traditions', in *Players, Playwrights, Playhouses: Investigating Performance 1660–1800*, ed. Michael Cordner and Peter Holland (London: Palgrave, 2007), 218–219.

[69] For a detailed account, see John Harrington Smith, 'Tony Lumpkin and the Country Booby Type in Antecedent English Comedy', *Publication of the Modern Language Association* 58.4 (December 1943): 1038–1049.

heroine to avoid marriage insisted on by a tyrannical maternal figure draws on both Shadwell's play, Cibber's *Woman's Wit; or, The Lady in Fashion* (1696) and the anonymous *The Lottery* (1728). Kate Hardcastle herself draws an analogy between the role she adopts and the part of Cherry, the landlord's daughter in Farquhar's *The Beaux Stratagem*, while Mr Hardcastle's nostalgic enthusiasm for the Duke of Marlborough's and Prince Eugene's campaigns is reminiscent of Judge Balance's attempts to engage Plume, hero of *The Recruiting Officer*, in similar discussions.

Burke's argument that this play of familiar fabular and characterological tropes also speaks a distinctly Irish lament leaves open the question of the comedy's meanings to other British spectators. James Evans argues persuasively that the contrast between Lumpkin and the London blades speaks to contemporary anxieties over masculinity, particularly noticeable in the discourse of macaronis, among whom Marlow despairingly enrols himself, on realizing how he has blundered with Kate.[70] While arguing that Marlow has to identify a form of manhood drawing on both the politesse of Hastings and Lumpkin's good humour, Evans draws attention to the series of defences Tony has received, identifying him as a 'natural man' whose artifice reflects critically on the apparently more sophisticated characters with whom he interacts – and oversets.[71]

There can be no doubt that Lumpkin was critical to the play's success, generating spin-offs such as John O'Keefe's eponymous farce *Tony Lumpkin in Town*, performed at the Haymarket Theatre Royal in June 1778. Bearing out the acuity of Evans's account, we read that appearing 'still more of a country savage than he is drawn by Dr Goldsmith', the *Universal Magazine* applauded Lumpkin's 'severe, but just, remarks on the modern macaronies'.[72] But Goldsmith's depiction of 'his own countrymen' offended William Woodfall, to whom the manners represented in *She Stoops to Conquer* were those of a distant date. Attacking Goldsmith's play as anachronistic, Woodfall argued,

> Our customs and manners have undergone a gradual alteration. A general correspondence arising from trade, and the progress of the arts, has brought the nation, as it were, together, and worn off those prepossessions and

[70] James Evans, '"The Dulissimo Maccaroni": Masculinities in *She Stoops to Conquer*', *Philological Quarterly* 90.1 (Winter 2011): 45–67.
[71] See Richard Bevis's *The Laughing Tradition: Stage Comedy in Garrick's Day* (Athens: University of Georgia Press, 1980), 80; Herbert F. Tucker Jr., 'Goldsmith's Comic Monster', *Studies in English Literature* 19 (1973): 493–494; and John Transgott, 'Heart and Mask and Genre in Sentimental Comedy', *Eighteenth-Century Life* 10 (1986): 137.
[72] *The Universal Magazine of Knowledge and Pleasure* 47 (June 1778): 367–368.

habits which made every little neighbourhood a separate community, and
marked every community with its peculiar character. The business of
comedy is therefore changed ... Some of our late writers have therefore
very judiciously had recourse to what is called *Sentimental Comedy*, as better
suited to the principles and manners of the age. A general politeness has
given a sameness to our external appearances; and great degrees of knowledge are every where diffused. An author therefore, has not that variety of
character, and that simplicity and ignorance to describe, which were the
capital ingredients in the old Comedy.[73]

Woodfall's hostility to *She Stoops to Conquer* arises from the play's representation of resistance to modernization, politeness, social uniformity and
the generic embodiment of those phenomena in sentimental comedy.
Structured by what Woodfall calls 'old Comedy' by Wycherley, Cibber,
Shadwell and Farquhar, the play asserts the value of traditional familial and
parochial relationships, questions the superiority of urban manners and
records the triumphant subversion of alien invasion by indigenous tactics
and knowledge. While Goldsmith's Irish affiliations provide one powerful
motivator for such comic revision, his lifelong sympathies for the victims
of oppression provide another. John H. Dussinger points out that he
began his literary career by translating Jean Merteille's *The Memoirs of a
Protestant, Condemned to the Gallies of France, for His Religion* (1758) and
followed this classic Enlightenment denunciation of religious persecution
with *The Life of Richard Nash* (1762), an account that suggests Nash
single-handedly created a coherent society out of Bath's diverse crowds
of genteel visitors, socially-aspirant bourgeois and all their impecunious
hangers-on and servitors. It seems likely that, as Dussinger argues, Goldsmith admired Nash's social and cultural creativity all the more because
(like Goldsmith himself) he had risen from relatively modest circumstances. Further, while Goldsmith did write for Smollett's Tory-inclined
Critical Review, his critical perspective on the disastrous effects of enclosure
and the growth of commerce is overt both in his remarks in *Lloyds Evening
Post* in 1762 and in *The Deserted Village* (1770), the latter published just
before he wrote *She Stoops to Conquer*. Although *The Deserted Village* was a
success, the critique of enclosure attracted negative commentary from
reviewers uncomfortable with the poet's hostility to 'improvement'.

    'The Revolution in Low Life' makes explicit Goldsmith's antipathy the
reduction of 'the laborious husbandsman', as 'lands are now either occupied by some general undertaker, or turned into enclosures destined for the

---

[73] *Monthly Review* 48, no. 7 (April 1778): 309–314.

purposes of amusement or luxury. Wherever the traveler turns, while he sees one part of the inhabitants of the country becoming immensely rich, he sees the other growing miserably poor, and the happy equality of condition now entirely removed'.[74] Goldsmith goes on to excoriate colonial trade and imperial expansion, complaining that such trade concentrates wealth in the hands of the few, so that 'Wherever we turn we shall find those governments that have pursued foreign commerce with too much assiduity at length becoming Aristocratical; and the immense property, thus necessarily acquired by some, has swallowed up the liberties of all. Venice, Genoa, and Holland, are little better at present than retreats for tyrants and prisons for slaves' (195). By contrast, the world being lost is one characterized by modest comfort and sociable commerce: 'I spent part of the last summer in a little village, distant about fifty miles from town, consisting of near an hundred houses. Though strangers to opulence, they were unacquainted with distress; few of them were known either to acquire a fortune or die in indigence. By a long intercourse and frequent intermarriages they were all become in a manner one family; and, when the work of the day was done, spent the night agreeably in one another's houses.' (195)

    She Stoops to Conquer performs the triumph of a just such a rural 'race of men' over the vertical invaders from London. We have already noted that *She Stoops to Conquer* draws on antecedent rural comedies whose plots are structured by the gulling of self-confident urbanites, with Tony Lumpkin's basic strategy of misdirection shaping an action within which Kate Hard-castle also improvises successfully to secure her chosen partner. Lumpkin's dominion over the plot is endangered by his partial illiteracy, but like Kate's, his improvisatory skills enable him to resolve his aunt's discovery of his duplicity and he successfully sets up a new and conclusive line of action. It is striking that at both moments Lumpkin takes incisive action, his tactics depend very precisely on local knowledge. In Act 1, Scene 2 in the alehouse, Tony commands the space into which the London travellers enter. He 'sits at the head of the Table, a little higher than the rest: A mallet in his hand': the 'mob' address him as Squire and applaud his performances; they depart when he tells them to go and the Landlord follows his lead in misdirecting Marlow and Hastings.[75] Responding to the

[74] Oliver Goldsmith, 'The Revolution in Low Life', in *The Collected Works of Oliver Goldsmith*, 5 vols., ed. Authur Friedman (Oxford: Clarendon, 1966), 3:195. Other quotations are cited in the text by page number.

[75] Oliver Goldsmith, *She Stoops to Conquer; or, The Mistakes of a Night*, in Friedman, *Collected Works of Oliver Goldsmith*, I.ii.4–5. All quotations are from this edition and are cited in the text by act, scene, line and page numbers.

latter's request for guidance, Lumpkin provides 'directions' of such length, complexity and threat – 'a damn'd long, dark, boggy, dirty, dangerous way' (1.2.17, 116) – that the Londoners are easily gulled into deciding to put up at what he spontaneously identifies as 'the old Buck's head' (1.2.12, 123), his stepfather's house renamed as an inn. When the scenario he has established seems to be unravelling, Lumpkin again deploys a specifically chorographical tactic to redirect the action when, at the end of the fourth act, he conceives of leading Mrs Hardcastle and her niece not forward forty miles to 'her old aunt Pedigree' (4.1.26, 191), but instead round and round their own neighbourhood. Off they go, 'down Feather-bed-lane ... crack over the stones of Up-and-down Hill' before he introduces them 'to the gibbet on Heavy-tree Heath, and from that, with a circumbendibus ... fairly lodged them in the horsepond at the bottom of the garden' (5.12.15–20, 203).

Lumpkin's final decisive action is enabled by his stepfather's belated admission that he is of age. In the speech he makes that formally resolves the plot, spatial identity is again highlighted: 'Then you'll see the first use I'll make of my liberty (taking miss Neville's hand). Witness all men by these presents, that I, Anthony Lumpkin, Esquire, of BLANK place, refuse you, Constantia Neville, spinster, of no place at all, for my true and lawful wife' (5.2.21–24, 215). Treading in his own father's footsteps, and more like his stepfather than either might be willing to admit, Lumpkin's identity is governed by his intense affiliation with his place and the customary habits and relations of what Woodward so disparagingly calls a 'little neighbourhood ... with its peculiar character'. Although despised by the other gentry, Lumpkin is admired and recognized by his inferiors as a chip off the old block: Old Squire Lumpkin 'kept the best horses, dogs and girls in the whole county' (1.2.15, 118) and in that, says the Second Fellow, '[Tony Lumpkin] takes after his own father' (1.2.11, 118). His lack of education in an institution at a distance with his peers has prevented his socialization into a gallant along the lines of Marlow or Hastings but not prevented his ability to command local respect and sociability.

Although Mr Hardcastle is presented as a model patriarch whose daughter (unlike Tony) is a credit to her parent, there are distinct parallels between Lumpkin and his stepfather. At the beginning of Act 2, Hardcastle attempts to instruct Diggory and his fellow servants, just removed from the barn and plough, in the art of proper service. The fundamental problem is to prevent the servants from feeling themselves to be 'part of the company' (2.1.22, 126) because clearly they are habituated to eating, drinking, talking and laughing with their master. They are part of

Hardcastle's 'family' in the broad sense delineated by Naomi Tadmor, a community that included servants as well as blood relatives.[76] The informality of the authority that Hardcastle extends over his manor is underscored again when he tells Marlow and Hastings that 'Half the differences of the parish are adjusted in this very parlour'(2.1.9, 135), suggesting a judicial regime whose ease reflects the extended family culture Goldsmith extolls in 'The Revolution in Low Life'.

Like Lumpkin, Hardcastle shares space in good fellowship, eating, drinking and making merry with his social inferiors. His servants laugh companionably at his old jokes, display a sense of ownership over his anecdotes and will doubtless partake of the celebratory supper their master announces at the end of the play, when 'we shall gather all the poor of the parish about us, and the Mistakes of the Night shall be crowned with a merry morning' (5.2.21–22, 216). The discursive and spatial intimacy with labouring-class characters displayed by both Lumpkin and Hardcastle stands in contrast to the way Marlow and Hastings treat servants; for the latter, all intercourse with the lower orders is mediated entirely by monetary exchange, and this assumption not only produces misrecognition but underscores the arrogance of the putatively genteel and polite. Marlow's confidence with labouring-class women depends on his assurance that the relationship is mercenary: both young men find Hardcastle's attempts to converse with them about matters of public interest ludicrous precisely because they regard such issues as beyond his preserve as an innkeeper, with whom their relationship is solely one of financial patronage. By having the young men misread Hardcastle in this way, Goldsmith invokes the recent highly charged controversy over vails, or fees paid to servants by visitors to aristocratic households. Gillian Russell notes that the practice of vail giving was most fiercely resisted by those living in the provinces, arguing that paying for meals or hospitality was particularly offensive to the newly established canons of sociability generated by Enlightenment culture.[77] Goldsmith's fundamental conceit – that a private gentleman's house might be mistaken for a public house – literalizes the anxiety articulated in the vails dispute, as a space putatively created for sociable commerce is entirely subsumed by economic exchange.

---

[76] Naomi Tadmor, *Family and Friends in Eighteenth-Century England: Household, Kinship and Patronage* (Cambridge: Cambridge University Press, 2001).

[77] Gillian Russell, '"Keeping Place": Servants, Theater and Sociability in Mid-Eighteenth-Century Britain', *The Eighteenth-Century: Theory and Interpretation* 42.1 (2001): 21–42.

She Stoops to Conquer suggests that such misrecognition and a concomitant disrespect for indigenes and 'the low' are the primary 'Mistakes of the Night'. Tony Lumpkin's repeated characterization as a monster – largely by his mother – sharpens this issue. Mrs Hardcastle is the most venal and foolish of the gentry characters, and the most invested in urban fashionability, undercutting the force of her judgement, especially in a context in which she clearly sees the notorious 'Ladies Club' as a social ideal. Lumpkin is described variously as a 'pretty monster' (1.1.7, 115), 'a good-natur'd creature' (1.2.25, 115), 'an awkward booby' (1.2.10, 121) and an 'unfeeling monster' (2.1.13, 154). The most virulent denunciation comes from the alehouse landlord, who calls him a 'damn'd mischievous son of a whore' (1.2.1–2, 125). Lumpkin's monstrosity, his alliance with the 'mob', his local knowledge, his occluded inheritance and his subversive plotting all suggest an affinity with Caliban, the archetypal dramatic indigene, excoriated and exploited by intrusive and domineering foreigners.

Two contemporary political references in the play strengthen the implicit critique of metropolitan and elite presumption and values. During the initial, cross-purposed conversation between Marlow, Hastings and Hardcastle, the latter explains that he has lost interest in politics, ever since 'our betters hit on the expedient of electing each other' (2.1.16–17, 134) and that while there was a time when he fretted over government 'but finding myself every day grow more angry, and the government growing no better, I left it to mend itself. Since that, I no more trouble my head about *Hyder Ali*, or *Ally Cawn*, than about *Ally Croaker*' (2.1.24–26, 134 and 2.1.1, 135). Hyder Ali was a highly effective opponent of the East India Company, whose affairs were being negatively ventilated in these years by Alexander Dow and others: Muhammed Ali Khan was a considerably less effective ruler allied with the British.[78] Hardcastle's identification of himself as an inferior deprived of a voice and interest in political discourse suggests his withdrawal from the larger national project of imperial expansion to an identity secured by the bounds of his parish. Described by his wife as 'Gothic' and a 'piece of antiquity', his favourite stories concern the glory days in which the Revolution Settlement was being secured from James II and Europe was defending itself against the Turks, rather than an era in which the British were themselves acting as the agents of oppression in South Asia. In distancing himself from the campaigns against Hyder Ali,

---

[78] See Lewin Bowring, *Haidar Ali and Tipu Sultan, and the Struggle with the Musalman Powers of the South* (Oxford: Clarendon, 1999); and Kate Brittlebank, *Tipu Sultan's Quest for Legitimacy* (Delhi: Oxford University Press, 1999).

Hardcastle echoes the distaste expressed in 'The Revolution in Low Life', where Goldsmith abjures colonial trade and power – 'Let others felicitate their country upon the increase of foreign commerce and the extension of our foreign conquests; but for my part, this new introduction of wealth gives me but very little satisfaction' (197). Those who are most invested in the fruits of colonial trade are Mrs Hardcastle, Miss Neville and Hastings because Miss Neville's fortune consists in jewels inherited from her uncle, 'the India Director' (2.1.12, 141). Unsurprisingly, the character most in thrall to urban culture, Mrs Hardcastle, is also the person with the greatest attachment to the morally dubious stones.

The play's gentle but pointed commitment to personal and political liberty is equally legible when Hastings is trying to persuade Miss Neville to elope to France, where, he says 'even among slaves the laws of marriage are respected' (2.1.7–8, 141). Referring here to the absolutism of France rather than chattel slavery, Hastings's remark alludes critically to the recent unpopular Royal Marriage Act, which prevented members of the royal family from making private marriages.[79] Here the rural plays' extensive exploration of 'unequal' marriages is identified with the conflict between feeling and interest that shaped and distorted the lives of even the most privileged. As the *Public Advertiser* (March 25, 1772) put it, 'The Royal Marriage Bill has now passed our *Most Faithful Commons* . . . ; so that every Descendant of our now more-than-ever-to-be-lamented Sovereign George the Second is in Vassalage and Slavery; and the Kings of this limited Monarchy are erected into Family Tyrants, to trample upon the Laws of Nature and Religion'. Hastings's remark suggests that a nation in which landed estate owners such as Hardcastle feel disenfranchised is on the way to becoming as oppressive as that of the great Catholic rival.

Although the parochial relations depicted by Goldsmith are intimate, they remain hierarchical. But the Epilogue to *She Stoops to Conquer* provides a final rather more ambiguous salute to the freedoms imagined and explored in rural comedy. Delivered by Mrs Bulkely, who played Kate Hardcastle, the verses recount the five acts of a barmaid's progress, from a first appearance as a simple country maid, through a position in a country inn, to one in a London chop house, followed by genteel marriage and an old age spent playing at cards. Rather than describing the kind of

---

[79] The account of the first production in *The Morning Chronicle*, March 16, 1773, records that when the Duke of Gloucester (who had married privately) entered the house he was received with 'great shouts of approbation. In one part of the play Hastings says to Miss Nevill – 'We'll go to France, for there even among slaves marriage is respected'. This the audience thought applicable to the royal Duke's situation, and marked their respect for him be a very particular plaudit'.

catastrophic decline towards a guilty and penurious death narrativized by Hogarth in *A Harlot's Progress* (1732), the Epilogue suggests that the restless female characters of *Sylvia* and *The Village Lovers* who decide to seek their fortune in London might indeed find a prosperous escape from country burial through marriage up the social scale.

The Lord of the Manor

In a now familiar pattern, the next major imperial crisis and its accompanying military conflict again saw rural drama centre stage. Gillian Russell and Daniel O'Quinn have both recently analysed the considerable success enjoyed by General John Burgoyne's dramatic reiteration of the *fete champetre* created for Lord Stanley's engagement celebrations at the Oaks, Epsom, as *The Maid of the Oaks.* Russell's commanding account describes the fete as an assertion of aristocratic, patriarchal authority in the context of scandalous publicity around noblewomen and its reiteration under Garrick's patronage at Drury Lane as the granting of cultural legitimacy over a new mode of multi-authored performance in the theatre. She argues, however, that Garrick's attempt to 'emulate and exceed' the theatricality of fashionable sociability was troubled by *The Maid of the Oaks'* dependence for its success on Frances Abington, with whom the play was strongly identified.[80] Daniel O'Quinn argues that *The Maid of the Oaks* attempted to generate a fantasy of imperial election through its regulation of sexual and martial masculinity, a hedging against increasing anxieties that would collapse with imperial failure in the American War.[81]

The *Lord of the Manor* was written and produced after Burgoyne's defeat at Saratoga, a personal and national disaster from which (he suggests in his lengthy Preface) the composition of the comedy was a much-needed distraction. The second sentence of the Preface addresses his concern that his anonymous authorship of the text has meant 'criticism has extended from poetical to political principles, and made a vehicle for party reflections upon persons who never saw a line of his writing.'[82] Stressing the play's primary function was innocent entertainment, he writes 'that these scenes were written for mere amusement — to relax a mind that had been

---

[80] Russell, *Women, Sociability and Theatre*, 141–152.
[81] Daniel O'Quinn, *Entertaining Crisis in the Atlantic Imperium 1770–1790* (Baltimore: Johns Hopkins University Press, 2011), 43–89.
[82] John Burgoyne, *The Lord of the Manor. A Comic Opera* (Dublin: H. Chamberlaine, 1781), Preface, iii. All other quotations are from this edition and are cited in the text by act, scene and page numbers.

engaged in more intense application', presumably the composition of his self-exculpatory *A State of the Expedition from Canada* (1780). Robert Jones has recently demonstrated just how doggedly (if unsuccessfully) Burgoyne worked at freeing himself from the obloquy that followed his American catastrophe, in letters home, in parliamentary speeches and in self-justificatory publications. Jones places particular stress on Burgoyne's high-risk decision to deploy both the language of honour and virtuous service and the discourse of sentiment in this endeavour, demanding from his auditors/readers both acclaim and pity. The fact that both pro-ministerial writers and radicals rejected his claims of honourable suffering suggests how carefully the proper bounds of masculinity were policed, to secure martial virtue from what was viewed as rash and dishonourable pretence.[83]

While Jones's focuses primarily on the construction and reception of Burgoyne's character and reputation as an illuminating limit-case of honourable masculinity, O'Quinn is more concerned with the mediation at work in the print reception of theatrical, aristocratic and popular entertainments which 'diverted' Londoners in the years around the American War. For O'Quinn, martial masculinity is also a central issue in the culture of these years but his analysis of imperial subjectivities is produced through examining the dense textual networks that shaped new kinds of genre, performances, productions and spectators. O'Quinn's emphasis on the 'diverting' quality of wartime entertainment is suggestive in the context of Burgoyne's later career, in which he was marginalized professionally and politically but increased in stature as a dramatist, with *The Heiress* an immediate hit which remained in the repertory through the nineteenth century. Articulating a commonly held view, one critic remarked that '*The Heiress* and General Burgoyne, the Author, may rejoice; if he proceeds as much as he has done, advancing as much beyond his *Lord of the Manor* as that was beyond his *Maid of the Oaks* he will rejoice not without good reason.'[84] Ironically, given Burgoyne's anxieties over his reputation, *The Heiress* was compared favourably to comedies by Sheridan and Foote as a depiction of high life written by a social insider.

Jones's and O'Quinn's arguments suggest that although conceived of as a personal and public distraction from the agonies of martial failure, *The*

---

[83] Robert W. Jones, *Literature, Gender and Politics in Britain during the War for America* (Cambridge: Cambridge University Press, 2012), 84–118.

[84] The Enthoven Collection, Victoria and Albert Museum, quoted in Gerald Howson, *Burgoyne of Saratoga* (New York: Times Books, 1978), 324, 284.

Lord of the Manor functioned as a justification and recuperation of elite British masculinity. Burgoyne certainly faced an immense challenge in his attempts at vindication. In *The New Maid of the Oaks* (1778), a satire written by radical Newcastle minister James Murray, Burgoyne is depicted as a stupid and brutalized Hamlet who actively encourages 'Brave Bear', an Indian ally, to scalp and massacre unfortunate American innocents. Murray's play was never performed but circulated in print and highlights one of the chief accusations against Burgoyne. Jane McCrea's death at the hands of an Ottawan ally served as a critical means of propaganda for the rebel cause in America and was an effective rhetorical tool for the radical opposition within Britain. Murray's play is particularly interesting for the way in which it heightens the contradictions in ministerial positions and patriotic dogma generally. In the final act, the rebel leader Horatius asks a series of questions central to radical concerns:

> Is English liberty confin'd to English ground,
> And not the Englishman? Happy soil indeed
> Has Heav'n curs'd all the globe, but that small spot,
> With bondage, and consign'd all mankind
> To slav'ry, except the tenants of a *wrat*,
> A *mole-hill*, scarcely visible to the moon? (III)

Horatius's queries put pressure on the assumption that British liberties are in fact cognate with the literal ground and earth of the British Isles. As we have seen, a central function of rural dramas from 1688 on is to reiterate the rootedness of political rights and liberties in the English countryside, the environment in which they are purportedly most ideally enshrined in the hierarchical but harmonious estate and its village. Without exception, rural comedies depict threats to the English heartland ranging from cits, Catholics, the French and the Pretenders to nabobs being successfully repelled. At the same time, however, the presence of the army in rural drama rehearses but does not necessarily disperse the anxiety generated by overseas wars, with their ceaseless demands for men and money. Further, for all the geniality of the relationship Farquhar establishes between Balance and Plume, audiences were well aware that relations between the magistracy and the army were frequently extremely tense. In a society without a police force and a long-standing loathing of a standing military force, the necessary dependence of law officers on the soldiery in times of civil emergency – the frequent outbreaks of riot – bred suspicion and resentment. For many army officers, most of whom hated riot duty, the

American War was the dreadful logical extension of their role in suppressing outbreaks of civil protest and direct action against high prices for food, enclosures, turnpikes and political repression. Tony Heyter argues that these were frequently causes with which magistrates and soldiers were in sympathy.[85]

Horatius's claim that English rights should be detached from their insignificant insular origins and recognized as a common human property cuts through the Gordian knot of ancient constitutionalism by deterritorializing liberty. Although the invocation of English identity might seem to ethnicize rights, his speech goes on to suggest freedom is a universal human inheritance, the proper claim of 'all mankind'. By locating the play so distinctly in Saratoga, where the scalping follows a village wedding 'wake' reminiscent of the country dances in other rural plays, Murray establishes the American loyalist world as fully parallel to England before showing it invaded by the most extreme savagery. But because Brave Bear is acting so clearly on Tullius's (Burgoyne's) orders, rather than underlining American difference, Celia's (Jane McCrea's) scalping suggests the incorporation of barbaric violence within Britain itself.

Burgoyne's apparent willingness to license savage violence by his Native American allies made his character a litmus test for the wider culture's tolerance of such practices, and as Robert Jones demonstrates, both radicals and pro-ministry writers were not slow to condemn his apparent sponsorship of cruelty.[86] In *The Lord of the Manor*, therefore, Burgoyne's Preface suggests he has tried to distract his audience from his infamy through an unimpeachably moral and humorous performance of that peculiarly English form, the comic opera. Nonetheless, his protests at the extensive critical reading of the play as party political generally and hostile to recruitment in particular seem disingenuous. While denouncing the notion that he 'introduced the character of Captain Trepan, for the purpose of impeding the recruiting service of the army' (iv), he announces that 'they who think the fallacies and frauds of receiving dealers about this town necessary evils, which ought to be connived at, as contributory to the military strength of the nation, are ignorant of facts, or blind to consequences' (v). As we shall see, not just recruitment and impressment but the Game Laws are directly addressed by a dramatist who seems determined to

---

[85] See Tony Heyter, *The Army and the Crowd in Mid-Georgian England* (London: Macmillan, 1978), 3–4 on policing duty. Stressing the perhaps counterintuitive degree of tolerance towards crowds, Heyter reports cases where both magistrates and officers were tried after killing rioters (32).

[86] Jones, *Literature, Gender and Politics*, 113.

align himself with a reformist and liberal agenda in the service of a continuing campaign of self-exculpation.

In *The Lord of the Manor* Burgoyne uses the venerable trope of manorial reform as a way to figure personal, national and imperial corruption and renewal. The family of a disinherited older son called Rashly is endangered by the change of ownership of the estate called Castle Manor where they live on a small farm. The new owner's son is a 'sportsman of fashion', a monstrous mixture of brutality and Francophile rakery called Young Contrast. Irritated by Rashly's lack of deference and assertion of his rights to hunt, Contrast and his valet La Nippe plan 'the father to jail; the lover to sea; my pointers, if you will, in Rashly's chamber; and his daughter in exchange in mine' (2.1.28). To Young Contrast, 'The game laws and the press act ought always to go hand in hand – and, were they properly enforced, the constitution might be more bearable to a man of fashion' (2.1.27). Young Contrast's plans are foiled by the ingenuity of Peggy, Sophia Rashly's maid; by the domineering camp follower Moll Flagon, who subdues Young Contrast when he's taken up as a deserter; and by Old Contrast's seduction by the innocent virtue of his (unknown) grand-daughters, Sophia and Annette Rashley. All the virtuous male characters are devised to display a certain rashness and obduracy, with Old Contrast, Rashly his son and Sophia's lover Trumore presented as men of hasty feeling, precipitate action and integrity. Their misjudgements and stub-bornness produce conflict and loss but all is eventually righted by a combination of plebeian female cunning and masculine sensibility. At the same time, every negative trope of masculine political, social and sexual tyranny and cruelty is concentrated in Young Contrast, a figure who resents the fashionability of the military, for as he says, 'the cockade predominates – the times have set ninetenths of our men of fashion upon being their own soldiers' (1.2.14). For all the satire on recruitment in Trepan's depiction, the opera closes by endorsing military service when Sophia's lover Trumore reiterates his intention to enlist.

While the plebeian women are important to the intrigue of *The Lord of the Manor*, the gentry ingenues serve simply as contrasting types of female attraction who draw out contrasting masculine responses of predation and protection. *The Lord of the Manor* is preoccupied by the crisis in martial masculinity embodied by Burgoyne himself – an indignant failure calling equally for praise and pity – and the associated problems that failure in the American War created in governance more generally. Questions of justice, policy and administration are played out in the opera through the two issues of hunting and recruitment, each of which tested notions of the law and honour. Each had complex associations by 1780. Many traditional blood sports such as cock fighting and bull baiting were outlawed during the Interregnum and hostility to such diversions (including hunting) was often associated with religious dissent. Fox hunting with hounds, so central to the image of the booby squire, became formalized only in the late seventeenth century but gained in popularity all through the period.[87] Several important Enlightenment figures including Locke, Voltaire and Rousseau were more or less hostile to cruelty to animals and in characterizing her booby squire in *The Beau Defeated* as a fanatic hunter, Mary Pix signalled his blindness to the attractions of sex and society.[88] In addition to the lingering associations of religious heterodoxy, hostility to the chase was mobilized in political critique, albeit from varied perspectives. Pope and Thomson attack hunting (in *Windsor Forest* [1736] and *The Seasons* [1726–1730]), associating the chase with Williamite and Hanoverian cruelty and tyranny, respectively.[89] Apparently responsive to the nascent sympathy for animals, Burgoyne was to join Sheridan in founding a Society for the Encouragement of Ancient Games, intended to foster interest in alternatives to the cruelties of bear baiting, dog fighting and hunting.[90]

As the extensive commentary on the Black Act of 1723 has shown, however, the Game Laws were also a central cause of conflict between rural plebeians, yeomen and gentry.[91] While there is evidence to suggest a Jacobite dimension to black violation of the prohibitions against poaching, the restrictions on labouring class access to game were a persistent source of confrontations between labouring-class people and gentry through the eighteenth century, although some of the latter were sympathetic to the need for reform. Using poaching as a test of estate management and political sensibility, the second scene of the first act of *The Lord of the Manor* highlights the conflict. When Young Contrast enters, furious that 'The manors are poached to desolation' (1.2.11) and complaining that in spite of his parasol he is becoming scorched as 'Mulatto in grain' (1.2.12), he hands his gun to one of his attendants and reels off a frightening series of orders: 'Searchem, get warrants immediately for seizing guns, nets, and snares, let every dog in the parish be collected for hanging tomorrow

[87] See Robert J. Malcolson, *Popular Recreations in English Society, 1700–1850* (Cambridge: Cambridge University Press, 1979), 89–119.
[88] See Raymond Girard, *Rousseau and Voltaire: The Enlightenment and Animal Rights* (Stanford, CA: Stanford University Press, 1985).
[89] See Williams, *Poetry and the Creation of a Whig Literary Culture,* 165–169.
[90] Howson, *Burgoyne of Saratoga,* 248.   [91] See Thompson, *Whigs and Hunters.*

morning – give them a taste of Norfolk discipline.' (1.2.12) Rashley intervenes, querying the wisdom of this brutal procedure and when explaining who he is, cites the country house ethos: '[I am] a tenant upon this estate these sixteen years, where I have been used to see harmony between high and low established upon the best basis – Protection without pride and respect without servility.' (1.2.12) Having established himself as a kind of creole, Young Contrast continues by querying whether Rashly is qualified to carry a gun. Rashly responds not by citing his property qualifications but by provocatively asserting a national, even a universal right to bear arms 'In my birth-right as a free-man – Nature gave the birds of the air in common to us all; and I think it no crime to pursue them, when my heart tells me I am ready, if called upon, to exercise that same gun against the enemies of my king and country.' (1.2.12) Rashley's assertion marries a radical protest against the Game Laws to an enunciation of patriotic loyalty, highlighting the difference from Contrast's despotic insistence that he requires 'unconditional submission in my supremacy of the game' (1.2.12). In a further exchange censored by the Examiner of Plays but restored in the printed text, Rashly describes the Game Laws as 'modern and unnatural excrescences, which have grown and strengthened by insensible degrees, till they lie upon the statute book like a wen upon a fair-proportioned body' (1.2.13). Young Contrast replies (in another speech expunged from performance) that 'Tho' our system be excellent for the preservation of game, it still wants a little foreign enforcement – in France the insignia of a lord Paramount of the chase are gallows with his arms upon every hill in his estate – they embellish the prospect better than the finest clump Brown ever planted.' (1.2.13)

Burgoyne's characterization of Rashly figures him as a patriotic and liberal in his sympathies but misrecognized as a potential criminal, in danger of wrongful imprisonment while his accuser is an arbitrary usurper, deeply un-English in his effeminacy and tyranny. Burgoyne's implicit self-justification continues in the third act, in which recruitment rather than the Game Laws is the focus of the analysis of good local governance. The act is notable for the satiric treatment of the recruiting officer, Captain Trepan, who describes himself as 'a manufacturer of honour and glory – vulgarly call'd a recruiting dealer – or more vulgar still, a skin merchant' (3.2.38). His manipulative use of verbal and visual advertising, gold, brandy, deceptive promises of new uniforms and arms and a decoy duck dummy recruit are all exhibited with cheerful gusto to the horrified Rental, Steward of Castle Manor. Rental's distaste for Trepan's practices is seconded by Sir John Contrast, new owner of the estate, Justice of the

Peace and therefore responsible for signing off on the new recruits. In the last scene, set in 'A large Gothic Hall' (3.4.48), Sir John expresses his distaste for attesting the men 'but no more of your occupation – I'm not for purchasing human flesh' (3.4.48). Sir John's characterization of recruitment as the purchase of human flesh by a 'skin merchant' sets up the clearest possible analogy with the slave trade, itself becoming increasingly a target of odium in these years. Sir John's judicial powers are then further tested by his younger son being brought in to be tried for desertion. Fittingly, Young Contrast was mistaken by Sergeant Crimp as a deserter 'with the best legs in England' (3.4.49) – legs which the audience knows to be the product of padding. Once 'enlisted', Young Contrast has been handed over to the camp follower Moll Flagon, who promises to 'make a soldier and a husband of him' (3.2.45), neatly reversing the sportsman's own arbitrary schemes of coercion to force Sophie and her father into the roles of whore and prisoner.

The Lord of the Manor's final judicial test comes in a confrontation engineered by Rental, in which the obdurate Sir John has to reconcile his promises of protection to Sophia and Annette with his long-standing hostility to his older son. Naturally enough, 'justice and nature' (3.4.51) win out over 'Caprice and passion' (3.4.51) as the family – and the estate – is restored to order. Trumore's engagement to Sophia is confirmed on the basis that virtue and mutual attachment should override disproportion (a point of personal importance to Burgoyne, who married well above his station) and the satire on recruitment is partially recuperated by Trumore's insistence on remaining a volunteer.

While *The Lord of the Manor* is clearly consonant with Burgoyne's own defensive campaign, its success in persuading audiences of his patriotic integrity was mixed at best. While the unjustly disinherited, impetuous, brave, independent and liberal Rashly seems designed as his avatar, spectators might have been as inclined to see the later Burgoyne in the role of Rental, the character who stage manages the final scenes and guides the principals (his social superiors) through the enactment of poetic justice. Certainly, Burgoyne was never to assume another important military role and the contemporary characterization of his dramaturgy as peculiarly genteel quite distinctly stressed his access to fashionable sociability rather than his possession of public virtue. As he was never himself the owner of a country house, always the entertaining visitor eventually denied even a property in honour, accused of employing by proxy the grossest savagery, it is hardly surprising that his depiction of 'Castle Manor' was so riddled

with overt reminders of the injustice, intractable hierarchy and violence
that subtended the security of the estate, the nation and the empire.

Plays and comic operas set in a countryside that arguably still serves as a
crucial element in the English national imaginary proliferated in the
theatres of eighteenth-century Britain. Frequently composed by military
men, plebeians and Irish writers, they presented a world apparently
governed by a tradition-bound, hierarchical order that purported to combine the ancient liberties and customary rights of the people with the
'natural' authority of their social, economic and political betters. But close
examination of these texts reveals that far from simply embodying encomia
to the nation's pastoral heart, rural plays from the Restoration to the end of
the eighteenth century (and beyond) address and question the most urgent
issues of their moment, ranging from rural poverty, class and gender
oppression, through the detrimental environmental effects of commercial
capitalism, imperial expansion and colonial war. Despite their apparently
emollient depictions of the manorial estates and villages that constitute the
shires and counties, rural plays repeatedly reveal the violence and exploitation both intrinsic to, and constantly impinging upon, the nation's
green heart.

Afterword

By the time Jane Austen wrote *Northanger Abbey*, it was possible for *The Spectator* and *The Tatler* to be dismissed as old-fashioned and even eccentric, residues of an age long past with nothing compelling to say to early nineteenth-century readers. Rather than registering *The Spectator*'s slow glide to cultural irrelevance, however, one might one see Austen's dismissal of the papers and her confidence in her own ability to represent her place and moment as an ironic tribute to her predecessors in social commentary. In *Spectator* 11, the paper devoted to Inkle and Yarico, Alithea cites the fable in which the lion complains that the human monopoly on discourse has resulted in his own species' persistent misrepresentation, a lament whose application to the situation of women – and women of colour in particular – has been well noted. Although the eighteenth century hardly shows an extensive improvement in the legal, economic or political position of women of any class or ethnicity in Britain, the period does witness a slow, halting expansion of women's participation in literature (as producers and consumers) and as cultural icons in the theatre. Along with a gradually increasing number of female historians and feminist theorists, novelists, playwrights and poets mounted ever more extensive if subtle protests against a highly restrictive gender order, preparing the ground for eventual political action. By bringing what Marilyn Butler would call the 'war of ideas' to the tea table as well as the coffeehouse, *The Spectator* and *The Tatler* deconstructed the division between household and polis, insinuating the public sphere into the realm of domesticity. While there are many instances of essays with disciplinary intentions aimed at controlling female conduct and female discourse, the papers also include critical reflections on gender inequity. Given a newly privileged position by periodicals as mediators if not monitors of sociable commerce, women would not hesitate to exploit the literary and social possibilities of these roles.

This book has argued that the late Stuart and Georgian theatre was engaged in a parallel process, as many kinds of people, including but not limited to bourgeois women, hitherto excluded from public discourse, were given unprecedented speaking rights in certain kinds of drama. What happened to the other figures whose complaints, protests and arguments resound in the many plays dedicated to condemning various forms of oppression in late Stuart Britain? One of the most fascinating aspects of England's 'enlightened' theatre is its deep connection with Ireland, with Irish writers deploying anti-colonial thematics and generating anti-colonial reception. A central figure in this study, Sir Richard Steele, was driven to create a united community of sentimental, patriotic playgoers because he wanted to be part of an inclusive Britain in which members of the different national communities enjoyed equal dignity, rather than suffering racist opprobrium. Written a generation later, Anglo-Irish Henry Brooke's *Gustavus Vasa*, known now primarily as the Licensing Act's first victim, in fact encodes a powerful critique not just of corrupt (Walpolean) rule but of imperial conquest and slavery. A celebration of successful rebellion against an oppressive colonial power, *Gustavus Vasa* not only cast a critical light on England's misgovernment of Ireland but rapidly assumed a privileged position in the repertory of the fledging American nation, with George Washington persistently identified with the Swedish Liberator. As his own Anglican bigotry was radically modified by long residence in the Irish countryside, Brooke shaped increasingly hostile depictions of colonial power and religious persecution in late tragedies such as *Montezuma* and *The Imposter*.

While Brooke's oeuvre reveals a slow modification of prejudice apparently shaped by living in Ireland, Arthur Murphy's career was governed by very different imperatives. Born and educated a Catholic, Murphy realized that success in London meant he needed to convert to Anglicanism. He was outwardly a charming and socially adept man, but the emotional costs of such coerced abandonment of faith are vividly revealed in his most powerful tragedy, *Alzuma*, a text whose denunciation of religious persecution and forced marriage remains powerful. The spiritual and sexual coercion associated with imperial conquest is equally a feature of Murphy's other serious plays, almost all of which focus on the losers in episodes of imperial conflict in locations ranging from China to Peru. It seems no accident that Richard Brinsley Sheridan's hugely successful *Pizarro* (1798) returns to a black legend that could be as applicable to Ireland's circumstances under English domination as those of indigenous Americans under the Spanish.

Thinking about eighteenth-century English theatre as a scene of Enlightenment helps bring the hugely important contribution of Irish writers into view, suggesting how their variously critical perspectives on England's expanding empire voiced the concerns of indigenes suffering from religious, economic and political oppression, not just across the Irish Sea but elsewhere. The various other kinds of plays explored here also brought sharp new attitudes to bear on Britain's novel commercial empire. The extraordinary interpenetration of freemasonry and theatre in Georgian London (and elsewhere) brings together one of the Enlightenment's most characteristic social formations and its foremost cultural arena. We have noted how freemasons supported theatre through patronage and charity, providing networks of sociable connection and institutional support while benefiting from the expertise of theatre professionals adept at helping stage the myriad ritual performances at the heart of the craft. Knowing that all the major authors of domestic tragedy were freemasons changes our understanding of these texts, all of which express profound anxieties about the new world of commercial capitalism in which older kinship structures and forms of economic relationship seem weak and vulnerable. The masonic promise of fraternity and solidarity, extended to all (men) regardless of sectarian persuasion, nation or race, is expressive of an idealistic cosmopolitanism that might suture up the ravages of incipient globalism. The domestic tragedies largely record the failure of such solidarity but also record the hope that innovative forms of cross-class, cross-cultural social bonding might provide succour in the face of a new world order.

British and colonial freemasonry would later resile from ecumenical cosmopolitanism (always more an ideal than a practice), but the craft's religious and ethnic inclusiveness is an important aspect of its enlightened character. The desire to create dialogue and discover comity between strangers and actual or potential enemies that is so striking in a play like *The Generous Freemason* is equally a crucial aspect of the significant number of dramas written to argue for religious toleration. Serious plays such *The Siege of Damascus* and *Edward and Eleonora* developed scenarios that were unfamiliar to theatre audiences, in order to make the case that religious differences between Christians and Muslims (and thus, by extension, Catholics and Protestants) might be best managed through amicable coexistence rather than conversion efforts or military conflict. Developing a topic hitherto generally dramatized through reiterations of the black legend of peninsular conquest in the Americas, tolerationist plays about Islam such as *Edward and Eleonora* reoriented the critique towards England itself, identifying the nation's participation in the Crusades as an egregious instance of cross-and-booty adventurism to be carefully avoided. It is sad but not surprising to note that by the last two decades of the century, the high-minded ecumenism of these plays no longer justified their production: instead, in the wake of the loss of the American colonies, *The Siege of Damascus* was read as a warning about the weakening effects of a divided polity while *Edward and Eleonora* was lauded for its patriotic depiction of royal connubiality.

One of the most important features of Enlightened theatre was the novel space and voice provided for those characterized as noble and ignoble savages. Dignified and articulate Wendat and Incan leaders appear repeatedly in eighteenth-century drama, sometimes fiercely resistant to colonial invaders, sometimes acquiescent in conversion and alliance. Close examination of source texts for these plays reveals that the arguments and perspectives voiced by these characters are not simply projections of European views but draw on indigenous beliefs, practices and histories. The embodiment of these figures in performance staged colonial encounters in terms that insisted on the ethical and political authority of their roles as leaders of societies whose territory, resources, culture and peoples were being appropriated. Although the protests of these figures often proved ineffectual within the dramatic vehicles and as moral provocation, their accusations retain salience in our own post-Enlightenment moment.

The exploration of the globe so characteristic of an enlightened and imperial stage was accompanied by a turn to England's interior. Villages, market towns, county seats, spas, manors, great houses and public houses all assume new dramatic visibility in the late Stuart and Georgian era. The incessant theatricalization of England's countryside, spiking during times of war, surely functioned in a dialectical relationship to the equally insistent dramatization of the exotic locations into which British power was increasingly projected. Sometimes nostalgic but almost always laced with sardonic scepticism about the naturalness of class and ethnic hierarchies, plays and ballad operas that focus on local 'savages' mobilize indigeneity and local affiliation against the invasive power of new money so often created in foreign trade or foreign wars. The epitome of this strand of rural resistance, Goldsmith's *She Stoops to Conquer*, returns us to the conclusion that the disruptive effects of colonial capital were often most acutely observed by the Irish, participant observers of the process in several domains.

Recent scholarship on late Georgian theatre has made clear that reformist agendas, pursued by such writers as Inchbald and Sheridan, persisted amidst reaction. In addition to the scandals of misgovernance in South Asia and the Americas, the most obvious focus of such dramaturgy was abolition, the reform cause par excellence in the late eighteenth century.

Slavery shadows this book: as has often been noted, the contradiction between Enlightenment ideals of human freedom and dignity and the contemporaneous expansion of the transatlantic slave trade seems to strip the former project of all claims to moral suasion. Certainly, there appears to have been a temporal disjunction between the Enlightenment focus on the evils caused by religious bigotry, absolute power and imperial oppression and the much slower realization of the horrors of slavery, whose evils were addressed theatrically at a much later point than forced conversion or colonial invasion.

It may be however that this issue requires more examination. Steven Pincus has begun to reveal that Britain's participation in the slave trade was an issue of profound disagreement between Whigs and Tories in the early eighteenth century, culminating in antithetical positions on acquiring the Asiento – the right to trade slaves to Latin America – in the Treaty of Utrecht. Two of the most popular and powerful dramatizations of Africans through the whole eighteenth century, Southerne's *Oroonoko* and Edward Young's *The Revenge* (1721) (the third being *Othello*), were written in the early English Enlightenment. One of the most striking aspects of these protagonists is that although Oroonoko is famously distressed by the prospect of killing his beloved wife, like Othello and Zanga he is a figure of heroic and frightening stature, so much so in fact that at the turn of the nineteenth century, in the midst of reaction, he was banished from the stage. When the play returned in 1817, Hazlitt expressed amazement that this terrifyingly revolutionary tragedy had ever been licensed.

As we have seen, plays of the early English Enlightenment deployed dramatic pathos to create sympathy for the ethnically or religiously alien victims of religious persecution or imperial power. Their protagonists were frequently women, their nations defeated. In Oroonoko and Zanga, however, spectators witnessed heroic characters infused with determined resistance if not also a desire for revenge on their enslavers. Less interested in interlocution or empathy than in their own pursuit of freedom and justice, these dramatizations of rebellion against and revulsion from enslavement suggest that the playhouse could imagine, where philosophy was fumbling, effective and persistent resistance to the worst form of European power. Rather than operating in conjunction with progressive opinion, even shaped as it was often by non-Western dialogue, *Oroonoko* and *The Revenge* serve as spectacular, specifically theatrical rejoinders to the moral, political and intellectual presumption of enlightened England.

Bibliography

PRIMARY SOURCES

Modern Editions

Addison, Joseph. *Addisoniana*. London: R. Phillips, 1803.

Annual Register and History of Literature 4 (January 1805).

Bond, Donald (ed.). *The Spectator*. 5 vols. Oxford: Clarendon, 1965.

Henderson, Nicholas. *Prince Eugen of Savoy*. London: Phoenix, 2002.

Jeffrey, Francis (ed.). *The Edinburgh Review*. 8.15 (April 1806): 148–154.

La Belle Assemble: Or, Court and Fashionable Magazine. 1.10 (December 1806).

Nichols, J. (ed.). *Literary and Miscellaneous Memoirs*, vol. 1. London: Printed for the Author, 1828.

Songhurst, W. J. (ed.). 'Quatuor Coronatorum Antigrapha: Masonic Reprints of the Quatuor Coronati Lodge No. 2076, London', vol. 10. In *The Minutes of the Grand Lodge of Free-Masons of England, 1723–1739*. Margate: printed by W. J. Parrott, 1913.

First Editions

'An Account of Alzuma, a New Tragedy, Now Acting at Covent-Garden Theatre'. *Universal Magazine of Knowledge and Pleasure June 1747–Dec. 1803* 52.361 (March 1773): 89.

Addison, Joseph. *The Drummer; or, The Haunted House. A Comedy*. London: Jacob Tonson, 1715.

The Works of Joseph Addison with Notes by Richard Hurd. 6 vols. Ed. Henry G. Bohn. London: George Bell & Sons, 1901.

Algarotti, Francisco. 'An Essay on the Empire of the Incas'. In *Letters from Count Algarotti to Lord Hervey and the Marquis Scipio Maffei*. Glasgow: Robert Ure, 1770.

'Alzuma, a Tragedy as Performed at the Theatre Royal in Covent-Garden'. *Monthly Review; or Literary Journal, 1752–1825* 48 (March 1773): 212–215.

Anderson, Robert. *The Life of Samuel Johnson, LLD, with Critical Observations on His Works*. Edinburgh: J. & A. Arch, 1795.

Baker, Thomas. *Tunbridge Walks; or, The Yeoman of Kent*. London: Bernard Lintott, 1703.

Banks, John. *History of Francis-Eugene, Prince of Savoy . . . Containing . . . Military Transactions . . .* London: John Banks, 1741.

   Preface to a New Play called Anna Bullen. London: Allan Banks, 1682.

Bedford, Arthur. *The Evil and Danger of Stage Plays, Showing Their Natural Tendency to Destroy Religion, and Introduce a General Corruption of Manners.* Bristol: W. Bonny, 1706.

Bickerstaffe, Isaac. *Love in a Village. A Comic Opera.* London: W. Griffin, 1763.

Brooke, Henry. *Poems and Plays by Henry Brooke, Esq., with the Life of the Author.* 4 vols. London: John Sewell, 1790.

   The Tryal of the Roman Catholics of Ireland. 2nd ed. London: T. Davies, 1764.

Brown, John. *Barbarossa. A Tragedy.* London: J. and R. Tonson, 1755.

   The History of the Rise and Progress of Poetry through Its Several Species. Newcastle: J. White and T. Saint for L. Davis and C. Reymers, 1764.

   The Mutual Connexion between Religious Truth and Civil Freedom; Between Superstition, Tyranny, Irreligion, and Licentiousness: Considered in Two Sermons. London: R. Dodsley, 1746.

Burgoyne, John. *The Lord of the Manor. A Comic Opera.* Dublin: H. Chamberlaine, 1781.

de Charlevoix, Pierre F. X. *Histoire et Description Generale de la Nouvelle-France.* Paris, 1744.

Chetwood, William Rufus. *A General History of the Stage from Its Origin in Greece Down to the Present Time.* London: W. Owen, 1749.

Chetwood, William Rufus. *The Generous Freemason: or, The Constant Lady. With the Humours of Squire Noodle and His Man Doodle.* London: J. Roberts, 1731.

Churchill, Charles. *The Rosciad.* 6th ed. London, 1766.

Cibber, Colley. *An Apology for the Life of Colley Cibber with an Historical View of the Stage during His Own Time Written by Himself.* 1740. Ed. B. R. S. Fone. Ann Arbor: University of Michigan Press, 1968.

   'The Prologue'. In *The Tragedy of Zara.* London: J. Watts, 1736.

The Constitutions of the Ancient and Honorable Fraternity of Free and Accepted Masons. London: Brother J. Scott, 1756.

Cooke, William. *Memoirs of Charles Macklin . . .* London: James Asperne, 1806.

A Criticism on Mahomet and Irene. In a Letter to the Author. London: W. Reeve and A. Dodd, 1749.

Davies, Thomas. *Memoirs of the Life of David Garrick, Esq.* London: Printed for the Author, 1780.

Defoe, Daniel. *The Honour and Perogative of the Queen's Majesty Vindicated and Defended against the Unexampled Insolence of the Author of the Guardian: In a Letter from a Country Whig to Mr Steele.* London: J. Morphew, 1713.

de la Vega, Garcilaso. *Royal Commentaries of Peru.* Ed. Paul Rycaut. London, 1688.

Dennis, John. 'The Causes of the Decay and Defects of Dramatick Poetry, and of the Degeneracy of the Publick Taste'. 1725. In *The Critical Works of John*

Dennis, 2 vols., ed. Edward Niles Hooker. Baltimore: Johns Hopkins University Press, 1943.

'The Character and Conduct of Sir John Edgar, Call'd by Himself Sole Monarch of the Stage in Drury-Lane; and His Three Doughty Governors. 1720'. In *The Critical Works of John Dennis*, 2 vols., ed. Edward Niles Hooker. Baltimore: Johns Hopkins University Press, 1943.

'A Defence of Sir Fopling Flutter, a Comedy by Sir George Etheridge'. In *The Critical Works of John Dennis*, 2 vols., ed. Edward Niles Hooker. Baltimore: Johns Hopkins University Press, 1943.

Liberty Asserted. A Tragedy. London: George Strahan et al., 1704.

'Remarks on a Play, Call'd the Conscious Lovers, a Comedy'. 1723. In *The Critical Works of John Dennis*, 2 vols., ed. Edward Niles Hooker. Baltimore: Johns Hopkins University Press, 1943.

Dodsley, Robert. *The King and the Miller of Mansfield. A Dramatick Tale.* London: Printed for the Author at Tully's Head, 1737.

Dryden, John. *The Works of John Dryden.* 19 vols. Ed. H. T. Swedenberg Jr. et al. Berkeley: University of California Press, 1956.

Farquhar, George. *The Recruiting Officer and Other Plays.* Ed. William Myers. Oxford: Clarendon, 1995.

Foot, Jesse. *The Life of the Late Arthur Murphy Esq.* London, 1812.

Foote, Samuel. *The Roman and English Comedy Consider'd and Compar'd with Remarks upon the Suspicious Husband.* Dublin: A. Reilly, 1747.

Gentleman, Francis. *The Dramatic Censor; or, Critical Companion.* 2 vols. London: J. Bell, 1770.

The Gentleman's Magazine: and Historical Chronicle 55.11 (November 1785): 909–910.

Gildon, Charles. *A Comparison between the Two Stages.* London, 1702.

Goldsmith, Oliver. 'The Revolution in Low Life.' In *The Collected Works of Oliver Goldsmith*, 5 vols., ed. Authur Friedman. Oxford: Clarendon, 1966.

She Stoops to Conquer; or, The Mistakes of a Night. In *The Collected Works of Oliver Goldsmith*, 5 vols., ed. Authur Friedman. Oxford: Clarendon, 1966.

Guthrie, William. *An Essay upon English Tragedy.* London: T. Waller, 1757.

Du Halde, Jean-Baptiste. *A Description of the Empire of China and Chinese Tartary, Together with the Kingdoms of Korea, and Tibet.* 2 vols. Trans. Emanuel Bowen. London, 1738, 1741.

Haywood, Eliza. *The Fair Captive. A Tragedy.* London: T. Jauncey and H. Cole, 1721.

Hennepin, Louis. *A New Discovery of a Vast Country in America, Extending above Four Thousand Miles between New France and New Mexico, with a Description of the Great Lakes, Cataracts, Rivers, Plants and Animals: Also the Manners, Customs, and Languages of the Several Native Indians and the Advantage of Commerce with Those Different Nations.* London: T. Bentley et al., 1698.

Heywood, James. 'To Sir Richard Steele, on His Comedy, Call'd *The Conscious Lovers*'. In *Letters and Poems on Several Subjects*. London: W. Meadowes, T. Worral, J. Ashford, 1726.

Hill, Aaron. *Alzira. A Tragedy*. London: John Osborn, 1737.

The Prompter (1734–1736). Ed. William W. Appleton and Kalmain Burmin. New York: Bejamin Bloom, 1966.

Hiram; or, The Grand-Master Key to the Door of Both Ancient and Modern Free-Masonry by a Member of the Royal Arch. London: W. Griffin, 1766.

Howard, Sir Robert, and George Villiers, Duke of Buckingham. *The Country Gentleman*. Ed. Arthur H. Scouten and Robert D. Hume. London: Dent, 1976.

Hughes, John. *The Siege of Damascus*. London, 1720.

Hume, David. *A Treatise of Human Nature*. 2nd ed. Ed. L. A. Shelby-Bigge and P. H. Nidditch. Oxford: Oxford University Press, 1978.

Johnson, Charles. *The Country Lasses; or, The Custom of the Manor*. London: J. Tonson, 1715.

Love in a Forest. A Comedy. London: W. Chetwood, 1723.

The Sultaness: A Tragedy. London: W. Wilkins et al., 1717.

The Village Opera. London: J. Watts, 1729.

Johnson, Samuel. *Irene: A Tragedy*. London: R. Dodsley, 1749.

Jones, Stephen. *Masonic Miscellanies, in Poetry and Prose*. Dublin: Brother Joseph Hill, 1800.

Lacy, John. *The Ecclesiastical and Political History of Whigland, of Late Years*. London: John Morphew, 1714.

Lacy, John. *The Old Troop; or, Monsieur Raggou*. London: William Crook and Thomas Dring, 1672.

Lahontan, Louis-Armand de Lom d'Arce, Baron de. *New Voyages to North America; Containing an Account of the Several Nations of That Vast Continent; Their Customs, Commerce, and Ways of Navigation* ... 2 vols. London: H. Bonwicke, T. Goodwin, M. Wotton, B. Tooke and S. Manship, 1703.

Le Blanc, Jean Bernard. *Letters on the English and French Nations*. 2 vols. London: J. Brindley, R. Francklin, C. Davis, J. Hodges, 1747.

Lillo, George. *Fatal Curiosity: A Tragedy*. Ed. William H. MacBurney. Lincoln: University of Nebraska Press, 1968.

The London Merchant; or, The History of George Barnwell. Ed. William McBurney. Lincoln: University of Nebraska Press, 1965.

Lucas, Charles. *A Nineteenth Address to the Free-Citizens and Free-Holders of the City of Dublin*. Dublin, 1749.

The Political Constitutions of Great Britain and Ireland. London, 1751.

Manley, Delariviere. *Secret Memoirs and Manners of Several Persons of Quality of Both Sexes. From the New Atalantis, an Island in the Mediterranean*. 6th ed. London: John Morphew, 1720.

McKenzie, Henry. *The Shipwreck: or, Fatal Curiosity. A Tragedy. Altered from Lillo*. London: T. Cadell, 1784.

Miller, James. *Mahomet the Imposter*. London: John Bell, 1795.

Mahomet the Imposter. A Tragedy. London: J. Watts and W. Dodds, 1744.

Mitchell, Joseph. *The Fatal Extravagance. A Tragedy*. London: T. J. Jauncey, 1721.
'To Richard Steele on the Successful Representation of His Excellent Comedy Call'd, the Conscious Lovers'. In *Poems on Several Occasions*, 2 vols. London: L. Gilliver, 1729.

Monthly Review, or Literary Journal 62 (March 1780): 185.

Murphy, Arthur. *Advertisement to Alzuma: A Tragedy*. 1773. Reprinted in *The Plays of Arthur Murphy*, ed. Richard B. Schwartz. New York: Garland, 1979.
Alzuma. A Tragedy. London: T. Lowndes, 1773.
The Gray's Inn Journal. 2 vols. Dublin: William Sleater, 1756.
Zenobia. A Tragedy. London: W. Griffin, 1768.

Ockley, Simon. *The Conquest of Syria, Persia and Aegypt by the Saracens*. London, 1708.
An Explaination [sic] of the Several Arabick Terms Us'd in The Siege of Damascus Written by Mr Hughes. With a Short Account of the Historical Seige, and the Life of Muhamet, as Far as It Is Necessary to Understanding the Story. London: J. Brotherton et al., 1720.
'The Pioneer'. In *Oriental Essays: Portraits of Seven Scholars*. London: Allen & Unwin, 1960.

'Plan of the Tragedy of Alzuma'. *Sentimental Magazine, or General Assemblage of Science, Taste and Entertainment* 5 (March 1775): 26–27.

Poems on Several Occasions ... 2 vols. Ed. William Duncombe. London: J. Tonson and J. Watts, 1735.

Pope, Alexander. *Correspondence of Alexander Pope*. 5 vols. Ed. George Sherburne. Oxford: Clarendon, 1955.

Preston, William. *Illustrations of Masonry*. London: William Preston, 1772.

S----cy, Ed. *The Country Gentleman's Vade Mecum*. London: John Harris, 1699.

Shiells, Robert. *The Lives of the Poets of Great Britain and Ireland to the Time of Dean Swift*. 5 vols. London: R. Griffiths, 1753.

Steele, Richard. 'An Apology for Himself and His Writings'. In *Tracts and Pamphlets*, ed. Rae Blanchard. London: printed R. Burleigh, 1714.
'The Englishman'. In *The Englishman: A Political Journal by Richard Steele*, ed. Rae Blanchard. December 17, 1713.
'A Letter to a Member, etc. Concerning the Condemn'd Lords, in Vindication of Gentlemen Calumniated in the St. James's Post of Friday March the 2nd'. In *Tracts and Pamphlets*, ed. Rae Blanchard. London: R. Burleigh, 1716.
The Tatler: The Lucubrations of Isaac Bickerstakke, Esq. 4 vols. London: H. Lintott et al., 1754.
Tracts and Pamphlets. 1714. Ed. Rae Blanchard. Reprint, Baltimore: Johns Hopkins University Press, 1944.

Steele, Sir Richard. *The Theatre 1720*. Ed. John Loftis. Oxford: Clarendon, 1962.

Summers, Montagu (ed.). *The Complete Works of Thomas Shadwell*, vol. 4. London: Fortune Press, 1927.

Swift, Jonathan. *The Publick Spirit of the Whigs*. London: T. Cole, 1714.

Temple, Sir William. 'Of Heroic Virtue'. In *Five Miscellaneous Essays by Sir William Temple*, ed. Samuel Holt Monk. Ann Arbor: University of Michigan Press, 1963.

The Tatler. 3 vols. Ed. Donald F. Bond. Oxford: Clarendon, 1987.

The Theatre: or, Select Works of the British Dramatick Poets. 12 vols. Edinburgh: Martin and Wotherspoon, 1768.

The Theatrical Register. York, 1788.

Thomson, James. *James Thomson: Letters and Documents*. Ed. Alan Dugald McKillop. Lawrence: University Press of Kansas, 1958.

'To Sir Richard Steele, on His Comedy, The Conscious Lovers'. In *Miscellaneous Poems by Several Hands*. London: D. Lewis, 1722.

Universal Magazine of Knowledge and Pleasure 61.425 (October 1777):169–173.

Vanburgh, John. *A Short Vindication of The Relapse and The Provok'd Wife*. London: N. Walwyn, 1698.

Victor, Benjamin. *An Epistle to Richard Steele, on His Play Call'd The Conscious Lovers*. 2nd ed. London: W. Chetwood, S. Chapman, J. Stagg, J. Brotherton, Th. Edlin, 1722.

A View of the Edinburgh Theatre during the Summer Season, 1759. London: A. Morley, 1760.

Voltaire, M. de. *The Complete Works of Voltaire*. Oxford: Voltaire Foundation, Taylor Institution, 1989.

   The Works of M. de Voltaire, vol. 13. Trans. T. Smollett, T. Francklin, et al. London: J. Newbest et al., 1762.

Wagstaffe, William. *A Letter from the Facetious Doctor Andrew Tripe at Bath to the Venerable Nestor Ironside*. London: B. Waters, 1714.

Watson, R. *An Apology for Christianity*. 2nd ed. Cambridge, 1777.

William, Earl Cowper. 'To the Memory of Mr Hughes'. In *The Poetical Works of John Hughes*, 2 vols. Edinburgh: Apollo Press by the Martins, 1779.

Williamson, J. B. *Preservation: or, The Hovel of the Rocks: A Play in Five Acts. Interspers'd with Lillo's Drama, in Three Acts, Call'd 'Fatal Curiosity'*. London, 1800.

de Zarate, Augustin. *The Discovery and Conquest of Peru*. Trans. and ed. J. M. Cohen. Harmondsworth: Penguin, 1968.

SECONDARY SOURCES

Abulafia, David (ed.). *The Mediterranean in History*. London: Thames & Hudson, 2003.

Adorno, Theodor, and Max Horkheimer. *The Dialectic of Enlightenment*. 1944. Reprint, London: Continuum, 1994.

Aitken, George A. *The Life of Richard Steele*. 2 vols. London: Wm. Isbister, 1889.

Aksan, Virginia. *Ottoman Wars, 1700–1870: An Empire Besieged*. Harlow: Pearson Longman, 2007.

Anderson, Benedict. *Imagined Communities: Reflections on the Origin and Spread of Nationalism*. Rev. ed. New York: Verso, 1998.

Andrea, Bernadette (ed.). *Delarivier Manley and Mary Pix: English Women Staging Islam.* Toronto: ITER, 2012.

Andrien, Kenneth J. 'The Invention of Colonial Andean Worlds'. *Latin American Research Review* 46.1 (2011): 217–226.

Aravamudan, Srinivas. *Enlightenment Orientalism: Resisting the Rise of the Novel.* Chicago: University of Chicago Press, 2012.

Armitage, David. *Ideological Origins of English Empire.* Cambridge: Cambridge University Press, 1998.

Aspden, Suzanne. 'Ballads and Britons: Imagined Community and the Contiguity of 'English' Opera'. *Journal of the Royal Musical Association* 122.1 (1997): 24–51.

Aveling, J. C. H. *Northern Catholics: The Catholic Recusants of the North Riding of Yorkshire, 1558–1790.* London: Chapman, 1966.

Ayres, Phillip. *Classical Culture and the Idea of Rome in Eighteenth-Century England.* Cambridge: Cambridge University Press, 1997.

Baigent, Michael, and Richard Leigh. *The Temple and the Lodge.* London: Jonathan Cape, 1989.

Baker, Eric. 'Lucretius in the European Enlightenment'. In *The Cambridge Companion to Lucretius*, ed. Stuart Gillespie and Phillip Hardie, 273–288. Cambridge: Cambridge University Press, 2007.

Ballaster, Ros. *Fabulous Orients: Fictions of the East in England 1662–1785.* Oxford: Oxford University Press, 2005.

Balme, Christopher. *The Theatrical Public Sphere.* Cambridge: Cambridge University Press, 2014.

Barrell, John. *The Dark Side of the Landscape: The Rural Poor in English Poetry.* Cambridge: Cambridge University Press, 1980.

Barush, Kathryn R. 'Painting the Scene'. In *The Oxford Handbook of the Georgian Theatre, 1737–1832*, ed. Julia Swindells and David Francis Taylor. Oxford: Oxford University Press, 2014.

Bekkaoui, Khalid. 'White Women and Moorish Fancy in Eighteenth-Century Literature'. In *The Arabian Nights in Historical Context: Between East and West*, ed. Saree Makdisi and Felicity Nussbaum, 131–166. Oxford: Oxford University Press, 2008.

Belcher, Wendy. *Abyssinia's Samuel Johnson: Ethiopian Thought in the Making of an English Author.* Oxford: Oxford University Press, 2012.

Bender, John. *Ends of Enlightenment.* Stanford, CA: Stanford University Press, 2012.

Bergman, Fred L. 'Garrick's *Zara*'. *MLA* 74.3 (June 1959): 225–232.

Bernbaum, Ernest. *The Drama of Sensibility: A Sketch of the History of English Sentimental Comedy and Domestic Tragedy, 1696–1780.* Gloucester, MA: Peter Smith, 1958.

Bevis, Richard. *The Laughing Tradition: Stage Comedy in Garrick's Day.* Athens: University of Georgia Press, 1980.

Bickham, Troy. *Savages within the Empire: Representations of American Indians in Eighteenth-Century Britain.* Oxford: Oxford University Press, 2005.

Bissell, Benjamin. *The American Indian in English Literature*. New Haven, CT: Yale University Press, 1925.

Black, Scott. *Of Essays and Reading in Early Modern Britain*. London: Palgrave Macmillan, 2006.

Blanchard, Rae (ed.). *The Englishman: A Political Journal by Richard Steele*. Oxford: Clarendon, 1955.

(ed.). *Richard Steele's Periodical Journalism 1714–16*. Oxford: Clarendon, 1959.

Bloom, Edward, and Lillian Bloom. *Joseph Addison's Sociable Animal*. Providence: Brown University Press, 1971.

Bolton, Betsy. *Women, Nationalism, and the Romantic Stage: Theatre and Politics in Britain, 1780–1800*. Cambridge: Cambridge University Press, 2001.

Bond, Richard P. *Queen Anne's American Kings*. Oxford: Clarendon, 1952.

Boulukos, George. *The Grateful Slave: The Emergence of Racism in Eighteenth-Century British and American Culture*. Cambridge: Cambridge University Press, 2008.

Bowers, Toni. *The Politics of Motherhood: British Writing and Culture, 1680–1760*. Cambridge: Cambridge University Press, 1996.

Bowring, Lewin. *Haidar Ali and Tipu Sultan, and the Struggle with the Musalman Powers of the South*. Oxford: Clarendon, 1999.

Braun, T. E. D. 'Alzire, ou les Americains'. In *The Complete Works of Voltaire*, vol. 14, 6–27. Oxford: Voltaire Foundation, Taylor Institution, 1989.

Braverman, Richard. *Plots and Counterplots: Sexual Politics and the Body Politic in English Literature, 1660–1730*. Cambridge: Cambridge University Press, 1993.

'Spectator 495: Addison and the "Race of People Called the Jews"'. *Studies in English Literature, 1500–1900* 34.3 (Summer 1994): 537–552.

Brewer, John. *The Pleasures of the Imagination: English Culture in the Eighteenth Century*. New York: Farrar, Straus & Giroux, 1997.

Brewster, Dorothy. *Aaron Hill: Poet, Dramatist, Projector*. New York: AMS Press, 1966.

Brissenden, R. F. *Virtue in Distress: Studies in the Novel of Sentiment from Richardson to Sade*. London: McMillan, 1974.

Brittlebank, Kate. *Tipu Sultan's Quest for Legitimacy*. Delhi: Oxford University Press, 1999.

Broadley, A. M. *The Craft, the Drama and Drury Lane*. London: Freemason Printing Works, 1887.

Bronson, Bertrand H. *Johnson and Boswell: Three Essays*. Berkeley: University of California Press, 1944.

Brooks, Richard A. 'Voltaire and Garcilaso de la Vega'. In *Studies on Voltaire and the Eighteenth Century*, vol. 30, ed. Theodore Besterman, 189–204. Geneva: Institut et Musee Voltaire, 1964.

Brown, Laura. 'The Defenceless Woman and the Development of English Drama'. *Studies in English Literature, 1500–1900* 22.3 (Summer 1982): 429–443.

Brown, Tony C. 'Joseph Addison and the Pleasures of Sharawadgi'. *English Literary History* 47.1 (Spring 2007): 171–176.

Brumstrom, Conrad, and Declan Kavanagh. 'Authur Murphy and Florida Peat: The Gray's Inn Journal and Versions of the Apolitical'. *Eighteenth-Century Ireland/Iris an du culture* 27 (2013): 123–141.

Brunstrom, Conrad. *Thomas Sheridan's Career and Influence: An Actor in Earnest*. Lewisburg, PA: Bucknell University Press, 2011.

Bruster, Douglas. *Drama and the Market in the Age of Shakespeare*. Cambridge: Cambridge University Press, 1992.

Buchanan, Michelle. 'Savages, Noble and Otherwise, and the French Enlightenment'. *Studies on Eighteenth-Century Culture* 15 (1986): 105.

Bulman, William J. *Anglican Enlightenment: Orientalism, Religion and Politics in England and Its Empire, 1648–1715*. Cambridge: Cambridge University Press, 2015.

Burke, Helen. '"Country Matters": Irish "Waggery" and the Irish and British Theatrical Traditions'. In *Players, Playwrights, Playhouses: Investigating Performance 1660–1800*, ed. Michael Cordner and Peter Holland. London: Palgrave, 2007.

Riotous Performances: The Struggle for Hegemony in the Irish Theater, 1712–1784. Notre Dame, IN: University of Notre Dame Press, 2003.

Burns, Ross. *Damascus: A History*. London: Routledge, 2005.

Burton, Hanna. 'Introduction: The Play in Historical Context'. In *Voltaire's Fanaticism, or Mahomet the Prophet: A New Translation*, ed. Melanie Ruthven. Sacramento: Litwin Books, 2013.

Canfield, Rob. 'Conquer or Die: Staging Circum-Atlantic Revolt in *Polly* and *Three-Finger'd Jack*'. *Theatre Journal* 59.2 (May 2007): 241–258.

'John Gay's *Polly*: Unmasking Pirates and Fortune Hunters in the West Indies'. *Eighteenth-Century Studies* 34.4 (Summer 2001): 539–557.

'Something's Mizzen: Anne Bonny, Mary Read, Polly and the Female Counter Roles on the Imperialist Stage'. *South Atlantic Review* 66.2 (Spring 2001): 45–63.

Carey, Brycchan. *British Abolitionism and the Rhetoric of Sensibility: Writing, Sentiment and Slavery, 1760–1807*. New York: Palgrave Macmillan, 2005.

Carey, Daniel, and Lynn Festa (eds.). *Post-Colonialism and Enlightenment: Eighteenth-Century Colonialism and Postcolonial Theory*. New York: Oxford University Press, 2013.

Carlson, Julie. 'Like Me: An Introduction to Domestic/Tragedy'. *South Atlantic Quarterly* 98.3 (Summer 1999): 331–624.

Carlson, Marvin. *Voltaire and the Theater of the Eighteenth-Century*. Westport, CT: Greenwood, 1998.

Carswell, John. *The Romantic Rogue: Being the Singular Life and Adventures of Rudolph Eric Raspe, Creator of Baron Munuchausen*. New York: Dutton, 1950.

The South Sea Bubble. London: Cressett Press, 1960.

Casey, Edward S. *The Fate of Place: A Philosophical History*. Berkeley: University of California Press, 1997.

de Certeau, Michel. *The Practice of Everyday Life*. Berkeley: University of California Press, 1984.

Champion, Justin. *Republican Learning: John Toland and the Crisis of Christian Culture, 1696–1722*. Manchester: Manchester University Press, 2003.

Choudhury, Mita. *Interculturalism and Resistance in the London Theater, 1660–1800: Identity, Performance, Empire*. Lewisburg, PA: Bucknell University Press, 2000.

Clark, Peter. *British Clubs and Societies, 1580–1800*. Oxford: Oxford University Press, 2000.

Cole, Lucinda. '*The London Merchant* and the Institution of Apprenticeship'. *Criticism* 37.1 (Winter 1995): 57–70.

Coleman, Deirdre. *Romantic Colonization and British Anti-slavery*. Cambridge: Cambridge University Press, 2005.

Colley, Linda. *Britons: Forging the Nation*. New Haven, CT: Yale University Press, 1992.

    Captives: Britain, Empire and the World. London: Pimlico, 2003.

    The Ordeal of Elizabeth Marsh. New York: Pantheon, 2007.

Cooper, Anthony Ashley, Earl of Shaftesbury. *Characteristics of Men, Manners, Opinions, Times*. Ed. Lawrence E. Klein. Cambridge: Cambridge University Press, 1999.

Cope, Kevin L. (ed.). *Compendious Conversation: The Method of Dialogue in the Early Enlightenment*. Frankfurt: Peter Lang, 1992.

Coppola, Al. 'Harlequin Newton: John Rich's *Necromancer* and the Public Science of the 1720s'. In *'The Stage's Glory': John Rich, 1692–1761*, ed. Berta Joncus and Jeremy Barlow. Newark: University of Delaware Press, 2011.

Crawford, Rachel. 'English Georgic and British Nationhood'. *ELH* 65.1 (1998): 123–156.

Curl, James Steven. *Spas, Wells and Pleasure-Gardens of London*. London: Historical, 2010.

Cypess, Sandra Messinger. *La Malinche in Mexican Literature, from History to Myth*. Austin: University of Texas Press, 1991.

Davies, Simon. 'Reflections on Voltaire and His Idea of Colonies'. *Studies on Voltaire and the Eighteenth Century* 332 (1995): 61–69.

Davis, Leith. 'Charlotte Brooke's Reliques of Irish Poetry; Eighteenth-Century "Irish Song" and the Politics of Remediation'. In *United Islands? The Languages of Resistance*, ed. John Kirk, Andrew Noble and Michael Brown. London: Pickering & Chatto, 2012.

De Krey, Gary. *A Fractured Society: The Politics of London in the First Age of Party*. Oxford: Clarendon, 1985.

Del Balzo, Angelina. 'The Sultan's Tears in *Zara*, an Oriental Tragedy'. *SEL* 55.3 (Summer 2015): 501–521.

Dessen, Alan. *Elizabethan Stage Conventions and Modern Interpreters*. Cambridge: Cambridge University Press, 1984.

Dobson, Michael. *Making of the National Poet: Shakespeare, Adaptation and Authorship*. Oxford: Clarendon, 1992.

Docker, John. 'Sheer Folly and Derangement: How the Crusades Disoriented Enlightenment Historiography'. In *Representing Humanity in the Age of Enlightenment*, ed. Alexander Cook, Ned Curthoys, and Shino Konishi. London: Pickering and Chatto, 2013.

Donovan, Kevin Joseph. 'The Giant Queller and the Poor Old Woman: Henry Brooke and the Two Cultures of Eighteenth-Century Ireland'. *New Hibernia Review* 17.2 (Summer 2003): 103–120.

Dudley, Edward J., and Maximillian E. Novak (eds.). *The Wild Man Within: An Image in Western Thought from the Renaissance to Romantics*. Pittsburgh: University of Pittsburgh Press, 1973.

Dunbar, Howard Hunter. *The Dramatic Career of Arthur Murphy*. London: Modern Languages Association and Oxford University Press, 1946.

Duques, Matthew E. 'John Dennis's Dramatis Personae'. *Notes and Queries* 62.262 (2015): 271–273.

Eagleton, Terry. *The Function of Criticism from the Spectator to Post-Structuralism*. London: Verso, 1984.

Eccles, W. J. *Frontenac: The Courtier Governor*. Toronto: McClelland and Stewart, 1965.

Ellingson, Terry Jay. *The Myth of the Noble Savage*. Berkeley: University of California Press, 2001.

Elliott, J. H. *Empires of the Atlantic World: Britain and Spain in America, 1492–1830*. New Haven, CT: Yale University Press, 2007.

Ellis, Markman. *The Politics of Sensibility: Race, Gender and Sensibility in the Sentimental Novel*. Cambridge: Cambridge University Press, 1996.

Ellison, Julie. *Cato's Tears and the Making of Anglo-American Emotion*. Chicago: University of Chicago Press, 1999.

Emory, John Pike. *Arthur Murphy, an Eminent Dramatist of the Eighteenth Century*. Philadelphia: University of Pennsylvania Press, 1946.

Evans, James. '"The Dulissimo Maccaroni": Masculinities in She Stoops to Conquer'. *Philological Quarterly* 90.1 (Winter 2011): 45–67.

Fay, Bernard. *Revolution and Freemasonry 1680–1800*. Boston: Little, Brown, 1935.

Festa, Lynn. *Sentimental Figures of Empire in Eighteenth-Century Britain and France*. Baltimore: Johns Hopkins University Press, 2006.

Fiengo-Varn, Aurora. 'Reconciling the Divided Self: Inca Garcilaso de la Vega's *Royal Commentaries* and His Platonic View of the Conquest of Peru'. *Revista de Filologia y Linguistica de Universidad de Costa Rica* 29.1 (2003).

Freeman, Lisa. *Antitheatricality and the Body Public*. Philadelphia: University of Pennsylvania Press, 2017.

Character's Theater: Genre and Identity on the Eighteenth-Century English Stage. Philadelphia: University of Pennsylvania Press, 2002.

Fuchs, Barbara. *Mimesis and Empire: The New World, Islam, and European Identities*. Cambridge: Cambridge University Press, 2001.

Fullagar, Kate. *The Savage Visit: New World People and Popular Imperial Culture in Britain, 1710–1795*. Berkeley: University of California Press, 2012.

Garcia, Humberto. *Islam in the English Enlightenment, 1670–1840*. Baltimore: Johns Hopkins University Press, 2011.

Gardner, Kevin J. 'George Farquhar's *The Recruiting Officer*: Warfare, Conscription, and the Disarming of Anxiety'. *Eighteenth-Century Life* 25.3 (2001): 43–61.

Garnett, Aama. 'Hume's "Original Difference": Race, National Characteristics and the Human Sciences'. *Eighteenth-Century Thought* 2 (2004): 127–152.

Garraway, Doris L. 'Of Speaking Natives and Hybrid Philosophers: Lahontan, Diderot, and the French Enlightenment Critique of Colonialism'. In *The Postcolonial Enlightenment: Eighteenth-Century Colonialism and Postcolonial Theory*, ed. Daniel Carey and Lynn Festa, 207–239. Oxford: Oxford University Press, 2009.

Genovese, Michael. 'An Organic Commerce: Sociable Selfhood in Eighteenth-Century Georgic'. *Eighteenth-Century Studies* 46.2 (Winter 2013): 197–221.

Gerrard, Christine. *Aaron Hill: The Muses' Projector 1685–1750*. Oxford: Oxford University Press, 2003.

The Patriot Opposition to Walpole: Politics, Poetry, and National Myth, 1725–1742. Oxford: Clarendon, 1994.

Gibbs, Jenna M. *Performing the Temple of Liberty: Slavery, Theater and Popular Culture in London and Philadelphia, 1760–1850*. Baltimore: Johns Hopkins University Press, 2014.

Girard, Raymond. *Rousseau and Voltaire: The Enlightenment and Animal Rights*. Stanford, CA: Stanford University Press, 1985.

Gordon, Helen. *Voice of the Vanquished: The Story of the Slave Marina and Hernan Cortes*. Chicago: University Editions, 1995.

Gordon, Scott Paul. 'Voyeuristic Dreams: Mr Spectator and the Power of Spectacle'. *Eighteenth Century: Theory and Interpretation* 36 (1995): 3–23.

Gose, Peter. *Invaders as Ancestors: On the Intercultural Making and Unmaking of Spanish Colonialism in the Andes*. Toronto: University of Toronto Press, 2008.

Gottlieb, Evan. *Feeling British: Sympathy and National Identity in Scottish and English Writing, 1707–1832*. Lewisburg, PA: Bucknell University Press, 2007.

Goulbourne, Russell. 'Voltaire's Masks: Theatre and Theatricality'. In *The Cambridge Companion to Voltaire*, ed. Nicholas Cronk. Cambridge: Cambridge University Press, 2009.

Gould, Eliga H. *The Persistence of Empire: British Political Culture in the Age of the American Revolution*. Chapel Hill: University of North Carolina Press, 2000.

Grace, Dominick M. '*Fatal Curiosity*, Fatal Colonialism'. *English Studies in Canada* 28.3 (September 2002): 385–411.

Grosrichard, Alain. *The Sultan's Court: European Fantasies of the East*. Trans. Liz Heron. London: Verso, 1998.

Guillory, John. 'Enlightening Mediation'. In *This Is Enlightenment*, ed. Clifford Siskin and William Warner, 37–63. Chicago: University of Chicago Press, 2010.

Habermas, Jürgen. *The Structural Transformation of the Public Sphere: An Inquiry into a Category of Bourgeois Society*. Trans. Thomas Burger with Fredrick Lawrence. 1962. Reprint, Boston: MIT Press, 1991.

Hamill, John. *The History of English Freemasonry*. London: Lewis Masonic, 1994.

Harland-Jacobs, Jessica L. *Builders of Empire: Freemasonry and British Imperialism, 1717–1927*. Chapel Hill: University of North Carolina Press, 2007.

Henbury, Phyllis. *The English Spa: A Social History*. London: Athlone, 1990.

Heyter, Tony. *The Army and the Crowd in Mid-Georgian England*. London: Macmillan, 1978.

Hill, Jacqueline R. *From Patriots to Unionists: Dublin Civic Politics and Irish Protestants Patriotism, 1660–1840*. Oxford: Clarendon, 1997.

Hiscock, Andrew. *The Uses of This World: Thinking Space in Shakespeare, Marlowe, Cary and Jonson*. Cardiff: University of Wales Press, 2004.

Holmes, Clive. *The Eastern Association in the English Civil War*. Cambridge: Cambridge University Press, 1974.

Hopkins, David. 'The English Voices of Lucretius from Lucy Hutchinson to John Mason Good'. In *The Cambridge Companion to Lucretius*, ed. Stuart Gillespie and Phillip Hardie, 254–273. Cambridge: Cambridge University Press, 2007.

Horejsi, Nicole. '(Re)valuing the 'Foreign-Trinket': Sentimentalizing the Language of Economics in Steele's *Conscious Lovers*'. *Restoration and Eighteenth-Century Theater Research* 18.2 (Winter 2003): 11–36.

Howard, Jean E. *Theater of a City: The Places of London Comedy, 1598–1642*. Philadelphia: University of Pennsylvania Press, 2007.

Howson, Gerald. *Burgoyne of Saratoga*. New York: Times Books, 1978.

Hudson, Wayne. *Enlightenment and Modernity: The English Deists and Reform*. London: Pickering and Chatto, 2009.

Hughes, Derek. 'Body and Ritual in Farquhar'. *Comparative Drama* 31.3 (1997): 414–435.

English Drama, 1660–1700. Oxford: Clarendon, 1996.

'Who Counts in Farquhar?' *Comparative Drama* 31.1 (1997): 7–27.

Hunt, Lynn, Margaret Jacob, and Wijnand Mijnhardt (eds.). *Bernard Picart and the First Global Vision of Religion*. Los Angeles: Getty Institute, 2010.

Hutcheson, Francis. 'Reflections on Our Common Systems of Morality'. In *On Human Nature*, ed. Thomas Moutner. Cambridge: Cambridge University Press, 1993.

Hynes, Peter. 'Richard Steele and the Genealogy of Sentimental Drama: A Reading of *The Conscious Lovers*'. *Restoration and Eighteenth-Century Theater Research* 40.2 (Spring 2004): 142–166.

Irwin, Robert. 'Labour and Commerce in Locke and Early Eighteenth-Century English Georgic'. *ELH* 76.4 (2009): 963–988.

Israel, Jonathan. *Radical Enlightenment: Philosophy and the Making of Modernity 1650–1750*. Oxford: Oxford University Press, 2001.

Jacob, Margaret C. *Living the Enlightenment: Freemasonry and Politics in Eighteenth-Century Europe*. New York: Oxford University Press, 1991.

The Origins of Freemasonry: Facts and Fictions. Philadelphia: University of Pennsylvania Press, 2007.

The Radical Enlightenment: Pantheists, Freemasons and Republicans. London: Allen and Unwin, 1981.

Jones, Robert W. *Literature, Gender and Politics in Britain during the War for America.* Cambridge: Cambridge University Press, 2012.

Joseph, Betty. *Reading the East India Company, 1720–1840: Colonial Currencies of Gender.* Chicago: University of Chicago Press, 2003.

Jusdanis, Gregory. 'Enlightenment Postcolonialism'. *Research in African Literatures* 36.3 (Fall 2005): 137–150.

Justice, George. *The Manufacturers of Literature: Writing and the Literary Marketplace in Eighteenth-Century England.* Newark: University of Delaware Press, 2002.

Keener, Fredrick M. *English Dialogues of the Dead: A Critical History, an Anthology, and a Check-List.* New York: Columbia University Press, 1973.

Kelsall, Malcolm. 'Terence and Steele'. In *Essays on the Eighteenth-Century English Stage*, ed. Kenneth Richards and Peter Thomson. London: Methuen, 1972.

Kenny, Virginia C. *The Country-House Ethos in English Literature, 1688–1750: Themes of Personal Retreat and National Expansion.* Brighton: Harvester, 1984.

Kidd, Colin. *British Identities before Nationalism: Ethnicity and Nationhood in the Atlantic World 1600–1800.* Cambridge: Cambridge University Press, 1999.

Kinservik, Mathew. *Disciplining Satire: The Censorship of Satiric Comedy on the Eighteenth-Century London Stage.* Lewisburg, PA: Bucknell University Press, 2002.

Klein, Lawrence E. 'Enlightenment as Conversation'. In *What's Left of Enlightenment: A Postmodern Question*, ed. Keith Michael Baker and Peter Hanns Reiss. Stanford, CA: Stanford University Press, 2001.

Shaftesbury and the Culture of Politeness: Moral Discourse and Cultural Politics in Early Eighteenth-Century England. Cambridge: Cambridge University Press, 2004.

Knight, Charles. *A Political Biography of Richard Steele.* London: Pickering and Chatto, 2009.

Kramnick, Isaac. *Bolingbroke and His Circle: The Politics of Nostalgia in the Age of Walpole.* Ithaca, NY: Cornell University Press, 1992.

Landry, Donna. *The Muses of Resistance: Laboring-Class Women's Poetry in Britain, 1739–1796.* Cambridge: Cambridge University Press, 1990.

Laramie, Michael G. *The European Invasion of North America: Colonial Conflict along the Hudson-Champlain Corridor, 1609–1760.* Santa Barbara, CA: Praeger/ABC, 2012.

Le Guin, Elizabeth. 'Opera Review: Charles Burney and *The Cunning Man*'. *Eighteenth-Century Studies* 44.1 (Fall 2010): 113–116.

Lewis, Jayne. '"The Sorrow of Seeing the Queen": Mary Queen of Scots and the British History of Sensibility, 1707–1789.' In *Passionate Encounters in a Time of Sensibility*, ed. Maximillian E. Novak and Anne Mellor. London: Associated University Presses, 2000.

Lindley, Keith. *Fenland Riots and the English Revolution*. London: Heinneman, 1982.

Livingston, Chela. 'Johnson and the Independent Woman: A Reading of *Irene*'. *Age of Johnson: A Scholarly Annual* 2 (1979): 212–234.

Lock, Georgina. 'The Siege of Damascus, 1764, at Mr Newcome's School in Hackney'. Paper, Paying the Piper: The Economies of Amateur Performance, University of Notre Dame, June 28–29, 2014.

Loftis, John. *Comedy and Society from Congreve to Fielding*. Stanford, CA: Stanford University Press, 1959.

The Politics of Drama in Augustan England. Oxford: Clarendon, 1963.

Macchi, Fernanda. *Inas Illustrados: reconstrucciones imperiales en la primera mitad del siglo XVIII*. Madrid: Iboamericana-Veruet, 2009.

MacKie, Erin. *Market a la Mode: Community and Gender in the Tatler and the Spectator*. Baltimore: Johns Hopkins University Press, 1997.

Malcolson, Robert J. *Popular Recreations in English Society, 1700–1850*. Cambridge: Cambridge University Press, 1979.

Mallipeddi, Ramesh. *Spectacular Suffering: Witnessing Slavery in the Eighteenth-Century British Atlantic*. Charlottesville: University of Virginia Press, 2016.

Maltby, William S. *The Black Legend in England: The Development of Anti-Spanish Sentiment, 1558–1660*. Durham, NC: Duke University Press, 1971.

Manning, Rita C. 'Rousseau's Other Woman: Colette in "Le Devin du Village"'. *Hypatia* 16.2 (Spring 2001): 27–42.

Mardock, James D. *Our Scene Is London: Ben Jonson's City and the Space of the Author*. New York: Routledge, 2008.

Marsden, Jean. *Fatal Desire: Women, Sexuality, and the English Stage 1660–1720*. Ithaca, NY: Cornell University Press, 2006.

Re-imagined Text: Shakespeare, Adaptation and Eighteenth-Century Literary Theory. Lexington: University Press of Kentucky, 1995.

'Richard Cumberland's *The Jew* and the Benevolence of the Audience: Performance and Religious Tolerance'. *Eighteenth-Century Studies* 48.4 (Summer 2015): 457–477.

Marshall, David. *The Figure of Theatre: Shaftesbury, Defoe, Adam Smith, and George Eliot*. New York: Columbia University Press, 1986.

Marshall, John. *John Locke, Toleration and Early English Enlightenment Culture*. Cambridge: Cambridge University Press, 2006.

Marshall, Louise H. *National Myth, Imperial Fantasy: Representations of British Identity in the Early Eighteenth Century*. London: Palgrave, 2008.

Marshall, P. J. (ed.). *The British Discovery of India*. Cambridge: Cambridge University Press, 1970.

Matar, Nabil. 'Islam in Britain, 1689–1750'. *Journal of British Studies* 47.2 (2008): 284–300.

Mather, James. *Pashas: Traders and Travellers in the Islamic World*. New Haven, CT: Yale University Press, 2009.

Maurer, Shawn Lisa. *Proposing Men: The Dialectics of Gender and Class in the Eighteenth-Century English Periodical*. Stanford, CA: Stanford University Press, 1998.

McCall, Tom. 'Liquid Politics: Towards a Theorization of 'Bourgeois' Tragic Drama'. *South Atlantic Quarterly* 98.3 (Summer 1999): 593–622.

McCrea, Brian. *Addison and Steele Are Dead: The English Department, the Canon, and the Professionalization of Literature*. Newark: University of Delaware Press, 1990.

McGeavy, Thomas N. 'John Hughes, 1668–1720'. In *Oxford Dictionary of National Biography*. www.oxforddnb.com.

McGirr, Elaine. *Heroic Mode and Political Crisis, 1660–1745*. Newark: University of Delaware Press, 2009.

McIntyre, Ian. *Garrick*. London: Allan Lane, 1999.

McNeil, David. 'Dialogues on Military Affairs'. In *Compendious Conversation: The Method of Dialogue in the Early Enlightenment*, ed. Kevin L. Cope, 129–137. Frankfurt: Peter Lang, 1992.

Miller, Christopher L. *The French Atlantic Triangle: Literature and Culture of the Slave Trade*. Durham, NC: Duke University Press, 2008.

Moody, Jane. *Illegitimate Theatre in London, 1770–1840*. Cambridge: Cambridge University Press, 2000.

Mullaney, Steven. *The Place of the Stage: License, Play and Power in Renaissance England*. Chicago: University of Chicago Press, 1988.

Murphy, Sean J. 'Charles Lucas'. In *Oxford Dictionary of National Biography*. www.oxforddnb.com.

Muthu, Sankar (ed.). *Empire and Modern Political Thought*. Cambridge: Cambridge University Press, 2012.

   (ed.). *Enlightenment against Empire*. Princeton, NJ: Princeton University Press, 2003.

Nash, Richard. *Wild Enlightenment: The Borders of Human Identity in the Eighteenth Century*. Charlottesville: University of Virginia Press, 2003.

Nenadic, Stana (ed.). *Scots in London in the Eighteenth Century*. Lewisburg, PA: Bucknell University Press, 2010.

Nussbaum, Felicity. *Rival Queens: Actresses, Performance, and the Eighteenth-Century British Theater*. Philadelphia: University of Pennsylvania Press, 2010.

   Torrid Zones: Maternity, Sexuality and Empire in Eighteenth-Century English Narratives. Baltimore: Johns Hopkins University Press, 1995.

O'Brien, Karen. 'Imperial Georgic, 1660–1789'. In *The Country and the City Revisited: England and the Politics of Culture, 1550–1850*, ed. Gerald MacLean, Donna Landry, Joseph P. Ward and Jo Ward, 160–179. Cambridge: Cambridge University Press, 1999.

   Women and Enlightenment in Eighteenth-Century Britain. Cambridge: Cambridge University Press, 2009.

O'Brien, Paula. 'Miller, James (1704–1744)'. In *Oxford Dictionary of National Biography*. www.oxforddnb.com.

Okie, Laird. *Augustan History Writing: Histories of England in the Early English Enlightenment*. Lanham, MD: University Press of America, 1991.

O'Quinn, Daniel. *Entertaining Crisis in the Atlantic Imperium 1770–1790*. Baltimore: Johns Hopkins University Press, 2011.

    Staging Governance: Theatrical Imperialism in London, 1770–1800. Baltimore: Johns Hopkins University Press, 2005.

O'Quinn, John. *Harlequin Britain: Pantomime and Entertainment, 1690–1760*. Baltimore: Johns Hopkins University Press, 2004.

Orr, Bridget. *Empire on the English Stage, 1660–1714*. Cambridge: Cambridge University Press, 2001.

    'Empire, Sentiment and Theatre'. In *The Oxford Handbook of the Georgian Theatre, 1737–1832*, ed. Julia Swindells and David Francis Taylor, 621–637. Oxford: Oxford University Press, 2014.

Osborn, James M. 'Spence, Natural Genius, and Pope'. *Philological Quarterly* 45 (January 1966): 123–137.

Pagden, Anthony. *The Enlightenment and Why It Still Matters*. New York: Random House, 2013.

    European Encounters with the New World: From Renaissance to Romanticism. New Haven, CT: Yale University Press, 1993.

    'The Savage Critic: Some European Images of the Primitive'. In *The Uncertainties of Empire: Essays in Iberian and Ibero-American Intellectual History*, 39–42. Aldershot: Variorum, 1994.

Parry, Graham. *The Trophies of Time: English Antiquarians of the Seventeenth Century*. Oxford: Oxford University Press, 1995.

Pedicord, Henry William. 'George Lillo and Speculative Masonry'. *Philological Quarterly* 53.3 (Summer 1974): 401–412.

    'Masonic Theatre Pieces in London, 1730–1780'. *Theatre Survey: The American Journal of Theatre History* 25.2 (November 1984): 153–166.

    'White Gloves at Five: Fraternal Patronage of London Theatres in the Eighteenth Century'. *Philological Quarterly* 45.1 (January 1966): 270–288.

Perkins, Merle E. 'The Documentation of Voltaire's *Alzire*'. *Modern Language Quarterly* 4 (1943): 433–436.

Perkinson, Richard H. 'Topographical Comedy in the Seventeenth Century'. *English Literary History* 3 (1936): 270–290.

Peter, Robert. '"The Fair Sex" in a "Male Sect": Gendering the Role of Women in Eighteenth-Century English Freemasonry'. In *Gender and Fraternal Orders in Europe 1300–2000*, ed. Maire Fedelman Cross, 133–155. London: Palgrave Macmillan, 2010.

Phillips, Mark Sabor. *Society and Sentiment: Genres of Historical Writing in Britain, 1740–1820*. Princeton, NJ: Princeton University Press, 2000.

Picart, Bernard. *The Ceremonies and Religious Customs of the Various Nations of the Known World*. 7 vols. London: William Jackson, 1733.

Pincus, Steven. *1688: The First Modern Revolution*. New Haven, CT: Yale University Press, 2009.

'Addison's Empire: Whig Conceptions of Empire in the Early Eighteenth Century'. *Parliamentary History* 31.1 (February 2012): 99–117.

Pink, Andrew. 'The Musical Culture of Free-Masonry in Early Eighteenth-Century London'. PhD diss., Goldsmiths College, University of London, 2007.

Pocock, J. G. A. 'Clergy and Commerce: The Conservative Enlightenment in England'. In *L'eta dei lumi: Studi storici sul Settecento europeo in onore di Franco Venturi*, 2 vols., ed. Rafaelle Ajello et al. Naples, 1985.

Virtue, Commerce and History: Essays on Political Thought and History, Chiefly in the Eighteenth Century. Cambridge: Cambridge University Press, 1985.

Pollock, Anthony. 'Neutering Addison and Steele: Aesthetic Failure and the Spectatorial Public Sphere'. *English Literary History* 74.3 (Fall 2007): 707–734.

Popkin, Richard H. 'Hume's Racism Reconsidered'. In *The Third Force in Seventeenth-Century Thought*. Leiden: Brill, 1992.

Porter, Joy. *Native American Freemasonry: Associationalism and Performance in America*. Lincoln: University of Nebraska Press, 2011.

Porter, Roy. *Enlightenment: Britain and the Creation of the Modern World*. London: Allen Lane, 2000.

Ragussis, Michael. *Theatrical Nation: Jews and Other Outlandish Englishmen in Georgian Britain*. Philadelphia: University of Pennsylvania Press, 2010.

Rasmussen, Dennis C. *The Pragmatic Enlightenment: Recovering the Liberalism of Hume, Smith, Montesquieu and Voltaire*. Cambridge: Cambridge University Press, 2013.

Reill, Peter Hanns, and David Phillip Miller (eds.). *Visions of Empire: Voyages, Botany and Representations of Nature*. Cambridge: Cambridge University Press, 1996.

Revel, Jacques. 'The Uses of Comparison: Religions in Early Eighteenth Century Culture'. In *Bernard Picart and the First Global Vision of Religion*, ed. Lynn Hunt, Margaret Jacob and Wijnand Mijnhardt, 331–347. Los Angeles: Getty Research Institute, 2010.

Richardson, John. 'John Gay and Slavery'. *Modern Language Review* 97.1 (January 2002): 15–25.

Rich Greer, Margaret, Walter D. Mignolo, and Maureen Quilligan (eds.). *Rereading the Black Legend: The Discourses of Religious and Racial Difference in the Renaissance Empires*. Chicago: University of Chicago Press, 2007.

Richter, Daniel K. *The Ordeal of the Longhouse: The People of the Iroquois League in the Era of European Colonization*. Chapel Hill: University of North Carolina Press, 1982.

Roach, Joseph. *Cities of the Dead: Circum-Atlantic Performance*. New York: Columbia University Press, 1996.

It. Ann Arbor: University of Michigan Press, 2007.

Robertson, John. *The Case for the Enlightenment: Scotland and Naples, 1680–1760*. Cambridge: Cambridge University Press, 2005.

Robinson, John Richard. *Recusant Yeomen in the Counties of York and Lancaster: The Survival of a Catholic Farming Family*. Kirstead: Frontier, 2003.

Rodger, N. A. M. *The Command of the Ocean: A Naval History of Britain 1649–1815*. New York: Norton, 2004.

Roelens, Maurice. *Avec un Sauvage*. Montreal: Lemeac, 1974.

Rosenfeld, Sybil. *Strolling Players & Drama in the Provinces, 1660–1765*. 1937. Reprint, New York: Octogon Books, 1970.

Temples of Thespis: Some Private Theatres and Theatricals in England and Wales, 1700–1820. London: Society for Theatre Research, 1978.

The York Theatre. London: Society for Theatre Research, 2001.

Russell, Gillian. '"Keeping Place": Servants, Theater and Sociability in Mid-Eighteenth-Century Britain'. *The Eighteenth-Century: Theory and Interpretation* 42.1 (2001): 21–42.

Women, Sociability and Theatre in Georgian London. Cambridge: Cambridge University Press, 2007.

Ruthven, Melanie. *Voltaire's Fanaticism, or Mahomet the Prophet: A New Translation*. Sacramento, CA: Litwin Books, 2013.

Sambrook, James. *James Thomson, 1700–1748: A Life*. Oxford: Clarendon, 1991.

Sayre, Gordon. *The Indian Chief as Tragic Hero: Native Resistance and the Literature of the Americas from Moctezuma to Tecumseh*. Chapel Hill: University of North Carolina Press, 2005.

Les Sauvages Americains: Representations of Native Americans in French and English Colonial Literature. Chapel Hill: University of North Carolina Press, 1997.

Schier, Donald. 'Aaron Hill's Translation of Voltaire's *Alzire*'. In *Studies on Voltaire and the Eighteenth Century*, vol. 67, 45–58. Geneva: Institut et Musee Voltaire, 1969.

Schmidgen, Wolfram. *Exquisite Mixture: The Virtues of Impurity in Early Modern England*. Philadelphia: University of Pennsylvania Press, 2012.

Schneider, Ben Ross, Jr. (ed.). *The London Stage 1660–1800*. Carbondale: Southern Illinois University Press, 1979.

Scouller, Major R. E. *The Armies of Queen Anne*. Oxford: Clarendon, 1966.

Scurr, Helen Margaret. 'Henry Brooke'. PhD diss., University of Minnesota, 1922.

Shaftesley, John M. 'Jews in English Regular Freemasonry, 1787–1860'. *Transactions of the Jewish Historical Society of England* 25 (1973–1975): 150–209.

Shevelow, Kathryn. *Women and Print Culture: The Construction of Femininity in the Early Periodicals*. London: Routledge, 1989.

Shields, Juliet. *Sentimental Literature and Anglo-Scottish Identity, 1745–1820*. Cambridge: Cambridge University Press, 2010.

Shouyi, Chen. 'The Chinese Orphan: A Yuan Play: Its Influence on European Drama of the Eighteenth Century'. In *The Vision of China in the English*

Literature of the Seventeenth and Eighteenth Centuries, ed. Adrian Hsia. Hong Kong: Chinese University Press, 1998.

Simms, Brendan. *Three Victories and a Defeat: The Rise and Fall of the First British Empire, 1714–1783*. London: Penguin, 2008.

Sioui, Georges. *For an Amerindian Autohistory: An Essay on the Foundations of a Social Ethic*. Trans. Sheila Fischman. Montreal: McGill-Queens University Press, 1992.

Smith, John Harrington. 'Tony Lumpkin and the Country Booby Type in Antecedent English Comedy'. *Publication of the Modern Language Association* 58.4 (December 1943): 1038–1049.

Smyth, James. *The Making of the United Kingdom: State, Religion and Identity in Britain and Ireland*. London: Longmans, 2001.

Snader, Joe. *Caught between Worlds: British Captivity Narratives in Fact and Fiction*. Lexington: University Press of Kentucky, 2000.

Snell, K. D. M. *Annals of the Labouring Poor: Social Change and Agrarian England, 1660–1900*. Cambridge: Cambridge University Press, 1985.

Solomon, Harry M. *The Rise of Robert Dodsley: Creating the New Age of Print*. Carbondale: Southern Illinois University Press, 1996.

Southerne, Richard. *Changeable Scenery: Its Origin and Development in the British Theatre*. London: Faber and Faber, 1952.

Stam, Robert, and Ella Shohat. 'Where and Whither Postcolonial Theory'. *New Literary History* 43 (2012): 376.

Steffensen, James L. (ed.). *The Dramatic Works of George Lillo, Including Silvia*. Ed. Richard Noble. Oxford: Clarendon, 1993.

Stromberg, R. N. *Religious Liberalism in Eighteenth-Century England*. Oxford: Clarendon, 1954.

Sudan, Rajani. *The Alchemy of Empire: Abject Materials and the Technologies of Colonialism*. New York: Fordham University Press, 2016.

Swaminathan, Srividhya. *Debating the Slave Trade: Rhetoric of British National Identity, 1759–1815*. Farnham: Ashgate, 2009.

Sweet, Rosemary. *Antiquaries: The Discovery of the Past in Eighteenth-Century Britain*. London: Hambledon, 2004.

Swindells, Julia. 'The Political Context of the 1737 Licensing Act'. In *The Oxford Handbook of the Georgian Theatre, 1737–1832*, ed. Julia Swindells and David Francis Taylor. Oxford: Oxford University Press, 2014.

Sypher, Wylie. *Guinea's Captive Kings: British Anti-slavery Literature of the XVIIIth Century*. New York: Octagon Books, 1969.

Tadmor, Naomi. *Family and Friends in Eighteenth-Century England: Household, Kinship and Patronage*. Cambridge: Cambridge University Press, 2001.

Tasch, Peter A. *The Dramatic Cobbler: The Life and Works of Isaac Bickerstaff*. Lewisburg, PA: Bucknell University Press, 1971.

Taylor, David Francis. *Theatres of Opposition: Empire, Revolution and Richard Brinsley Sheridan*. Oxford: Oxford University Press, 2012.

Thompson, E. P. *Whigs and Hunters: The Origin of the Black Act*. New York: Pantheon, 1975.

Toomer, G. J. *Eastern Wisdom and Learning: The Study of Arabic in Seventeenth-Century England*. Oxford: Clarendon, 1996.

Tracy, James D. *The Rise of Merchant Empires: Long-Distance Trade in the Early Modern World*. Cambridge: Cambridge University Press, 1990.

Transgott, John. 'Heart and Mask and Genre in Sentimental Comedy'. *Eighteenth-Century Life* 10 (1986): 137.

Trevelyan, George Macaulay. *England under Queen Anne*. 3 vols. London: Longman, 1930.

Tucker, Herbert F., Jr. 'Goldsmith's Comic Monster'. *Studies in English Literature* 19 (1973): 493–494.

Turner, Henry S. *The English Renaissance Stage: Geometry, Poetry, and the Practical Spatial Arts, 1580–1630*. Oxford: Oxford University Press, 2006.

Urban, Eva. 'Lessing's Nathan the Wise: From the Enlightenment to the Berliner Ensemble'. *New Theatre Quarterly* 30.2 (May 2014): 183–196.

Varner, John Grier. *El Inca: The Life and Times of Garcilaso de la Vega*. Austin: University of Texas Press, 1968.

von Maltzahn, Nicholas. '"Acts of Kind Service" and the Patriot Literature of Empire'. In *Milton and the Imperial Vision*, ed. Balachandra Rajan and Elizabeth Sauer. Pittsburgh: Duquesne University Press, 1999.

Warner, Wolf. 'Eighteenth-Century Sensibility and Its Ambivalent Position in the 'Herstory' of Gender Roles: Cibber's *The Careless Husband*; Lillo's *Silvia*; and Richardson's *Pamela*'. In *Framing Women: Changing Frames of Representation from the Enlightenment to Postmodernism*, ed. Sandra Carroll, Birgit Pretzsch and Peter Wagner, 25–50. Tübingen: Niemeyer, 2003.

Watkins, John. *Representing Elizabeth in Stuart England*. Cambridge: Cambridge University Press, 2002.

Wechselblatt, Martin. 'Gender and Race in Yarico's Epistles to Inkle: Voicing the Feminine/Slave'. *Studies in Eighteenth-Century Culture* 19 (1989): 197–223.

Weber, David. *Barbaros: The Spanish and Their Savages in the Age of Enlightenment*. New Haven, CT: Yale University Press, 2005.

Weinbrot, Howard D. *Britannia's Issue: The Rise of British Literature from Dryden to Ossian*. Cambridge: Cambridge University Press, 1993.

Widmayer, Anne F. *Theatre and the Novel from Behn to Fielding*. Oxford Studies in the Enlightenment. Oxford: Voltaire Foundation, 2015.

Wilkes, Thomas. *The History of the Theatres of London and Dublin*. 2 vols. Dublin: G. Faulkner and J. Exshaw, 1761.

Williams, Abigail. *Poetry and the Creation of a Whig Literary Culture, 1681–1714*. Oxford: Oxford University Press, 2005.

Williams, Raymond. *The Country and the City*. Cambridge: Cambridge University Press, 1973.

Wilson, Brett. *A Race of Female Patriots*. Lewisburg, PA: Bucknell University Press, 2012.

Wilson, Catherine. *Epicureanism at the Origins of Modernity*. Oxford: Clarendon, 2008.

Wilson, Kathleen. *The Sense of the People: Politics, Culture and Imperialism in England, 1715–1785*. Cambridge: Cambridge University Press, 1998.

Wood, Nigel. 'Goldsmith's "English Malady"'. *Studies in the Literary Imagination* 44.1 (Spring 2011): 63–85.

Worrall, David. *Harlequin Empire: Ethnicity and the Drama of the Popular Enlightenment*. London: Pickering and Chatto, 2007.

Yang, Chi-Ming. *Performing China: Virtue, Commerce and Orientalism in Eighteenth-Century England, 1660–1760*. Baltimore: Johns Hopkins University Press, 2011.

Yeazell, Ruth. *Harems of the Mind: Passages of Western Art and Literature*. New Haven, CT: Yale University Press, 2000.

Young, Brian. *Religion and Enlightenment in Eighteenth-Century England: Theological Debate from Locke to Burke*. Oxford: Oxford University Press, 1998.

Zamora, Margarita. *Language, Authority and Indigenous History in the Commentarios reales de los Incas*. Cambridge: Cambridge University Press, 1988.

Index

CPSIA information can be obtained
at www.ICGtesting.com
Printed in the USA
LVHW050430130122
708310LV00021B/2826